SHATTERED DREAMS

ABOUT THE AUTHOR

IRENE SPENCER lives in Anchorage, Alaska, with her husband of nineteen years, Hector J. Spencer. During the twenty-eight years of her polygamous first marriage, Irene gave birth to thirteen children (all single births) and adopted a newborn daughter. Irene has 118 grandchildren and 37 great-grandchildren.

SHATTERED DREAMS

My Life as a Polygamist's Wife

IRENE SPENCER

HODDER

First published in Great Britain in 2008 by Hodder & Stoughton
An Hachette Livre UK company

1

Copyright © Irene Spencer 2007

The right of Irene Spencer to be identified as the Author of the Work
has been asserted by her in accordance with the Copyright, Designs
and Patents Act 1988.

A CIP catalogue record for this title is available from the British Library

ISBN 978 0 340 96361 6

Printed and bound in Great Britain by Clays Ltd, St Ives, plc

Hodder & Stoughton policy is to use papers that are natural, renewable
and recyclable products and made from wood grown in sustainable
forests. The logging and manufacturing processes are expected to
conform to the environmental regulations of the country of origin.

Hodder & Stoughton Ltd
338 Euston Road
London NW1 3BH

www.hodder.co.uk

To my precious children, who made
all my sacrifices worthwhile:

> Donna, André, Steven, Brent, Kaylen, Barbara, Margaret,
> Connie, LaSalle, Verlana, Seth, Lothair, and my little
> angel, Leah, and my special gift from God, Sandra, who
> are both now in Heaven but live also in my heart.

To my husband,

> Hector J. Spencer, for allowing me to pursue my dreams,
> for loving all my children, and for always displaying
> a servant's heart. Thank you for making me not only
> your favorite wife but your only wife.

ACKNOWLEDGMENTS

A special thanks to:

God—who drew me to himself through my suffering, heard my prayers, and rescued me from the years the locusts had eaten.

Donna Goldberg—my beautiful, faithful daughter without whose love and support I might not have lived to tell my story. God gave her to me to be my strength when I was weak, to need me when I felt unneeded. Without her persistent dedication and passion, this book never would have happened. I owe it all to her and her wonderful spirit. She truly is an angel.

Thomas J. Winters—my incredible literary agent. Praise God for delivering him right out of the heavens and landing him into my life (via sitting next to my precious granddaughter, **Margaret LeBaron Tucker,** on an airplane).

Debby Boyd—an earthly angel, for using her wings of expertise and helping my dreams take flight.

Rolf Zettersten—of Hachette Book Group USA, and the staff, for seeing value in my manuscript.

Gary Terashita—for letting my story touch his heart and for making it all happen so perfectly.

Susan Kahler—for her invaluable input and editing skills.

Maxine Hanks and **Duane Newcomb**—for being the first to read my manuscript and for giving me valuable help and encouragement.

Bud Gardner—for validating me as a writer and inspiring me to reach for the stars.

Marilyn Tucker Beesemyer—who has been a dear friend and a pillar of strength I've admired throughout my journey. Seeing my potential years ago, she planted seeds of encouragement in me to write my own story.

Rhonita Tucker—who has compassion for those whose ideas and ideals differ from her own. Her light extinguished the shadows, and her smile created a warm atmosphere in which I could grow.

Linda Craig—my best friend for over forty-five years, who promised she would never, ever marry my husband, no matter what. I appreciate such loyalty. I'll never have a more faithful friend who has walked my walk.

Rebecca Kimbel—my dear sister, who was always there to rescue and encourage me. I've appreciated her wisdom, love, and willingness to think outside the box.

Brandy Goldberg—my gorgeous granddaughter, for faithfully and tirelessly typing and retyping my manuscript. I've enjoyed the wonderful time of bonding and the laughter we've shared. You're the best!

Humor enables one to live in the midst of tragic

events without being a tragic figure.

—E. T. "CY" EBERHART

PROLOGUE

I edged sideways down the aisle of the crowded Greyhound, careful not to bump anyone with the bulky brown suitcase, which held my every possession: two or three plain cotton dresses, my undergarments, and toiletries—the sparse but precious contents of my hope chest. It may have been no great wonder, back in 1953, that a sixteen-year-old could stuff all she owned into one bag. But the fact that I was transporting my entire life to a new and faraway place felt momentous indeed.

Checking my ticket for the correct seat number, I stopped at 12D, raised myself up on my toes, and pushed the case onto the luggage rack above a heavyset woman who smiled apologetically as she half stood and let me take the empty window seat next to her. I nodded and started to squeeze past, halting for one last look out the window opposite, where my brother, Richard, and his pretty wife, Jan, stood in the docking bay, still waving me a halfhearted good-bye. I tried to smile back, may have smiled back. But when they dropped their hands to close comforting arms around one other, I turned away for good and let the tears streaking my cheeks fall toward my own window. How I hoped it would show me a future beautiful and dependable and worth all the sacrifice.

With a loud snort of exhaust, the bus eased out of the station and turned down State Street toward the main highway heading south out of Salt Lake City. South to Texas, then to Mexico. South to the ranch that would become my home. And south to my new husband,

Verlan LeBaron—twenty-three, tall, blond, and handsome (even if his hairline had begun its retreat prematurely). With him, thus far, I'd spent exactly three nights, all of them covert, and those memories were now weeks old. Yet here I was, smuggling myself out of Utah, out of the country in fact, and entrusting myself entirely to his hands with nothing but a few vague and breathy promises of a better life to spur me on.

Afraid this might be my last glimpse of home, I took tearful pains to register the landmarks streaming past—the Hotel Utah, the tall brownstones, the Mormon owned and run ZCMI department store, and Temple Square, with its giant, gray granite buildings, secretive walls, lush gardens, and the gold-leafed statue of the trumpet-blowing angel Moroni—the divine messenger who'd revealed the location of the Book of Mormon to our prophet Joseph Smith back in 1823. Most beloved of all was the majestic backdrop the Wasatch Mountains formed as their gigantic cliffs rung the valley in which Brigham Young and his companions nestled our city. The ache in my heart became a sharp hurt as this symbol of steadfastness and strength, which had long anchored my horizon, eventually drifted out of sight. I offered a silent prayer: *God, give me the courage to stand as firm as my Mormon forefathers.*

Leaning back in the swaying seat, I closed my eyes, hoping to ward off the surge of homesickness already enveloping me. My mother, along with most everyone else I loved, didn't even know of my marriage. I'd told even fewer I was moving to the LeBarons' Mexico homestead. We—Verlan and Charlotte and I—didn't consider it safe to tell. Besides, by keeping it secret, I avoided all the subversive "I told you so's" I was sure would have greeted my news. Still, how would I fare in such a strange place with only these two to care about me? That in itself was no given at this point—that either of them would really care. One was the husband I barely knew; the other was the wife who had him first.

As the gloom crept over me, I pressed a hand against my fluttering stomach and tried massaging the knotted fear within. I determined to concentrate on truly pertinent worries, like making it through the next twenty-four hours, until I arrived in El Paso and crossed over the border into Mexico. Since my every step now was an act of sheer obedience to God, perhaps I could presume he'd protect me through it all. In the meantime, I'd have hours to pray for the strength I'd need to take the next steps: *Oh God, help me to be unflinching in this sacred commitment I've made . . .*

The din of the vibrating bus motor eventually lulled me calm enough to look at my fears a bit more objectively. I'd been trying hard to be brave, and in that I'd largely succeeded so far. (I never much lacked for courage.) But my fundamentalist Mormon faith taught wives to be sweet, patient, and above all, never, ever jealous. I had to be honest. It was not simply the prospect of seeing my new husband again that spawned my dark cloud of worry. More than anything else, I dreaded moving in on the wife who'd staked her claim to him two years prior to mine. In truth, I'd barely claimed him yet at all. And, though I was livelier than she was and quite determined to fulfill him, just how was I going to get my fair share of him with her always around? . . . *and help me to be sweet, patient, never, ever jealous . . .*

I told myself I should be thankful she was no stranger to me. She was my half sister, after all. Somehow, this didn't help. I still felt like being selfish, and I felt plenty bad about feeling it. God commanded our people to live "plural marriage" or be damned forever. The revelation came directly through the prophet Joseph Smith in 1843: "I reveal unto you a new and an everlasting covenant; and if ye abide not that covenant, then are ye damned; for no one can reject this covenant and be permitted to enter into my glory." (Doctrine and Covenants, 132:4) Polygamy was a necessary sacrifice we all had to make in order to attain Godhood and avoid Hell. So I'd been told.

Yes, I'd been told it and told it and told it.

As the bus wandered past still-familiar fields of brown and green, I wandered back through my childhood in search of the words so persuasive to me. Perhaps they would persuade me now.

BOOK ONE

CALLED
TO BE A
GODDESS

CHAPTER ONE

As we were growing up, polygamy was the ruling tenet of our lives. This "Celestial Law" was so integral to who we were and what we were trying to accomplish that most often, we referred to it simply as "the Principle." Everything else we were to do or not do, be or not be (a great deal, as it turns out) was ancillary to this: men were to have as many wives and as many children as they possibly could during the few years they walked this Earth. It was upon the conclusion of those trying, earthly years that we would all reap the divine rewards for our obedience to the Principle.

As children, we were not just taught to honor the Principle, we were taught to claim it as our birthright. We were born into it; no conversion was necessary. "You are God's chosen ones, his special children of the covenant" we were told at home and at Sunday meeting, during visits to and from friends, and in all the literature we were allowed to read. We consequently viewed with great suspicion the few strange souls who occasionally tried to join our ranks from the outside. More likely than not they were mere deviants, men who got off on the idea of God-sanctioned sex with multiple women who were bound by oath to endure it. These were not children of the Principle. Children of the Principle understood that polygamy was all about future glory.

I WAS BORN INTO a fourth-generation polygamous family on February 1, 1937, a day that lay frozen under the white shroud of a typical Utah winter. I ended up a middle kid—thirteenth of the thirty-one born to my father, fourth of the six born to my mother. I was Mother's long-awaited first daughter. After me, she had two more.

Mother was the second of Dad's four wives. Rhea Allred, his first wife (a powerful position within many polygamous families), was a smashing brunette with beautiful brown eyes who believed heartily in the Principle and was determined to live it. My grandfather Harvey, who fathered both Rhea and Mother by different wives, wouldn't let Dad marry Rhea until he promised just one thing: to live plural marriage. Outside our Mormon fundamentalist circle, this would have been an unthinkable stipulation to put on a prospective groom, particularly one wanting to marry your daughter. But among children of the covenant, a commitment to polygamy had to come first. Dad complied, initially by word and later by action.

So my mother, Olive, was my aunt Rhea's half sister. In obedience to the Principle, Aunt Rhea urged and ultimately persuaded Mother to marry her husband—my father, Morris Q. Kunz. This was one of the more vexing contributions polygamous women were called on to make: the recruitment of new wives into their husband's households. After all, only so many women were born into the Principle, and each man was commanded to wed as many of them as he could. There was terrible competition. Weary husbands needed assistance, particularly as they aged and grew thicker in the middle as well as thinner in the wallet. A righteous woman who mastered the sin of jealousy and could effectively court others on her husband's behalf was a prize worth having. Generally, she could accomplish it only with her eternal rewards square in her sights. Devout Aunt Rhea managed to do her part. So Mother and Rhea were half sisters who then became sister wives.

Twenty-one on her wedding day (relatively old by polygamist standards), Mother was a lovely, blue-eyed blonde. One might think two beautiful wives would be enough for any man, but in polygamy, nothing is ever enough. A couple years after he married Mother, Dad married Ellen Halliday, who he'd met only days earlier. And another two years after that, while Ellen was still taken up with the birth of their second child, Dad married fifteen-year-old Rachel Jessop, his fourth wife. He was two months shy of twenty-eight at the time.

THE PRINCIPLE WAS NEITHER a license for male promiscuity (though it sometimes felt like it) nor a gratuitous call to suffering (though it quite often felt like that). In harmony with our teaching that "as man is, God once was, and as God is, man may become," the Principle was, quite simply, the way of God.

Many early Mormons believed this planet was given to Adam as a reward for his own obedience to the Celestial Law on some other world. Adam, known prior to his earthly incarnation as Michael the Archangel, was granted the status of a god because of his righteous life. Earth was to be his domain, and the wives and children he acquired on that other world were to help him populate this one, which he would then rule over as God the Father, spoken of in the Christian scriptures. Adam came to Earth with one of his celestial wives to begin mortal life for their spirit children. Their primary mission was to procreate and populate their world, providing bodies to all their spirit children so those children would have the opportunity to work out their own salvation.

Adam chose Jesus, the firstborn of his innumerable offspring in the preexistence, to be the second member of the Trinity (the third being the Holy Spirit). While here on Earth, before he was sacrificed for the sins of humanity, Jesus himself had at least two wives, Mary Magdalene being one of them. When Jesus returns to resurrect the dead, he will exalt to the highest level of celestial glory all male children of the covenant who have succeeded well in living the Principle. They will become gods of their own worlds.

A man who acquires at least two wives in this life is thought worthy of being such a god, and one with seven or more (called a quorum) is practically assured of it. The wives and children sealed to a deserving man while on Earth will assist him in populating the world he is given to rule over in the next link of this godhood chain. The larger his family here, the better head start they'll have there. (There were even mechanisms in place for marrying off dead women by proxy. This was thought to add to the prestige of the polygamist men to whom these women were married.)

Women cannot become gods in their own right. A woman's hope lay solely in being a wife and mother—one of many wives to her husband; mother of many, many children. She thereby contributes to her husband's future kingdom and will ultimately share in his glory as a goddess, an immortal being who will rule under him and alongside her sister wives for eternity. A woman is dependent on her husband god to "pull her through the veil" of death into heaven and divinity. Polygamous women whose husbands for some reason do not merit becoming gods can be sealed to other worthy men. Unmarried women and monogamous women can look forward to being angels in the next life. Angels are forever single and childless, ministering servants to the gods, and part of the celestial audience attendant at others' earthly weddings.

This was the "gospel" of the early Mormons as we were taught it.

DAD WAS A FIREMAN whose family, understandably, grew much faster than his paycheck—an almost universal problem among polygamists. On Dad's salary, there was no way he could afford separate households for each of his wives. This also was common. Wives always needed, wanted, and at times demanded privacy for themselves and their own broods, but polygamous husbands could rarely afford that for very long, especially as they got deeper into living out the Principle. Different compromises were struck in different households. In ours, for a time, the solution was a half-finished fourplex that accommodated all Dad's wives. He built it himself with the help of a few friends on some acreage he bought in the small Mormon community of Murray, Utah, just outside Salt Lake—a spot his four families came to call "the Farm."

For a few months during the construction of the fourplex, my mother, brothers, sisters, and I lived in our neighbor's chicken coop. I was only four years old the night lightning flashes from a threatening line of thunderstorms woke me. Soon the rain was seeping through the coop's torn, tar-papered roof, soaking me to the skin. The next day we moved into our house, though its rooms still lacked even partitions or plaster. We used blankets for dividers, but at least Dad had his whole family under one roof. Aunt Rhea and Mother lived upstairs, while wives three and four lived below. Eventually, each would have her own all-important and much-utilized kitchen. We thought our fourplex a fairly comfortable arrangement for everyone concerned. Still, my four "mothers" suffered in ways I was too young to understand.

It took just one night for us to discover that our old mattresses had been contaminated while we'd been sleeping in the chicken coop. When we moved into the house, the bedbugs came right along with us. We children cried, thrashing around all night, scratching our bites until they bled. Mother turned on the lights and killed the vermin as we squirmed beneath the covers. (I can still remember the unique stench of squashed bedbugs.) The next morning, Mother hauled the mattresses into the August sun and searched each one individually. She stretched the seams where the creatures hid and multiplied, and then she poured hot, scalding water from her teakettle down the folds on the mattresses' sides. After the hot sun dried them, Mother returned them to our bedroom, but the pesky bugs kept snacking on us, and she finally realized they had migrated into the framed walls, hiding where the two-by-fours were nailed together. She fought them continually until the day we moved away.

DESPITE THE LONG HOURS he put in, Dad's modest income always fell far short of our needs. To make up for it, Mother and her sister wives had to be on their toes and working as a team. Creativity and compassion also came in pretty handy. On many occasions, they had to pull together for mere survival.

One opportunity for some major pulling together came in 1942—a year in which the winter arrived early and set in heavy along the Wasatch Mountains. A late-September snow that year caught three

pregnant wives unexpectedly. Rachel, Ellen, and Rhea were all with
child and couldn't work outside in the cold. This left my mother to
do all the harshest chores for the ever-growing family.

In this bitter cold, Mother gathered fuel for the stove. She re-
cruited three of the older children from Rhea and Ellen's families
and two of her own. Though they lacked rubber boots for their feet
or hats for their bare heads, their mothers tried to bundle the workers
up, pulling odd stockings over their hands for gloves. These stretched
up to their elbows and were held in place by their tattered, secondhand coats.

Thus attired, the ragtag work team emerged from our fourplex
and traipsed along silently in the fresh-fallen snow, each member carrying a gunnysack. They snuck into a neighbor's orchard, lured there
by its stark, bare trees, and then scoured the white fields for already
fallen, more flammable plunder. Breaking branches into small enough
lengths to fit into the cloth sacks, they worked for over an hour as the
small children's hands became numb. Mother spurred them to hold
their sacks open wide so she could fill each one, shoving in just the
amount each child could carry home. When I saw the red faces and
stiff, cold hands of the work crew as it returned home, I was glad my
mother ignored my tearful pleas to go along.

Each morning, Mother would repeat her foray. Gunnysacks in
hand, she'd take a few of us on a "walk," and we'd pick up old shoes,
pieces of crates, and broken branches along the way, always trying
to gather enough fuel for the day's needs. When we were lucky, the
scavenged odds and ends would burn long enough in one stove for
each wife to have a turn cooking. Sometimes there wasn't enough
for them to light four separate fires in their kitchens. This was just
as well. The warmth from that one woodstove generally took the
chill off the room in which we huddled together for comfort during
those cold winter months.

The four wives humbled themselves before God daily, asking and
waiting for him to supply their needs as it became more apparent that
Dad could not. At some point, we were left with cornmeal as our
only staple, though once each week, we could get a two-day supply

of watered-down milk. Mother finally decided that it just wasn't good enough. One day she announced she was taking three of the older kids with her, and they would return only after they'd found something with which to feed the family. Aunt Rhea took her aside and scolded her for building up our hopes falsely, but Mother was determined to procure anything she could to nourish the famished tribe. Having done God's bidding for eleven years now, she expected him to come through for her in this dark hour. Tucking three heavy paper grocery bags under her arm, she led the way out the door and headed toward the nearby fields, where new houses were fast going up.

Mother sang praises to the Almighty as they marched along. She recited a Bible verse, asserting "ye have not, because ye ask not." With what little personal experience in prayer the children had, they implored their maker to send them some rations.

As they approached the construction area, Mother saw a man with a wheelbarrow coming in their direction. She received a premonition and exclaimed to the kids, "I know that whatever that man is dumping on the ground is the answer to our prayers!" My siblings waited quietly while the man returned to his garage, then came back out with his wheelbarrow full a second time. He dumped the contents on top of the first load and then went back inside. He hadn't seemed to notice the little clan standing by, stomping their feet and eyeing his debris. Mother waited about ten minutes, until she was satisfied the man had completed his job. She had no clue what he had deposited, but she knew it would soon be hers.

When she thought it safe, they made a run for it. Mother wanted to cry with joy as she knelt before the heap. Sure enough, God gave us heavenly manna—a magnificent pile of dirty, sprouting potatoes. If she managed it right, this windfall would feed Dad's family for two full weeks. The gleeful kids loaded up their paper bags. Mother instructed them to walk the potatoes home slowly so the bags wouldn't tear open and scatter our treasure down the street. They should then return to the potato pile with our empty wicker baby buggy and two strong gunnysacks, being extra quiet on the way back so as not to draw the attention of any of our nosey, monogamous Mormon neighbors. Mother couldn't bear letting those disapproving tongue-waggers see us scrounging out such a minimal existence.

But the emotions of the three hungry children ran high. They made a clatter probably heard for a block as they raced along behind the ragged buggy, preoccupied with tantalizing visions of hot potato soup.

THE MORMON CHURCH SLOUGHED off many of its basic beliefs beginning late in the nineteenth century, largely under pressure from the civil authorities who outlawed the practice of polygamy, which many Mormons considered integral to their faith. For a brief time after 1890, when they issued the first manifesto renouncing plural marriage, even some of the church leaders continued to privately profess and practice the Principle. They had sent believers to form polygamist colonies across the western United States and as far away as Mexico with orders to safeguard the faith. But political pressures eventually prevailed. A second manifesto, in 1904, ended the practice of polygamy within the Mormon Church, now called the Church of Jesus Christ of Latter-day Saints, or just Latter Day Saints (LDS). The command to live plural marriage was suspended; LDS men were to have only one wife.

Torn between God's law and man's law, those who refused to give up plural marriage had to go into hiding. Some of them fled to Mexico; others went underground within their own communities. Despite the transformed doctrines of the LDS Church, these spiritual refugees considered themselves the true Mormons, the faithful followers of Joseph Smith and his initial converts. Their mission now was urgent—to preserve the faith in a time of dark apostasy. More than ever, they believed, the Principle must be lived and lived strictly. Known as fundamentalists, we were their descendents.

By the time I came along, fundamentalist Mormons were a huge embarrassment to the LDS Church. And the fundamentalists, in turn, both resented and envied the LDS. We considered ourselves the chosen ones, the pure in heart, the true "Zion." And the LDS, having abandoned the Principle, were merely worldly. In a way they were worse than the world, since they'd once known the light and gave it up. We prayed for their return.

In the meantime, we hid. And while we hid, we had to eat and breathe the Principle, continually pumping ourselves up in it so we could withstand the world and the church thinking it wrong. We shielded ourselves from outside influences and tried hard to value persecution as proof of our righteousness. One form persecution took was exclusion from our own temple, the temple the prophet Brigham Young (successor to Joseph Smith) longed to see finished throughout the years he'd faithfully lived and taught plural marriage. The only polygamists ever allowed in now were those masquerading as LDS members or who had not yet personally acted on the Principle.

Yes, the LDS apostates chose the easy path, leaving us to slink about in the shadows. And then they had the nerve to treat *us* as undesirables.

HOW WELL I STILL remember my first day of school. Before that morning, I'd only left the Farm to visit the homes of family friends, to go to Sunday meetings (also at friends' homes), and on one very special occasion, to attend a family picnic at Murray Park. The expedition to Lincoln Elementary School would be my debut into the world—an event mandated by the state, anticipated by me, and feared by my family. The adults in our household worked hard to prepare us.

"You are the special, chosen ones," they told us even more often than usual. "Very few of your classmates will be children of the covenant, so you'll have to be careful of them. Don't let them influence you. Don't listen to their talk or play their games or read their books. Remember, you are chosen; you must keep yourselves pure.

"Now, don't feel bad if they call you names. We have to welcome persecution. It just proves you're the chosen ones, not them.

"Oh, and don't talk to anyone about the Principle."

When the time came, we—the eldest thirteen of the twenty-one children born to my father thus far—left our fourplex in a pack and began the trek to the school. I walked between Joseph and Mary, holding their hands, as excited as we were united. The three of us had all turned five and were going to begin kindergarten. I had on my new, blue and white checkered dress (homemade from printed flour sack material), my brother Richard's worn tennis shoes that were a size too big, and ribbons in my braided hair.

Our older siblings told us younger ones to walk fast and ignore the insults from the teenage kids who ran past, throwing rocks at us and yelling, "Ha, ha, there go the pligs!" I didn't understand what "plig" meant (it was short for "polygamist"), but by the way my brothers and sisters acted, I knew it must be a dirty word. It was a label I'd be branded with for years to come. Knowing myself to be a "special child of God," I was always left to wonder why these kids would be so cruel to me.

My ten-year-old brother, Roger, escorted Joseph, Mary, and me to the unfamiliar kindergarten classroom. It was the teacher's first year at that school. Roger gave her our birth certificates and a paper with our address and phone number on it. After he left for his own class, the teacher smiled, looking at our papers, and asked, "You're triplets, aren't you?"

I, being the bravest of the three, answered, "No, ma'am."

"Are any of you twins?" I shook my head no. A bewildered look crossed her face. "How can you be brothers and sisters and all be five?"

I wondered how the teacher could be so stupid. "We've all got the same father. We live in the same house. But Mary's mom is Ellen, Joseph's mom is Rachel, and my mom is Olive."

I'll never forget her horror. She stammered, "You—you—you mean your father has . . . three different wives?" She looked shocked.

I answered obediently, "Yes, ma'am."

Gasping, she continued, "You mean to tell me he lives with all three wives . . . in the same house?"

I thought maybe she was slighting my dad's first wife, Aunt Rhea, so I clarified. "Oh no, my dad has four wives." Then I added, bragging, "But tonight it's his turn to sleep with Mom."

The new teacher got up from her desk and curtly left the room to confer with the school principal, who it turned out was familiar with polygamist children because they'd infiltrated his school in the past. While we waited for the teacher's return, the whole class kept staring at the three of us. Young as I was, I felt something was amiss. I began to suspect we weren't being given the respect "chosen children of God" deserved. By lunchtime, my classmates had poked such fun at me—about my floppy tennis shoes and our many mothers—that I was finally reduced to tears.

Later that same year, I was kneeling down and accidentally stepped on my fading flour-sack dress, tearing the seam at the waist and revealing my flour-sack panties. I was sick about being seen that way by the other children. My teacher supplied a couple of safety pins to hold the torn skirt in place, but the damage had been done.

Our polygamy and our poverty made us different, but it also bonded us to each other, especially as our sense of conspicuousness and persecution heightened. We got by on bare necessities, sometimes wanting even for those, while the other kids routinely enjoyed what we knew were great blessings: a new pair of shoes to start each school year, store-bought clothes now and then, and the acceptance of our teachers, administrators, and one another.

I began to hate school and to long for the safety of home.

WE HAD ONLY ONE CAR, which Dad took every day to work. His wives rode the bus when they had to go shopping or do other errands, and the rest of us rarely went anywhere except to school and to meet or visit with other fundamentalists. Extracurricular school activities were generally off-limits as well.

All we were allowed to read, aside from what we were assigned by our teachers, were the Mormon scriptures and a running exposition of those scriptures titled *Truth Magazine,* published monthly by one of our dear fundamentalist brethren. By Mormon scriptures, I refer loosely to the Book of Mormon, divinely received, translated, and passed down by our prophet Joseph Smith; the Doctrine and Covenants, a collection of literature on the Mormon faith and revelations on church governance; the Christian Bible, as corrected by Smith in the Inspired Version; and other Mormon books, such as the *Pearl of Great Price,* the *Journal of Discourses,* and later *The Teachings of the Prophet Joseph Smith.* These formed the inventory of our indoctrination.

My aunt Rhea was the spiritual engine within our household. She was pious, serious, and devoted to the Principle. Sure it was the only way to please God and attain glory, she meant for the rest of us to be pious, serious, and devoted to the Principle as well. Whenever I got up early enough in the morning, I could find Aunt Rhea still poring over her scriptures or the newest *Truth Magazine,* steeling herself on the proper ends and means for living plural marriage.

These truths, moreover, were the topic of most every conversation I was privy to whenever friends came by for visits or when we went visiting. The adults discussed the Principle while they cooked and while they sewed, and we prayed about it daily as a family. At Sunday meetings, we children were divided and taught the Principle in age-appropriate doses and concentrations, while in the main room the grown-ups were reminded weekly why they were doing what they were doing and how to do it better. Every precept at every level of our comprehension seemed to support that central call on our lives—to live polygamy. Here is just a sampling of the truths that, over time, became even more real to us than our hunger or our jealousy or the disdain of our neighbors:

1. As chosen vessels of God, we were held in Heaven to come forth in these latter days to live the Celestial Law. In fact, while our spirits were still with God in the preexistence, we chose to be born at this precise time for the very purpose of living polygamy.

2. We were to stay separate from the world, keeping ourselves innocent of its culture, values, and various entanglements.

3. We were to obey God at all times and costs, even if we had to break the laws of the land to do it. The prophet Brigham Young emphasized that we should welcome persecution, for if it ceased, we could be sure we had fallen from God's favor.

4. All men who reached the age of eighteen were to be received into the higher priesthood if they also believed the Mormon scriptures, prayed faithfully, obeyed the Word of Wisdom (did not smoke or drink coffee, tea, or alcohol), and pledged to practice plural marriage. These men (also referred to as brethren) were thereby competent to participate in priesthood activities and to get married, lead their families, and receive God's divine revelations.

5. Women were only to marry men who held the priesthood, because no one else could pull them through the veil. Once married, wives had to obey their husbands strictly.

6. The brethren were to be respected and obeyed, their wisdom and dictates never questioned. (After all, they were the vehicles of God's priesthood and served as his mouthpieces.)

7. We were to be loyal to the brethren and protect them from the scrutiny and interference of outsiders at all times. In short, we were never to talk about our fundamentalist brothers and sisters to anyone.

These various components of our gospel may not have been set out for us quite so bluntly, but this was their gist. It was a handy bunch of mandates for safeguarding such a countercultural lifestyle. But sometimes it was an awful lot to put on children.

WHEN I GOT OLDER, my father and four of his wives lived near another large, polygamous family named Kelsch. My association with these kids was mostly on Sundays, when both families met together in the Kelsch home to be taught the gospel.

One particular Saturday morning, seven of Dad's kids took off running to Murray Park, with eight of the Kelsch kids trailing our heels. We wanted to be first in line for free swimming lessons, so we got there early and waited almost an hour for the swimming pool to open.

Finally, a slim, severe-looking woman in a blue one-piece bathing suit unlocked the gate. She instructed us to stay in line and keep the noise down.

Joseph, Mary, and I signed up first. The three of us were now ten years old. Next was my sister Rula, who was twelve, sisters Nan and Norma, who were both eight, and Millie, seven. We seven gave the woman our same address.

This went along pretty well and without incident until the eight Kelsch kids started signing up. Two were six, two were eight, two were ten, and two were twelve. It was then the swimming teacher realized all fifteen kids had only two last names and two addresses. She threw her pen down with an air of authority and said, "Somebody here is trying to be funny. I'll send every one of you home, and you can't swim unless you tell me the truth."

The air went dead. We'd been cautioned never to tell anyone we were polygamists unless it was an emergency. I reasoned instantly that since Mother and Dad couldn't pay for swimming lessons and these were free, the truth had to be told. As far as I could see, this was an emergency.

Acting as spokesperson, I stepped closer to the table. I lowered my voice, trying to avert any more of the uncalled-for attention we'd already received. "L-L-Lady," I stuttered, hoping she was smart enough to understand, "we all have different mothers, but we have the same dad." To avoid further complication, I added, "We really do have the same address. It's the same with these Kelsch kids, and . . ."

She looked more dumfounded with each word I spoke. Picking up her pen, she tilted her head at a quizzical angle and interrupted me midsentence. She pointed to the two ten-year-old Kelsch kids. "You're half brothers?" she asked, astounded. They nodded.

"Now, you two are half brothers, right?" she asked the twelve year olds. They, too, nodded.

She got excited, clearly thinking she'd finally figured this mess out. She thrust her pen at each age group in rapid succession, using it to separate them as she went along. "Now, you're half?" They nodded. "You're full and you're half?" Her pen went back and forth. Finally, she yelled at little eight-year-old Dale Kelsch, whose mind by this time had wandered onto other things. "Hey, kid, are you full?"

He looked up at her in total earnestness and said in a timid voice, "No, ma'am, I'm hungry."

We all broke up laughing as the lady sat there with a dazed look on her face. Finally, in disgust, she waved her arms, giving us all permission to go into the pool.

After that confusion, I realized why Dad always refused to allow us to call one another half brothers or half sisters. To him, and eventually to us as well, all his children were simply brothers and sisters.

AS I GOT OLDER, I began to stew about some of our fundamentalist doctrines. If Adam was God, for example, whom did he disobey? I was told such questions showed disrespect and a lack of faith. "Be quiet and believe," I would hear from my older brothers and my devout aunt Rhea.

Another time I actually raised my hand in a Sunday school class and asked how it could be that the godly brethren we knew—all of whom were someone's sons—could one day receive their own worlds to populate and rule and at the same time be required to help their fathers to populate theirs.

The question was disallowed, and I learned quickly that our faith had a lot more to do with righteous practice than understanding. My worries turned from the beliefs themselves to how well we were living them. Were we succeeding? And when my turn came, would I know what to do and be able to do it?

CHAPTER TWO

A teaching that was to have a grave impact on how I lived my life can be summed up quite simply as follows: people fail the Principle, but the Principle itself never fails. The way it was put to us was really more like a challenge, even a dare: plural marriage will damn more people than it saves precisely because so few who attempt it will be able to live up to such a high calling. When families splintered, when spouses delved into unrighteousness, when children of the covenant lacked the courage to live polygamy for themselves, it was always the fault of human weakness and sin, never a problem with the Principle.

Over the years, in a great variety of ways, we saw so many of our number fail—some of them our own parents, or worse still, our leaders. The odd effect on me and on many others was to make us resolve all the harder to be among those who prevailed. If glory was that hard to attain, it must be well worth having. Besides, what was our alternative?

I WAS TOO YOUNG to comprehend the problems among my father and his four wives, but soon after I started kindergarten, my mother moved out of the fourplex. A short time later, both Aunt Rhea and Aunt Rachel also left Dad. Yes, even Aunt Rhea. At my age, it was baffling to me why three of our four mothers suddenly left.

Years later, when I tried to find out why, Mother admitted to me that Dad had a drinking problem. This, along with his inability to support them financially or meet any of their emotional or physical needs, forced Rachel, Rhea, and Mother to move out and struggle on alone.

After that conversation with Mother, she never talked much about Dad to me, except to make sure I remembered about his drinking problem and also that I knew he swore and smoked. "If he couldn't even keep the Word of Wisdom, how could he expect to become a god?" Mother said. My father had violated those relatively minor rules, even while living the higher and harder law of polygamy.

I regretted that I never got to know my father any better. It was terribly lonely to be raised without him. I needed his love and acceptance. When my mother left him, I was torn between him and my loyalty to her. After that, I didn't get to see him very often, and when I did, I was afraid of him.

The most vivid recollection I have of my father was the time he picked me up at our little rented house after work and took me to spend the night with him and Ellen. (Of his wives, she alone had elected to stay with him.) I was barely six, and without Mother there, I was too frightened to eat much supper. Dad must have sensed my discomfort because he allowed me to sleep in his big brass bed with him and Aunt Ellen. He hugged me, telling me how special I was. "Don't ever forget me, Renski. I know your name's Irene, but you'll always be Renski to me. Come visit your ol' man whenever you can." He held me close as I fell asleep in his arms.

I'll never forget that night. I came halfway out of a deep sleep, sensing something warm and wet. Then I heard Dad's angry shouts. "Damn it, Ellen, get this kid out of here. She's pissed all over me!" He shoved me out of bed. "Hell sakes, Ellen, put this kid on the damn pot," he yelled as he jumped up and went to the kitchen to heat some water so he could take a bath. I could still hear him grumbling. "I've got to leave for work by five o'clock!"

Aunt Ellen wearily slipped off the wet panties that clung to my bottom. I was groggy and could hardly move, but I hoped to escape Dad's further wrath by letting her place me on the chamber pot. (We still didn't have an operational indoor toilet.) I had to hold myself carefully over the two-gallon "chamber" so the stifling stuff inside wouldn't touch my bum. I tried hard to balance myself, but somehow the whole stinkin' pot tipped over and spilled in all directions. I could do nothing but sprawl right in the middle of the awful mess. I was horrified.

"Good hell, Ellen, get that damn kid in here! Wash her off in my bath water so I can take her home before I'm late for work."

On the way back to my mother's, I hardly said a word. I couldn't even look at him. I thought Dad didn't like me anymore. He must have noticed my quivering lip, because he reached in his pocket and gave me a quarter. My deep longings for a father soon began to fade.

AFTER ALL THE COVENANTS my mother and dad made to one another before God and angels, plus one or two witnesses, it was dire poverty that finally eroded their commitment. That, and Dad's inability to meet Mother's most profound needs as a woman. According to a journal I found many years later, after her death, this failure broke my mother's heart.

She tried to live polygamy, but found her life joyless in it. Waiting for her turn alongside Dad's other three young wives, Mother found her time with him was too limited. His passions were spent by the time he came to her door. His emotions were consumed by alcohol before he came to see any of them. Mother was afraid of him even while she yearned for him. Sometimes she wondered why God didn't want women and children to be happy, too.

My mother lived in a religious no-win situation. She was devoted to a tradition that defeated her. And she passed this dilemma along to us. Though she loved the Mormon Church, "it was out of order," she said. It ceased to proclaim God's law of polygamy, and this not only confused people about God's requirements for exaltation but it also left the faithful in the lurch. Perhaps the church's failure even contributed to the downfall of some, like her and Dad, who couldn't quite get to the polygamy finish line despite years of sacrifice and struggle.

Mormons who rejected the LDS's manifestos of 1890 and 1904 were instructed to bear all the children they could and thereby multiply the numbers of the faithful, but no one seemed to much consider who would support these abundant offspring. Each man married whomever he could persuade to become a producing member of his "family kingdom," and each wife then set about fulfilling her maternal role. Not to worry, "God would provide." But far too often, God came in the form of county and state welfare. With six young children to raise, my mother was forced to live on welfare for eight years after leaving Dad. Her heart ached that she could never give us the things she thought we needed.

Mother tried unsuccessfully for several years to get an official "release" (divorce) from Dad, but this could only be done by the "priesthood holder" who married them in the first place. This man told Mother he'd gladly release her, but only on the condition she marry him instead. It didn't take her two seconds to realize she'd rather be single forever (forever, because in heaven she'd be an angel instead of a goddess) than marry this disgusting, obese old man. It had been unbearable enough being wife number two. Why now stoop to being the seventh wife of a high priest?

Soon after she first left him, Dad came and pled with Mother to take him back. She was so painfully lonely that in a moment of weakness, she finally agreed, and she returned to the fourplex. This lasted for only a short time. Not many months later, Mother was alone again, now pregnant with her sixth child.

All of my mother's pregnancies were rough. She'd often spent a month or more confined to her bed, trying to not miscarry. As every delivery approached, she feared she would die. Aunt Rhea was the one whose nurturing and gentle coaching helped Mother pull through each painful ordeal. Afterward, while Mother recuperated (the custom then was for women to lie in bed for ten days after giving birth), Aunt Rhea would bathe her and rub lotion on her arms and legs. The tender treatment she received from Aunt Rhea gave her license at times to pretend she was weaker than she was and incapable of resuming her duties—a situation Dad generally responded to with

impatience, which made Mother feel even more alone and more rejected by him. Soaking in the loving attention Aunt Rhea showered
on her, she resented the fact that her own husband never rubbed or
caressed her and rarely touched her at all. Mother often felt her sister
Rhea was the only person who really loved her.

With no Aunt Rhea down the hall, no vitamins, and what little
nourishment she could get after her welfare checks were spent on
us, Mother's final pregnancy thoroughly taxed her naturally thin, frail
frame. Still, she somehow carried my sister Erma to term. The baby
was delivered by cesarean section at the county hospital in May 1943.
It had been four years since Mother delivered her last child. Erma
was a cute, red-faced doll who won her heart instantly. Mother doted
on her and immediately repented of ever thinking the pregnancy
had been a mistake. But when she thought about caring for her new
daughter, desperation enveloped her.

Mother was a dreamer who never made peace with her life. I
remember her as multitalented—a singer, typist, seamstress, poet, and
teacher. And I remember her as a servant, always doing for others
when she had any energy at all to spare. But to her own children she
was distant and inaccessible, caught up with regrets about how things
might have been, caught up with her poverty and isolation and need.
At times she got depressed, and then we had her even less. My brothers and sisters and I felt she'd abandoned us, perhaps not as much as
Dad had, but she'd emotionally abandoned us just the same.

IN JULY 1944, state and federal authorities arrested nineteen men
throughout Utah for the practice of plural marriage. My father was
one of them. The raid was intended to stop polygamy by making an
example of these men. This was the biggest crackdown on polygamists in a decade, and the State of Utah said its actions were necessary to curb abuses of women, children, and welfare agencies. Soaring
numbers of applications for government aid came in from women
claiming to be single moms, but who continually turned up pregnant. Girls as young as fourteen were bearing children by men old

enough to be their fathers. Polygamy was on the rise, and something needed to be done.

At the tender age of seven, I appeared with a large group of polygamist families in a double-page photo spread in *LIFE* magazine. The story was so unusual, the editors gave it prime placement. Not since the 1890s, as far as anyone could remember, had a national publication addressed the oddity of American polygamy.

Among those arrested, fifteen signed a statement promising to abandon their plural wives and the practice of polygamy, and these men were released. My father and three other staunch believers refused, determined to sit in jail forever, if necessary, rather than make bastards of most their children. Dad, with only one wife still willing to live with him, said he remained committed to the laws of God, including polygamy.

The polygamists who signed the statements mostly went right on practicing polygamy, apparently undaunted by the arrests and their own disavowals, though perhaps a little less esteemed by the surprised rest of us. But Dad and his three steadfast friends who did exactly what we all expected them to do spent two and a half years in the Utah State Prison. He called it "Crowbar College."

Mother was never allowed to visit Dad inside the prison, because she wasn't legally married to him. Only Aunt Rhea, his legal wife, could go in. But Mother once took her children to see him anyway. Hoping for a miracle that would gain us entrance, she persuaded a friend to drive us to the prison grounds on visitors' day. Once there, while other families went in and out, she waited with all six of us in the crowded parking lot. When Dad finally came into the prison yard with the other convicts, we watched as she led little Erma over to the fence to meet her dad for the very first time.

I remember him stooping down with tears streaming down his anguished face and putting a quarter through the squares in the wire to coax little Erma to let him kiss her. Mother then scooped Erma up in her arms and walked rapidly toward the car before Dad could see that she was crying, too. He was the only love she'd ever known, but in order to survive, she needed to quit loving him and move on with her life. She learned that desire brings pain with it, so she vowed never to desire a man again.

The long ride home that afternoon seemed to take forever. None of us frightened kids said a word as Mother sat beside us, weeping silently all the way.

I WAS TWELVE when Mother applied for homestead rights in an arid, sparsely settled region near the Utah-Nevada border called Trout Creek. The homesteading program involved the receipt of 150 undeveloped acres in the Utah sticks in exchange for nothing but a commitment to improve them. Mother planned to farm on her homestead, though we later discovered it was too sandy to sustain much in the way of vegetation. All the water with which we tried to irrigate disappeared instantly into the deep sand, sinking too quickly to be grabbed up by seeds or roots near the surface. Our farm was like a giant sieve. But Mother, who had by this time settled for a civil divorce from Dad (granted on the basis of her being a common-law wife), felt she finally had to get away from Salt Lake City and focus her attention on her neglected children. At first, Trout Creek seemed the place to do it.

Aunt Rhea, always worried that my mother was relying on me too heavily around the house and yet depriving me of proper religious instruction and example, insisted I come live with her and her seven children for the school year. Having obtained the official release from my father that my mother had been unable to get (two different elders married the two sisters to my father), Rhea was now living in Farmington, Utah, a little north of Salt Lake. I was there when Mother moved to Trout Creek with my sisters, Becky and Erma. (My brothers had already left home. Roger was married and living in Salt Lake City; Douglas and Richard worked as hired hands on a ranch some thirty miles away.) During the Christmas holidays that year, Mother came to see me. I was so homesick, I prevailed upon her to let me go back with her to Trout Creek so I could be a part of her fresh start in life.

A Mr. Walter Faber began building Mother a two-bedroom frame home on her sandy property. He was a former Mormon who brought his family to Trout Creek to found some sort of new religious sect, though not a polygamist one. My mother accepted his tremendous generosity as a neighborly kindness. As for her land, Mother was determined to clear a piece of it herself with a borrowed tractor and at least plant a large vegetable garden. By the time I arrived, she and my eleven-year-old sister Becky had already dug a well to supply the new homestead. They had to excavate fourteen feet before finally reaching water.

While Mother's house was being built, we moved in with the Faber family, and I enrolled in Partoun School—the only seventh grader in a one-room secondary school. When summer came, I was able to get work at a ranch owned by Chet and Nelda Young, acquaintances of my brothers'. I tended the Youngs' five children and helped with the housecleaning. Their ranch was about ninety miles from Trout Creek, so I didn't see any of my family the entire summer. At the end of it, I came home with a hundred dollars in my pocket, and I finally got to move into our brand-new house.

When I saw my sister Becky, I took her in my arms and cried. Just being together in our own home was heaven. We were six hours west of Salt Lake City, in the middle of nowhere, and I was ready to be a family again. I missed my three older brothers, but at least I had Becky and Erma and Mother. Still just thirteen, I yearned for the comfort and security of some togetherness after all the ways our family had been torn apart over the years.

That first night, I helped out with the chores until the warm autumn sun went down, and then I retired to gab with my sisters. Becky begged me to sleep outside with her, where we could talk and have our privacy, and Mother happily gave her consent. Since seven-year-old Erma was still rather shy around me, I insisted she be included. Snuggling up close together while we slept would give us a chance to express the sisterly love we felt for each other.

Becky helped me pull the old blue and white striped mattress off the metal bed in our room. We puffed along dramatically as we dragged the unwieldy thing across the yard, stopping often to rest, and then we giggled like idiots when we finally dropped it in among the sagebrush about thirty yards from the house. The sagebrush might at least muffle our voices and laughter. We slipped into our nighties and tucked our clothes under the foot of the mattress, settling in for bed. Soon it was pitch black except for a dazzling spray of stars across the desert sky.

One thing kept nagging at me and preventing me from sleeping. Earlier in the evening, a neighbor from a nearby ranch showed up for a visit. I took an instant disliking to him, mostly because of how he kept his eyes glued on my mother. I just knew his supposed friendship with her was really about what the Bible calls lust. He also laughed too loud, with an awful bray, was ugly and unkept, and when he wasn't looking hungrily at Mother, he flitted his eyes about the room in a manner I found, well, shifty. Furthermore, when I gave him blatant hints to leave, he'd ignored them, showing a total lack of manners. He was still inside with Mother when we gathered on the mattress outside.

I felt uneasy about the whole thing. Yes, Mother was forty years old, but could she keep this fellow in line? I well knew no man could be fully trusted except for the brethren who held the priesthood and made a covenant with God to live plural marriage. Horace Nielson, still a bachelor at forty-eight, couldn't possibly qualify. He wasn't even a fundamentalist.

According to Brigham Young, who had at least twenty-seven wives, "Any young man who is unmarried at the age of twenty-one is a menace to the community." A man had to be responsible and get married, taking many wives in order to bring God's "special spirits" into the world. If Horace loved the Lord, why didn't he have at least six wives and thirty or more kids by now?

I lay on my stomach, talking to Becky. Every once in a while, I'd raise up and squint into the darkness to try and see if Horace's old green Chevy was still in our yard. Becky tried to convince me it was gone, but I sure hadn't heard it leave. I got more indignant by the minute. Mother was going to have to take a few cues from me.

From now on, she'd have to put her foot down and tell Horace to stay away. After all, the scriptures said to avoid the very "appearance of evil."

Getting drowsy, I surrendered the whole matter after awhile, but I bolted wide awake when I heard coyotes howling in the distance. Becky and Erma assured me we were safe, that they heard the howling all the time, and I finally dozed off into a dreamless sleep.

I awoke to the biting chill of the morning air. Slipping into my sandals, I headed for the outhouse while my sisters still slept. Parked on the cold, unplaned seat, I wondered how many people left this privy with slivers in their butts. I giggled, then caught myself. I was being silly and light-minded again. Many a well-meaning friend or relation brought this fault to my attention. I'd tried to overcome it, asking God many times to forgive me, but somehow he'd never cured me. Shivering, I ran back to bed and crawled in between the girls.

When I saw smoke rising from the tin pipes of the kitchen stove, I grabbed my bundle of wrinkled clothes from under the mattress and slipped into my blouse and jeans. Then I started toward the house. Unable to talk me into staying outside with them, Becky and Erma, still in their nightgowns, raced behind me.

As I approached the kitchen, the familiar aroma of Mother's hot-cakes made my mouth water. I burst through the door, yelling, "I get the first ones before the stove gets too hot!"

There sat bald-headed, disheveled Horace in front of a half-eaten stack of Mother's prime pancakes, smothered with butter and her homemade syrup. And there sat Mother right beside him. As if that weren't enough, Horace had the nerve to invite me to sit down and have breakfast in my own home. I was undone. I hated him. Horace, that horse's ass, had gone too far.

I looked him in the eye like a snake about to strike. I usually tried not to be mean to anybody, but at Horace that morning I let swear words fly out of my mouth that I'm ashamed now to repeat.

He got the message. He looked at Mother as though he expected her to stick up for him, but she wasn't prepared to take sides. Then he got up slowly and went out to his car without a word.

Mother looked like she wanted to cry, but she scolded me instead. "I can't believe a daughter of mine would talk like that!"

Horace's motor revved a few times out in front of the house. Mother took the cue. She ran out the door and climbed in beside him. As they pulled away, she called out, "I'm going to Nielson's Ranch. I'll be back later." Horace and his siblings owned the ranch, such as it was.

After they left, neither Becky nor Erma said a thing. Though too angry to eat, I did cook up the remaining batter for my sisters. After that, I put a bucket of water on the stove to heat for the dishes, stripped everything from the cupboards, and scrubbed all the shelves. Then I rearranged the dishes in an orderly fashion, all the while seething.

As Becky and Erma wisely stayed out of my way, I accomplished even more over the next two hours. I swept the ever-present sand out of the kitchen and living room and mopped the gold and white linoleum beneath to a perfect shine. Then I shook out the two shag throw rugs and placed them back in front of each door so we could at least wipe our feet before tracking the sand and dust inside.

I took two galvanized pails out to the well, where an old, leaky bucket with a big metal bolt wired onto one side was tied by a rope to a round wooden winch. I lowered the antique contraption into the well six times in order to fill my two pails. Back in the house, I carefully placed the pails of clean, fresh water side by side on the counter next to the sink. I'd done a lot more work than I'd started out to do.

Finally, I heard a car drive up. I glanced out the kitchen window and saw Mother getting out of Horace's Chevy. Still furious, I worried about facing him again, about what I might say.

Through the open screen, I heard Mother ask plaintively, "Should I just tell her?"

"Well, use your own judgment, Olive."

By the time they got to the kitchen door, I'd jerked it open and squared off against the both of them. "TELL ... ME ... WHAT?" I demanded. I was already pretty headstrong back then, though I didn't realize it at the time.

Mother whispered apologetically, "Irene, don't be so angry ... please ... I wanted to tell you last night ..." She faltered. "But ... I didn't know how. Horace and I are married!"

I saw it all in an instant. They deceived me, every one of them—not just Mother and Horace, but Becky and Erma, too. So much for our private little slumber party under the stars. It was Mother and Horace who'd needed the privacy, and they'd needed it from me. My sisters had simply been their pawns. Whom could I trust now?

My eyes burned, and my vision blurred. I whirled around, bolted out the door, and took off running through the fields, through the mesquites and sage, running faster and faster, trying to gain momentum to escape. My grand homecoming, the fresh start we'd waited and worked for, was a mirage. Mother had gone off and married a monogamist, and a creepy one at that.

I kept right on running. I was gasping for breath and my legs ached, but I pushed myself further until I found a large mesquite tree growing out of a sand dune. I prostrated myself facedown in the shade of its branches and sobbed. I howled and I cursed. Finally, I begged God to be kind and let me die.

For hours, I lay there in the sand. As the shade disappeared, the midday sun beat down on me and drenched my blouse with sweat. Perversely, I enjoyed the discomfort.

During my long repose, I thought about my whole life. I didn't like the sad, lonely childhood I saw as I reflected. Now I couldn't wait to be grown up. If God wouldn't let me die, perhaps he'd bring along a worthy man one day who would take me out of this mess. He'd have to be a man who would love me the way a woman ought to be loved, the way my mother should have been but never was and probably never would be. Maybe with such a man, I would finally feel secure.

I'd lost my mother, and I was even confused about the Principle. Thirteen years old has never been so lonely.

THE FOLLOWING SUMMER, I was glad to get away from Trout Creek and work again for Chet and Nelda Young at their ranch near

Milford, Utah. Over the three summers I eventually spent with them, the Youngs were always wonderful to me. They offered a family atmosphere in which I felt loved.

Nelda taught me the things my mother neglected, partly because Mother didn't do them herself. Mother was a terrible housekeeper and cook. But Nelda showed me how to make homemade bread and butter, cook, mend, hand stitch, and darn stockings. She even taught me how to separate dirty clothes into light and dark batches in order to keep the whites bright—a finer point of laundering with which Mother never bothered.

At first, it seemed Nelda constantly had to make me redo things I'd messed up. But she patiently trained me that first year, and then they invited me back again for two more summer stints. In the end, I must have done something right. Mostly it was Nelda, though. I couldn't have asked for a better teacher. The education she gave me prepared me for raising my own family.

While we worked, Nelda helped me memorize hymns. I gained new confidence in my singing. They didn't ostracize me for my fundamentalism, but their example of another way was just one more factor contributing to my religious questioning around this time.

Back at Trout Creek, my mother was just as glad I was gone for the summer. She figured it would solve a lot of her problems. I knew before she did that her marriage was a big mistake. Horace was what we called a "jack Mormon"—one only in name. He practiced no religion, was completely unspiritual. It showed in his life.

As it turns out, the reason Mother married Horace was not love, but cancer. She'd been feeling bad for a long time, and the doctors who finally diagnosed her told her she didn't have long to live. She kept this from everyone. Desperate not to leave her children in the hands of any welfare agency, however, she married Horace. Trapped out on his family ranch with nothing but brothers and sisters and crops for company, he homed in on her the moment she arrived in Trout Creek. She'd accepted his pushy marriage proposal without really knowing him, hoping that when the time came, he'd at least prove superior to foster care. She didn't tell her children about her cancer until much later, after she'd miraculously conquered the disease.

In the meantime, Horace proved an even lousier parent than he was a husband. He resented Mother's kids, and we resented him. His childish, hurtful antics shock me even now. For example, he put all sorts of silly restrictions on the food we could eat, though he served himself royally. He also wouldn't let Mother buy us clothes we needed, even with her own money. And when Mother got her certification through a correspondence course and began teaching school, he suffered so from the loss of her constant attention that he apparently determined he wouldn't share her with us at all. That's when he went from childish to abusive.

Once during this time, little Erma was burning up with a fever. Horace came in and found Mother rocking her gently in our old wooden rocker. With no warning at all, he jerked Erma out of Mother's arms and shoved her, sending her sprawling across the sandy floor.

"You leave my woman alone, ya hear?" he bellowed. "She's mine!"

For the first time, hate filled Mother's eyes.

After that, Horace frequently sent my sisters outside so he could get Mother all to himself. She began to realize why I'd instinctively hated the man. Turns out, she traded polygamy for a lethal possessiveness.

Horace worked many miles away on an assembly line at the Tooele Ordnance Depot. He would wear his steel-toed work shoes home. Once when he came in and found little Erma hugging Mother, he knocked her away and commenced kicking her with those awful shoes until Mother finally fought him off. He liked to pick on Erma because she was the easiest target.

Once when I was there, Horace tried pulling the same sort of tantrum on me. It wasn't long before he ordered me out of "his" house. But I stood my ground, as always.

"Your house?" I yelled. "Hell, this is our house! Mother built this house. If you were any kind of man, you'd build your own house."

"You're all just bastards!" he screamed, starting to get up out of his chair to come at me.

I was at the stove stirring the coals with a poker at the time. I whirled around, brandishing my red-hot sword in his face. "You better take that back!" I yelled.

He went ashen. He flailed his arms about, almost falling off the chair as it tipped back against the wall. "Don't . . ." he pleaded. Then he yelled, "Olive! Olive!"

Luckily for him, Mother came running. "Irene, stop it. That's enough," she ordered. Mother was even more afraid of Horace than she'd been of my father.

Some nights, Becky and I could hear him through the wall, beating her. She'd cry out, begging him to stop, but he went right on hurting her. I'd see her bruises the next morning, and I'd plead with her to leave him, to no avail. For the time being, Mother was determined to live with her mistake.

Once I found her crying on her bed, and she told me it was because she failed so miserably at the beautiful principle of polygamy. She made me promise I wouldn't tell Aunt Rhea what she'd done—marrying Horace. How could I possibly refuse her?

It was so awful living there with him that Becky and I often ran away from home. Neighbors would take us in for weeks at a stretch. Most of them had known our stepfather a long time. They understood. But Mother always found us eventually and brought us back, probably telling herself it was the best thing for us.

I began to yearn for a different home.

CHAPTER THREE

I finally got Mother's permission to move to Hurricane, Utah, where Aunt Rhea now taught school and lived with the four of her children who weren't already off pursuing plural marriages themselves. Without telling my aunt I was coming, I caught a ride to Salt Lake City with some friends, then rode a Greyhound bus all by myself the whole six hours to Hurricane—a dusty, windblown town below the climbing plateau to Zion's Canyon. At fourteen now, I overcame my fears and made that scary, grown-up trip because I was desperate for some kindness and stability—commodities Aunt Rhea always seemed to have in extra measure. Despite my surprising her, she seemed pleased to see me, and she allowed me to spend the year with her while I attended the ninth grade. I felt some lingering guilt about leaving my sisters back in Trout Creek, where Horace could torment them, but I had to live my life. Besides, he and I fought so much, I thought they might all be better off without me there.

I don't think Aunt Rhea knew about Mother's marriage to Horace at this point, but she knew things were not as they should be with her sister in Trout Creek. She took it as her personal duty to set an example and to help Olive's spiritually undernourished kids to embrace polygamy. So, once I got to Hurricane, she poured it on, mostly just by being herself—getting up early to study the scripture, praying continually, always talking up the gospel (relative to exaltation through plural marriage), relating her many dreams and visions of things that were sure to happen in the future. I thought she went a little overboard at times, but she cared about me and took me in, so I listened. To this day, I wonder if she really understood how messed up I was that ninth-grade year. Probably so, because she put energy into straightening me out.

It seemed there were certain aspects of the Principle I had yet to learn or that I'd simply never focused on before, and Aunt Rhea meant to fill me in, help me focus. After all, I was getting to the age at which I might sorely need to know these things.

Part of the beauty of polygamy, she claimed, was the advantage it gave women who wanted to marry (all right-thinking women, in her opinion). Within the Principle, girls generally got to choose their husbands, not the other way around. Indeed, it really eliminated all the competition among the fairer sex. If a girl wanted a man who was already married, no problem. She could just make her desires known, and the other wives were supposed to welcome her into the fold. The bigger the family here, the bigger the kingdom there, so everyone was supposed to rejoice when the family expanded, whether with wife or with child. Since each new wife was supposed to contribute several new children, perhaps they were even the greater asset. And to the gentlemen, the brethren who were looking toward godhood, more wives of course meant more celestial prestige. Why would they ever turn anyone down? The proverbial wisdom floating around polygamous circles stated it bluntly: if a man didn't love or desire a particular girl who wanted him, he should marry her anyway and just hope for love the next time around. One of the many brethren waiting in the wings would surely snap up any available woman he did not.

Next, Aunt Rhea said, I must understand the role of a plural wife. It was singular—to have children. The reasons were many: to obey God's commandment, to make our husbands more deserving of exaltation, to thereby attain exaltation for ourselves, and to help populate the worlds we would rule throughout eternity. The prophet Brigham Young had given it yet another emphasis: "There are multitudes of pure and holy spirits waiting to take tabernacles [bodies]. Now what is our duty? To prepare tabernacles for them; to take a course that will not tend to drive those spirits into families of the wicked, where they will be trained in wickedness, debauchery, and every species of crime. It is the duty of every righteous man and woman to prepare tabernacles for all the spirits they can.... This is the reason why the doctrine of plurality of wives was revealed, that the noble spirits which are waiting for tabernacles might be brought forth." To these ends, polygamous wives were encouraged to have a child every year for as long as they could. I was young and strong, and my prime years for childbearing were fast approaching.

Finally, Aunt Rhea taught me the law of purity. It first entailed abstaining from most any physical contact with the opposite sex prior to marriage. Even kissing was disallowed. Once married, contact was allowed within strict limits. I discovered that sex had the same singular role within polygamous families that wives had—procreation. Aunt Rhea said each of us possessed a "divine procreative power" we were to use only for divine procreative purposes. If a husband and wife indulged in sex for any other purpose, they could even commit adultery with each other. Consequently, it was forbidden during pregnancy, lactation, and menses, as well as after menopause. I wondered even then if it was okay to enjoy sex whenever it had to be done in order to bring forth the requisite annual child. But I didn't dare ask my pious aunt.

She told me the story of a wonderfully devout, polygamous woman who had sex only nine times in her whole life, and she had nine kids to show for it. "Isn't that beautiful, Renski?" my aunt said at the end of that story. "She was such an obedient, spiritual soul. I just wish we all could be so righteous!" I suspected she meant me, and I wanted to be that good, too. But of course, I had yet to be tested.

TWO OF AUNT RHEA'S daughters, Donna and Myra, were already married—the second and third wives of the same man. I was very close to Donna even though she was seven years older. She and Myra, along with two of my aunt Ellen's daughters, lived about twenty-eight miles south of Hurricane, all the way down on the Utah-Arizona border in a growing polygamist homesteading settlement called Short Creek.

Under the direction of a man claiming to be a prophet of God, at least forty fundamentalist men moved their polygamous families into this far-flung, out-of-the-way place to escape the gaze of observers and the law. Some built houses, while others lived temporarily in whatever shelter they could find, such as trailers with lean-tos or large army tents. Three of my sisters lived in cleaned-out chicken coops, the other in a half-finished house. The idea was for the settlement to become self-sufficient so that its members could live as independent of the outside world as possible. Nothing like Short Creek had been around in my younger years, but there was precedent for it. Joseph Smith called this sort of communal living the "United Order." The people at Short Creek said they were making a concerted effort to live the United Order. To this end, every household displayed a photograph of their prophet in the way Catholics might display a picture of the pope. Each family also hung a plaque to remind them: THE KINGDOM OF GOD OR NOTHING.

I visited my sisters at "the Creek" often, which gave me a chance to get acquainted with almost everyone in town. Most of the colonists were related to one another, either by blood or by marriage. Contrary to the way Aunt Rhea told me it should work, older men in Short Creek often traded their young daughters to each other for wives. I knew of several instances in which a man married a widow or a divorcee with several children, and then he also married her young girls when they reached puberty (sometimes even before). Of course, those lusty men always claimed they never did a thing without a revelation from God.

Soon I became friendly with the Short Creek girls my own age. During the time I knew them, several disappeared from public view, only to reappear months later with new babies in their arms. Most of these girls were secretly married off to men old enough to be their fathers. It was done in secret just because that was the polygamous way; subsequent marriages were always kept quiet so members of the community could claim ignorance if anyone from the outside ever questioned them about specific relationships. None of these young wives and mothers ever mentioned the word *love* when they finally whispered the truth to me. Not once.

One fourteen-year-old girl who'd just had her first baby confided in me that she'd never even had a menstrual period until after the baby was born. Her husband had married her at that young age so she could bear as many children as possible. This was important to him because he wanted to become a god with his own kingdom in heaven, where he and his wives and children could be numberless and beget spirit children to populate other worlds.

Conveniently, the Short Creek elders sent most of the young, unmarried men away on what were called "work missions," where they were to earn money for the colony while they learned trades, mostly in construction. During these two-year stints, the young men were advised to live with other fundamentalists who would give them free room and board. Their entire paychecks were then sent back to the leaders for the support of the giant polygamous families back home and to "advance the work of God."

This seemed well and good in theory, but I couldn't help noticing how God seemed biased against these young men. While they were away, he gave revelations to the older men to marry all the young, healthy, beautiful girls. Then when the young bachelors returned from their work missions, they were rewarded with the leftovers—girls who were obese, homely, handicapped, or ill. Understandably, many of these young men questioned God's supposed will for them. Still, they mostly complied, assured that they could marry girls they desired later on.

As I took these things in, naughty little thoughts crept into my mind. I began to think of the brethrens' so-called godly testimonies as testi*phonies*.

Every Friday, several of us would go to dances at the Creek. I danced the Scottish polka, the Virginia reel, the two-step, the waltz, and the John Paul Jones. I generally had the time of my life dancing with the married men, every one of whom was available. God must have gotten his wires crossed, however. Within a matter of months, he'd given twelve different men a revelation that I should be his next wife. I wondered why God didn't spare us all the confusion by giving me the revelation. Meanwhile, Donna and Myra wanted me to marry their husband so we could all be together in eternity.

I became increasingly concerned about God's future plans for me. How could I know for myself what he wanted me to do? Was I even to take the polygamous path my mother took? If I did, I would somehow have to do it more successfully, more righteously. And if I took that path, would I let others, like these brethren at Short Creek, tell me who God meant to bind me to forever? My heart told me no— no to all of this. I recalled the day I'd cried alone for hours under the mesquite tree after Mother finally told me she'd married Horace. All I wanted that day was one person to love me, and love me well. That was still what I wanted in the depths of my soul. And when I pictured it—my future husband and me—there were no other wives in other bedrooms down the hall. But Aunt Rhea and dear Donna and all these brethren who I'd been taught to trust as the mouthpieces of God were telling me it should be otherwise. I so wanted to belong. If only God would testify to me personally that polygamy was his call for me.

One Sunday at the Creek, I heard a sermon by Brother Hammon that profoundly impacted my thinking on all this. "Mary, the mother of Christ, was only fourteen when he was born," the brother told us. Now, he said, time is running out before Christ returns, so any girls who feel led to do so should "follow in the Virgin's footsteps" immediately by marrying and having children before it's too late.

However, from here on out, none of us were to do any more courting on our own. Instead, the leading brethren would seek special revelations from God so each girl would be sure to marry the partner God chose for her. It seemed all the revealing God had been doing to the individual brethren had gotten thoroughly out of hand; he'd been telling many of them to marry the very same attractive young girls, and this was clearly not the direction righteous polygamy was to take. The elders of the Short Creek colony felt they had to step in and referee as best they could, so they decided that all God's divine revelations on the topic of marriage would henceforth be disseminated only through them.

One of these leading brethren, Uncle Rich, took me aside one evening to speak with me about his son, Bill, who had his eye on me. Uncle Rich preached to us both for over an hour. He felt I should be "sealed" (married) to Bill, and he insisted we go straight to his house so he could perform our marriage ceremony. I flatly refused. I told him I was too young and that I was still under my mother's jurisdiction. He pompously refuted that, saying because my mother left my father, she had no authority over me. For that matter, my father had no authority over me either, because he refused to follow the other brethren and move down to Short Creek. Consequently, I should be obedient to him, Uncle Rich, God's true servant. When I remained defiant, he ordered Bill never to see me again.

I'd grown up believing the brethren, the men who held the priesthood, talked directly with God. After all, Joseph Smith talked with him. I'd thought fundamentalist elders, especially, were good men who consulted God's will for everything they did. Now I'd begun to wonder. But of one thing I remained certain. Polygamy itself was God's way. If sin happened to raise its head in the course of our trying to live out this gospel, it wasn't the gospel's fault. Any failure was merely the result of human weakness.

In the end, I determined that if I lived plural marriage, I was going to do it on my own and God's terms, not those of some old man. Nobody would boss me around, except God. And even he had better tread lightly.

CLEVE LEBARON LIVED IN Hurricane, not far from Aunt Rhea. Years earlier, he helped my mother because she was an unmarried woman living on a small income. He may even have wanted to marry her, but she'd never been able to obtain that divorce from my father, so she was off-limits to the brethren. She probably wouldn't have married him anyway, since everyone knew the LeBarons had insanity in their family. Still, Cleve brought us sacks of beans and potatoes and whatever fruit was in season. One day in late 1951, a friend and I stopped by his home in Hurricane to say hello.

When I walked into his parlor that afternoon, I found a tall, strikingly handsome stranger there already. His hair was blond and his eyes were a brilliant blue. Cleve asked if I knew him. I didn't, but I found myself so irresistibly drawn to those eyes, I didn't bother answering. We stared at each other far longer than was necessary when a bolt of knowing tingled down my spine, and an inner voice told me, "This is the man you are going to marry." I couldn't believe it. Could this finally be the revelation from God I'd been begging for? I wanted it to be so.

Cleve interrupted my reverie. "This is my nephew, Verlan LeBaron, from Mexico."

A kaleidoscope of thoughts flashed through my mind in an instant. I recalled that some of the LeBarons lived in Mexico, colonizing there in order to escape America's stricter enforcement of its anti-bigamy laws. I'd also heard about the "special priesthood" the LeBaron clan claimed to possess as direct spiritual descendents of Joseph Smith. They told people the prophet to be revealed through them would thereby be higher in rank than the president of the LDS Church. Then there was all the talk of the insanity running through the LeBaron bloodline. Why, I'd even seen crazy Ben LeBaron at a Salt Lake City polygamist meeting where the brethren had to bodily throw him out because he was yelling, "I'm greater than Jesus Christ!" On another occasion, rumor had it that Ben commenced doing one hundred push-ups in the middle of a busy street in downtown Salt Lake. When police officers came to arrest him, he'd challenged them boldly. "None of you can do that, so it proves I'm the One Mighty and Strong!" Now here was Ben's brother smiling up at me.

Verlan stretched out his hand, and I took it. He held on tightly as he raised himself to his feet. A beautiful, broad grin showed his perfect white teeth. I was captivated.

"Hi," he said, pausing to look me over. "Are you Charlotte's little sister?"

I nodded and answered, "Yes, I'm Irene. I live with her and my aunt Rhea." I wondered how he knew Charlotte.

"Could you give me directions to your house then? I've come down from Provo to spend the weekend and see her."

The very first twinge of jealousy panged my heart. *Oh God,* I thought, *you just said he'd be* my *husband. Oh well, I'm only fourteen. Maybe I'll still have him in my future.* I was content enough thinking Verlan might be in my plans, but I seriously wondered if I could cope with nineteen-year-old Charlotte in them.

Weeks later, the newly engaged Charlotte and twenty-one-year-old Verlan were outside Aunt Rhea's house in his gray Pontiac, about to leave for Short Creek. Three of my half brothers and sisters and I begged them to take us along. Charlotte gave us a most definite no and added hotly, "We've been invited as a couple, and we're going alone."

Charlotte was very serious and pious like her mother, and I loved to tease her. So I whispered to John and Sam, and then grabbed Karen's hand, pulling the four of us into the backseat of the car. We acted as if we had every right to be there. "Well, let's go then," I said. "We're all couples!"

Charlotte turned and gave me one of her icy stares. I got the message. Giggling, we all scampered out of the car. They drove off without so much as a wave or smile.

Because Verlan had no prior wives, their wedding three months later was a public celebration. I handled it well enough. But I cried when I went home that night. If I were ever to become a polygamist wife, there would be so many difficult things to bear. Even then, I resented Verlan making love to my half sister. I wondered how he could ever love me if he were busy making love to her.

I recalled what Brigham Young said—that plural marriage would damn more people than it would save. Then why even try it? I longed to have a man just for myself, but according to my religion, that was selfish and shortsighted. If I loved monogamy, I might be happy in this life, but not for the "eternities."

In the scriptures, God warned that the "angels did not abide my law; therefore, they cannot be enlarged, but remain separately and singly, without exaltation, in their saved condition, to all eternity; and from henceforth are not gods, but are angels of God forever and ever." (Doctrine and Covenants, 132:17). I'd been lonely enough in this life without having to spend all eternity "separately and singly." I worried that if I didn't follow God's law of polygamy, I'd completely lose out.

I often wished I'd been born Catholic, like a friend of mine. She seemed so much at peace after each confession. I really didn't know what sins I had that would amount to much, but I figured the main ones were swearing and being light-minded. If only that was all standing between me and glory. But I knew better. I was one of the special children of God.

I remembered the scripture: "For of him unto whom much is given much is required." I wanted to become a goddess and receive the highest exaltation in heaven. Would I throw that away in order to satisfy my small, selfish desires in the present? The possibility that I might, quite terrified me.

The choice was mine. If Mother was any indication, I'd get no second chance to make the right one. Yes, here I was, in the very same place she'd been, with just the two options, both of them terrible: suffer now or suffer later, be loved today or be exalted tomorrow. How I wished God might have thought to forge us at least one other way.

CHAPTER FOUR

Toward the end of May, Mother met me in Salt Lake City. She was still married to Horace, and the two of them drove me back to the Trout Creek homestead. I was now fifteen. When we got home, Mother mentioned that Horace had a twenty-eight-year-old nephew named Glen Spencer, who was a shy, available bachelor. I'd actually seen him before because he was the local postmaster. Glen also worked on the Nielson ranch, which meant he had limited time for a social life. Out near Trout Creek, there weren't many girls for him to socialize with anyway.

Mother didn't seem at all concerned that Glen was so much older than me, that he was Horace's relative, or even that he wasn't a polygamist. Like his uncle, Glen was a jack Mormon. His family was once devout, perhaps, but he didn't practice Mormonism. He was certainly no fundamentalist, no holder of the priesthood. Mother knew this meant he wasn't marriage material for any girl wishing to live the Principle. But she wanted me to have some company, and she thought he was nice, so she encouraged me to give him a chance.

Since I had nothing better to do, I moseyed on over to Nielson's ranch not long after I got home. I met up with Glen, and he invited me to go with him to work in the hay field. The day passed quickly in spite of the summer heat. I acted completely myself, being silly and cutting up most of the day.

That night, Glen and I lay on the lawn beneath a big oak tree in front of the ranch house. We talked until almost midnight. He was kind and attentive to me in a way no man had ever been before—my father and Horace most especially. I was able to explain my dilemma to him, and he understood and commiserated. In his view, he said, God gave us free agency as a gift, not as a tool with which to taunt and confuse us. Why would he give us desires he wanted us to deny? After all, isn't God love? I recall these things making perfect sense to me at the time.

What drew me to Glen even more, though, was the familiar loneliness I sensed in him. It seemed a loneliness perfectly matching my own. All at once, in a single day, I'd found another soul who might give my life meaning, someone I thought would completely understand me. We were so compatible, we spent the rest of the summer together.

His being thirteen years older than me made no difference to either one of us. We were inseparable. He loved me in a way I'd never been loved before—fully and unconditionally. I could be my silly self, and Glen thought it was wonderful. With him, I didn't have to curb what so many others unflatteringly described as my light-mindedness. He never reprimanded me. Instead, I could sing, laugh, talk, cry, or be funny without ever worrying if it was out of line. This man loved me for me.

I was surprised by immense joy. When Glen and I would lie together on the lawn, we'd hold hands. His kisses set me afire. When he held me, I melded to him deliciously. Aunt Rhea's law of purity seemed to have no application here. I even dared to thank God for letting me experience something so wonderful as Glen's kisses. I never wanted to be anywhere else but in his arms.

Best of all, we dreamed and planned for the day we would belong to each other and to no one else. Somehow, our love blocked out all my fears of eternal Hell. Heaven couldn't be better than what I'd found here with Glen, and Hell couldn't be worse than going back to not having him. I literally closed my mind to God, to the Principle, to everything that might say no to this. When Glen and I were together, I could forget the rigid rules that placed our love squarely out of bounds.

But alone at night, I was haunted by the well-ingrained fundamentalist Mormon dogma. I asked God if he might consider changing his harsh rules, perhaps grant me an exemption. I wanted him to
understand Glen, who I thought was as good, if not better, than I. Was
it his fault he wasn't born a Mormon fundamentalist, wasn't born
under the covenant? It didn't mean he wasn't a very special person.
What I wanted to have with Glen was not plural marriage anyway; I
wanted monogamy, exclusivity. Adding another wife would destroy
what we were together, spoil the intense two-way connection that so
enthralled me. It was unthinkable. No, I did not want God to let Glen
become a last-minute child of the covenant. I wanted God to exempt
us from the Principle altogether.

I wondered about my supposed premonition that I was going to
marry Verlan LeBaron. He was personable and good-looking, and he
held the priesthood—all qualifications any obedient woman would
want. My beliefs drew me to Verlan, but I was in love with Glen. Perhaps I also saw Glen as a way out of polygamy, a choice that would save
me from ever having to think about a husband of mine being off in
another room making love to one of my sister wives. I decided I preferred to be Glen's only wife, to grab joy now and face Hell later, so I
consented to our marriage. But I did so with considerable trepidation.

We only told a few people of our plans—mostly those who
wouldn't oppose them. I wrote to my sister Donna and asked her to
bring my hope chest to Trout Creek if by chance she came our way.
She was one of the sisters living at Short Creek. I had a strong bond
with Donna, and I valued her opinion. Though she was devoted to
polygamy, I trusted her not to brand me as an outcast if I chose a different path. Perhaps I suspected Donna might try and talk me out of
marrying Glen, and if she could do it, I wouldn't have to face God's
wrath for marrying him.

OUR DAY FINALLY ARRIVED — September 1, 1952. Glen and I and
both our mothers were loaded into Uncle Charlie's old beige Kaiser,
ready to leave for Salt Lake City, where we'd be married five days

later. Glen's uncle Charlie, who was paying for the wedding, had just finished rearranging our suitcases in the trunk. As soon as he got into the driver's seat, he laid his head on the steering wheel. His face was colorless. "I'm sick," he announced. "Can't we all get up early and leave tomorrow?"

I was furious. Someone else should drive. Or Uncle Charlie could even stay home. We had so much shopping to do in Salt Lake, so many details to take care of before the wedding and the reception at my brother Richard's. But since all of it was to be Uncle Charlie's gift, we pretty much had to agree to go the next day. Mother and I slept at Nielson's ranch so we could leave as early as possible.

At 4:00 A.M., I was jarred awake by a loud pounding on the door. The pounding continued, so I quickly slipped into my jeans and scampered to the front door before anyone else was disturbed. When I drew back the bolt and opened the door, there stood Donna and her husband, Clyde.

Under a cool, starless sky, the three of us convened in their car for a private conference. I listened intently as Donna revealed a premonition she'd received. They traveled all night to warn me. "Thank God, honey, you're still here!" she said. "I've come to bring you to your senses." She spoke excitedly. "Irene, God sent us! You must not marry an unbeliever who can't exalt you. You're a child born into the Principle. Please don't give up your birthright. God is counting on you."

My whole world teetered. I wished I'd never been born a child of God. But since I was, I had to consider if he might actually have gone to all this trouble to warn me not to make a grave mistake. Had Charlie's sudden illness possibly been God's doing? Had he really given Donna this premonition? Was this my one last chance to correct my path and serve the Lord?

By now, Glen had come outside and strolled by the car several times, hoping we'd invite him to participate in our conversation. He thought he was included in all my plans, but he also knew what a strong hold my family had on me. He paced a few yards away from us, waiting to be called over to the car.

I watched him while I silently rehearsed the fateful, awful words

Donna insisted would end what she called my "predicament." I couldn't see myself saying them, not ever. But then here was my beloved sister who'd driven all night to catch me before I abandoned our beautiful doctrine and threw in with the common, monogamous riffraff who would never be exalted. Would I really choose love over God, a selfish life of freedom over a life of noble, god-honoring obedience? Would I really let down Donna and Aunt Rhea and so many others I loved?

Suddenly, I felt ashamed. Of course I couldn't shirk my duty to God. At any cost, God must always come before love, before my personal feelings. I thought of the words of one of our favorite hymns: "Sacrifice brings forth the blessings of heaven." If God required that I sacrifice Glen, then I had no right to question it. He was God, after all. And I'd been taught that God's faithful ones would be tested, like Abraham, whose son God ordered sacrificed on the altar. How had I dared ask for exemption from God's testing, from obeying his will?

With my heart bursting and paralyzed with misgivings, I got out of the car and walked slowly through the darkness to where Glen waited. He looked at me somewhat angrily as I approached. "What the hell's going on?" he asked.

My mind whirled. I opened my mouth to deliver my speech, but my tongue froze. My mind went blank. "Glen," I finally stammered, "I know you won't understand, because I don't . . ." I started to cry so brokenheartedly, I couldn't finish my sentence. I buried my head in his shoulder, sobbing uncontrollably. But these few words had already told him all he needed. My mind had been twisted back around. I'd been reprogrammed in a single, predawn session.

"Let's get out of here," he said. "Don't listen to them."

I finally managed to say it. "I can't marry you, Glen, because . . . because you can't exalt me." I pushed away from him and shoved the diamond locket he'd given me as a token of our engagement into his hand. Then I ran back to Donna's car.

I sobbed to Donna, "If you've come to save me, then let's get out of here, now." Through the trees and tears, I watched Glen, standing there all alone, as we drove out of sight. What in God's name did the future hold now?

Donna and Clyde took me all the way to Hurricane and dropped me off, along with my now sad little hope chest and my other belongings, at Aunt Rhea's. She was thrilled to see that I'd been snatched from the jaws of such terrible sin. She assured me their fervent prayers got me back.

Since school had already started in Hurricane, I enrolled in the tenth grade, two days behind schedule. On the second day of class, I picked up a registered letter at the post office and walked the three blocks home before opening it. Shaking so hard I could hardly breathe, I tore open the envelope and read Glen's forgiving note: "Dear Irene, I know that you left against your will. I know that you do love me. I'd crawl to China on my knees for you! I'll meet you anywhere. I'll send you money so you can come to Salt Lake. I'll never stop loving you. Glen."

I wanted to leave right then and run to him for safety. Then I worried this was just another phase of God's testing. Somehow I had to erase all thoughts of Glen from my mind.

I didn't return to school for my afternoon classes. Instead, I sat and cried for hours, unable to do anything else. I was so mad at God. It hurt too much to be obedient, especially since God kept allowing temptation to be thrown in my face. I wished I'd never been born, or at least that I'd never been taught this rigid "gospel."

At 2:00 A.M., I was awakened once again by an incessant pounding at the door. When I opened it this time, my brother Richard grabbed me and pushed the door wider so my mother and sister Becky could come in. "Get your things, Irene. We're leaving right now," he ordered as he charged upstairs.

"I'm not going," I said, following him up to my bedroom. "I want to stay here and finish school."

He yanked my clothes from the closet, hangers and all, looking quickly around the bare room. "Where's the rest of your stuff?"

Aunt Rhea was up by this time, and now I heard her yelling at someone downstairs. When I went to see who it was, I was shocked to find Glen in the entryway with everyone else. He'd come in during all the confusion. "Leave her alone!" Aunt Rhea yelled at him. "You're nothing but a whoremonger!"

I knew that wasn't true, but I didn't dare say anything in Glen's defense. I cowered before my aunt, afraid she would stop loving me if I crossed her. I didn't know what to do—go or stay. My heart ached to go and be with Glen, to let him love and protect me. Only my fear of God and Aunt Rhea restrained me.

Then it seemed God intervened. Charlotte, Verlan's wife, had been trying to fend off a miscarriage, and she just happened to be staying in Aunt Rhea's other guest room so her mother could tend to her. I suddenly got it into my head that perhaps I could make the correct decision about Glen if I knew what God's intentions might be for me otherwise. Driven by necessity, I entered Charlotte's dark room to ask her the burning question point-blank.

I found her already awake, of course, roused by all the pounding and yelling. "Does Verlan plan on marrying me?" I asked her.

She barely had to think. "Yes, of course he does, Irene. We pray about you often, feeling that the Lord is saving you to be a part of our family."

At that moment, after all the terrible ambivalence I'd found almost worse than either of my choices, this felt like a great relief to me. I patted her hand, thanking her for helping me clarify my agonizing decision. I would go with my insistent family, but I would not marry Glen.

Ironically, unbeknownst to me, Verlan was down in Mexico at around that same time, asking sixteen-year-old Lucy Spencer to marry him. She agreed but said she was supposed to be his third wife, not his second. Though she loved him, he'd have to get a second wife before she'd marry him. It was a strange response, to be sure. But there was little romance and rarely any rhyme or reason to polygamy. By all appearances, I was going to be Verlan's second wife.

Mother tried to calm Aunt Rhea while I packed my few things and obediently left with them for Trout Creek. I sat next to Glen on the way home, but I rejected his advances. I even refused to hold his hand, though it hurt to be so cold to him. As we drove, Mother and Richard got right to the point. They both wanted me to marry

Glen. Richard had joined the LDS Church, and he said I should join, too, and then get sealed to Glen in the Mormon temple. As far as the Principle went, they both claimed that other wives could simply be sealed to Glen by proxy, after his death, and that way I could be his only wife during our earthly lives together. But their advice came too late. I already had my answer. I knew what God was going to make me do. So I rode along in silence, loving Glen, but vowing to do my duty to Verlan and God.

When we finally stopped for breakfast, I got the opportunity to tell Glen the truth. While the others went inside, he asked me to stay in the car to talk with him. Trying to keep my voice from breaking, I said, "I can't marry you Glen, because God wants me to marry someone else."

"Who is it?" he asked, astounded, almost angry.

With a lump rising in my throat, I whispered shamefully, "It's my brother-in-law, Verlan."

"Your brother-in-law?" he blurted out in disbelief. Then, despairingly, he asked, "Has he ever kissed you?"

"No."

"Has he ever told you he loves you?"

"No," I answered defensively. "You'll always be the love of my life."

At that, he took me in his arms, and tears came to his eyes. "Please, Irene, don't let them talk you into this. You'll regret it for the rest of your life!"

"I have no choice, Glen. God wants me to do it." We clung to each other, crying, neither of us willing to let go.

I would live to regret not listening to that anguished prediction of his. Turns out, when I'd finally heard a real premonition, I completely failed to recognize it as one.

GLEN PROVED TOO GREAT a temptation for me that fall. If I didn't get away from Trout Creek, I thought it likely I would change my mind. My brother Douglas's October wedding in Salt Lake was a good excuse to leave. Aunt Beth, another of Mother's sisters, invited me to stay with her in nearby Murray during the festivities. She was always willing to make room for me despite having her own brood of twelve.

During my stay at Aunt Beth's, Charlotte and Verlan came up twice from Provo to see me. The first time, the three of us went to a movie; the next, we went to the park for an afternoon picnic. During these outings, Verlan spoke no words of love or commitment to me. And certainly, he never touched me. Everyone just seemed to take it for granted that I'd marry him. Compared to the wonderful candidness and sensitivity Glen always showed me, this made me feel like a toddler being dragged around by her father and mother. It left me empty inside, alone.

What I wanted was for Verlan to express his feelings for me, to assure me I would really be loved as a woman. I wanted a kiss, anything that might convince me this would be okay. I guess I didn't yet believe God would actually make me choose between love and obedience. If I trudged up the mountain and lay my sacrifice upon the altar, if I pulled back my knife arm and was truly willing to plunge it in, maybe, just maybe, a voice would tell me it had all been nothing more than a horrible test. I held out hope that if I obeyed God by giving up Glen's love, he would reward me with Verlan's love to take its place.

But neither Verlan nor God offered me any such words of love or assurance. Verlan didn't even speak to me about the logistics of our getting married—when, where, by whom. I thought maybe it was because he held the priesthood, and he was righteously trying to let God lead, make all the arrangements. As for a touch that might spur me on, I knew that believers weren't to even kiss until they were married. What did I expect from Verlan at this point? I kept quiet about my growing uneasiness. God would work things out in his wondrous way.

THREE MONTHS LATER, MY mother insisted I return with her to Trout Creek. She'd heard rumors I'd been seeing Verlan, and she meant for that to stop.

"No way do I want you in that family," she told me. "Verlan may be nice enough, but there's insanity in that bunch. You have to think about that, Irene! I'll never accept him or allow you to marry him."

So I went home again, more confused than ever. Mother kept praising Glen to me, reminding me of how I'd be his only wife. I wouldn't have to suffer as she had. She even tried to entice me with worldly riches. Someday, she said, Glen and I would probably inherit the whole Nielson ranch.

For his part, Glen gave me a respectful berth. He didn't come around the house, and when I saw him at the post office, he barely talked to me. I knew it was sadness and hurt as much as kindness holding him back. It made me love him all the more.

Soon I started going over to the ranch to watch wrestling with him on television. I said we could only be friends, but he couldn't maintain his detachment with me right there on the couch beside him. He would tell me how he loved me, how he loved God, too. He said he could make me happy, and that God would surely want that. "No one is ever happy in polygamy," he said. I had to admit, the last part seemed true. I could see, on those evenings, that Glen and I had no choice but to run off together before anyone could stop us.

And then I would go home, and the panic would set in. God had shown me just what I was to do. He hadn't only put Glen off-limits; he'd put me on another path altogether. What would happen if I willfully refused to go down it?

One night, desperate to end the turmoil to which I'd been subjecting us both, I agreed to elope with Glen. Ely, Nevada, was just four hours west of us. We could get married there. Mother would gladly go along to give her consent. But I had trouble convincing Glen I would really go through with it. "I'll believe it when I see it," he said.

I promised him we'd do it "the day after tomorrow."

The next day was my sixteenth birthday. I went to get the mail, and as I sorted through the stack of letters, I found one for me with Charlotte's return address in the corner. The handwriting on it was unfamiliar; it had to be Verlan's. *Oh God, what are you doing to me now?*

I tore the envelope open and read this simple verse: "Extra special birthday wishes, joy and smiles the whole day through, happiness forever after, all for extra special you!—Verlan and Charlotte."

I read it over and over. Was Verlan trying to tell me something between the lines? Did he really think I was "extra special"? Was he "joyful and smiling" because he thought I'd be his? By "happiness forever after," was he actually offering to one day pull me through the veil of death and make me a goddess with him for all eternity? If he did not mean any of these things, why had he personally signed the note? I was plunged again into indecision.

Perhaps this was another of God's signs pointing me to Verlan. If so, I'd have to obey this time. No more wavering. As I thought it over, I became increasingly certain God made this card arrive precisely on my birthday and the very day before my reckless elopement. God was giving me this one last chance to fall in line with his will.

I immediately sat down and wrote to Nelda Young, asking her to come and get me. She was someone I could depend on, someone who could help me out of my predicament with Glen. "I'll make it up to you," I told her. "Love, Irene."

When Glen saw me later that day, he knew he'd been right to doubt me. The elopement was off. "Good hell," he said in complete exasperation. "The Devil has beaten me again, believe it or not, by only one day!" He just stood there staring at me, shaking his head. I was so embarrassed by this newest about-face, I avoided him until Nelda came for me a couple of days later. How could I expect him to understand what I didn't understand fully myself?

MEANDERING THE WAY UTAH winters are wont to do, February was apathetic to the fact that I was on constant high alert for further word from Verlan and God. None came that month. There were anxious moments when I was sure time ceased to pass altogether. Otherwise, why didn't someone contact me? Verlan and Charlotte had to know the quandary I was in. If it hadn't been for my busy work schedule at Youngs' ranch, I might have been tempted just to go out and bury myself under the snow, never to be heard from again. Frazzled almost beyond words, I finally got up the courage to write to Charlotte. (I didn't feel I could be so forward as to write directly to her husband.) I basically told her I wasn't sure how much longer I could hold out.

Secretly, I decided that if it was God's will for me to marry Verlan, Verlan would grasp the need either to let me know he loved me or to do something else that would give me some hope. If he didn't grasp it, and soon, I'd take it as God's release, and I'd go back and marry Glen. I thought this a very reasonable condition to put on Verlan, whether he knew about it or not. Surely God would honor it.

I was waiting for a reply when a friend from Trout Creek un-expectedly arrived at Youngs' ranch early in March. Leonard Parker looked grave as he delivered a somber message. "Horace's brother, Slim, died this morning. Do ya wanna go to the funeral?"

I most certainly did. I was dying to be back at Trout Creek. I told myself that any girl in my situation had a right to be homesick for her family. With a promise to Nelda to return to the ranch in three days, we immediately left for home.

The closer we got, the faster my heart beat. I reminded myself that Verlan never gave me one word of hope, except for that little card, and I couldn't even be sure he meant that as anything more than "happy birthday." Now that we were closing in on Trout Creek, on Glen, I could have kissed Verlan for ignoring me over the previous weeks.

When we arrived at Mother's house, I grabbed my suitcase and got out of the car, but I lingered by Leonard's window until he finally gave me a quizzical look. "Would you mind very much doing me an-other favor?" I began. "I'd be really grateful if you'd drive over to the Nielson ranch and find Glen for me. Don't let anyone else hear you, but tell him I'm home and waiting for him."

With my heart pounding in my throat, I watched the cloud of dust billow behind Leonard's car as he drove the two miles through the mesquite and sagebrush before he disappeared into the grove of trees at Nielson's ranch. Would Glen be home? Would he be too angry to come to me after the terrible way I'd treated him?

While I watched and fretted, I saw the beige Kaiser leave the ranch. The dust blew up faster and higher than I'd ever seen it before. His car barely came to a stop in front of me before he jumped out and took me in his arms. His kisses smothered my doubts, and his tender words of love swept them away. This was the man I really loved.

After Slim's funeral, Glen insisted on driving me all the way back to the Youngs' himself. I promised him I'd give Nelda my notice immediately and have her bring me home as soon as I finished my month of work. I would see him again on the first of April. When we parted, I felt like my old, lighthearted self for the first time in months.

March, like February, brought no correspondence from Verlan or Charlotte of any kind. This now hurt me only the tiniest bit. Mostly it was a huge relief. I dismissed them from my mind and returned home to Glen at the end of the month, just as I'd promised. As for the birthday card I'd taken as a sign from God? Discerning God's voice was clearly an art I hadn't quite mastered. At long last, my mind was made up. I would marry Glen.

I settled back in at Trout Creek, and we began making new plans for our wedding. Fairly late one evening, about three weeks after my return, Glen and I were relaxing at Nielsons', cozily holding hands on a brown leather couch, watching television. I'd just agreed to go with him the next day to take some supplies to the sheepherders on another ranch. He actually talked me into riding over there on his two motorcycles. With a satisfied smile, he got up and went into the kitchen for some refreshments.

Just then, I heard a car circle in the yard out front. I didn't think Glen heard it, and somehow I knew not to bring it to his attention. I just quietly got up, opened the door, and slipped out into the warm night.

Two figures were approaching me from the dark.

"Verlan?" I called out.

The next moment, he was standing there beside me. My ten-year-old sister Erma had come with him to show him the way. When he reached me, he grabbed my hand. "I'm so glad we found you!" he said. "Let's go back to your place, where we can visit. Charlotte, her mom, and your mother are all waiting there for us."

The moment I heard and saw Verlan, it was as if I lost all power of self-direction. He came, and I was going to have to comply with God's law after all. God had not played along with my little condition. He blew right through my deadline and yet still meant to have his way. I felt like the crime victim who finally understands that for all her spitting and scratching and name-calling, she *is* going to be tied up and thrown into the van.

I couldn't go back in and face Glen, even just to tell him good-bye. What else would I say? "Um ... another man just drove up into the yard, so I'll be going now. Have a good life." How could Glen ever forgive me or even understand?

In a daze, I followed Verlan to his car. I was alert enough to notice he seemed truly happy to see me, but I hardly cared anymore. He hugged me before opening my car door, but he still didn't say exactly why he'd come. When we got home, I sent Erma ahead of us into the house.

Once we were alone, I wasted no time. "What did you come for?" I asked.

"Well ... uh ... hopefully you can go back with us and ... uh ... stay ... maybe ... forever!" Not exactly the romantic approach I once hoped for, but it seemed the best that Verlan could muster.

After all the flip-flopping my mother saw me put Glen through, and after all her threats and warnings about the LeBarons, I didn't want her to know I was still considering Verlan as a husband. So I hurried into the house, where Aunt Rhea and Charlotte greeted me warmly. I served them tuna sandwiches and peaches as we chit-chatted until late about everything except why they had come.

The next morning, I got up early as usual to milk our cow. Verlan met me at the corral a few minutes later, wearing a big, silly grin. "I wish you were milking my cows," he teased. I couldn't help but smile at his awkward attempt to be charming.

Then I heard Glen's motorcycle powering up the dirt road from Nielson's ranch. I hurried back toward the house, not wanting him to catch me with the man God chose for me over him. Glen came to a stop in our yard but kept revving his engine. He eyed Verlan's gray Chevy. As I crossed over to him, he looked toward the corral and saw Verlan.

"Is that your damn brother-in-law?"

"Yes, it is," I said, thoroughly humiliated for what I was doing to him yet again.

"Then you can go to Hell, the both of you!" he snarled. His Harley almost ran me down as he shot past, trailing a spume of choking dust behind him. Utterly crushed, I watched until he was out of sight. I was terrified he thought I actually wanted this.

When Verlan saw Glen leave, he came out of the corral and put an arm around me. "Aw, don't feel so bad, Irene. Things will work out. Go inside now, and ask your mother permission to come with us. I don't want to take you away from here without it. If it's okay with her, we'll leave tomorrow."

An hour later, I followed Mother down several rough cement steps leading into the cellar we'd built together two years before. I remembered how I'd helped her mix and pour those cement walls. The two dark rooms now held all our bottled fruit and other supplies—row upon row of wooden shelves crammed with cases of jams, jellies, molasses, mayonnaise, oils, vegetables, tuna, and Spam. On one of the shelves, there was even a special case of Franco-American spaghetti just for me. I sat down on a metal army cot we sometimes used for naps or when the boys came to visit.

"You wanted to talk to me?" Mother asked somewhat wearily.

Scared and embarrassed, I decided just to blurt it out. "Mother, I know you don't approve, but I'm going to marry Verlan."

I'm sure she'd suspected this, but she started crying nonetheless. "Please, Irene, I suffered so much trying to live the Principle. Don't do this. You've got a chance to have a husband of your very own. You're already breaking Glen's heart with this nonsense. Besides, Verlan will take you away to Mexico, where I'll never see you again!" she finished angrily. Then she started sobbing.

Suddenly I'd had enough of her sanctimony and duplicity. This was a woman who'd told me throughout my childhood that I had to live polygamy or else be damned. Now, just because it had been hard for her, because she failed at it, she was simply changing her mind. I don't know quite how I managed it, but I somehow remained impervious to Mother's supplications. I couldn't let her tear me down. I would live the life she'd been unable to, following in the footsteps of my faithful forefathers and foremothers, who gave up everything to obey the Principle. Like them, I would just square up my shoulders and march into God's celestial glory. I would do it by sharing my husband.

When I'd gone into that cellar, I'd been about 90 percent sure what I was going to do. When I emerged, I was 100 percent sure. Finally, I had endured one of God's testings. A small victory, perhaps, but it gave me hope. I thought I felt a little more like a goddess already.

CHAPTER FIVE

On the long drive to Salt Lake City, I sat in the backseat with Aunt Rhea. At some point during the trip, she took my hand and made a grand revelation. "Irene," she said, "the Lord has shown me in a vision that you'll be married within eight days. I think it is so wonderful."

How shocked I was that God had spelled this out to Aunt Rhea, but he'd only communicated to me with cryptic winks and hand signals. All my ceaseless, futile praying for some clarity, and he chose to tell Aunt Rhea not only what would happen to me, but in how many days. Why, Verlan hadn't even proposed to me. Among the group in the car, it seemed understood that we were driving all that way to get a priesthood authorization for my marriage to Verlan, yet all Verlan actually said to me about it was that he wanted me to milk his cows. And now here was Aunt Rhea announcing to us all that I'd be married eight days hence. I was humiliated.

But when we arrived in Salt Lake, Verlan drove directly to my uncle Rulon Allred's chiropractic office. This was finally a real indication Verlan was serious. Besides being my mother's brother, Uncle Rulon was the prophet leader who later formed the fundamentalist church, the Apostolic United Brethren, which grew quickly from a few rebels to several thousand by 1953. All of us in the car were members of this group rather than the group at Short Creek, though we also supported them to an extent, and many of our loved ones belonged out there. Uncle Rulon was the successor to Joseph Musser, who was the successor to Lorin C. Wooley, who had been "called by God" to continue polygamy after the LDS Church finally banned the practice way back in 1904. So visiting Uncle Rulon was like visiting God himself.

They decided I should stay in the car while the three of them—Verlan, Charlotte, and Aunt Rhea—went in and talked to Uncle Rulon. This was because I was underage, and we'd come to see Uncle Rulon at his secular business, and, well, we were talking about polygamy, after all. It was my first intimate taste of the terrible and constant hiding that always was such a huge part of the practice of plural marriage. As childlike and angry as it made me feel, I compliantly stayed behind while the others went inside. Later, they told me what happened.

In hushed tones, Verlan stated his reason for coming. My dear uncle thereafter flatly refused Verlan's request. "No," he said, "she's too young to marry without her parents' consent. I've already been ordered by her father and older brother not to allow the union. I simply can't perform the marriage under these circumstances. I suggest you be patient and let the Lord work things out. Give it a couple of years." Richard apparently got to Dad, and the two of them went to Uncle Rulon and made their case against Verlan based on the LeBarons' mental instability as well as their supposed secret priesthood. I know now Uncle Rulon had high hopes for Verlan, even then. He thought Verlan would redeem the LeBaron name one day. But Uncle Rulon still didn't want to be the one responsible for marrying us against my family's wishes. In two more years, I'd be eighteen and responsible for my own choices.

Back out in the car after this meeting, Verlan was in a quandary. Aunt Rhea had just told us that we'd be married within eight days. Now the reigning high priest and servant of God told us to wait two years. Verlan had no alternative. For the time being, he left me at Aunt Beth's in Murray and returned with Charlotte to their home in Provo.

I'd gotten a reprieve. The question was, what was I to make of it?

TWO DAYS LATER, through the influence of a good friend, my Aunt Beth made arrangements for me to interview for a job at Sears. We agreed the experience would be good for me. If all went well, I'd make myself a little money and work toward becoming self-sufficient.

While I was getting dressed for the interview, I received a most welcome phone call that distracted me in a number of ways. "Yes, Glen," I said. "I'd be glad to meet you at one o'clock in the Sears candy department before my interview."

I left early, hoping to spend at least an hour with him. Along the way, of course, my inner voices started their familiar, conflicting cross fire. After listening for a while, I finally resolved that this would have to be good-bye, regardless of Glen's intentions. Anything else, any more of the constant back and forth, would be much too painful.

Just one glance at him undid me. We hungrily embraced, all my solemn vows to honor Verlan forgotten. Neither of us spoke of love or the future or much of anything else. I ditched my interview, and we sought refuge in a movie theater. There, in the dark, Glen and I hung on for two more blissful hours. Later he took me by the B&B Bowling Alley, where a friend of his greeted us warmly and informed Glen his "order" had been delivered. Glen followed him into the office while I waited at the counter.

Soon I heard his soft, sad voice behind me. "Irene, these are for you to remember me by," he said, presenting a gorgeous bouquet of yellow daffodils. In my mind, as I write this, I can still see every delicate petal point, the exquisite, buttery trumpet at the center of every blossom. All too soon, I knew, they would wither and fade away, just as Glen would. I thanked him with tears and an embrace.

Leaving there, we walked along in silence for blocks, just holding hands. Then we stopped and waited for a bus that would take me out of his life forever. I felt I was losing my best friend, that when I did lose him, just like my fresh-cut daffodils, I would lose something life-giving. Then the bus came. As it pulled up to the curb, a knot of people began descending through the rear door. We walked slowly toward the front, allowing all the other passengers to board first while we clung to each other a minute longer.

"Hey," the driver shouted, "if you're going with me, you'd better hop on."

We kissed once more, knowing it would have to last us forever. With a breaking heart, I boarded the bus and took a seat by the window. After a block, I could still see my beloved standing forlornly on the corner.

A week later, while I was still very much in mourning, my cousin Evelyn burst into the bedroom we shared at my Aunt Beth's and threw a letter on the bed that came for me in that day's mail. The handwriting on it made my own hands shake. It was postmarked from California.

Inside, I found a single sheet of paper. When I pulled it from the envelope, my picture and a lock of my golden hair fell from its folds onto the bed. Glen had promised to always keep these in his wallet. I didn't have to read the letter to know what his returning them meant. Sobbing like the world had come to an end, I finally got up the courage to read. "Dear Renski, I'm in California trying to forget you. I know I never will. I want you to know one thing for sure. If things go wrong for you, now or later, I'll always be waiting for you. Love, Glen."

The regrets, the grief, the tremendous sense of loss—it all washed over me at once. I couldn't accept it. For a moment, I lost all sense of reason. I wanted to do something rash, something passionate and selfish and without any regard for God or his precepts. If Glen would only come and rescue me, we'd run far away, where we could hide from the world and just be together. Would anyone really begrudge us that?

But God would always know where I was, and he didn't approve of unbelievers.

Or was there some tiny chance he might?

UNCLE RULON, MY MOTHER, Aunt Rhea, and Aunt Beth had all been raised in a polygamist family. Their father had two wives and twenty-two children. Although the women in such fundamentalist families worked every bit as hard or harder than the men, everyone revered the men as leaders. They were the ones who held God's priesthood. Furthermore, no one, man or woman, made any important decisions in his or her life without first consulting the presiding priesthood leader. When I was growing up in the Murray and Salt Lake City areas, I often called Uncle Rulon's chiropractic office and asked the nurse (who happened to be one of his seven wives) if I could speak with him. I especially needed his counsel after my mother left my dad.

In addition to being our leader, Uncle Rulon was something like a father to me growing up. I recall how he would lift me onto his broad shoulders and then romp and whirl around the room with me hanging on to his blond hair. Tall, stately, and very handsome, he was universally thought of as a godly man.

On the day I received Glen's letter returning my lock of hair, I called Uncle Rulon with a heavier than usual question pressing on me.

"How's my sweet niece today?" he asked, concerned.

"I'd be doing better if I could talk to you. Could you give me a few minutes of your time if I come over to your office?"

"Come right on over, dear," he said. "I'll have time during my lunch hour. I'm not too rushed today."

I hoped the cold water I splashed on my face would relieve the swelling around my puffy eyes. I didn't want Uncle Rulon to think I was still a "bawl baby" at sixteen. I also didn't want a tearstained face to make Uncle Rulon doubt my resolve to be obedient to God. Besides, God might not count my sacrifice as worthy unless I offered it without flinching.

At his office, I explained my dilemma to Uncle Rulon as he took small bites of a tuna sandwich and weighed out the facts I presented to him. My voice broke several times as I expressed my love for Glen, cataloged Glen's wonderful attributes, and proclaimed what a good man he was. In light of all that, might there be some way I could marry Glen and yet stay right with God? Perhaps if Glen were willing to convert . . .

My uncle interrupted with his most comforting voice, gently but firmly excluding the possibility that Glen might ever be a suitable husband for me. I fought off despair as Uncle Rulon then agreed heartily with the premonition I thought I'd had about Verlan the first day I met him. "There's no question Verlan is the better man, my dear," Uncle Rulon said, "if for no other reason than he was born under the covenant." His words tore at my heart.

"You definitely can't let an unbeliever like Glen stand in the way of your salvation," he sagely counseled me. Then, glancing quickly at his watch, he added, "I approve of your decision. You're a valiant woman. I appreciate your willingness to serve the Lord." His voice cracked when he added, "Your dear Mother suffered terribly trying to live the Principle. I hope you won't have as hard a time. Whatever happens, will you promise me one thing?"

I nodded.

"Promise me you won't come back in five or ten years, asking me, 'Uncle Rulon, why did you let me do it?'"

He was asking me to promise I'd stick with it, that I'd never veer off the polygamous road once I started down it. It would be hard, to be sure, but I had vast stores of wisdom to fall back on and bolster me along the way. What else had all the years of lessons and talking and praying about the Principle been for? I was a child of the covenant; I could do this. I had to do it. It was my duty and my birthright. Besides, I'd gone voluntarily up the mountain with my Isaac in tow. In my deepest heart, I could not believe God would ask this of me unless he meant to reward me with something just as good in the here and now.

"Yes, I promise," I said.

"Well," he said, rising from his chair, "tell Verlan I'd like to talk to him. See if you can find me at home this Sunday, just before meeting."

We hugged. Then, squaring my shoulders, readying myself for the long march into God's celestial glory, I ran to the bus station and bought a one-way ticket to Provo.

IT'S NOW BEEN OVER fifty years since I've seen Glen, but he lives on vividly in my heart. Sometimes I can even sense his presence, especially each springtime, when I see his illusive form in the golden yellow daffodils.

BOOK TWO

STANDING ON PRINCIPLE

CHAPTER SIX

A promise can be a powerful thing. When I boarded the bus bound for Provo, it had only been a few hours since I'd received Glen's letter returning his mementos of my love for him. But in those few hours, a promise had been made. I already felt as if I was living a different life, though committing to it didn't mean it was going to be easy. My first challenge was to get my new life out of the starting gate.

I did lots of hard thinking in the forty miles to Provo. What exactly did Uncle Rulon want to tell Verlan? Would he now consent to our marriage immediately? If so, how did I feel about having brought about that change of heart? And how would Verlan feel? Then there was Charlotte. She might have some feelings about it, too. More pressing still, how was I to tell Verlan the priesthood leader wanted to see him? I didn't want Verlan to think I'd been too forward by visiting privately with Uncle Rulon.

The trip was scary in itself. Here I was, traveling out of town without anyone in the world knowing, although Uncle Rulon promised to call Aunt Beth so she'd know my whereabouts. Why, I hadn't even a clue how to get to Verlan and Charlotte's from the bus station. So, after the bus pulled into Provo, I got off quickly and surveyed the other passengers as they descended the steps. I approached a fat, gray-haired woman of about forty-five and showed her the paper in my hand with Charlotte's address on it. She eyed it for a minute, thinking. "Well, young lady," she said, pointing east, "it's about twenty blocks that way. Do you need a cab? I can go into the depot and call one for you."

"No thanks," I said, taking the paper from her chubby hand. It was my only link to Charlotte and Verlan; I couldn't afford to lose it. I walked in the direction the woman pointed, hoping the street signs would make enough sense to me, hoping to find someone else I felt comfortable approaching if the need arose. With my apprehension running so high, the continual uphill walk exhausted me more than it should have. Every few blocks I had to rest on a bench at a bus stop. It gave me opportunity to fret even more.

Making my way up the hilly avenues heading east, I passed red-brick homes with beautiful landscaping. I picked one out and imagined it was mine—a place of beauty, with a man inside to fulfill my dreams. I was the only woman who lived in my fantasy house. And, of course, this brought me back to Charlotte, whom I would get to face in just a few moments under the most awkward circumstances. The thought made me need to sit down again. Would she be angry with me for infringing on her rights? I vowed to censor my every word so as not to distress her in any way.

We were half sisters, yet I'd never felt close to Charlotte, who was by nature serious and spiritual and never seemed to waver on our fundamentalist faith. In contrast, I loved to laugh and be silly, and I struggled powerfully with our gospel, as Charlotte well knew. I'd surmised she'd never much appreciated what she likely saw as my nonsense and excessive laughter. Despite what she told me to the contrary that night at Aunt Rhea's, I found it hard to believe I was the girl Charlotte really would have wanted to get the position of second wife to her husband. Perhaps I should have phoned ahead.

The concern was academic at this point. I found the white-plastered house with the same bold black numbers as the ones I'd written on my paper. I rang the bell and heard a baby's cries inside. When Charlotte answered the door a few moments later, her pretty face showed complete surprise.

"Irene, what are you doing here?" she asked as she invited me in. I stepped into the foyer, and she embraced me. Then she shot questions at me. "How did you get here? Did you come alone?"

I tiptoed around with my answers, hoping she wouldn't catch on that I'd come to see her husband, but her brown eyes looked sadder and sadder the longer I talked. I was sure she was figuring out my scheme. Out of small talk, I played with seven-month-old Verlan Jr., holding him on my lap, cooing at him, conversing with him in baby talk. He looked so much like his father. Secretly, I wondered if my children by Verlan would be as handsome.

For the longest time, neither of us mentioned that taboo subject— Verlan. Instead, our conversation centered on siblings, mothers, and new additions to our huge family through marriages and births. Charlotte finally invited me to sit down and eat dinner with her, explaining that "Verlan won't be home until eleven. He attends BYU in the daytime, where he's in his second year of college. At night he works at the state mental hospital." Since I knew so little about Verlan, I clung to each detail. He was still such a mystery to me.

I helped Charlotte with the baby and the housework, but the hours passed slowly and quietly once we'd run through all the headlines about relatives. Finally, at precisely eleven, Verlan came through the back door into the kitchen. His blue eyes danced when he saw me. He shook my hand, squeezed tightly, and held on a little longer than I thought was legal. "What a nice surprise to have you here!" he said.

When Charlotte left the room to check on the baby, Verlan's pleasing voice lowered to a whisper. "What's going on? Are you bringing good news or bad?"

Before answering, I couldn't help but pause a moment to appreciate how clean-cut he looked with his blond hair, dark blue slacks, and blue and white plaid shirt. When I realized I'd been staring, I blushed, but Verlan seemed not to notice. "Well," I said, "it depends on how you look at it." Then I added nervously, "Uncle Rulon wants to see you on Sunday."

"Do you know why?"

"He simply told me to tell you to come and see him."

Just then Charlotte returned with a pillow and blanket, and we both stopped talking. She looked past me to her husband, and asked, "Are you ready to eat? If so, I'll serve you now."

Charlotte handed me the pillow and blanket, and invited me to retire in her living room. I laid the pillow on the couch and quickly unfolded the blanket. Then I pulled my dress over my head and spread it neatly across the wooden rocker. I didn't want Verlan to see it wrinkled the next morning. I took off my freshly polished white shoes and curled up on the sofa in my panties, bra, and slip for the night. I hadn't brought a thing with me.

The next day was Saturday; Verlan had the weekend off from both school and work. Here I was, without even being invited, taking up Charlotte's precious time with him. I felt just as ridiculous being there as I would have expected Charlotte to feel if she'd come down and horned in on Glen and me. It was an awkwardness I'd one day find as normal as sleeping and eating, but at this point it was still a new thing, and I despised it.

In the midst of my feeling this way, when Charlotte's back was turned, Verlan winked at me in a furtive attempt to flirt. I froze with apprehension. I was shocked at how stupid men could be about a woman's feelings.

I wondered why I'd even come, since I was so constrained here. I wanted to go home before Charlotte got really upset with me. I'd just about decided to when Verlan handed me his infant son. A wide grin flashed across his handsome face. "Keep him happy for a few minutes," he commanded. Then, ushering Charlotte into the bedroom, he said, "We need privacy for a few minutes." I couldn't imagine what would happen next. The minutes dragged as I watched the hands move on the white wall clock. After some time, I laid the baby down to nap.

Nearly half an hour later, Verlan emerged, but no Charlotte. "How about going to a movie?" he asked excitedly.

I shrugged. "Let's go if you want. Is Charlotte ready, or does she need help with the baby?" I asked.

He gently pushed me toward the kitchen door. I looked around, hoping Charlotte and the baby were coming along behind us. They were not. Verlan reassured me. "It's okay. The two of us are going alone."

My pangs of fear made me feel like I was getting diarrhea. How could I just walk out with Verlan, without Charlotte? No wonder she'd stayed in her bedroom. I imagined her there in pain and tears.

When we were outside, Verlan suggested I get in the car first and duck down; he would follow a few minutes later. "I don't want the nosy neighbors to see me driving away with a woman who isn't my wife," he said. "We have to be cautious. These gentiles don't understand our divine laws."

Once we were alone in the gray Chevy and out of view, I sat up and told Verlan I didn't need to be entertained. I needed to get to know him better. He seemed fine with this change of plans, so we drove over to Provo Lake and sat in some shade with both car doors open to allow a cooling cross breeze. For three hours, he did most of the talking—nothing really important, mostly just bragging about this and that. He described some of his brother Wesley's inventions. He told me about his sister Esther's piano playing and her musical awards. He talked about his brother Ben, who'd taken first place in a high-jump competition in school and about Wesley's setting a record in pole vault. I learned he had nine living siblings. He was the youngest, but after he was born, his mother lost twins, Joseph and Mary, at birth. He didn't mention Ben's mental breakdown until I brought it up. He assured me it had just been stress. Then he admitted that one of his sisters, Lucinda, had a few mental problems. "But I'm sure God will eventually heal her," he said.

After a while, I noticed none of the topics Verlan brought up included me. I began to wonder if I had the wrong idea about him. Was he really interested in me? If not, why had he brought me out to the lake alone? Did he think this was courting? I'd experienced courting, and this didn't much resemble it. When Verlan spoke about his future plans, I wasn't even mentioned in them. If God wasn't going to give me a big fat reward for sacrificing Glen, I thought he could at least give me some tiny assurance that obedience wasn't going to be exclusively about suffering. All I wanted at this point was a lifeline, something I could cling to for hope.

The only lifelines I could find that night were Verlan's pleasing personality and striking good looks. That is, I liked him. I watched his face as he spoke, wondering if he could capably guide me here and in the afterlife, if he could really exalt me one day and make me a goddess. I'd just placed my fate in the hands of God, so I guessed it was time to start trusting him.

Finally Verlan stopped talking and reached down to take my hand in his. He smiled. "We must be heading back to the house," he said. "I don't want Charlotte to feel bad that we've been gone so long." He relinquished my hand and closed the car door on his side. I followed suit. He started the motor, threw the gear into reverse, flashed a broad grin, and said, "You sure are pretty." After a pause, he added, "I hope you don't feel I'm too forward in saying so."

I didn't answer. Who cared if I was pretty? God was going to make me share a husband. I'd have to face Charlotte, to somehow deal with her presence, not only when we got home that night but for our whole lives. I had both fear and resentment to look forward to. I decided then and there that sister wives should live miles apart.

The mood at home was somber. Charlotte's sulkiness affected us all. While Verlan went in to talk to her, I stayed in the living room by myself, trying not to eavesdrop. I scrutinized every detail before me, especially the framed pictures of Charlotte and Verlan's wedding. The way he smiled into her beautiful oval face made me feel as if I should leave and just go back to Trout Creek, where I had a love of my own. Instead, I retired to their uncomfortable blue sofa and listened to my stomach growl. When I realized Charlotte and Verlan were not going to reappear, I went to bed hungry and lonely and more than just a little angry. Several times during the night, I woke up and wondered what I was doing there. And why, I asked God, did love hurt so much?

The following morning, I took a shower, combed my hair back into a ponytail, and put on the same dress I'd worn the previous two days. Charlotte looked cheery in her green and white striped dress when she came in. She sewed all her own clothes and dressed very conservatively. "Your dress is sure pretty," I complimented her. She didn't answer.

"Sit down here in the kitchen," she said flatly, making no eye contact. "The French toast will be served here shortly."

I sat down, trying to think of something to say to her. Rarely had I ever lacked for words, but in Charlotte's presence, I was tongue-tied.

Verlan soon breezed in and saved the day. "Good morning. What a wonderful day! Let's eat breakfast quick so we can leave as soon as possible."

Charlotte loaded the spatula with three pieces of French toast and stacked them on a serving plate. "We're ready for prayer," she announced. Verlan fell to his knees beside his chair, inviting his wife to kneel close to him. I folded my hands and knelt by my own chair as he led us in the invocation.

After we hurriedly ate, we collected the baby's things and made our way to the car. The three of them rode in front, forming an idyllic family picture. Then there was me—the spoiler in the backseat. It saddened me, embarrassed me, and made me angry all at the same time. The pain on Charlotte's face told me the arrangement wasn't going to be any easier on her than it was on me.

We arrived at Uncle Rulon's home ahead of schedule. Worshippers were just starting to straggle in for the Sunday meeting. A couple dozen cars were parked in the circular driveway in front of the three big homes in which Uncle Rulon had established his seven wives and their respective offspring. This compound also served as the nerve center of our church network, which was spread along the Wasatch Front, from Ogden to Payson.

Uncle Rulon had been watching for us, and he excused himself and came out to meet us. Instead of inviting us into the meeting, he walked us back out to the car. In whispers, he cautioned us, "I don't want anyone to know what's going on here." Then he pulled a piece of paper from his shirt pocket and handed it to Verlan. "Go to this address at seven o'clock tonight," he said. "Don't get out of your car."

He looked at Verlan to make sure he was taking note of each detail. "Someone whom I've authorized will take you to a secluded place and perform your marriage ceremony. Let me emphasize, you must never reveal who did it."

Seeing our surprise, he added, "You did want to get married, didn't you?"

"Married . . . uh . . . yes," Verlan managed eventually. "But . . . I hadn't planned on it today. I thought you said we had to wait two years. I have classes in the morning. I never expected this to happen so soon." He looked accusingly at me, then back to Uncle Rulon. "I thought you just wanted to talk to us." After a long pause he continued, clearly thinking out loud. "Maybe we could do it this Friday. I have the weekend off. That would give us more time. Would that be okay?"

"That'll be fine," said Uncle Rulon. "I'll make the necessary arrangements for Friday at seven. But remember—do not get out of the car. And never tell who did it." Uncle Rulon then looked to Charlotte and me, his eyes questioning us. We both nodded in the affirmative. Verlan also assured and thanked him.

Seeming satisfied, Uncle Rulon shook our hands and suggested we not come into the meeting. Relatives would be suspicious, seeing the three of us there together. We could hear voices inside already lifting up the first hymn to the Lord, but Uncle Rulon waited to make sure we were safely in our car before he said, "I'm so very proud of you all, of your willingness to serve the Lord in these perilous times. God bless you." Then he waved us away.

We were silent as we drove off, each of us lost in thought. I could tell Verlan felt the burden of this new reality. The fulfillment of his dream of living plural marriage was less than a week away. But he was ill prepared to deal with two women in such an awkward circumstance. Fortunately, Aunt Beth lived only five miles away.

I promised myself I'd remain silent until Verlan and I were alone. We would discuss our plans at the first private opportunity. I had planned my wedding before, and I had dozens of questions about this one, even though it appeared, from what Uncle Rulon said, the three of us would make up the entire guest list.

How I wished Charlotte would say something—anything. Despite her marrying Verlan only after he promised her he intended to comply with the holy Principle of plural marriage, I sensed her devastation at it actually coming to pass. Seeing her face now, I wondered if she'd changed her mind. Feeling guilty and foolish, I reminded myself I was just doing what all the godly people I knew said God required of me.

Verlan broke the painful silence. He turned and smiled at me. "What kind of ring do you want?" he asked.

I was flabbergasted. Why couldn't we wait and discuss this in private? I turned red with humiliation, saying nothing. But he was intent on prying the information out of me right in front of my sister, his wife. "I could get you a small diamond," he offered.

That broke Charlotte's prolonged silence. She looked at Verlan as though questioning his sanity. "You never got a diamond for me! You promised me that all you'd ever buy were gold bands," she reprimanded coldly.

Not wanting to participate in such a dispute, I clenched my teeth and prayed we'd get to Aunt Beth's before Charlotte turned on me. After a brief silence, Verlan tried again. I caught his blue eyes questioning mine in the rearview mirror. "What kind of a band do you want?" he said.

I saw that to keep the peace, I'd have to conform to decisions they apparently had made together before I'd arrived on the scene. I wondered what other rules they had made for me. Following rules wasn't really my best thing; they could just ask God about that. From this point on, would I have to get every decision approved not just by my husband but by Charlotte as well? "A band will be okay," I answered, "But I'd like it to be as wide as possible."

"Like Charlotte's?" Verlan asked.

Where was his tact? It was bad enough our having to share the same husband without our rings being identical as well. Charlotte apparently felt the same way.

"Nobody is copying my ring," she said. "Get it any width except mine."

In full agreement, I said, "Just get the ring a width narrower."

To everyone's great relief, we soon pulled into Aunt Beth's yard. Verlan helped Charlotte out of the car with her baby, and she walked ahead of us into the house. He grabbed the opportunity to whisper in my ear, "We'll be here Friday at 6 P.M. Don't tell anyone what's going on, and don't bring anything with you. No toothbrush—nothing! I don't want anyone getting any ideas. Tell Aunt Beth we're taking you to a movie."

Yes, along with everyone else, I would have to hide my marriage from Aunt Beth, whose life was the most shining example of the Principle I knew. As her husband's third wife and the mother of twelve, plump, jovial Aunt Beth gave the impression that plural marriage was a snap if you just loved God. It grieved me that the practice of polygamy had evolved in such a way that even the Aunt Beths in one's life had to be kept in the dark about your marriage if you weren't a first wife. It was for everyone's good, of course, so if ever questioned by authorities, she could honestly deny having any incriminating personal knowledge. The future of my own family and of the extended polygamous family network could be jeopardized if anyone found out about my marriage. Still, I felt terrible about having to freeze her out.

Verlan told my aunt their visit would be brief. "We just came by to bring Irene home," he said. Then he quickly changed the subject, not wanting Aunt Beth to suspect he was interested in me. She told us about all the babies being born, her latest travels with her family, and shared a few of her newest jokes. She was always a delight to visit.

Eventually, she took note of Charlotte's brooding silence. Turning to her, Aunt Beth asked comfortingly, "Is this June heat getting to you today? You look like you don't feel well."

"I'm doing just fine," Charlotte snapped. Verlan took it as his cue to stand up and motion for his wife to follow him out. He shook Aunt Beth's hand, then gave my hand a little squeeze as he and Charlotte said good-bye.

I went up to my room and collapsed, my nerves shot from the hours and days of constant tension. Plus, I had other reasons to be anxious. Most notably, I was supposed to be getting married in five days, but Verlan still hadn't actually proposed to me. He hadn't even said he loved me. His behavior was such a stark contrast to everything I'd experienced with Glen, I could barely fit "Verlan" and "marriage" into the same sentence in my mind. I was so twisted up, I spent the next four days in bed.

It gave me time to obsess on a variety of levels. For example, at the wedding, when I apparently would kiss Verlan for the very first time, should I turn my head to the left or to the right? Then there was the fact that we hadn't made any wedding plans, with the possible exception of the troublemaking ring. What were we even going to do on Friday? If our communication was this bad before the wedding, what would it be like after?

The whole week, I was sick with apprehension, and my mind kept racing in all directions. Would he remember the ring? Would it fit? Oh, heavens, what if Aunt Beth wouldn't let me go to the movie? What kind of honeymoon would I have without a toothbrush or nightgown or even clean underclothes?

On Tuesday, I ran my fingers across the calendar. Wednesday ... Thursday ... Friday. Friday, July 3, 1953, would be my wedding day. I couldn't believe the irony when I realized my mother married my father on the very same day in 1931. Was this mere coincidence, or had God planned it this way?

A second wife herself, my mother had a lonely, underground wedding, just as it appeared mine was going to be. And, in an effort to obey God, she, too, married her half sister's husband. In the end, she'd been rewarded with depression, sickness, and years of loneliness. Plural marriage shattered my mother's dreams. She never got the love, honor, and attention she desired and deserved. I reminded myself that people fail the Principle; the Principle does not fail us. But would Mother agree with that?

Here on the threshold of my polygamous life, I longed to run back to Trout Creek and take her down into the cellar for another talk. This time I'd do more listening. I'd try and find out just where she'd gone wrong. I'd ask her what advice she could give to a brand-new second wife. But of course, I couldn't run home. So I resolved to be happy with my wedding and my life no matter what. If I just loved the Lord with all my heart, I could surely pull it off.

Thinking about Trout Creek, however, got me thinking about Glen and the beautiful wedding we'd planned. We would have had guests, refreshments, joy, and many, many expressions of our love and affection for each other.

Oh, but those were dangerous thoughts! I couldn't make myself marry Verlan on Friday if I let myself think about such things on Tuesday or Wednesday or Thursday. Forcing Glen from my consciousness for the thousandth time, I kept repeating to myself, "I must be strong. I want celestial glory!"

The days passed slowly.

CHAPTER SEVEN

When I stepped on the scales Friday evening, I had lost ten pounds, having been too nervous to eat for days. I ironed my new gingham dress and polished my white shoes while I worried about whether Aunt Beth would give me a hard time for going out. She'd been bringing herb teas and hot broth up to my room all week, trying to cure my supposed flu.

I'd always envisioned myself being married in white—the sign of purity, of virginity. I was a virgin. I opened the Mormon scriptures and read: "And again, as pertaining to the law of the Priesthood—if any man espouse a virgin, and desire to espouse another, and the first give her consent, and if he espouse the second, and they are virgins, and have vowed to no other man, then is he justified; he cannot commit adultery . . . with that that belongeth unto him and to no one else." (Doctrine and Covenants, 132:61) I read the passage over again thoughtfully. Charlotte had been a virgin and she was now willing to give me to her husband, Verlan.

I read the next verse: "And if he have ten virgins given unto him by this law, he cannot commit adultery, for they belong to him, and they are given unto him; therefore he is justified." (Doctrine and Covenants, 132:62). *Oh God,* I prayed, *please don't ever let him find ten!* I needed love, someone who needed and understood me. How would Verlan possibly manage all that if he was busy with nine others? Furthermore, if I couldn't be somebody's only wife, I at least wanted to be his favorite wife. How would I ever have a chance if Verlan fulfilled this scripture? Charlotte would be quite enough competition, thank you very much.

I looked nice in my new turquoise and lavender dress. It wasn't what I'd dreamed of wearing on my wedding day, but was any of this what I had dreamed? I finished by pulling my curled hair back into a ponytail and hoped Verlan would be pleased with the results.

I found Aunt Beth sitting in the living room downstairs. "Where are you going looking so pretty?" she asked.

I kept my eyes from hers. "To the movie."

"Hmm. What time will you be home, dear?"

I frankly didn't know, so I just said, "Late." Then I quickly added, "But don't wait up for me." If anyone would have understood, it would have been Aunt Beth, but Uncle Rulon and Verlan said no telling anyone.

I heard Verlan's car pull up, which mercifully ended the questioning. I went out to meet them so Verlan and Charlotte wouldn't have to come to the door and stir Aunt Beth's suspicions. Walking toward Verlan's car, I motioned for them not to get out. I was fast catching on to the polygamous way.

I took my usual place in the backseat, with the three of them—Verlan, Charlotte, and their baby—up front. Verlan pointed to Charlotte's beige suit (her wedding suit, in fact) hanging in the window. "I thought you'd look nice in this," he said, "so we'll stop first chance we get, and you can change." I guess my best dress wasn't good enough for Verlan after all.

Charlotte said nothing, so I presumed my wearing her wedding suit was not her idea. Still, I wished she'd give me her opinion about it. When we stopped at a gas station, she mutely carried the suit into the filthy restroom, and I followed. Because everything in there was too dirty to touch, Charlotte had to hold everything while I changed clothes. We found the suit fit me well enough, though I filled it out a little more than she had. I was grateful for the ten lost pounds at that point.

"Let's hurry," she said. "It still may take us a while to find the place. We can't be late."

I removed the elastic band and let my shoulder-length hair fall around my face. Charlotte produced a lipstick. Though we'd been warned by the brethren not to use such "evil trash," I was thankful she'd brought it. We both felt God would be lenient this once. After all, how often did a girl get married? Besides, no one else would ever know. The only witnesses at my wedding would be the three of us and the mysterious priesthood elder who would perform the ceremony.

Soon we pulled up to the address my uncle gave us. Uncle Rulon had told us not to get out of the car. "Now be quiet," Verlan cautioned us. "Keep the baby's noise down. I just hope this is the right place. The number is right, but I'd sure feel silly if the wrong person came out to see why we're sitting in his front yard."

I knew we had to be careful, but frankly, I was more concerned with the fact that Verlan ought to have put me up front with him. After all, I was the bride. I felt like a fool sitting alone in the back.

I didn't know who felt worse about this marriage, Charlotte or me. It all felt so awkward. I could see the suffering on her face. She only spoke when spoken to and appeared on the verge of crying. It made me feel sick inside.

Verlan reached under the seat. Then he turned around and handed me a small white box. "This is for you," he said with a smile.

I opened it. Inside was a red rose corsage. "I hope you like it," he said as he reached into the box and took out a white carnation boutonniere for himself.

I had no idea where to pin it. This was the first corsage I'd ever been given. Verlan took Verlan Jr. from Charlotte just long enough for her to pin it properly in place.

As 7:00 turned to 7:15 and then 7:30, Verlan couldn't stand the suspense. He kept checking his watch. "Why doesn't he come out?" he thought out loud. "He's already half an hour late. I wonder what's wrong."

Just then, a stocky, middle-aged man came out of the house and walked over to our car. I recognized him, having seen him occasionally in Sunday meetings. He opened the back door and got in beside me. "Sorry to be so late. I hope I haven't inconvenienced you," he said. "Go to the Mormon temple. They won't allow us inside, of course." He laughed at that, his fat jowls moving up and down. "But at least you can tell your future posterity that you were married on the Salt Lake temple grounds."

Once we'd parked the car at the temple, we got out and searched the grounds for a place secluded enough that we could rest assured no Latter Day Saints would see what we were doing and pitch a fit. If we'd been LDS church members, we'd have been ushered through an elaborate secret ritual inside the temple, but as fundamentalists involved in plural marriage, we were strictly forbidden anywhere the general public couldn't go. That night, the temple grounds were crowded with tourists.

Disappointed, the brother said, "We can't perform such a holy ordinance here, under these circumstances. We have what the Mormons have lost. They may not let us in God's house, but they'll never keep us from fulfilling his laws. Let's drive down below the state capitol to a place called Memory Grove. We'll find a nice, secluded spot and get this taken care of."

A short time later, we parked the car and all walked through Memory Grove until we crossed a small bridge. Several trees hid the creek below from our view. We climbed down a hilly embankment under the protection of the trees, just in case any hikers passed by, and found a place we thought was fully hidden from anyone's view. Then God's servant clasped his hands behind his back and cleared his throat.

"This is a solemn occasion," he intoned. "As a brother holding the priesthood, I have not only the right but also the duty to obtain the sanction of the Lord to perform this holy ordinance. I know you're in a hurry, so I won't prolong my remarks. But I do want you to know that God is looking down upon us this very moment. He is pleased with what is about to take place."

Then he carefully took Charlotte's sleeping baby from her arms and nodded to Verlan. "Stand here with your wife on your left," he said. "Now your new bride on your wife's left. Okay . . . uh . . . I must apologize. I just realized I don't know your names." We told them to him in the order he'd just positioned us.

"I think I have it," he said, no longer flustered. "Now, let's begin. Do you, Charlotte Kunz LeBaron, take Irene Golda Kunz by the right hand and give her to your husband to be his lawful wedded wife?"

With a catch in her voice, Charlotte answered, "I do." Then she took my right hand and placed it in Verlan's. Stepping to one side, she allowed me to take my rightful place next to my soon-to-be husband.

"Do you, Verlan MacDonald LeBaron, take Irene Golda Kunz by the right hand . . ." It was about to happen. ". . . before God, angels, and these witnesses . . ." I could no longer change my mind. From then on, I would always be a plural wife. Maybe I'd be arrested as my father had been. Maybe I'd even have to go to jail. Then I thought of Glen. I'd wanted so badly to tell him how much I still loved him. But God had to come first. I reminded myself that I had to be strong if I wanted a celestial glory.

"I now pronounce you husband and wife, for time and all eternity. You may kiss the bride," the brother concluded. Somewhere in there, Verlan and I actually said "I do." Now he kissed me for the very first time, ever so lightly. Then he turned to kiss Charlotte, praising her for fulfilling her role in this holy Principle. I thought Verlan's lips lingered just a little bit longer on Charlotte's than they had on mine.

To the brother's surprise, Verlan took out a gold band from his pocket and nervously placed it on my finger. For obvious security reasons, rings weren't usually given to plural wives. Mine was a perfect fit.

Then Verlan handed me the wedding band Charlotte bought for him and placed on his finger two years earlier. I hesitated, knowing how bad it would make her feel. The brother instructed me to put it on Verlan's finger, so I did.

Suddenly, it was all over. I was a wife. I looked around me and took everything in from this pivotal new perspective.

No one has ever known better than I did in that instant how big a crowd three really is.

I sat beside Verlan as we drove the elder back to his home. Verlan thanked him, reassuring him we'd keep his trust and never reveal his identity.

I felt jittery, taking Charlotte's place next to Verlan. Then, to my shock, he reached over and patted my knee right in front of her. "One more errand, and we'll be on our way," he said.

He drove back to the temple and parked at a meter, then helped Charlotte and Verlan Jr. out of the car. She said nothing to me, but I could see her tears as she turned and walked away.

"I'll be right back," Verlan said nervously to me. By the time he caught up with her, she was openly crying, so he put his arm around her and tried to comfort her. I could see her shoulders shake as sobs racked her body. Then they walked slowly toward the Greyhound bus station across the street. This was his "one more errand." He was sending her back to their apartment in Provo, where she would spend the weekend alone with her baby while he celebrated his honeymoon with me. My heart was aching for her.

"Verlan," I called out after him. He turned and waved, signaling that everything was under control. I yelled louder, "Verlan, please come here."

He didn't want me attracting attention, so he came running back. "What is it?"

"Please, Verlan, just take me home . . . please don't do this to her!" I begged.

"She'll be okay," he reassured me. "Really, I'll get her happy again." He ran back, taking long strides, and caught up with her just as the light changed for them to cross the street.

Fifteen minutes went by. I was tempted to run away and get lost in the temple crowd. I felt so confused. Before their marriage, Charlotte made certain Verlan meant to live the Principle. Why, then, did she seem so devastated? I wasn't taking him away from her. We were just going to share him, as good fundamentalist wives do. I'd been taught a man would love you more if you gave him another wife. She had done that very thing. Besides, she'd had him all to herself for almost two years. Surely he loved her more. He hardly even knew me.

His "errand" apparently complete, I saw him jaywalking through traffic to hurry back across the street. Grinning broadly, he almost skipped over the curb and winked at me as he approached the car.

Finally, he plopped down beside me in the driver's seat and kissed me for the second time. Only now, he wasn't so nervous or quick about it.

Starting the motor, Verlan patted my leg again and announced, "We're going north to Ogden, where nobody knows us. We have to be careful, you know. I can't take a chance on having anyone find out I married you!" He explained he was in the United States on a student visa to attend college. "If any snoopy officials find out I've got two wives, I'll be arrested, and I could lose my residency rights." He let out a sigh. "But let's try to be happy, okay?"

With Charlotte out of the way, I began to see a different side of Verlan. Now he was free to treat me like a wife without having to worry about hurting her feelings. "I'm the luckiest man alive!" he exclaimed. "Today I finally entered the Principle. I really did it. I'm on my way to exaltation!" He held my hand, stealing kisses as he rattled on. "You are the *key,* Irene. The key to plural marriage. No matter how many wives I have, you'll always be the key that got me into this Principle!"

So much for being loved, cherished, even liked for myself. A damned key was what I was. I suppose he thought I would be thrilled to have been useful to the cause. But then, that would actually have required him to focus on something besides his own future glory.

On our way to Ogden, Verlan stopped at a fruit stand in Bountiful. "Stay in the car," he instructed. "Do you want a cold soda?"

I shook my head no.

He returned with a large paper bag, which he laid on the backseat. Then we drove on. He tried sharing his 7-Up with me, insisting I at least take a swallow. I was thirsty, but I knew I wouldn't be able to get it down. I was increasingly anxious about what was coming next. I watched, frightened, as Verlan carefully scanned every motel sign we approached.

"Which one would you like to stay in, Irene?"

I couldn't even cope yet with the general concept. Every time he'd slow down, I'd say, "Let's go to the next one, okay?"

Before we realized it, we were heading out of town and had to turn around. Verlan pulled into the first motel we came to after that. Dick's

Motel. "You stay out here while I go and register for our room," he ordered. "Take off that corsage. Don't act like you're my wife [as if I knew how to do that]. If I'm caught with an underage girl, I could be in big trouble."

I was sixteen years old, about to have sex for the first time, and had no personal belongings with me of any kind, but all he could think to be concerned about was himself. What in heaven's name had I gotten myself into?

"Oh, don't look so hurt," he apologized. "We just have to be cautious, that's all."

He came back with a key and drove us over to room 9. Obeying his orders, I stayed in the car while he checked out the room. Apparently satisfied, he walked quickly to the rear of the car and took out his suitcase, looking around carefully to make sure no one saw us. "Follow me," he said quietly. "But wait till I turn the lights out." He darted into the room, flipped the switch, and motioned with his hand in the semidarkness for me to come in.

Once inside, he locked the motel door behind us. After checking to make sure there were no sizable curtain cracks, he flipped the lights back on and placed his suitcase on the foot of the bed, opening it with a broad smile. "Charlotte made this for you," he said, pulling out a paper sack and playfully throwing it to me. "I've never seen it before," he assured me. "You can be the first to show it to me when you put it on. If you don't mind, though, I'll use the bathroom first."

When he had gone, I opened the sack. Inside was a nightgown. I'm sure I must have turned ten shades of red even though I was the only one in the room. It was just the thought of Charlotte knowing and planning what I would wear on my wedding night. Since I hadn't been allowed to pack a thing, I was certainly grateful to have something to put on, but I hated that it had to be something Charlotte made. Like a shadow, her presence permeated the room. It seemed to me she was everywhere.

I sat on the foot of the bed, listening to Verlan take a shower and brush his teeth. When he came out in his striped pajamas, I blushed and turned away. "You can go in now," he said cheerfully.

I ran in and closed the bathroom door behind me. But I was afraid to get into the shower. The mere thought of being naked with Verlan just on the other side of the door made me blush all over.

I opened the paper bag again and took out the long cotton nightgown with elbow-length sleeves. It had cute, colorful little figures of violins and birds on it. I hoped Verlan wouldn't think of Charlotte when he saw me wearing it. I double-checked the lock on the bathroom door, and then I took the fastest shower of my life.

Afterward, standing there in my new nightgown, nervous and sweating, I hesitated for several minutes, trying to summon the courage to open the bathroom door and go out to my husband. Suddenly I felt the need to go, but I didn't dare for fear he'd hear the splash. To buy some time while I figured out what to do, I turned on the tap so the water would run into the sink and Verlan would think I was still just prettying up. Then I worried he'd think the sink splash was me using the toilet, so I quickly turned the tap back off. Oh God, what had I gotten myself into?

From the other room, I heard Verlan whistling, and I froze. "Are you ever coming out?" he asked.

"Turn the lights off first, and I will," I said.

He did as I asked, but pleaded, "Let me take a peek at your nightgown."

I slowly opened the bathroom door and stood there one brief moment for him to get a glimpse, and then I flipped off the bathroom light switch, darkening the room.

Somehow, despite my heart now beating double fast and extra loud, I heard Verlan whisper to me, "Come on over here, Irene. I'm waiting for you." I was paralyzed with fear. "Well, are ya' comin'?" he asked in the darkness. I groped along, feeling the wall with my right hand while my left hand searched to find the bed. Then I stumbled over his legs.

"Oh, I'm sorry," he said, pulling me down beside him in a kneeling position against the bed. "Let's have prayer first."

God forgive me, I thought. I had to admit, prayer was the farthest thing from my mind.

Verlan grasped my hand tightly in his and prayed out loud: "Dear Lord, thank you for giving me such a beautiful wife. Thank you for this special Principle that gave her to me. We are indeed blessed, Lord . . . bless Charlotte, comfort her, help us to always be united. Amen."

I climbed onto my side of the bed, and Verlan crawled over me to get to his side. I could barely breathe as I tried to recall all the ins and outs of the law of purity Aunt Rhea taught me. Would we be able to do this without committing adultery? Would I be able to do it at all? There was so much to fear.

I checked to make sure my new nightgown was clear down to my ankles. Verlan pulled me close, making sure he didn't touch my breasts. It seemed he was almost as embarrassed as I. We lay in that position for nearly an hour, and all that time he talked on and on about our future.

"I'll move back to the family ranch in Mexico just as soon as I get ahead a little," he said. "Down there we can live plural marriage freely. I don't want to have to hide the fact that you're my wife."

That sounded ideal to me. I gave no thought at all to my mother's constant warnings of insanity, fanaticism, and isolation down in Mexico. Instead, I imagined a sprawling ranch house with a white picket fence, a big red barn, a generator for lights, and fields of luscious green alfalfa—just like the Youngs' place. Verlan explained how the early Mormon polygamists moved to colonies in Mexico, taking their plural wives out of the United States to avoid arrest. Mexico had its own bigamy laws, but enforcement there was far more lenient. Perhaps this was because the culture was so open to men having mistresses. At any rate, Verlan promised that when we were safely below the border, he would openly acknowledge me. Then I'd receive the same rights and privileges as Charlotte.

He further told me how thrilled he was to have me as his wife, to finally be on his way to fulfilling all his dreams. "Can you imagine?" he said in wonder, "I now have two of the seven wives I've dreamed of having!"

Lying there in his arms as he revealed his innermost hopes and dreams, I fixated on that last one. Seven wives? I'd never thought a man having seven wives was a big deal, but now that I was a second wife, I was stunned.

"Just think," he said, "if I can have a quorum of seven wives, and each one of them has at least seven kids, I can easily have fifty children! Irene, I want you to help me build my kingdom! I'm so glad you're a part of it."

I sank deeper by the minute. This wasn't the kind of honeymoon I'd expected, even from Verlan. I had just taken the biggest step of my life. I was a brand-new wife who had sacrificed her true love and married for God's Principle, but I still desperately wanted some assurance I'd be cherished. What did I get instead? A long-winded lecture about other wives to come.

Apparently satisfied with the picture he painted, Verlan sighed, gave me a quick kiss, and then turned over on his side and said, "Good night."

I didn't know whether to cry or run away to where I could scream. I was overcome with regrets, with bitter remorse. I gave up passion for this? Glen hadn't been able to keep his hands off me. His kisses were always long and fiery, while Verlan's were just . . . just chicken pecks. In vain, I tried not to compare the two in my mind.

The remainder of my lonely wedding night, I lay awake, wondering if I'd done the wrong thing. Or was it possible, despite his infinite wisdom, that God was the one who made the mistake?

Eventually, the early morning sun began to filter beneath the dingy curtains, and I came out of my sleepless, all-night stupor. I thanked God it was daylight. Beside me, Verlan stirred, stretched languorously, and climbed out of bed. I pretended to be asleep until I heard him close the bathroom door. Then I quietly got up and put on my bra and gingham dress. I looked at my haggard face in the mirror. Spotting his pocket comb on the dresser, I used it without permission, figuring that since I'd given up everything, whatever he owned should be mine, too.

Opening the bathroom door, Verlan saw I was awake and chirped, "Good morning, Irene." He walked over and kissed me. "Boy, you're sure quiet this morning. Are you hungry?" He went over and pulled a package of sweet rolls and a carton of warm milk out of the paper bag he'd brought from the fruit stand. It was some spectacular wedding breakfast.

"No, I don't feel like eating yet," was all I said. Normal people had big, colorful weddings and family feasts afterward. I knew we had to be discreet and that Verlan didn't have lots of money, but he could at least have made arrangements to take me out to a nice restaurant. I wondered if he was ashamed of me, only pretending to be cautious. Or did we truly have to be this austere?

After Verlan ate, he casually took a bunch of books from his suitcase and sat in the only chair in the room. "I hope you don't mind," he said, grinning. "I have a lot of homework to do. I'm having a big test on Monday. This is my second year at BYU, you know." Without another glance in my direction, he started turning pages and scribbling notes. I sat on the bed doing nothing until he finally asked me to read psychology to him. Then he read to me. I consoled myself with the fact that we were at least sharing something. Eventually, he slammed the psychology book shut and asked me to drill him for a test.

I wondered why he didn't take a break and pay some attention to me—kiss me, or at least give me a little hug. He must have noticed my disappointment. With a sly look, he said, "That's enough studying for now. I do need to draw a design for my art class, but that can wait." He suddenly jumped up and threw me back on the bed, kissing me on the face and neck. "I really need to get this done first!"

I thought we might have finally gotten around to "it." But Verlan released me as suddenly as he grabbed me, and he sat back down to thumb through another book, looking for ideas to make a design for his art lesson.

Angry and frustrated, I said dryly, "Why don't you just copy the design on the border of the wallpaper?"

"That's perfect!" he squealed with delight. "Why didn't I think of that? Thanks, Irene." I numbly watched as he colored in the shades of blue and green, matching the wallpaper design. When he finished, he laid down his pencils and announced, "We have to get going if we want to see a movie and go out to dinner."

After the breakfast he'd offered me, I couldn't imagine what he might have in mind for dinner. But by now I was starving as much for food as for attention. I tried to shrug off my mounting depression. Already my honeymoon was half over, and I was still a virgin!

During the movie, Verlan played with my fingers and held me close. I was all jittery inside, my mind one minute on consummating my marriage with Verlan and the next minute on Glen. Would I ever forget him? I couldn't tell you now what the movie was about. I couldn't have told anyone even then. My attention was focused on the noises inside my head and stomach.

After the movie, Verlan found a small family restaurant and proudly ordered "two big steaks." The wedding feast was finally on. The jukebox was our wedding orchestra, and the meal, when it came, looked fabulous, with all the trimmings. I couldn't swallow a bite. Verlan insisted several times that I try and eat my steak, but I was in an overwrought state of mind unlike anything I'd ever experienced. I just couldn't do it.

He apologized as he deftly reached over and stabbed my steak with his fork. "I hope you don't mind," he said. "I don't want it going to waste."

"Go ahead. Help yourself," I heard myself say. As I watched him devour my steak, I thought how obvious it was he'd been married before.

The jukebox eventually played Eddie Fisher's haunting "I'm Walking Behind You." It was lovely but heartrending. As I listened intently to the familiar lyrics, I imagined each word being sung just to me. It was Glen singing them. His final words to me in his letter carried that same sad message: "If things go wrong dear, and fate is unkind, look over your shoulder, I'm walking behind . . ."

Fighting back tears, I excused myself and headed for the ladies' room. I told myself that "fate" couldn't be unkind to me forever. If God put me in this, he'd have to see me through somehow.

Back at the motel, Verlan turned off the overhead light in our room, leaving on just a small table lamp. After we crawled into bed, he snuggled up close to me and began talking about his schooling, his childhood, and his religion. After a long time listening to him go on and on, I could no longer contain my disappointment. Dreading the answer, I asked him the question that had preoccupied me for the past twenty-four hours.

"You really don't love me, do you?"

He got my drift. Amazed, he rolled over on his side and wrapped his strong arms around me. "Of course I do," he said. "I just want to take things easy. But I'm glad you want me." Before I knew what was happening, he pulled me out of the bed onto my knees. "Come on, Irene, let's pray first."

I knelt there beside him, so shaken I could hardly breathe. We held hands, and he began, "Our Heavenly Father, help us stand firm under all our trials. Let your spirit be with us." He paused. "Bless us now, in what we're about to do, and forgive us wherein we offend you. Amen."

I kept my head bowed through Verlan's prayer but shuddered at its conclusion. Here he was asking God, God's angels, and all the sublime hosts of heaven to watch us. With that sort of audience, I could hardly bear Verlan's touch, let alone doing the deed for the first time. I snapped off the light.

It was all over so quickly that, but for the pain, I wasn't even sure I'd been there for it. Was that what all the fuss was about, what I'd waited sixteen years for? If so, I wondered if I'd be able to tolerate it well enough to conceive my annual child.

Seeming to sense my disappointment, Verlan asked if I knew about the law of purity.

"Yes, I do," I answered, thinking what a very good law it was.

"My father lived it," Verlan said, "and I wonder if you intend to."

"Absolutely," I assured him.

Clearly pleased, he nodded his agreement and then rolled over on his side. Within minutes, he was snoring softly. All I could do was lie there in confusion.

The next day, when Verlan took me for a walk, I finally became acquainted with his version of romance. The midday sun filtered through the tall, leafy trees as we strolled along, hand in hand, looking for the spot in Memory Grove where we'd been married two days before. Standing there on that same piece of ground, hidden by the same trees, Verlan wrapped me in his arms, kissed me warmly, and said, "Thanks for being so wonderful." Then, for the first time, he said, "I love you, Irene."

Our interesting time together was drawing to an end as we headed back to Murray. Verlan would soon be on his way home to Provo and to Charlotte. Before he dropped me off at Aunt Beth's, he handed me an eleven-dollar check, insisting I give it to her and confide in her that we'd married. He asked me to tell her to please keep it a secret from anyone else. "Tell her the money is for your living expenses, and I'll send her some more later. If she prefers you not stay with her now that you're married, I'll figure something else out." Then he checked his rearview mirror to make sure no one was behind us, reached across the seat, and briefly kissed me good-bye. We drove the remaining blocks in silence.

In front of Aunt Beth's house, Verlan kept the car running, stopping just long enough for me to grab the paper sack that contained my now-soiled nightgown and jump out. He waved a friendly smile and drove away.

My unforgettable honeymoon was over.

I dreaded seeing my aunt after basically lying to her when I supposedly went off to the movies two days before. If I'd lost her trust with that action, I'd have no havens left and would be forced to move in with Charlotte.

All was quiet as I tiptoed into the house and up to the bedroom I shared with sixteen-year-old Evelyn. I assumed my aunt and her dozen children were at Sunday meeting. I immediately took off my gold wedding band and put it in a stationery box I tucked under my panties in the bottom of my dresser drawer. Then I hid my nightgown in a safe corner of the cluttered closet.

Without warning, Evelyn opened the door and came into the room. Looking at me smugly, she asked, "Well, did he give you a ring?"

From the outside, this was how a polygamous union looked: people you knew and loved simply disappeared for a while, and then they showed back up a few days later, scrambling to hide the evidence while you were free to suspect all you wanted without knowing anything for sure. I'd seen it many times, but I'd been foolish enough to think that no one would notice when I did it myself. I was shocked that Evelyn was onto us.

"If you're asking if I married him . . . um . . . well . . . yes," I said, knowing I shouldn't. "But please don't tell anyone. What does your mom think about me running off like I did?"

"Mostly she feels bad 'cause you didn't trust her enough to confide in her."

"I figured your mother would understand when I was finally able to tell her. After all, she entered polygamy as your dad's *third* wife. I can tell her now, but no one else is supposed to know. It has to be kept a secret for Verlan's sake."

As soon as Aunt Beth returned from Sunday school, I gave her Verlan's check and told her all about my marriage. She was very understanding, though she worried about our hiding such a special occasion from my mother.

VERLAN HAD TOLD ME to go see him the following Friday. As instructed, I took the bus to Provo, wondering all the way how Charlotte would feel about seeing me again now that I'd slept with her husband. I was certain she wouldn't want me hanging around her house, interrupting her life. And, though I wanted to see Verlan again, I thought a hotel, or perhaps Aunt Beth's home, would be a far more appropriate venue for a visit than the home he shared with Charlotte. How would I ever get to know him in another wife's presence?

The whole situation made me feel sick to my stomach. Verlan had told me to relax and leave it up to him. He'd know how to handle it, he said, assuring me he understood women. I had my doubts.

I arrived after dark, and Verlan wanted to get us all settled immediately for the night. So he pulled the heavy mattress off his and Charlotte's bed, carried it four feet away, and dropped it roughly on the floor. Then he told Charlotte to sleep on it right there in the same room with us while he and I took the box spring still on the bed frame. Incredulous and humiliated, we both complied, because that's what fundamentalist polygamous wives did—comply with whatever absurd, insensitive things their husbands came up with.

Lying there on the box spring next to Verlan, my discomfort was indescribable. If I so much as breathed deeply, the bed squeaked. Verlan and I didn't talk, touch, or even move. Down on the ground, Charlotte also made no sound, though I couldn't imagine how she could keep from bawling. I thought I might be about to bawl myself when Verlan said suddenly, "Well, I can see this won't work." He jumped out of bed in his pajamas and ordered Charlotte off the mattress. Then he dragged it all the way down the hall to the living room, while Charlotte stood meekly by with a bewildered look on her face.

Completely disgusted, I followed him. "Please, Verlan," I whispered, trying to keep my voice calm. "I don't like to share her home with you this way. I'll wait until I can have a place of my own. Please, go sleep with her."

"No!" he retorted in a loud whisper. "I haven't seen you for a week, and I intend to be fair."

"This isn't fair to any of us," I pointed out.

"Look, Irene, we're all new at this," he said. "But we'll figure things out as we go along."

Verlan went in and reassigned Charlotte to the box spring, then returned to me in the living room. He peered briefly through the part in the drapes and checked the door lock before he crawled onto the mattress beside me. "There've been rumors going around that the government is planning raids on polygamists," he warned, "so I have to be extra careful, especially with you being underage and all."

That was all very interesting, but I had a few more pressing matters to settle at the moment. "Where am I going to live, Verlan?" I asked him.

"Oh, God will take care of that. Let's just take things one day at a time and trust in him." He patted my hip and gave me a brief kiss. Then he turned over on his side to go to sleep.

I hadn't finished. "Verlan, I need to figure out my life! What are our plans? I can't live like this. I want a home and some privacy." He said nothing, but I still wasn't done with him. "I won't ever come here again and be made to feel like a complete fool in my sister's house," I warned.

"Shh, shh . . . that's enough. Now go to sleep," he mumbled.

I'd have felt more validated if he'd slapped me. Unheard and untouched, I cried myself to sleep. Later Verlan told me Charlotte cried all night in the other room, visualizing us making love.

I'D BEEN MARRIED NOW for two whole weeks. This time, Verlan promised to come to Aunt Beth's house to see me. He'd be there around 7:00 P.M. Fortunately, he believed me when I told him I wouldn't go see him again at Charlotte's. Or maybe she forbade it. Either way, I thought this a superior arrangement until we got a place of my own.

When Verlan finally showed up, he insisted we go to a drive-in movie. I begged him to stay home so we could retire early and get to know each other a little better. Didn't he want us to spend some time together without a crowd around? But in the name of obedience, I gave in again.

Returning from the movie, we crept upstairs, hoping not to wake anyone. Cousin Evelyn, who'd thoughtfully decided to sleep somewhere else, made up the bed with clean sheets and even left a vase on the nightstand with two beautiful red roses in it. Verlan quickly undressed in the dark and crawled into bed. Still shy, I followed suit. I don't recall Verlan inviting a celestial audience to watch, bless, or forgive us that second time.

That was the night I discovered what the fuss was all about.

CHAPTER EIGHT

On our first trip together as a threesome, we went to visit Aunt Rhea in Hurricane. Everything was going along fairly well until Horace Knowlton, a polygamist friend and lawyer in Salt Lake City, came by and gave us some alarming news. He told us the same thing Verlan told me that night in Provo—the government authorities were gearing up to go after polygamists. But our friend knew details Verlan didn't, and these details would very much change the immediate course of our lives. He'd heard from reliable sources that a raid was planned for the very next day against the polygamist settlement of Short Creek, less than thirty miles south of where we were visiting. Short Creek was where Aunt Rhea's daughters, Donna and Myra, lived with their husband, Clyde.

For a decade, the little town of Short Creek served as a refuge for polygamists who desired to practice their conspicuous lifestyle in a secluded community uncorrupted by the worldly, secular society of the Latter Day Saints and others. It was a place where fundamentalists controlled practically everything, instead of being at the mercy of those who opposed them. This refuge had grown to house about four hundred people, including men, women, and swarms of children. The population varied considerably, as polygamous families constantly moved in and out according to their various needs or sometimes due to "orders from above" coming to them through the colony's prophet.

The elders of Short Creek knew the community's practices were in flagrant violation of state and federal bigamy laws, but they'd so far escaped enforcement of those laws by keeping to themselves and by locating the town exactly on the Utah–Arizona border. This made it strategically convenient for slipping back and forth from one state to the other whenever the need arose. By spreading themselves across two states, moreover, the polygamists living in Short Creek avoided being exclusively subject to either state's laws. The clear responsibility of neither state, then, the Creekers had thus far been left alone by both.

But disturbing rumors like the ones Verlan heard recently began to circulate. Polygamists always speculated that raids like the one in 1944 and the one now planned for Short Creek were launched whenever the LDS Church and the State of Utah got particularly embarrassed about our escalating numbers. We were prolific if nothing else. And our population increase did have very real and negative implications for state governments, mostly in the form of welfare costs, since polygamist husbands, like my father, were rarely able to support all their wives and children. It was common for subsequent wives like my mother to draw welfare as supposed single moms while they continued to produce a child each year or so with a husband who circulated constantly from wife to wife. (When I was growing up, my mother had a hiding place inside a haystack near our home for when the welfare authorities came around, checking for fraud.) Then there were the rampant charges of child abuse, both in the form of giant families full of neglected children and teen and preteen girls being taken as wives.

When they got word that this new raid was in the works, most of the settlers at Short Creek decided to stand firm. We feared for them terribly. All of us well remembered the 1944 raid that resulted in the imprisonment of my father, Uncle Rulon, and so many others. Though I'd only been a child of seven at the time, I doubted I'd ever be able to forget the terror and sadness I felt when I thought they were going to take me from my mother and put me into foster care. The officials conducting the raid had in fact interrogated her, but they didn't bother her once she assured them she'd left my father.

The next morning, Sunday, July 26, 1953, the long-dreaded raid at Short Creek took place. In the wee hours just before daylight, we watched from Aunt Rhea's upstairs bedroom window as convoys of police cars and government vehicles snaked along the highway south out of Hurricane. Like a midnight funeral procession, they quietly ascended Hurricane Hill, headed for Short Creek. We lost sight of them after that.

Subsequent newspaper accounts of the raid informed us that Governor Howard Pyle of Arizona—under strong public pressure to enforce the antipolygamy laws and thereby blot out "a community dedicated to the production of white slaves"—worked for months to mobilize a number of government agencies and officials, including the FBI, the National Guard, state troopers, the highway patrol, sheriffs, and judges, among others. Even some Utah authorities took part in this all-out effort to correct what was variously labeled "an insurrection," "a conspiracy," and a "monstrous and evil growth."

At the appointed predawn hour, they approached the little town of Short Creek from both the Arizona and Utah sides, expecting to surprise everyone. Instead, the loud boom of a dynamite explosion greeted them while they were still some distance away. To those in the convoy, of course, this could only mean trouble; to the Creekers, it was a signal from loyal lookouts telling them the raid was imminent. Because of the warning, those who wanted to hide had the time to do so. But the majority of townspeople took it as their cue to gather for final instructions on how to receive the invaders.

Cautiously, the heavily armed patrols descended on Short Creek, expecting militant hostilities. They'd been warned the fundamentalist lawbreakers were desperate, as well as armed and dangerous. To their surprise, they found most of the saints gathered in front of the church, unarmed, praising God and singing, "My country 'tis of Thee, sweet land of liberty . . ." The Creekers surrendered without a fight, martyrs for their faith. The real drama was caused by all the hysterical children afraid of losing their parents.

During the next few days, the saints were held captive. Under strict surveillance, they were fed National Guard rations and escorted back and forth to the outhouse. Stragglers who hid or tried to flee across state lines were gathered up, while the judges and other officials began sorting out the preliminary fates of the various categories of perpetrators and victims they'd found within the settlement. These included nonpolygamous adults or those who still had only one spouse, polygamous husbands, adult polygamous wives, underage polygamous wives, and 263 children, some of whom clung to their mothers, wailing in fear of being separated and carted off to foster homes. Impossible decisions had to be made, and many mistakes were committed in the process. Some of the adults who were participants in plural marriages were freed to go home with their children, while some who were suspected to be polygamists but weren't remained in custody.

It was a disagreeable situation for all concerned, especially the mothers and children. Seeing their sad plight, some of the officers felt so bad, they apologized and expressed sympathy. But they had their orders, after all. They arrested most of the settlers as bigamists.

The men and a few of the women were taken to Kingman, Arizona, for incarceration, while approximately 40 women and 166 children were loaded into chartered buses and transported farther south to Phoenix, where they were put into temporary shelters until their relocation could be arranged. Naturally, they all wondered if they would ever see their families reunited again.

Fear struck the hearts of Mormon fundamentalists everywhere. There were an estimated thirty to forty thousand polygamists scattered across the West in Utah, Arizona, Idaho, Nevada, and other states, along with Canada and Mexico. All now felt vulnerable. Money was scarce; supplies were short. Many families were so large that going into hiding was next to impossible. Groups of saints began moving quietly out of big cities in the dead of night onto farms and ranches. Hoping to escape persecution, they went into Montana and California for concealment.

But the government's aggression did nothing to curb the fundamentalist fervor for plural marriage. Instead, it bonded families even closer together, strengthening their will to be loyal to God and valiant in living their revered Principle. Fundamentalist leaders simply directed all their followers to lay low until the storm subsided. Members were praised for their self-control and nonviolence. Instilled with a righteous pride, they actually welcomed the persecution, vowing to advance God's cause at all costs. Women were even counseled to relinquish their children rather than their religious freedom to obey God's commandments. The Short Creek settlers who'd been jailed did their part, too. Seeing themselves something like Paul in biblical times, they held prayer meetings asking for deliverance and sang praises to their maker. Now that liberty was on the line, the fundamentalists were demonstrating that they were willing to give their all for polygamy.

As for Verlan and Charlotte and me, we were so fully involved with the polygamist clans around the area, we considered ourselves to be in the same serious danger. We held a family council and decided Verlan should immediately quit school at BYU and move back to his family's ranch in Chihuahua, Mexico, taking Charlotte and her baby with him. I would join them in a month or so. Obediently, I agreed, wishing God's blessings on them as I saw them off. Somehow, on the other side of this crisis, I hoped to find stability and some freedom from all the hiding.

My brother and sister-in-law let me stay with them in Salt Lake City until Verlan sent instructions and bus fare for me to come to them. When it was time, I asked Richard to take me to the bus depot. He pleaded with me not to go, assuring me my life with the LeBarons would be misery. He begged me instead to stay in Utah with him or Mother.

I wouldn't hear a word of it. I'd been called, and I'd been chosen. I'd also made a promise. Besides, as I'd thought about it, I decided I was thrilled to be moving down to Mexico. What a romantic image I had conjured in my mind. It would be a wonderful adventure.

CHAPTER NINE

I was going to be met in El Paso by two of Verlan's older brothers, Joel and Floren, who were traveling the 185 rugged miles north by bus to the bustling Ciudad Juárez, just across the border. Joel registered in a cheap motel and was waiting there while Floren came to the bus station in El Paso to retrieve his young wife, Anna, her two small children, and me. Anna had been on my bus all the way from Salt Lake City, but we'd pretended not to know each other until we crossed into New Mexico. It had only been four weeks since the raid at Short Creek, so we took extra precautions just in case any of the authorities might be watching.

As the bus eased into the El Paso terminal, I saw Floren standing there, scrutinizing each passenger climbing off. I'd met Floren a few times when he'd come to see Aunt Rhea's older daughters. I was about ten at the time. I remembered him as a pleasant, fun-loving fellow, so I felt lucky to have him for a brother-in-law. Pushing my worn suitcase out the bus door before me, I threw myself into his arms. Anna was hugging him, too. He released his hold on me, kissed her warmly, and held her for another brief moment. After loving on the kids, he waved down a taxicab. It took us across the border into old Mexico.

Joel met us in the lobby of Hotel Rivas. He was about six feet tall and had a medium build and straight blond hair. He was very congenial, his blue eyes conveying good humor as he talked. Joel reminded me so much of Verlan, I immediately liked him.

After a hurried breakfast at a small café, we boarded a grimy Chihuahuense bus. I took a seat at the very rear of the dilapidated old vehicle, next to Joel. Nearby, Anna and Floren were cuddling and catching up after a nine-month separation. She was Floren's only wife so far, but they had marital troubles while living in the States, where they met. She left him, and he'd gone home to Mexico. The needs of the children motivated her attempt to reconcile.

I feared my clean dress would be soiled on the filthy, torn canvas seats, but I kept quiet about it. The large, rusty screws holding down the seats were almost vibrating out of the floor. The driver was trying to force the old bus into third gear, but it wouldn't (or couldn't) switch. He pumped the clutch like mad, grinding the gears, but still he couldn't seem to gain any momentum. We bounced along ever so slowly. The alien landscape of sand and mesquites barely crawled past as we headed south along the dangerously narrow, potholed highway.

It seemed as if we spent more time letting people on and off the bus than we did actually traveling. At the first stop, a weather-worn Mexican gentleman who I figured was about seventy boarded the bus. He was wearing crumpled white cotton trousers and a long-sleeved white shirt. What I noticed most was the wide red sash tied around his ample stomach. Since all the seats were taken, he stood with his back to us, clinging with one hand to the luggage rack above as the bus bounced along. As more and more people got on, he was forced to back up until he was standing directly in front of me. When he finally turned around, to my utter amazement, I found myself face to face with two live roosters tied by their legs to his big red sash. They looked as embarrassed about the whole thing as I was, but the old man never cracked a smile.

Next, a round-faced Indian-looking woman with a long black braid down her back got on the bus. She disrespectfully shoved everyone out of her way, squeezing herself onto the already overcrowded seat next to me. With her bare feet, she held a squealing little pig under her seat. I'd never seen anything like it.

In an effort not to gawk at the strange characters all around me, I asked Joel to translate the Spanish words I saw on two bold signs posted at the front of the bus. "NO BRINQUE EN LOS ASIENTOS," he said, trying to hide a smile. "It means 'don't jump on the seats.'"

I gasped, "What kind of place is this?"

Joel laughed. "The other one says NO ESCUPE EN EL PISO. That means 'don't spit on the floor.'"

Before I could stop myself, I blurted out, "In the States, they would junk this bus! Why do they even allow this old heap on the road?"

"Well, it's because we're going second class," Joel chuckled.

"Second class!" I exclaimed in disbelief. "Why are we going second class?"

"Because there's no third," he answered, straight-faced.

Just then, Floren got my attention. "Hey look, quick!" He pointed to a crude adobe (mud-brick) house with a flat dirt roof. "That's exactly like the house you're going to live in."

I laughed out loud. "You and Joel sure have a good sense of humor. I can see I'm going to survive in Mexico after all!"

Two hours later, we got off the bus at a completely isolated junction called Sueco. Other than the road, I saw nothing in any direction except sagebrush and mesquite bushes. The crumbling asphalt pavement ended thirty feet or so away, where a dirt road took over, winding off to the west toward a range of mountains.

The hot August sun beat down unmercifully. Neither Floren nor Joel seemed to mind it in the least. The brothers were too involved batting at one another with paddle balls—small red balls attached to paddles by rubber cords. Soon the balls at the end of their cords got all tangled up, so Anna demanded they put them away "before they're ruined for the kids."

Joel pretended he didn't hear her as he whacked Floren on the head. They both giggled like little boys.

Anna and I sat on our dusty suitcases, wondering why it was taking so long for the next bus to come by. Two hours passed. I was anxious to get to my new home. Finally I asked Joel when the next bus was due.

He never cracked a smile. "Tomorrow morning at nine," he said.

"Don't tease me, Joel. I want to get to the ranch."

"Really, the next bus won't come till the morning. But we'll hitch a ride on the first truck headed in our direction."

One by one, cars came and went along the highway, but none of them turned toward our dirt road. The broiling sun kept beating down, and I perspired heavily. Finally Joel saw a gray Dodge pickup approaching. Recognizing it, he hailed it down when it turned our way. The driver agreed to give us all a ride, so Joel and Floren shouted for Anna, the kids, and me to get into the cab of the truck. Laughing, they threw our suitcases into the back and jumped in behind them. They seemed to be having a grand old time.

I sat next to the driver, feeling very nervous—a well-to-do Mexican decked out in western attire. Since he spoke no English and I spoke no Spanish, we rode in awkward silence. At least it was awkward for me. An hour crawled by while choking, hot dust whirled in through the open windows. At one point, Anna and I turned to look at each other, and we both burst into hysterical laughter. We were so covered with white dust, we looked like we had on powdered wigs and white mascara. The driver stared at us like we'd taken leave of our senses, but he never said a word.

We finally came to a little town that we learned was called El Valle, the valley, officially known as San Buenaventura. It was a typical small town founded by ranchers and farmers—not much more than a wide place in the road where a few small buildings and adobe houses had been thrown up. The driver slammed on his brakes, and we skidded to the left, coming to a precarious stop in front of a moss green–colored store facing the roadway.

Joel hopped out of the truck and rattled away plaintively in Spanish to the driver, who eventually yielded to his request. What luck! Joel had talked him into going an hour out of his way to take us on to the ranch, some dozen miles further.

The closer we got, the greater my anticipation at finally getting to see the beautiful ranch that would be my new home. I fully expected the earthiness and poverty and oddity I'd seen of Mexico so far to all simply disappear at the LeBarons' gate. My apprehensions had only to do with seeing Verlan and Charlotte again, Verlan because he was the husband I still barely knew, and Charlotte ... well, for obvious reasons.

Half an hour later, with no warning, the truck lurched off the dirt road through large mesquites, bouncing over what seemed to be no more than a cow trail and scattering chickens in its wake. Joel and Floren stood up in the bed of the truck, hollering and waving their arms. "Welcome home, ladies! Welcome home!"

Excitedly, I challenged Anna, "Let's see who spots the ranch house first." We both leaned forward, peering through the powdery windshield. The truck slowly came to a halt in front of a large corral.

Verlan and his brother Ervil were milking cows when they heard the truck approaching. They stopped and jumped over the corral fence in their excitement to greet us. Verlan ran past Ervil, yanked open the truck door, and greeted Anna warmly. Reaching out his long arms, he helped me down next, laughing when he saw his dust-covered young bride.

As he gave me a little hug, he whispered in my ear. "Nobody here knows we're married except Joel and Floren. Remember, you're just my sister-in-law."

I could not have been more crushed. I'd come over a thousand miles, the last hundred on washboard dirt roads, to escape this very thing. Verlan said we'd be free here to live our fundamentalist religion and be a family. I felt broadsided and minimized by this unexpected demand for further secrecy, just when I'd expected to finally be validated. For the time being, I couldn't even question him about it. I had to play along.

Verlan tapped my suitcase against the rocky path to shake loose some of the dust and said, "Come on, Irene, let's walk home." I followed him, still looking for the ranch house.

As we walked along the dirt path, I told Verlan how worn out and dirty I felt from the long trip. All I wanted was a nice warm shower and a clean bed. That's when I began to wonder just where my bed might be, now that I'd been labeled a mere sister-in-law. It had been almost five weeks since I'd slept with Verlan. Would we sleep together here if no one was supposed to know I was married to him? And what about Charlotte? Would I have to pretend to be but a guest in her home? I had just assumed all this time that I would have my own private quarters in the LeBaron ranch house.

We'd only gone a few yards when Verlan stopped at a small adobe house exactly like the one Floren pointed out on the way down. It had a flat dirt roof, with uneven wooden frames for windows and gunnysacks rolled up at the top of the frames to keep out the dust and cold. I stood in front of it with my mouth hanging open, dimly aware that Verlan was speaking to me. I was turning to face him when I heard him drop my suitcase to the ground. Somewhat sheepishly, he said, "Welcome to the ranch, Irene. This is your new home."

Ranch? He called this a ranch? My cheeks flushed with sudden anger. Anyone with any brains at all knows that a ranch has a nice, framed white cottage with a neat picket fence and a large red barn. There had to be some rational explanation for all this. Verlan was surely kidding me, like his brothers had all the way here. But the look on his face told me it was no joke.

Somehow I kept my cool and held back the gathering tears. With monumental restraint, I managed to say, "I just want to take a shower, Verlan. Would you please show me to the bathroom?"

"Uh . . . er . . . wait right here!" he said. He dashed into the house and returned with a bar of coarse, homemade soap, a washcloth, and a ragged towel. Thrusting the soap into my hands, he raised the handle of the solid, cast iron pump next to the house and chirped, "We don't have electricity, of course. But look here, we do have running water." As he spoke, he forced a steady stream of water from the well with the strong pumping motion of his long arm.

Ignoring this new revelation for the time being, I unbraided my thick, dusty blonde hair and held my head under the pump, gasping for breath as the cold water washed the dirt down the wooden trough. I rinsed the caked dust and grime off my arms and legs as best I could, standing first on one foot, then on the other. After that, I scrubbed my filthy feet. Wrapping my hair into a towel turban, I flipped my head back and followed Verlan into the house.

Things went downhill from there. As Verlan pushed the crude, heavy front door open, it scraped the cement floor with a harsh grating sound. The first thing I noticed in the gloom was a wobbly wooden table in the center of the room. The only thing on it was a kerosene lamp. A pale yellow enameled cookstove with a rusty stovepipe protruding through the unfinished, wood-beamed ceiling squatted in the far corner. In another corner, a stack of unpainted orange crates were arranged into some semblance of shelving for cups and dishes. A galvanized, five-gallon bucket filled with well water stood next to a rough-hewn wooden washstand masquerading as a kitchen sink. A long, crooked counter of sorts stretched across one wall, its shelving partially covered by a piece of cloth. I saw no discernible food anywhere on these shelves, just a few mismatched canisters. There was no refrigerator in the room or other appliances of any kind. There were no knickknacks or pictures on the walls, no clock, no linoleum or rug on the floor—nothing that might help turn the simple shelter into a home. Through the kitchen window I could see a small wooden outhouse set some forty feet behind the house at the end of a dirt path.

Here it was, 1953. How could people still be living like this? Immediately I prayed, *Oh Lord, how long before I can get back to civilization?*

Charlotte appeared from one of the two bedrooms adjoining the primitive kitchen on opposite sides, and she welcomed me with a hug, asking if I was hungry after my long trip. Ten minutes earlier, I'd been starving, but now I had no appetite at all. "No thanks," I answered, "I just need to brush out my hair." I didn't dare mention bed to her. I felt so disappointed and out of place, once again nothing but an intruder in my husband's home. Miserable, I didn't know where to turn.

By now it was dark. Verlan lit the lamp on the table. He opened the door to the second bedroom with his foot. I couldn't help noticing that the hinges on the door were made from old tire treads simply nailed to the door frame. Motioning me inside, he placed the dim oil lamp on a white wooden chair next to the bed. He'd borrowed a clean sheet from Charlotte to cover us for the night. Before we lay down, he threw a handwoven serape blanket over the bare mesh metal springs.

"Where's the mattress?" I asked incredulously.

"Oh, these bedsprings are woven," he said. "With this blanket over them, you'll never know the difference." Kissing my cheek, he added, "I'll be right back. I want to go tell Charlotte good night."

I assumed he just wanted to see if she was already in bed before he blew out the lamp. I slipped into my long nightgown, thinking how Charlotte made it especially for me and allowed me to marry her husband. Despite all the gospel teachings I'd received on being a faithful, compliant plural wife, a sudden surge of jealousy and resentment overwhelmed me. How could I have any privacy with nothing but a kitchen separating Charlotte and me? I was willing to share a husband, but I would not share a house. Tomorrow I would stomp my foot on the lousy cement floor and inform Verlan I wouldn't be spending another night under her roof.

Grudgingly, I climbed into the rickety bed. The rough weave of the wool blanket scratched me as I lay there, waiting for my husband to return. I looked around in the dim light at the bare, empty room. Its adobe walls weren't painted or even plastered. It had no pictures, no closet, not even a dresser in which to unpack my meager belongings.

Verlan finally came back in, carrying a white enamel chamber pot in his hand. He blushed as he said, "This will be under the bed if you need it."

It had only been a few weeks since I'd been too bashful to use the toilet with a door separating us. I told myself I'd bust before I used that thing in the same room with him. I was so embarrassed, I couldn't speak.

He bolted the back door that opened onto the bedroom. Crossing the room, he pushed another wooden bar into place, locking the door that went into the kitchen. "For privacy," he said. Checking to see that his matches were handy for later, he cupped his hands above the lamp's glass chimney and blew out the dancing flame. I lay there in anticipation, waiting for my husband to get into bed and take me into his strong arms.

In the darkness, Verlan peeled off his worn work clothes and put a pair of pajamas on over the thin cotton undergarments he'd received in the LDS temple a few years earlier, before he'd begun his life of polygamy. This white, one-piece knit bodysuit resembled a pair of long johns, only it had no buttons. It simply tied closed across the front with three strings. It covered Verlan from his neck to his wrists and ankles. Only Mormons in good standing could receive these holy garments, which were ceremonially awarded with a promise of protection and an explanation of their symbolic meaning. Except for Verlan to bathe, the garments never came off, not even during intimacy. That's where the ties up the front came in.

Verlan snuggled up to me and cooed in my ear, "You can keep these pajamas of mine in your room from now on. I've got another pair in Charlotte's bedroom." He could say the most devastating things without even realizing it. After asking about my trip and my family, he got busy trying to convince me he hadn't actually lied to me about the ranch; he'd merely failed to tell me everything. I would eventually learn this was Verlan's usual method of conflict resolution: he did what he wanted, and then he charmed the pants off whoever was unhappy about it.

"Irene, you must be very cautious from now on," he told me next. "You have two Mexican sisters-in-law, Luz and Delfina. They may not treat you right if they find out you're actually my wife. We won't lie to them. We just won't tell them the whole truth. After all, you *are* my sister-in-law. You see, neither of them have the spirit of the gospel, like you do. We won't tell them until we have to."

I later found out that these two wives were actually Catholic, and they had no desire to be plural wives or to have polygamy thrown in their faces. But I didn't care about any of that now. I just wanted to be loved. I hadn't traveled all the way to a foreign country to be lectured. I wanted to be held and kissed, to be assured of my husband's love. But Verlan made no loving advances. As he talked, he kept his hand on my stomach, making damn sure not to touch my breasts.

Then he raised up over me, gave me a light peck on the lips, and yawned. "Good night, Irene," he murmured. "I'm so lucky to have you for a wife."

The smoldering volcano inside me suddenly erupted. "Your wife?" I yelled. "You're treating me more like a concubine!"

"Shhh," he tried to silence me. "Please. Charlotte will hear us."

"Where do I fit in, Verlan? Where are my rights?" I fought to remove the hand with which he'd now covered my mouth. "No! You won't shut me up! I didn't run off and leave my family to come down here to the end of the earth so that you could roll over and not even make love to me!"

"Shh, shh," he begged almost desperately. "Hold still, pleeeease. You're shaking the springs! She'll think I *am* making love to you!"

I pulled away, crying.

"Please don't cry, Irene. She'll see your swollen face tomorrow morning, thinking I've mistreated you."

"I don't care what she thinks. I'm sick and tired of being second fiddle," I wailed.

"Irene," he whispered, trying to calm me. "Why would you ever say you're second fiddle?"

I sat up, gritting my teeth, and snapped, "Because you fiddle with me second!"

I could feel Verlan's despair. How would he ever handle two wives in the same house? Finally calming me, he persuaded me to lie back down next to him. He kissed me repeatedly, trying to dry my tears on his pajama sleeves. "Forgive me if I don't make love to you," he said. "Try to understand. I don't want to hurt Charlotte. But look, since we have been apart so long, I'll give you two nights in a row. What would you think of that?"

"Big deal!" was what I thought. The tears welled back up. Would we never make love again for fear of hurting Charlotte? Could that really be how plural marriage was supposed to work? Surely not, if I was supposed to manufacture a child each year. The knot in my stomach got bigger and tighter. I couldn't help but think how different things would be if this were Glen lying next to me.

Verlan held me as he abruptly began praying. I tried to cry softly so as not to interrupt. "Thank you, Lord, for Irene's safe arrival," he said. "Give us strength to bear up under our trials and tribulations. Let Irene know she is needed and loved." With a final "Amen," he pulled me closer. "I do love you," he whispered in my ear as he drifted off, apparently content that God had answered his prayer. Within a few minutes, Verlan's rhythmic breathing told me he was sound asleep. I lay there wide awake, staring into nothingness, exhausted from the day's shattering events.

Soon I heard tiny squeaks, then odd rushing noises. I listened for a while but couldn't figure out what this could be, so I shook Verlan awake. "What are those noises?" I asked nervously.

"What noises?" he said groggily.

We both listened. They came again. "Oh, that," he said, patting my arm as he rolled over toward the wall. "You'll get used to it. It's just mice running up the walls." Burying my face in the pillow, I turned my back to him and wondered how long it would be before *I* was climbing the walls.

THE BAD THING ABOUT expectations is the huge thud that always seems to follow on their heels. I'd envisioned an idyllic, Utah-like hacienda where I'd have my own home far from Charlotte and live openly and proudly as Verlan's wife. The reality so far was much more akin to what Mother and Richard predicted. This thud left me in a deep state of shock. If not for the promise I'd made to Uncle Rulon and the fact that I knew not one word of Spanish, I think I would have resolved in that moment to thumb my way right back to El Paso the next day.

So far, I'd lived up to my side of this most difficult bargain. But for some reason, God wasn't doing his part.

CHAPTER TEN

The next morning, Verlan decided he'd show me around the "ranch." We'd already had a hectic morning chasing a large, evil-looking rat around the house before Charlotte and I managed to corner and kill it by bashing it with a cast-iron frying pan. I was somewhat shaken by that experience, but I would soon get used to rats, and all sorts of other vermin as well.

After breakfast, Verlan and I had only walked about the distance of a city block before we met up with Ervil's wife, Delfina. Delfina was a tall, light-skinned Mexican woman with short black hair and lively brown eyes. She appeared to be pregnant. After Verlan introduced us, she smiled and laughed as she spoke to me in Spanish. Verlan told me she'd said I was pretty, with my beautiful, honey-colored hair, and she hoped I'd be happy here.

Next, Verlan led me to a ramshackle, two-room adobe hut situated behind three other homes where his brothers lived. "My sister Lucinda lives here. She's been sick for years, but don't be afraid. She's harmless as long as she's locked up." He was apparently worried he'd gone too far in downplaying the situation, so he added, "The last time she was out, she went after Mother with a butcher knife, but luckily Delfina grabbed it away before anyone was harmed."

When Lucinda saw us approaching, she put her arms through the wooden, two-by-four bars across the window. "Who's that girl?" she called out, waving to us.

Verlan pushed me up to the hut near the window. From there I could see her sandy, reddish hair going every which way as she threw her head back, laughing at nothing. Her blouse gaped open, revealing a saggy breast, and her skinny arms were deeply freckled from the sun. I noticed then that one of the rooms to which she was confined had no roof. I thought she was probably in her early thirties.

"This is my sister-in-law, Irene," Verlan said.

Lucinda was incoherent. She talked a blue streak, never finishing one sentence before trailing off into another, laughing without warning. She made no sense at all. I had never dealt with an insane person before. It scared and depressed me to see her caged like a wild animal. I turned almost immediately to leave.

I was still trying to recover from this shock while walking back toward the house when a tall, lanky, sandy-haired man approached us. "I want you to meet my brother Alma," Verlan said. Alma was the eldest LeBaron brother living on the Mexico ranch.

Verlan and Alma shook hands, and I said hello. I stood close to Alma with my hands on my hips, waiting for him to say something, but he didn't return the greeting. I could feel his judgmental eyes scanning me up and down.

"Nice girls don't put their hands on their hips," he said, finally breaking his silence. Then he turned and sauntered off down the path. Verlan just shook his head, smiling at me apologetically.

"How come I've never heard of him before?" I asked, thinking that a natural history museum probably wouldn't have as many skeletons in its closet as the LeBarons did.

"Well," Verlan chuckled, "I thought maybe I'd scare you off if I told you all the family secrets at once."

Oh, my goodness, my mother was right. Alarmed, I stuttered, "Is . . . he crazy, too?"

"Not really," Verlan laughed. "They thought he was about three months ago, but only for a few days. You and I missed out on the action. Our cousin Owen, who was visiting from Canada, claimed that God was directing all his activities. He convinced his two wives and their children to parade nude around the ranch. Alma went along with them, climbing those hills over there across the main dirt road, and naked, they all waited for hours on their rooftop for flying saucers to arrive and take them up to the heavenly realms. But when the Mexican police showed up before the spaceships did, well, Alma figured he and Owen had somehow been deceived."

When Verlan saw my shocked expression, he added, "Don't hold it against him, Irene! He's repented!"

Verlan was trying to make light of it, but I felt my depression quickly deepening. Maybe it was a good thing, after all, not to tell anyone I was Verlan's second wife. I wasn't sure I wanted to be that closely associated with these LeBarons.

THAT EVENING, Ervil took Verlan aside. I couldn't help overhearing him ask, "Say, who's responsible for your sister-in-law?"

"I am," Verlan answered. "She's here to keep Charlotte company."

A broad, satisfied grin spread across Ervil's chiseled features. "Well," he announced proudly, "God gave me a revelation last night. Irene is to be my second wife!"

Verlan's shocked tone was not at all friendly when he shot back, "Leave her alone, Ervil. She's already *my* wife!"

The silly grin vanished. Blushing a deep red, Ervil now apologized, "Ah, I was just jokin', Verlan, just jokin'."

By bedtime that night, I knew Verlan had some serious problems. Charlotte's constant expression screamed displeasure. She'd been civil to me but had not tried to make any conversation. Verlan spent twenty minutes in her bedroom telling her good night. Then, he'd finally locked the kitchen door and crawled into bed with me. He surprised me then with his incredible powers of positive spin.

"Things seem to be running pretty well, all considered," he said. "I have two wives in the same house, and no major fights yet. Thank God both you and Charlotte were raised with the same fundamentalist Mormon principles. I know it's hard on you, but you're so lucky to be sisters. I'm sure you'll get along fine together."

Yes, I did love Charlotte, I assured him. But the truth was I couldn't feel free with both of us living under one roof. "In fact," I said, "I want a house of my own, even if it's just one room."

Verlan claimed disappointment that I could even entertain such thoughts. "You'll never learn to overcome your faults and jealousies if you're not faced with them on a daily basis," he lectured. "You have to overcome your negative thoughts, purify yourself. Don't put yourself in a position to jeopardize your salvation by indulging your sin."

Over the years, I discovered this to be the standard response of polygamous husbands whenever their disgruntled plural wives made the demand I had. Even that night, at the start of our marriage, I thought Verlan's rebuke sounded awfully convenient.

"Besides," he said, getting to the crux of the matter, "I can't afford another home. What money we make here is just enough for survival, not enough for selfish wants."

That said, Verlan quickly changed the subject. He told me about Ervil's revelation, about how Ervil said he *knew* I was to be his wife and not just his sister-in-law.

"Yes, I heard him," I said. "I couldn't help but laugh at his false revelation." I wished Verlan would shut up long enough to *know* me like Adam *knew* Eve, in the biblical sense. After all, what about his duty as my husband?

I playfully rubbed my toes against his bare foot, leaning against him as I stroked his neck, running my fingers through his hair. My youthful body ached with desire. Shivers ran down my spine. He didn't respond in the least, rejecting all my advances. Finally, I asked fearfully, "Verlan, don't you love me at all? What am I doing wrong?"

"Of course I love you," he whispered almost painfully. "Just because we don't make love doesn't mean I don't love you! Sex shouldn't be such a big deal in our lives. You know we want to reach for the highest goals. If we want godhood, we have to keep the law of purity."

I didn't want to listen to any more of his explanations, but he continued with his sermon: "We have to learn to control our passions and use them only for procreation. We've already done it twice in the last few weeks. Let's not overdo a sacred thing."

I turned my back to him, hoping to block his painful words. I couldn't bear being rebuked for wanting love from my husband. I was screaming inside. Of course, I knew I'd brought some of this on by my hasty assent to the law of purity on the night we'd first consummated our marriage. After that first painful sexual experience, I'd have been willing to abstain altogether. Surely the Devil led the world astray with such a disgusting activity. I couldn't imagine why God would allow it except when absolutely necessary, for procreation. At the time I agreed, I thought it would be easy for me to keep my vow.

But all that was before the night Verlan spent with me at Aunt Beth's. I'd never known such ecstasy before that. I felt like I'd ascended through glory after glory until I'd finally been thrown into seventh heaven. Why would God have invented something so wonderful and then put such harsh restrictions on it? It didn't seem fair.

I fell to thinking about my mother. How had she lived so many years without any physical love? As sorry as Horace was, I repented that I'd begrudged her the love of a man. Why hadn't I listened to her wisdom, her warnings to me? Why hadn't it ever occurred to me that God might have been speaking to me through her and Richard and even my father, rather than through Aunt Rhea and Donna and Uncle Rulon, that God might have been telling me to shun my childhood indoctrination into polygamy and accept his good gift of Glen? The Fifth Commandment says to honor thy father and mother, that thy days may be long upon the Earth. I hadn't listened to my mother or father, so I guess I had all this coming to me. Now perhaps God would do me the favor of shortening my days upon the Earth.

There in the dark, with Verlan snoring in one ear and the patter of tiny feet in the other, I knew I'd wandered into dangerous thought territory. To get back to a tolerable mind-set, I told myself Verlan was simply a man who loved God more than I did. I could honestly respect him for that. At least he wasn't lustful, like other men. Not about certain things, anyway.

His desire was to obtain at least seven wives—a quorum, he called it. He believed that would secure his eternal godhood. Meanwhile, I was to be patient and obedient; after all, we had an eternity to work out our problems as husband and wife. We'd been commanded by God to multiply and replenish the Earth so we could enlarge our heavenly glory. I would therefore have to be long-suffering.

Still, we had to have sex in order to have all those children, didn't we?

I often lay sleepless, with Verlan softly snoring beside me, wondering if the problem was really me. Was something wrong with me? Did he find me offensive in some way? I knew I wasn't a beauty, but then no one had ever said I was ugly, either. Many men already wanted me at sixteen. In fact, compared to other girls my age, I'd been led to believe I was fairly pretty. I had golden blonde hair down past my shoulders, with thick braids. I sometimes wore it parted in the center with a wave on each side. I was five foot six, with blue eyes, and I wasn't overweight.

My major shortcoming was never being serious. Life might be hard, but I had to unbend sometimes or I'd become an old prune. I was prone to find humor even in tragedy.

I vowed to quit being so terrible so Verlan would love me. More than anything now, I wanted to become his favorite wife.

CHAPTER ELEVEN

The following afternoon, Verlan and I headed for what he called the cheese house, where we found Ervil hard at work. Ever since Verlan told me they made cheese on their ranch, I'd been anxious to learn how to do it, but I was not prepared for what I saw. The right sleeve of Ervil's dirty gray shirt was rolled all the way up to his armpit. I watched with fascination as the dark hairs on his long arms swished through the clabbered milk while he gently stirred, round and round, explaining how simple it was to make cheese.

"It's sure nice to have you guys here," he said after a while. I was too busy looking around the incredibly filthy room to listen to what he was saying. Torn wire screens over the window frames kept more flies in than out. Sour whey lay in puddles on the rough cement floor, the smell sickening me. Grimy and flyspecked straining cloths, stiff with dried sour milk, lay on the table. It seemed like a thousand flies buzzed about the room. I was thankful neither Verlan nor Ervil could read my mind.

I glanced at the mixing tub. Whey rose to the top with clots of scum. Ervil's huge hands pressed the forming curds to the bottom of the large, galvanized tub. Then, with a small tin saucepan, he dipped the yellow whey from the tub and dumped it into five-gallon buckets. He stirred the cheese continually as he spoke. Finally, turning the tub on its side, he poured the remaining whey into a leaky bucket.

"Give me the salt there in the window," he ordered. I grabbed the rusted Crisco can off the windowsill. The salt was coarse and dirty with dust that had blown in. There were also several mice turds in it. Noticing my grimace, Ervil told me not to be so squeamish. "Just pick them out," he said.

I handed the can to Ervil instead. After dumping the top part of the dirty salt into the bucket of whey, he salted the cheese. Then he and Verlan relaxed on the wooden table, snacking on some of the fresh curds Ervil had just made. It struck me as funny . . . two big men, like little Miss Muffet, with their feet propped on a bucket, eating their turds and whey.

Verlan told Ervil he needed to know what he could plan on, now that his family was growing. The four brothers who lived on the ranch—Alma, Ervil, Floren, and Verlan (Joel lived up in the mountains with his Mexican wife, Magdalena, buying and selling corn)— had already decided to work together and divide everything equally. This was another example of the United Order the people at Short Creek had tried to live—a Mormon version of socialism first encouraged by Joseph Smith back in the nineteenth century. It required everyone's full participation. All goods, work, costs, and profits were divided evenly, at least in theory. This was the LeBaron brothers' plan.

Ervil made it clear that our family would be obligated to take its turn making cheese. Then he added, "Your wives are no doubt used to higher living standards, but we'll still have to split the money evenly four ways."

Ervil put cheesecloth down in the homemade metal press and dumped in the curds. Whey ran over onto the sticky floor. Looking at me as though his instruction was for me alone, he said, "Every cheese that turns out good will bring in a hundred pesos or more. That's anywhere from eight to ten dollars. You need to make sure the milk buckets and tubs are washed in soapy water. They must be scalded every time they're used. If they're not kept clean, the cheese may go sour."

From what I'd seen, all the cheese must go sour.

He went right on. "The ones that do go sour are the only ones our families will be allowed to eat. We'll divide the imperfect ones among us equally."

Verlan instructed me to clean the place up while both men left to attend to other chores. So I began my new job. I scrubbed the stale whey from the cement floors with an old, broken broom. I hauled in heavy buckets of fresh water from the well. Then I washed and scalded all the equipment. I turned the clean tub upside down and hid the salt can so it wouldn't be dusty or crapped in the next day. I took the stiff strainer cloths back to the house, where I could wash them out well for future use. The cheese house took on a new look. I was proud of my small accomplishment.

When the men returned and saw the results of my labor, they immediately delegated me chief cheese maker. It was a job I learned to appreciate. I felt useful here, and it kept me from being bored beyond what I could bear. I could plop myself on the wooden table anytime I wanted and munch on fresh curds I knew were made under sanitary conditions.

ON SATURDAYS, THE LEBARON brothers took turns riding the bus twelve miles to El Valle, where they would sell three or four cheeses and return with salt, sugar, oil, rice, perhaps a few oranges, and various other indispensable items to be divided among the four families. I understood that Verlan was strapped by this arrangement, but oh, what I wouldn't have given for a place of my own. I was so desperate to live freely with my husband, I even coveted the relative sanctity of the cheese room. Verlan said he wanted to keep his wives united by us all living together, so I should never mention the subject to him again.

At twenty-three, he was seven years my senior. I'd long been conditioned to obey my elders, but it was hard to obey my husband, whom I loved and admired as a peer. He was over six feet tall and blond. His strides were so long, I often complained about not being able to keep up with him. His hands were large and callused, and he had long, hairy arms covered by his holy garments even in the

Mexican summertime. Usually a broad smile lit up his handsome face, and he could be quite charming when the mood struck him. When he was upset, his blue eyes seemed to puncture me. Though stern at times, more often he was understanding. He listened to my frequent rants and raves without ever seeming to take them to heart. When I was finished yelling at him, he would usually ask with a grin, "Are you over it now?"

Verlan loved to work. Most mornings he'd get up at 6:00 A.M., rain or shine, and he kept busy all day long, trying to accomplish as much as he possibly could before having to go to bed. Soon I learned he was also a strict disciplinarian, demanding that the various houses he owned throughout the years be kept clean both inside and out. Even after his wives thought they'd gotten everything spotless, Verlan could always find one little thing that wasn't quite right, and he'd demand we take care of it immediately. Aside from that idiosyncrasy, he was fairly easygoing. He loved my jokes and tolerated my playful naughtiness as we laughed together often.

TWO WEEKS AFTER my arrival at the ranch, I was in my bedroom alone. It was Charlotte's turn to sleep with Verlan. Since we had no screens on the windows, I had a sheet pulled up over my head to keep the flies from bothering me. The early morning sun shone brightly through the window frames. I drifted in and out of sleep, enjoying the cool morning breeze.

Without any warning, I heard heavy footsteps below the open window directly behind my bed. Then I heard someone take such a deep breath that the sheets seemed to billow up and down with his inhale and exhale. I froze in a panic. Was it one of those terrible bandidos my mother warned me about? The heavy breathing grew even closer and louder. My mind tore through the possibilities. Surely any moment now, a dagger would be thrust through my heart. Or perhaps I'd be raped right here in my own bed.

I was so paralyzed, I couldn't even scream. Why did Verlan have to be sleeping with Charlotte when I needed him here, protecting me?

Even if I could scream, Verlan and Charlotte wouldn't be able to save me in time. More heavy footsteps. The breathing grew even louder. I simply had to do something, or die trying.

It took all my courage to throw back the sheet and whirl around to face my predator in the window. There he was . . . a shaggy gray burro. With his head now hanging in over my bed, he snorted and brayed loudly right in my face, "Hee haw, hee haw, hee haw."

I flung myself off the bed, pulling the tangled sheet along behind me, and ran into the kitchen, screaming with horror. As soon as he heard my cries, Verlan came flying out of Charlotte's room, ready for battle. But when he realized what had happened, he started laughing uncontrollably.

I felt so foolish. The bandido was just an old donkey, but I was the one who felt like a jackass.

I WENT OUT BACK to the outhouse. As I sat shooing flies, I realized it was my time of the month. Generally, I hated periods, but this one made me smile. Since I wasn't pregnant, I'd get to have sex again.

I didn't want to bother Verlan, but I needed products immediately. We couldn't afford toilet paper, so how could I ask him for sanitary napkins? This was the first time I'd ever discussed such a personal matter with a man. When I timidly informed him of my plight, he first tried to humor me. "If my mother could make her own napkins, surely you can," he said.

I blushed and said, "Let's be serious."

"Just stitch together soft knit rags lengthwise, and in minutes you will solve your problem," he said.

I was taken aback. He was serious! "You may think you know what you're talking about," I said, "but why sew them up if I'm just going to throw them away?"

"Because rags are a luxury," he answered. "You can't discard them." He enlightened me further as my jaw dropped open in disbelief. "You'll have to wash them out so you can have them for next time."

I ran into my room, locked the door, and threw myself across the foot of the bed, pouting. Soon I decided it might be more effective to pray. *God, I'm willing to sacrifice, but only if you require it of me. It's bad enough to be cursed with menstruation, but are you really going to make me wash my rags?* I lay still, hoping God would realize this was an emergency, and I needed an answer fast. My mind wandered to the Bible. I was certain this sacrifice was not mentioned in the Old Testament.

These thoughts were interrupted by Verlan rapping his knuckles on my locked door. He tried not to laugh as he said, "Honey, didn't you tell me you wanted to be a pioneer like your grandmother? This'll just help build your character."

"Character? Hell!" I retorted. I opened the door, holding it ajar just enough to look out at him, and lowered my voice so Charlotte couldn't hear what I said next. "I will never, ever, ever wash them!"

"What makes you so sure, Irene?" he laughed.

I knew the scriptures would back me up, so I declared triumphantly, "Because God did away with blood sacrifices!"

He had no response to that. Smiling, he shrugged his shoulders and walked away.

CHARLOTTE WAS ALWAYS CIVIL to me, but we were never friends and never confidants. I continued to feel that she disapproved of my overall manner, and frankly, we now had just too much else between us to ever work through it all. We never tried. We simply stayed a respectful distance from each other, though I think I was probably a little more respectful than she was by virtue of her being older and being first.

By now I discovered Charlotte was pregnant with her second child. We still shared the same house, but I didn't feel I belonged there. I tried to fit in, but I resented Charlotte for always taking liberties I didn't feel I could take. High on that list was her habit of calling Verlan endearing names in my presence, as if she owned him.

I complained about it to Verlan one night when we were alone. I told him I wasn't being given any recognition. I didn't feel I was really his wife.

He tried to console and reassure me. "I'm the master of this household," he said. "You are both equals. You can feel free to call me whatever you want."

I told him I always felt intimidated because of Charlotte's proper attitude and the fact that she'd married him first.

"There's no problem; just speak up. Call me whatever you want, as long as it's ladylike," he chuckled.

The following day, it was Charlotte's turn to do all the cooking. After dinner that evening, she placed a lemon pie on the table for dessert. This was a rare treat.

Verlan smiled at me as he served himself. Then he knocked his knee against mine under the table as though telling me it was time to speak up and test my equality. I swallowed hard and addressed him bravely. "Sweetheart, would you please pass me the pie?"

Charlotte froze. Then, without a word, she pushed herself away from the table and ran to her room in tears, slamming the door behind her.

Verlan looked at me in disgust. "Now see what you've done!" he said. Then he got up and went in to console her.

I was furious. I felt like calling him names all right, but not endearing ones. I cleared the dishes and went off to my own room, enduring thirty minutes of sheer agony while I waited for Verlan to join me. Would he put her in her place? Would he make her understand our equality? Finally he came to bed. I knew his silence meant trouble, but I was in hot water already, so I spoke first. "What's the matter? Can't she take it?"

He chose his words carefully. "Irene, she feels bad because you called me 'sweetheart.' That's her special name for me. Try to understand. You'll just have to find another name she doesn't use."

I blew up. "Okay, let's see . . . she calls you honey, sweetheart, darling, dear, and sweetie! Just what names are left? Tell me, Verlan, what's left?"

He lowered his voice, hoping I'd do likewise. "We'll just find one that's not hers."

I thought hard for a minute. "I know. Here's one she'll never use!"

I announced victoriously. "It'll be different from hers, but it's the only one I'll ever use. And I'll call you this forever."

"Good," he sighed with relief. "What is it?"

"It's 'lover'!"

Terror crossed his face. "Oh, no! That's too worldly! You can't use that!" he sputtered.

"Whether you like it or not, from now on, you'll always be 'lover' to me!"

He shook his head in disgust. Turning his back to me, he was soon fast asleep. I lay in the dark seething, all my thoughts bitter as resentment swept over me. Whose side was he on? Did I have a husband who wouldn't defend me?

I realized then he could never treat us as equals. I'd suspected it all along. I really was second fiddle.

CHAPTER TWELVE

After a few months at the ranch, I seldom wrote to Mother. She would occasionally write to me—updating me on family milestones, telling me about her work with handicapped kids, and expressing her love—but she rarely asked me any questions. I guess neither of us wanted to get too specific about what befell me in Mexico. It was just about as bad as she'd predicted, maybe worse. I thought it would break her heart to know the ins and outs of my circumstances, so I told her very little.

For instance, I never mentioned how completely isolated we were from the outside world. We had no reading materials, no newspapers, no radio. Charlotte owned about ten religious books, but I'd soon read them all many times, cover to cover. When I lived out in the sticks with Mother at Trout Creek, I at least got to listen to the radio, and I was also able to read lots of classics as well as Mother's monthly *Reader's Digest*. But here, I had none of that. With no friends and no real family besides Verlan, I longed for a few novels or a radio to distract me.

On Sundays, I got some relief from the intense boredom. We would hitch up the horses to our rugged old wooden wagon, take a pot of cooked beans and a couple of loaves of fresh-baked whole wheat bread, and travel five miles to a small settlement we called Spencerville because it was owned by the Spencer family. There were usually about thirty of us there, including Floren and Ervil's families. We would gather outside the Spencers' tiny, three-room adobe farmhouse for Sunday services. The men took turns preaching. Later we ate lunch; then some of us would gather around an old-fashioned organ. Seventeen-year-old Lucy, the oldest Spencer daughter, would play it for us as we sang hymns all afternoon until we were hoarse.

I tried hard to ignore the flirtatious smiles constantly passing between Verlan and Lucy. I had no right to be jealous. Verlan told me all along that Lucy planned on being his third wife. I secretly hoped she'd change her mind, but that didn't seem likely. Besides, Verlan needed three praying wives to be more worthy of godhood. And, according to the Principle, I was to minister unto my husband. That meant it was my duty to court Lucy for him. I often muttered under my breath, "I'll be damned if I will."

The Mormon scriptures say, "If any man have a wife ... and he teaches unto her the law of my priesthood [polygamy] ... then shall she believe and administer unto him, or she shall be destroyed." (Doctrine and Covenants, 132:64) Well, I didn't have to wait for God to destroy me. Jealousy was beating him to it.

SINCE CHARLOTTE AND I offered each other very little companionship, and since Floren's wife Anna was generally off somewhere with Charlotte, I spent many of my afternoons with my Mexican sisters-in-law, Luz and Delfina. Luz was Alma's wife, Delfina was Ervil's. Neither of them spoke much English. After being around them for four months, I learned to talk better with my hands than with Spanish. I still understood so few words, I became quite discouraged. I would grow weary of trying to communicate with them. Boredom would then force me to visit Verlan's crazy sister, Lucinda. She may have been out of her mind, but I could at least get her to respond to me in English. I went to see her almost every day, taking her a wildflower or some sort of goodie now and then. For three months, I listened to her fragmented prattle, trying to piece together her tragic, unfulfilled life. The terrible despair in her eyes said more than all her jabbering.

Lucinda, too, had entered polygamy. She, too, had been a second wife and tried to conduct herself and her marriage as she'd been taught by our fundamentalist faith. In the process, something went terribly wrong. I asked God many times why he allowed her to lose her mind when she tried so hard to obey him. I never heard a hint of joy in her words or her voice—no dreams fulfilled, no happiness.

She would beat the gnarled, craggy sides of her adobe cell whenever I asked her probing questions about her youth. Each time I mentioned her husband's first wife, Martha, she would grab a large spoon and begin to dig violently into the hard clay walls, trying to make a hole through which she could escape.

I feared jealousy did this to her. As time went on, I grew more and more certain of it because I could feel the seeds of craziness in my own mounting jealousy. If I didn't overcome this sin, Satan would destroy me, too. From now on, I would have to be nicer to Lucy or risk being damned. Besides, Verlan would love me more if I served him better.

THE LONGER VERLAN AND I managed to stay "pure," the more I longed to be held and loved physically. He insisted he loved me, but his words didn't match up with his actions in any manner that made sense to me emotionally. Every other night, after he started his soft snoring next to me, I'd cry myself to sleep.

I pled with him to change his strict rule about sex. My mind consented to the doctrine, even agreed with it, but my body kept demanding to be touched. I was a tortured example of the old Bible dictum we've all heard a hundred times about a willing spirit plagued by weak flesh. As long as Verlan remained aloof to it, my weak flesh threatened to destroy me.

In an effort to bring him over to my way of thinking, I tossed out all the significant Mormon scriptures I could think of. For example, "Men are, that they might have joy." (2 Nephi 2:25). Surely, women are, that they might have joy, too, I argued. "Sex would give me joy."

"Irene," Verlan answered sternly, "sex is not to be used for pleasure, only for procreation. You know that. If we allow ourselves to enjoy the sex act, God will punish us for the sins of the flesh."

I fought with him almost every time he came to my room, but he continued rejecting my loving advances. "Sex once a month is sufficient for anyone," he reminded me, determined to drive his point home.

One night I was particularly determined to have my way. "I thought God was no respecter of persons," I challenged him.

"He isn't."

"Then why is he spoiling you? You're the one who seems to be having all the fun!"

"You know I didn't make the rules. Besides, I'm just doing it for duty's sake."

I was so frustrated, I couldn't speak. I beat my fists into my pillow and then used it to smother my sobs so Charlotte wouldn't hear them. I couldn't even scream when I wanted to.

Of course Verlan didn't understand my new urgency. How could he? I'd only known for about a week that I was pregnant, and the law of purity completely forbade sex during pregnancy. The longer I kept enjoying our monthly "procreating" without telling Verlan that I was pregnant already, the more obvious it would eventually be to him that I'd violated the law of purity with knowing intent. I felt I had to tell him about the baby the next day, so tonight would be my last chance to experience a truly passionate love. After that, nothing for nine endless months, plus however long I nursed.

Harsh as it was, that was the rule. I often likened it to a person who goes her whole life without sweets. Then one day she gets invited to a birthday party where she's given a giant slice of a delicious, moist, chocolate-frosted cake. After two fabulous bites, someone yanks it right out of her mouth and tells her, "Stop! Turn off your taste buds." Well, my taste buds just wouldn't turn off.

As I continued to sob into my pillow, Verlan pulled me close and whispered, "Just say your prayers more often, Irene. God will help you overcome this."

LUZ AND DELFINA'S SUSPICIONS of me grew even faster than my expanding stomach. Why, even my swollen breasts revealed more to

Above: Polygamists exposed in *TIME* magazine in 1944. My father, Morris Q. Kunz, was one of the "fundamentalists" who was sentenced for being a polygamist. He served over two years in the Utah State Prison. (John Florea/ Time & Life Pictures/Getty Images) *Below:* Me at age 15 in 1952.

Me, my siblings, and my mother.

Above, left: Verlan, age 18. *Above, right:* July 1956: This was considered our wedding picture, taken three years after our marriage. *Below:* Pregnant with my daughter Donna, June 1955.

Above: With Verlan in November 1954 after Leah's death. *Left:* The headstone of my first daughter, Leah.

LEAH LEBARON
BORN · AUGUST 7 · 1954
DIED AUGUST 7 1954
BELOVED DAUGHTER
AND SISTER

Above: Charlotte, Verlan, and me; November 1954. *Below:* Holding Brent, with Donna, André, and Steven; 1960.

Above: Lucy, Charlotte, Aunt Rhea, me, and thirteen of Verlan's children; 1961. *Below:* The first three wives: Charlotte, me, and Lucy; 1961

Above: From left: Lucy, Beverly, Charlotte, Verlan, Esther, and me in 1965.
Below: Verlan with his first five wives and twenty of his children, 1965

Above: My inheritance in the promised land of Baja California, Mexico, where I lived with ten children after selling my new home in the mountains of Chihuahua, Mexico; 1966. *Below:* Verlan, on left, discussing his wives' weekly food rations with the Bishop; 1966.

Above: The New Utopia, where saints gathered in Los Molinos, Baja California; 1967. *Below:* Hector J. Spencer and Verlan in front of one of the windmills in Los Molinos, Baja California.

them than Verlan had. Tongues wagged. There were vile insinuations of adultery, which of course was a sin far worse than polygamy, even to these Catholic girls.

Verlan wasn't about to be scandalized, especially among his own people. So he finally had to tell them everything. Always one to put off conflict, Verlan intended to confess his polygamy when the time was just right, but my stomach beat him to it. The truth simply popped out, quite literally.

My pregnancy caused great consternation within the family. Once their suspicions were confirmed, Luz and Delfina fought their husbands bitterly. They warned Alma and Ervil not to dare follow in Verlan's polygamous footsteps.

Products of a plural marriage themselves, the LeBaron brothers all believed in polygamy. In fact, their fundamentalism led them to seek religious refuge in Mexico. But Verlan was the first of them to actually practice the Principle. Until now, they'd all been busy homesteading their forsaken outpost—establishing their family kingdom in the wilderness, their version of the United Order, like the prophets of old. Plural marriage was a vital component of their plan, but it was a component not yet implemented.

An unspoken competition raged between the brothers over who would succeed at it first. Although the youngest, Verlan had been best positioned to circulate socially while he'd attended BYU. He worked through the polygamous family network in Utah to find his second celestial bride—me.

As it turned out, then, my becoming Verlan's second wife really was a huge deal. Our marriage not only launched Verlan into the Principle, it launched the entire LeBaron clan into the practice. This won me animosity from everyone. While Verlan's older brothers wanted to see the family live the higher law of celestial marriage, Alma, Ervil, and Floren preferred to get there before Verlan. They resented me for giving Verlan an edge over them. And their wives resented me for bringing home the dreaded reality of polygamy—an offense to their morality and religious scruples, but even more so to their womanhood.

Even after my status as Verlan's wife was discovered, the brothers'

wives still fully accepted Charlotte into their circle, continuing to
treat her like a sister-in-law, but they completely shunned me. Now I
truly was a stranger in a strange land.

SOON I'D OUTGROWN all my clothes; nothing would fit. Verlan
somehow managed to buy me three pieces of material in El Valle,
and Charlotte helped me to cut out and sew up two maternity outfits. I liked my navy blue skirt with the tiny pink-flowered smock
best. I saved it to wear to Spencerville on Sundays.

I wore a pair of Verlan's white knit shorts in place of my shrinking
panties. As my stomach expanded, I found them, with their fly opening, so much more comfortable. I promised him I'd stop wearing
them as soon as he bought me something bigger of my own.

Verlan talked to Lucy's mother, Sylvia Spencer, and she came to
my rescue. She led me into her own cluttered bedroom, where she'd
stacked several boxes of used clothing she was saving for her twelve
children to use.

I had to try hard not to look too ungrateful when she handed me
a big pink pair of silky, old-fashioned bloomers. I was only seventeen;
I deserved better than that. But I knew "pride goeth before a fall," so
I swallowed my pride. The ugly bloomers would stretch nicely as my
tummy grew. Besides, they'd be a perfect match for my homemade,
flour-sack half-slip and the even stranger looking bra I'd made from
a sugar sack. After all these years and the work and miles in between,
here I was wearing flour-sack clothes again.

I clopped around in torn, worn-out shoes I left behind when I
walked too fast. I was supposed to be thankful for these, too. A store
in Nuevo Casas Grandes sold Alma a whole load of outdated shoes
for next to nothing. He meant to supply all of us first and then make
a profit selling the leftovers to the poor Mexicans up in the mountains. When I saw the weird assortment, I laughed and told Verlan,
"I wouldn't want the whole load even if you gave 'em to me! They
look like the shoes my grandma used to wear. I refuse to be seen
in them."

"Irene, be grateful," he insisted. "These are a blessing to us. No one will see them on you except our family. Luz and Delfina are already wearing them, so don't be so ridiculous." It was bad enough being pregnant, let alone barefoot, so I reluctantly accepted them.

One afternoon when I was four months pregnant, Verlan crept up behind me and pulled my body close to his. He kissed the sides of my face as he positioned his hands on my bulging tummy. "Is the baby kicking?" he asked excitedly. "Tell me when it does. I want to feel it."

My response came as a complete shock to both of us. "This baby will die when it's born." When I heard those words tumble out of my mouth, I was angry with myself for having said them. But a strange knowing went through me that I could not deny.

Verlan pulled me even tighter, and I realized he was crying. Never had I seen him shed a single tear. I felt terrible. I never wanted to hurt anyone again, much less him. He sobbed, gasped several times, and said, "Don't you ever say such an awful thing again." When I felt his sorrow, I closed my mind to the awful premonition and promised never to mention it again.

MY NAVY MATERNITY SKIRT wasn't exactly dirty, but I decided to wash it along with the matching smock with the dainty flowers on it. As I soaked the top, gently squeezing it, all the tiny flowers faded and then dissolved completely in the water. I was dismayed. My pretty smock was now a dingy gray. I had to rub around the collar and beneath the sleeves to remove the few forlorn little flowers that remained. Then, as soon as the dark blue skirt hit the water, the water turned to ink. I rinsed it quickly in clear water and wrung it out, but my heart grew sick when I flattened the skirt to hang it on the rope clothesline. It was streaked with dingy blue and gray lines, like something poorly tie-dyed. My new outfit was ruined. The only other dress I could fit into looked even worse, since I'd worn it every day herding cows, making cheese, baking bread, and canning fruit. Now my nice Sunday skirt and smock looked nearly as bad.

My first trip to the doctor was to be the following day, and I had nothing to wear. Verlan insisted that I iron my ruined skirt and smock. When Charlotte saw me, she offered to let me find something of hers to wear, but I'd gained so much weight that nothing she had would fit me. The skirt and smock would have to do.

This was going to be my first trip to the city since arriving in Mexico. Nuevo Casas Grandes, or Casas as we called it, was only forty miles away, but I had never been there. Alma offered us a ride over so we could save the bus fare, but we'd have to hitchhike home because he'd be going on to the mountains to sell his horrid shoes.

As I prepared to leave for town, my dignity was still very much in question. I knew I had to have a medical checkup in order to see that the baby was in the proper position, and I'd meant to go to the doctor looking nice in my new outfit, rather than looking like a poor pregnant peasant. Yet here I was in ruined clothes and old, ugly grandma shoes. I wiped the caked mud off them, hoping I would remember not to cross my legs and reveal the big holes in the soles. I'd put pieces of cardboard inside them so the rocks wouldn't bruise my feet.

I'd never been to a doctor before. One reason was I'd always been healthy. Besides that, pligs didn't go to doctors unless something was serious. I had no idea what I was in for. I thanked God the doctor would be Mexican so I wouldn't be able to understand him. While he examined me, he could talk to Verlan, and that might keep his attention off me just a little.

"What if I don't go, Verlan?" I asked in a desperate attempt to get out of it.

"You have to. We're having the baby at home, remember? Aunt Sylvia said she'd deliver it only on the condition that it's down in the right position so it'll be born headfirst. She already lost one that came breach. She doesn't want to take any chances."

"I'll die if I have to go there looking like this."

"Well, the baby may die if you don't," he countered angrily.

Verlan almost dragged me into the Dodge pickup, where he sat by Alma, and I sat by the window. Frightening mental images fluttered through my mind. I'd heard, for example, that doctors in the States actually looked at your . . . well, you know. Horrors! I hoped these Mexican doctors were different. If he felt my tummy and that was all, I could stand that. But I thought I'd die if he saw my homemade underclothes. The red and blue letters, F-L-O-U-R, hadn't completely washed out of my half-slip because we couldn't afford bleach. My mind raced ahead almost as fast as the truck. Would the doctor see I had a homemade bra, too? I couldn't interrupt Verlan with my silly fears. If I did, Alma would hear, so I turned to God. *Whatever you do, God, please don't let this foreigner see these old-fashioned, hand-me-down pink bloomers!*

It took us forever to get there on that old, bumpy dirt road. Finally, in the distance, I saw the "big city" of Casas. Boy, did these LeBarons stretch things! It wasn't a city; it was more like one of the small western towns I'd seen in the movies. There was a railroad and railroad station, the Hotel California, a little church, the bank, and a dry goods store called El Madrigal de la Luz. I saw improvised stalls where Mexican vendors were selling straw hats, leather belts, sarapes, and fruit. A few other old-fashioned buildings lined the sides of the main road, and a splattering of adobe houses completed the town. That was it.

Alma let us out at the town park. Verlan held my hand as we crossed the narrow street. Then he showed me the stairs at the back of the bank that led up to the doctor's office. "I want you to go up alone," he said. "This is Dr. Hatch's office. He's a Mormon, and he's the finest doctor in town. Even better, he speaks English. I'm sending you to him because you deserve the best."

I was appalled. "I'm not going up there without you," I protested. "Certainly not looking like this!"

Verlan merely folded twenty pesos into my hand and gently pushed me onto the first step. "Go on, Irene. Go on up."

I stood there, speechless. Then I collected my thoughts for one last-ditch effort to escape my fate. "Your family only found out about me three months ago," I said. "Are you now prepared to tell the Mormons?"

"Heavens, no!" he exclaimed excitedly. "Don't you dare tell him who you're married to! I'll be excommunicated from the Mormon Church if you do." Contrary to my experience as a child in Utah, Verlan grew up within the LDS Church in Mexico, and he still had many Mormon friends. In his usual fashion, he wanted to delay as long as possible their discovering that he'd chosen to live according to his fundamentalist heritage and training.

"What will I tell him?"

"Just go up there and say you're Irene Kunz. Make sure you don't mention me."

Seeing that I wasn't going to get out of this, I took a long, deep breath, sent one last silent prayer up to God, and climbed the stairs, trembling and alone.

Dr. Hatch was a pleasant, ruddy-faced man of about thirty-five. He offered me a chair, and I sat down in front of his desk, thanking God this put my skirt and shoes out of his line of vision.

"You're new around here, aren't you?" he asked as he took a new file out of his bottom desk drawer. Before I could answer, he continued, "Well, we'll just get a little information on you first. Your name?"

"Irene Kunz," I answered quickly, hoping he wouldn't probe much further.

He wrote it down, paused, and looked me straight in the eye. "It is LeBaron, isn't it?"

I froze. Verlan's own family had barely found out. How could word have traveled so fast? He interrupted my thoughts. "It *is* LeBaron, isn't it?"

"Uh … er … yes," I admitted. "But I don't go by that name."

"Now that we've got that cleared up," the doctor said, "what can I do for you?"

"I want to make sure my baby is in the right position because I want to have it at home."

"How far along are you?" he asked.

I kept my eyes on the floor. "A little over seven months. I think."

"Well, just slip off your bloomers and lie down on the table."
Heavens, did he have X-ray vision? But then he added, "Oh, I guess
they don't call them bloomers anymore. They're called panties, aren't
they?" He turned his back to give me a few moments of privacy.

I had to pull the faded, tight-fitting skirt up over my hips and
swollen belly to remove my—he'd been exactly right—bloomers. I
quickly folded them and hid them under the wooden chair. I eased
up onto the table, covering myself up with the sheet he'd given me.

"Are you ready?" he asked.

I knew I'd never be ready, so I lied. "I guess so," I said.

Dr. Hatch turned around and walked toward me with a rubber
glove on his right hand. With his free hand, he pulled up some metal
stirrups from the sides of the table, guiding each of my shoes into one
of them. "Slide your buttocks down to the end of the table," he commanded.

I was dying a thousand deaths. He could see not only my flour-
sack slip and my ragged soles but my whole rear end as well. I turned
scarlet. Why, even Verlan hadn't seen this much of me, let alone some
stranger.

The kindly doctor tried to ease my nerves. "Don't be so embarrassed," he said. "I have so many people come in here, I don't even
notice whether they're men or women." But I didn't believe him.

His gloved hand suddenly probed painfully deep inside me. As he
explored, moving his fingers here and there, I grew increasingly mortified. I wondered if this was somehow violating God's sexual code.

Removing his hand from me and the glove from his hand, he said,
"The baby is in perfect position." After that, he walked over to the
window and peered down on the park below. "Take your time getting dressed, young lady. I'll give you a minute."

It only took me a few seconds. "I'm dressed," I said, still embarrassed.

"Oh, there's one more thing. Sit back up here on the table. I need
to check something else before you go." He instructed me to undo
the two top buttons of my faded smock.

"Oh, no you don't," I wanted to say. I held the smock tightly to my throat.

"It's okay," he said patiently, "I just want to see how your nipples are. You do plan on breast-feeding, don't you?"

Continuing to guard my breasts with a trembling hand, I insisted my nipples were okay. He gently but firmly moved my hand and unbuttoned the blouse himself. I fought back tears as he pulled my large, swollen breasts from the homemade bra. Now he'd seen it all.

My ordeal was finally over. "How much do I owe you?" I asked, a bit steadier now that my pathetic underclothes were finally back under my other sad garments.

"Usually, I charge ten pesos. That's eighty cents. But I see you need it worse than I do, so this time it's on me."

One final humiliation. "Thanks," I muttered, bolting out the door as the tears began streaming down my red cheeks. I was going so fast and was so blinded by my misery, I came close to stumbling on the flight of stairs.

Verlan was waiting for me nervously. Always sensitive to the plight of others, he grabbed me when he saw my tears and said, "Don't cry right here, Irene. All these people are looking. They'll wonder what I've done to you. Please," he begged.

"Well, get me out of here," I sobbed.

We walked side by side for about a half block and entered a small restaurant, taking a seat at a table in the back, away from the other customers. Then he said to me, "Irene, please don't take this so hard. Let's get happy. I'll buy you anything you want."

I hadn't tasted meat for ten months, so I said, "I want a big, thick, juicy steak." Suddenly I was famished.

He rattled off something in Spanish to the waitress. I understood none of it except her response, and that was easy because she simply shook her head and said no.

Verlan laughed. "I guess it's just not your day. They don't have steak." He ordered his favorite dish for both of us—cheese enchiladas. He didn't have to ask what soda I preferred, since I'd been begging him for it for almost a year. The waitress returned with two ice-cold

Cokes. We ate our enchiladas leisurely. I savored each bite, finding the fried egg on top a special treat.

We held hands across the table while Verlan knocked my ugly shoes playfully with his worn ones, and said, "I'm so sorry for what happened at the doctor's office and that you didn't have anything nice to wear. I'm sure Dr. Hatch didn't mean to embarrass you. You're so beautiful to me, I'd love you even if you wore a gunnysack."

My condition made him more sensitive. I was so starved for his love that this sweetness went straight to my heart. Maybe God did have a better future planned for his faithful servants, after all. I resolved to go home and try harder to be happy.

"God loves you, Irene. The worst is over," Verlan said tenderly. How I hoped it was true.

After lunch, we sat in the pleasant little park, watching people and eating Popsicles in the shade. Verlan didn't rush me because this was "my" trip to the city. Eventually, we had to think about hitchhiking back home. It was too far for me to walk to the edge of town, where the main road came through, so Verlan woke up the town's only cab driver to take us that far in his dilapidated vehicle. Then we waited for an hour in the broiling sun until a large blue truck stopped for us. It was loaded to the top of the side racks with hundreds of cases of soda pop. Verlan asked if we could have a ride. The driver and his assistant smiled and nodded their heads. Verlan told me to get up front, and he climbed on top of the cargo, sitting near the cab.

I felt uneasy riding between the two young Mexicans, not knowing what they were saying to each other. As the truck bounced over the dirt road, the tires fell into every rut, sending us swaying and jerking so much, I was afraid we'd tip over. The heat was stifling, and I could barely breathe through all the dust.

Before long I was feeling terrible. I held my aching stomach and wondered if my pains might be premature labor. But they grew more intense as we jolted back and forth. Both men watched helplessly as I clung to my rumbling, swollen belly, the pains growing worse and worse. I desperately needed out of the truck. But I couldn't make them understand it wasn't labor I was groaning about. I was having an attack of diarrhea. "My God," I said to no one in particular, "I've got Montezuma's Revenge!"

Grabbing my stomach even harder, I cried out loudly and prayed for them to stop. I couldn't remember the Spanish word for stop, but I knew I had to run for a bush. I scanned the road, desperately hoping that over the next knoll there'd be a tall mesquite bush behind which I could relieve myself. I took deep breaths, but one more bump and the inevitable would happen.

We topped the next summit. To my horror, it fell away into a pretty green valley full of Mexican workers busily digging trenches on each side of the road. There was not a bush in sight. My sobs so frightened the driver, he stopped the truck right there.

I leapt out, sobbing in agony as everyone watched me wobble to the back of the truck. Verlan jumped down from his perch, exclaiming, "What's the matter, honey?"

"I've got diarrhea," I cried. "I've got to go, Verlan. I can't wait!"

He glanced around. By this time, all the workers were leaning casually against their picks and shovels, not twenty feet away, watching the show. With complete disgust he said, "Go then. Just go!"

I had no choice. I tugged my tight blue skirt up over my waist, pulled down my pink bloomers, and let loose. My revenge took off in every direction. The spectators whooped and hollered, waving their straw hats wildly. Even the driver came around to the truck's rear end and saw mine.

Verlan was mortified. He usually never swore, but he couldn't help himself this time. "Damn it, Irene, get back in the truck! Let's get out of here."

"I can't get back in there with those men. Please, Verlan," I begged.

"Damn it! Get back in," he ordered.

"It'll kill me if I do!" I pled.

He gritted his teeth and laughed, humiliated. "Irene, I'll kill you if you don't!"

I reluctantly obeyed. Sitting next to the window, I covered my face with my hands and cried all the way home.

. . .

SOON AFTER MY TRAUMATIC checkup in Cases, Verlan received a summons to appear before the LDS Church court in Colonia Dublán to be tried for his membership. The Mormon Church in Mexico was as intolerant of plural marriage as the Mormon Church in the States. Dr. Hatch had confirmed to the church that Verlan was practicing polygamy, and at his trial they excommunicated him. He said he didn't blame me for it, but I felt as if I'd triggered the events costing him his membership.

Afterward, Verlan told us he'd made a heroic effort to defend plural marriage. He reportedly told the LDS high councilmen that it was the Mormon Church that should be on trial for abandoning polygamy, rather than him being on trial for practicing it. Verlan's answer to one particular question from them finally clinched a verdict against him: "Are the two ladies who were carrying your babies when Dr. Hatch examined them both your wives?"

"I'll tell you one thing for sure," Verlan said. "No lady ever carried my baby who wasn't my wife." The truth was plainly out.

Poor Verlan knew that sooner or later this would happen, but he was still perturbed when it did. He'd gained a second wife and entrance into the Principle, but he'd lost the mother church through which God originally commanded Mormons to live polygamy. He believed the Mormon God was unchangeable, so why didn't the LDS leaders still proclaim and obey God's laws? Brigham Young condemned anyone who wouldn't live polygamy. Now Verlan was excommunicated from the church because he did.

The scriptures always consoled him. He especially loved this one: "All things work together for good to them that love God." (Romans 8:28) Verlan simply followed his conscience by living plural marriage. The difficulty was in hiding it for so long, being so fearful of what others would think, say, and do. Now that the whole world knew what Verlan's conscience drove him to do, and all those who would condemn us for it already had their way with us, we were finally free to live in the relative open without fear of further reprisals. We could throw off the terrible hypocrisy that had so invalidated me, especially, as Verlan's second wife. Now we could live the Principle proudly, as God surely intended it to be lived. I prayed this was the good to which all things had been working.

RELIGIOUS DEVOTION characterized Verlan throughout all our trials. He always remained faithful to his beliefs, putting his God and church doctrine ahead of his wives and children. Twice a day, he'd call us all together for family prayers, and we would gather around him as he read to us from the scriptures and the Journal of Discourses. He was dedicated to the original teachings of the early, nineteenth-century Mormon Church. He always made sure we knew that God came first and that he had to do whatever God required of him.

CHAPTER THIRTEEN

By now our income was next to nothing. The cows dropped way down in their milk production; some were even dry, expecting their calves. Feed was scarce. It would be three long months before the rainy season, when there would again be plenty of tall grass.

Anna was expecting a baby a week after me. She promised Floren she was leaving him as soon as her baby was born. This was no life for her, she said. She wanted to live a little, not always struggling just to survive. I could understand completely. The LeBarons' primitive existence was killing me, too. I envied her spunk.

Verlan talked for several months of the possibility of our moving back to the States, perhaps to Salt Lake City to be a part of Uncle Rulon's group again. He knew we needed a better social and material life. But he was wary about leaving. His late father, Alma Dayer LeBaron Sr., had expressly warned all his sons to stay in Mexico to raise their families. He believed that his sons would someday participate in a great work that would take place there. One of them, in fact, was going to be called into a secret priesthood as a direct spiritual descendent of Joseph Smith himself. In the meantime, we were nearly destitute.

"We need to pray that God will intervene," Verlan humbly whispered to Charlotte and me one night. "Ask him to either save our financial situation or show us where we ought to go." So we knelt in a little circle, holding hands. Each took a turn pleading with the Lord to guide us. Then we went to bed, hoping for the best.

As usual, Verlan was up before daylight. He hitched the horse to an old plow and dragged it to a field he planned to plow all day. He usually came home at noon to eat, but it got to be 1:30, and we still hadn't seen a sign of him. I took a spoon and our last bottle of cherries out to the field so he could have something for lunch. I knew he was discouraged, and I wanted to cheer him up. I hoped to surprise him.

I found his horse tied to a barbed-wire fence, the plow lying on its side. Only eight rows had been worked. I knew this wasn't right. I called his name several times, but got no answer. Maybe he'd been bitten by a rattler and died. I started crying as I looked for him among the mesquites. Eventually, I went home to wait, and I got Charlotte upset, too.

About 9 P.M., Verlan finally came in, with Floren and Anna close behind him. "I had to get us all together to tell you the wonderful news," he blurted out.

He was so excited, I didn't have the heart to scold him, especially if God might be behind the day's events. We pulled the wooden chairs around the table, sat down, and braced ourselves for the good news. Verlan was smiling so happily. I knew whatever he had to tell us must be really good.

"God has answered our prayers!" he began. "I prayed most of the night for God to bless us, to open up a way for us to stay in Mexico if it was his will. Then this morning, I'd just started plowing when a pickup stopped on the road. An American got out and came over to where I was plowing. He introduced himself as Dick Loomis, asked me if I knew how to make cheese. 'Boy, do I ever!' I said. He took me to a ranch called Terrenates about sixty miles from here, near the town of Flores Magón."

"He wants me to start working for him immediately. We're going to be buying cows, shipping them in from the States. We'll set up a factory that makes the best cheese in Chihuahua. And that's not all. We'll have an eleven-room house for our family, with electricity!

Imagine that. And hot running water. It's furnished, too. They have a vegetable garden. We can have all the vegetables we want out of it. I was told they would kill a steer once a month, so we'll get free meat. Besides that, we'll have all the milk, cheese, and eggs we need. Plus ... now listen to this," he beamed, "I'll get paid two dollars a day!" Flush with excitement, his eyes sparkled. "Floren and I can both live in the house with our families. We can live high on the hog! With Joel and his wife in the mountains, and Alma and Ervil here at the LeBaron ranch, we can all live better lives."

We knelt in prayer, thanking God for his goodness and for our deliverance.

Later, when we were in bed, I let Verlan know I was somewhat disappointed. "I was hoping we could all go back to the States, but of course this is next best."

"You'll even have to sacrifice a little more, Irene. I really hate to ask it of you, but for now you'll have to move up to Spencerville into my Aunt Annie's two-room adobe house. It'll just be till the baby comes. I'll be going to the States for cows and equipment. In fact, I'll be leaving tomorrow to start my new job."

"But what about the baby, Verlan? Won't you be here for the baby?" I implored.

"Be patient. God will look after you. I can't pass up this opportunity. Besides, Charlotte will be with you if I can't make it back in time. You've got to learn to have greater faith and trust in God." Then he gently kissed me good night and rolled over, and his loud snoring soon drowned out my sniffling.

THE CALENDAR ON THE WALL said it was August 6. My due date was the twelfth, but I was more than ready to get this thing over with. Swollen all over, I felt huge and unattractive. I hated my two faded maternity outfits. I couldn't wait to cut them into small pieces and turn them into toilet paper.

I'd been sick ever since I got home from my checkup. My head throbbed all the time. I even passed out once. Everyone told me it was just nerves. Ervil actually accused me of being a coward. I guess I was. I decided I needed a doctor at my first delivery, even if the doctor was a man. After all, I'd been feeling that something was wrong ever since the day I made that strange statement to Verlan. So I'd begged Verlan to let me have our baby in the hospital. As always, he tried to allay my fears to the point of flat discounting them. "Having a baby is the most natural thing in the world. In fact," he laughed, "every mother on Earth has gone through it."

That's when Ervil shared his thoughts on the subject. "Delfina has had her three girls at home. It's as easy as a cow having a calf!" I thought it interesting that all these reprimands were coming from men.

I cried alone every night, or so it seemed. I didn't want to be a chicken, but I was homesick for Utah. I felt I needed my mother. But my biggest concern was having the baby without Verlan there. He'd left two weeks earlier for the Terrenates ranch after moving Charlotte, her babies, and me over to Spencerville. "You'll be in good hands," he'd told me.

Aunt Sylvia, the midwife (also Lucy's mother), lived only a mile down the road from the two-room adobe hut we borrowed from Aunt Annie. Charlotte sweetly offered to stay with me to see that the delivery went well. What more could I ask? I still felt jittery. My legs and feet were so swollen, I could hardly walk. I imagined complications; what if something went wrong? Although I kept my word and never mentioned my earlier premonition again to anyone, I worried about it constantly and begged God to let it be false. I wanted a live, healthy baby.

I drank lots of herb teas at Aunt Sylvia's insistence. She thought it might reduce the swelling in my hands and feet. I tried to cheer myself up by thinking how my grandmother bore some of her children in Mexico, with only a midwife attending her. I wanted to be like her. I came from good pioneer stock. Would I be less valiant than she was? I prayed constantly, placing myself squarely in God's hands.

I'd just finished washing the breakfast dishes when terrible diarrhea pains hit me. I scampered to the old outhouse and quickly sat down, but the pain kept up, so finally I waddled back to the house. I looked at Aunt Annie's clock; it was noon.

Charlotte saw me crying as I sprawled on the bed. "Are you in labor?" she asked. I answered by rocking back and forth, rubbing my stomach and thighs. It was one continuous pain. Aunt Sylvia came immediately. From that point on, I remember very little except that I lay there for hours, feeling like I was dying.

Charlotte's mother, my Aunt Rhea, arrived from the States just minutes after my labor pains began. Marden, one of the Spencer boys, brought her down from Utah for a visit. After he dropped her off, he left immediately for Terrenates to get Verlan. It had rained for days, and the muddy roads were washed out in several places. I knew it could be hours before he came.

At 4 P.M., Alma brought a Dr. Ramirez from nearby El Valle. (Dr. Hatch lived a couple of hours away, near Casas.) This doctor was really rough with me. I thought I'd split as he plunged his fingers inside me. "She'll go eight or ten more hours yet. Send for me again if you need me," he said and left. What he clearly meant was, "Handle it. What are you calling me for?"

The clock nearly stopped after that. Every ten minutes seemed liked an eternity as I drifted in and out of consciousness. Ten o'clock eventually came and went. I expected Verlan hours before, even with the washed-out roads to deal with. I strained to listen for bouncing trucks in the rain, wondering if each one could be Verlan coming to help me through this. Deliriously, I called his name over and over.

Aunt Sylvia grew concerned about my groggy, semiconscious condition. She asked Charlotte why I didn't work with them. Trying to rally me, Aunt Rhea rubbed my legs vigorously and massaged my hands. Charlotte held my head as Aunt Sylvia tried to force some coffee down me in hopes it would revive me. But I refused to drink it. I'd been taught that coffee was a no-no. All I wanted was for them to leave me alone and for Verlan to come. Before, I'd merely needed him; now, I was desperate for him. As I drifted in and out, I could hear the women's muffled voices.

"Irene, it's coming. The head's appearing. You've got to cooperate with us," Sylvia demanded.

Charlotte coached me, "Push, keep it up, come on now, that's a good girl!"

My mouth was parched. Charlotte gave me sips of water. The bearing-down pains brought me out of my stupor as I cried out with each one.

They prodded me. "Push, Irene, push. Just a few more times, and we'll have it."

"Help me, help me!" I cried as the baby's head crowned. With Charlotte on one side of me and Aunt Rhea on the other, I grabbed their hands in trembling fear and pushed with all my strength.

"Pant, Irene, pant," Charlotte ordered. I did, but I felt like hot acid had been sprayed inside me. With one more push and a blood-curdling scream, the baby's head came out.

"Push one more time to get the baby's shoulders out," Aunt Rhea commanded me. "The hardest part is almost over." Hanging onto their hands, I pushed again and then felt one huge release as the baby flopped into Aunt Sylvia's hands.

"It's a girl!" Charlotte exclaimed. "A darling baby girl!" She kissed my forehead, wiping it again with a cool, wet cloth. I glanced at the clock; it was ten minutes past midnight. I'd endured twelve hours of sheer hell. Then I noticed the silence.

"Why isn't she crying?" I yelled frantically. Pulling up on my elbows, I watched Aunt Sylvia squeeze a rubber syringe, drawing the phlegm from the baby's nostrils. "Please," I begged God, "let her cry!" Then Sylvia spanked her little bottom, and my precious baby let out her first cries. I could see her still attached to my body by the thick, wrinkled umbilical cord that had nourished her for nine months. She cried like her little heart was broken. "Give her to me, please," I begged.

Aunt Sylvia said, "Calm down, she's okay. Let's cut the cord first. When we get her cleaned up, then you can take her."

"No, now," I insisted. I silently feared that God was going to snatch her away from me. Just to calm me down, Aunt Sylvia gave in. She placed the darling treasure on my stomach. I held her by her little arms, listening to her whimpers. Then, as I let go of her arms to turn her on her side, she grabbed my index finger. I wondered how any woman could ever abort such a priceless, adorable gift from God.

"You're Mommy's precious little angel," I cooed.

"I'll call her Leah," I announced. Satisfied that God had heard my months of anguished pleas, I relaxed, handing her back so Aunt Sylvia could cut the cord.

When she was through, Aunt Sylvia wrapped my baby in a towel and handed her to Charlotte. "You get the privilege of doing the rest," she said.

Charlotte took her and said, "Irene, she's beautiful." She proceeded to clean her rosy body with cotton dipped in warm olive oil. When I made it clear to Charlotte that I didn't want this tiny baby out of my sight, she assured me I could have her back as soon as she finished with her.

While Charlotte tended Leah, Aunt Sylvia finished with me. "Push again. This is just the afterbirth. It won't hurt," Aunt Sylvia informed me. I reluctantly pushed, expelling it. I watched, fascinated, as Aunt Sylvia examined the placenta inside and out, looking for any torn or missing pieces. "It's okay. Now we can clean up this messy bed."

I was looking at my flat tummy, thanking God it was all over, when suddenly Charlotte cried out for help. Handing the baby to Aunt Sylvia, she exclaimed, "This baby keeps acting like she's passing out!"

Aunt Sylvia cleaned out Leah's nostrils and mouth again with the syringe. Then, holding up her back with one hand and her tiny heels with the other, Aunt Sylvia forced the baby's little knees back and forth onto her chest. She slapped her bottom several times, with no response.

"God!" I cried, "Don't do this to me! Please, God, don't do it!" But I just knew he wasn't listening.

I heard Charlotte's sobs first, then Aunt Rhea's. Aunt Sylvia told me what I already knew. "She's gone, Irene! Yes, she's gone!"

I was too paralyzed to cry. I just lay there in shock, numbly watching Aunt Sylvia clean up the bed, rolling me from side to side to put a clean sheet under me. Then I watched Charlotte dress my dead baby in a long-sleeved undershirt as though to keep her warm. Over that, she put on a tiny white satin dress that I'd made from scraps. It had delicate pink roses embroidered on the yoke.

Charlotte scanned the room for a place to lay her out. She covered the wooden lid of the toy box with a receiving blanket, placing Leah's tiny lifeless body on it. "What else do I do?" she asked Aunt Sylvia helplessly.

"Watch me. I'll teach you how to lay someone out," she whispered as she tore two narrow strips from one of the new flannel diapers. Placing one under the baby's chin, she pulled her little mouth closed, tying a bow on top of her head. Then she crossed Leah's little hands on her chest, saying, "Hold these in place while I tie them." She searched in her purse for two small coins. "Look, Charlotte, her eyelids are half open. Push them closed like this. Now place a coin on each eye. When rigor mortis sets in, you can remove them, and her eyes will stay closed. At the same time, take the cords from her hands and head; her mouth will stay shut, and her hands will stay in place on her chest."

I watched in disbelief. I could barely endure life; I was in no shape at all to deal with death. It just couldn't be happening to me. I lay there in silence as emotional numbness overtook me.

Later I heard a pickup coming closer through the drizzly night. It had to be Verlan. Charlotte stepped outside into the dark to meet him. I could hear the excitement in his voice. "Was it a girl?" he asked. Then there was silence, followed by rapid footsteps that seemed to batter my poor heart all the way to the door. He stepped inside quietly. I could see his intense grief through the dim lamplight. He knelt beside my bed and gathered me in his arms. Seeing my expressionless face, he remembered my premonition. "How did you know?"

"I just knew," I answered. "I just knew."

He buried his head in my chest, sobbing like a child. "Why wasn't I here? I missed her by twenty minutes! Irene, you're too young for this!" he cried.

Getting up from his kneeling position, he walked over to the toy box, glancing at our little Leah. I watched his tears fall as he immediately returned to lie down beside me on the bed in his damp clothes. He held me as though he feared I'd be snatched away, too.

I couldn't say anything. I could only lie there, still as a corpse myself. Verlan wept the tears I could not. I watched his anguished body heaving, convulsing with deep sobs, until he finally fell asleep. A few minutes later he awoke and stumbled back over to the toy box to examine our baby more closely. He stroked her silky brown hair, touched each delicate finger. He shook his head, sighing deeply as he noticed that her fingernails were already turning black.

Then he returned to my bed, caressing me and crying softly until slumber again relieved his grief. I watched his rhythmic breathing as the empty lamp flickered a time or two and then went out, as did the light in my heart.

When a rooster crowed the next morning, Verlan awoke to our harsh reality. It was 6 A.M., and he had much to do to prepare for the funeral. Borrowing a pick and shovel, he hired two Mexicans to go to El Valle and dig the grave. We didn't have a vehicle of our own, so he took the workers in the Spencers' pickup. He stopped along the way at the *presidencia* to notify the authorities of our baby's birth and death. He'd already sent a twelve-year-old Mexican neighbor off on horseback to take a note to Joel, five miles away at the LeBaron ranch.

On receiving the heartrending news, Joel notified the other family members. He then gathered up some tools and nails, saddled up his horse, and left for Spencerville. It was about 10 A.M. by the time he arrived at our hut.

From my bed, I numbly watched Joel through the screen door as he selected the best pieces from a pile of warped, wet boards for the coffin. He measured the unplaned pine; then with a dull handsaw, he cut each board to the proper size. I watched every move he made as the coffin took shape. Each nail he drove in I envisioned being pounded deep into my own throbbing heart.

After Joel made the lid, he hammered nails into each corner, but he inserted them only halfway through the wood so that later, when Leah's body was inside, the lid could be nailed down tight. He carried the rough little box into the kitchen, where Aunt Sylvia helped Charlotte pleat my white flannel diapers and tack them into place to form a lining that would cover the knotted boards and protect Leah from pine splinters.

When he got back to the adobe hut, Verlan picked up our little Leah and placed her in my arms for the last time. I looked at her precious, ashen face. I didn't blink, couldn't blink. I stared hard and long at my baby. The years would hopefully lessen the pain, but her beautiful features would always be there, indelibly etched in my mind.

After my final look, Verlan picked her up and gently put her in the rustic casket. It was past noon. He knew he had to get going. The Spencers' truck pulled up. Delfina, Anna, Floren, Ervil, and all fourteen of the Spencers came into my room. They huddled together, ten of the children sitting on the foot and sides of my bed. No one knew what to say, but the adults moved single file past Leah's casket. Joel offered a prayer. Then Floren and Verlan guided the lid into place on the casket, and Joel pounded the nails on through, making sure the lid was down tight.

Verlan motioned for Floren and Ervil to carry the casket outside to the truck. Single file, the rest of our family and friends followed them. Charlotte and Aunt Rhea were waiting in the cab of the truck, purposely leaving me alone with Verlan.

He took a blue receiving blanket from the dresser. "I'm taking this with me. I want to cover the casket with it." He kissed me several times, not wanting to leave.

We were interrupted by Karen, an eleven-year-old sister of mine and Charlotte's, who arrived with Aunt Rhea the day before. "I'm going to stay with you while everyone else goes to the funeral."

Verlan left with the blanket, but he'd hardly shut the door behind him when he whirled around and came back in to me, crying. He held both my hands in his. "I'll make it up to you, Irene. I promise!" I could only look at him with no emotion.

. . .

IT WAS DARK when Verlan walked in with a small cardboard box he placed on my bed. "How's my sweetheart doing?" he asked, kissing my cheek. "You can't believe how God works things out." I waited for the story he was clearly dying to tell.

"I'm sorry we're back so late," he said. "When we got to the graveyard, the men didn't have the hole deep enough, so it took us awhile to get it to the required depth. I jumped into the grave, and Joel and Floren lowered the casket down to me. Charlotte handed me the little blanket, and I spread it over the box. For some reason, I didn't want her to be cold." He sighed.

"Then Joel and Ervil pulled me out. Flying gravel hit the wooden casket with loud thuds, but soon it was all covered. When the grave was completely filled, my brothers stomped the dirt down firmly." He paused. "Please don't feel bad, Irene. I just wanted you to know I did the best I could. We made a nice little mound on top with the remaining dirt. I measured from both cemetery walls, so we won't lose her grave before I can afford a sack of cement to make a good marker for it. Be sure to help me remember that it's three long steps from the north wall and seven steps from the east wall."

He stopped to see if I was taking it okay. All I could do was lie there and stare up at him.

"I promise, Irene, I'll make her a headstone. Now, let's get happy, get our minds on other things. I've got a surprise for you! God touched Juan Fernandez's heart for us. I had everyone stay in the truck while I went into his mercantile store. I was embarrassed because he'd cut off our credit last month after I charged oil, cotton, and the flannel for the diapers. I told him I knew we owed him forty dollars, but I'd pay him interest if he'd just give in this once and extend our credit. I told him about our baby's death and that I needed to get something for you. He couldn't have been nicer. In fact, he sent you his condolences." Verlan patted my hand and continued, "I hid the box under Charlotte's feet in the front of the pickup. I didn't want Delfina and the others to see what I'd bought. I don't need to be criticized for buying luxuries."

Charlotte entered my room and sat on the foot of my bed. "Are you ready for this?" Verlan asked excitedly. I tried to appreciate his efforts, but I really didn't care about anything. I doubted I'd ever smile again.

When I didn't answer, he urged me, "Please cheer up, Irene." Then he reached into the box with both his big hands and brought out six bottles of Coke. "These are all yours," he said. Then he scattered eight American candy bars across the bed. He had the biggest grin on his face, just waiting for my reaction.

I picked up a Baby Ruth and a Butterfinger, rubbing my fingers over them in disbelief. It was illegal to sell such American products here. These items had been smuggled in. "You actually bought this contraband?"

"Yeah," he said, nodding his head, hoping for approval. "I did it just for you. And that's not all! There's something else." He handed me a shoe box.

Did I dare open it? Was the box some sort of deception, camouflage for something else?

Too excited to wait for me, Verlan took the lid off, pulling out a pair of beautiful black patent leather shoes. Never had a gift been more appropriate or more meaningful.

My numbness vanished. The pain I'd been clinging to dissolved, and my tears gushed freely. God may have forgotten me, but Verlan hadn't.

CHAPTER FOURTEEN

Three months after Leah's death, I got to go home to Utah to visit my family. Seeing the gorgeous, snowcapped Wasatch Mountains again helped to heal me just a little from my long ordeal in Mexico. Seeing my mother helped even more. She wept as she lamented how much I'd been through over the past year and the fact that she hadn't been there to help me through my baby's birth and death. I didn't have the heart to tell her about the rest of my sufferings. In part, I still felt so foolish about charging off and marrying Verlan despite all my family's well-founded warnings that I would terribly, terribly regret doing so.

Over the first two weeks of my visit, I gained several pounds. Alarmed, Mother complained about my constant eating. I knew I couldn't tell her why. How would she believe that I'd gone for over a year without tasting peanut butter, jam, margarine, Jell-O, tuna, mayonnaise, or so many of the other things I used to take for granted. At Mother's house, I couldn't help gorging luxuriously on raisins, nuts, fresh fruits, and ice cream. I was afraid I might not ever see such sumptuous goodies again.

The result was fairly disastrous. One night I awoke with my side killing me. The pain shot clear down to my knees. I couldn't wait until morning to see a doctor, so Mother rushed me in the dead of night to see Uncle Rulon, whom my family went to for medical as well as spiritual emergencies.

"It's your appendix," Uncle Rulon concluded. "It's about to burst. You need an operation immediately. I'll find you a surgeon."

I told him I couldn't be operated on because I had no money to pay an American hospital bill. Besides, I was now Verlan's responsibility. I'd had Leah without Verlan there, and that was hard enough. I meant for him to be with me through all other medical crises I might have to endure. I left Uncle Rulon's office against his strong advice and made plans to return to Mexico.

But the prospect of cutting short my vacation devastated me. I longed for more time with my family. Even more fervently, I longed to escape life in Mexico. Circumstances there were too unbearable. Now, faced with having to run right back to those circumstances, I found myself entertaining unthinkable things. The pain in my side didn't help.

A divorce could settle everything. Then I could start a new life back here in Utah. I could eat what I wanted, wear normal, twentieth-century clothes, and maybe even hook up with Glen again. Almost as soon as the vision formed, I felt ashamed for concocting such a wicked plan. How I wished I had someone wise and objective I could go to for counsel.

Maybe if I prayed harder, I'd feel better about going back. I rationalized that Verlan was honest, upright, good looking . . . and he loved the Lord, after all. I just wished I could believe he really loved me.

I remembered a lecture on faith I'd once heard. Any religion that doesn't require the sacrifice of all things earthly doesn't have the power to lay hold of things eternal, the lecturer assured us. I'd given up everything material. Was I now willing to sacrifice my feelings also? I wanted a celestial glory, didn't I? Then I shouldn't complain. Of course I had to return.

The Cox family, from Cane Beds, Arizona, offered to take me with them to Mexico. I rode the thousand-mile trip in the back of a three-quarter-ton pickup with only a canvas over the top. With nine people aboard, it was almost impossible to relax on the mattress. The chill of the November night, plus the pain in my stomach, kept me awake and worried that my appendix would rupture any minute from all the endless jolting. Once we got to the Mexican border, we went from highways to dusty, ungraded dirt roads for the final two hundred miles to the LeBaron ranch.

On my arrival, Verlan, Charlotte, and I left immediately for Casas to find a doctor to perform the operation. When we arrived there late in the evening, we were told that Dr. Hatch had gone deer hunting. Doctors Salas and Fregozo would have to do the operation the following morning.

I was admitted to the clinic on Thanksgiving Day. Almost immediately, Charlotte and Verlan took off with a friend, Ossmen Jones, to eat Thanksgiving turkey. I couldn't believe he'd leave me among strangers at a time like this. It seemed I could never be alone with my husband when I really needed to be. Charlotte was present at my wedding to place my hand in his. Worse, she'd been around after my baby died so Verlan and I couldn't even mourn in private. Now, when I desperately needed Verlan to reassure and comfort me, he was off with her again. I'd never had an operation, never even been in a hospital. It seemed to me my life was in danger, and on top of that, I felt abandoned and alone. I was seventeen and petrified. In lieu of my missing husband, I wanted my mother.

To prep me for surgery, the nurse painted my stomach and my legs down to my knees with disinfectant. Then Arturo Muñoz, the young Mexican English-speaking anesthetist, arrived on the scene. He didn't look a day over twenty. He put a rubber band around my left arm and thumped my vein with his finger until it bulged out enough to insert a needle. He shot some fluid in and asked, "Do you feel sleepy?" Before I could say a word, I was out cold.

I THOUGHT I COULD hear voices. I listened again. Yes, Verlan was talking to me. "Irene, Dr. Hatch is here to see you."

The light was too bright, almost blinding. I squinted until I could focus on the doctor, but he looked odd to me. At first I thought I might be imagining the scratches and cuts all over his head and face. His eyes were swollen and bruised. "Oh ... Doctor ... Hatch," I said, still all drugged up, "what ... happened ... to ... you?"

He patted my arm reassuringly. "I went hunting, and my horse fell off a cliff with me still on him."

I grasped his arm, trying unsuccessfully to sit up. With a concerned, pathetic look, and to Verlan's great embarrassment, I said, "Oh . . . the . . . pooooor . . . horse!"

I CARRIED LEAH FOR nine months, and throughout that time Verlan and I kept the law of purity. He hadn't made love to me once during my pregnancy. Nor had he done so afterward, while we were grieving. Counting the three plus months since Leah's death, it had now been a full year since I'd had sexual intimacy. A part of me was dying. In that sense especially, I felt Verlan was still more a stranger to me than a husband.

My incision from the appendectomy healed slowly, but my fights with Verlan were hot and constant. When he'd come to bed, we'd always argue about sex.

"You've read too many steamy novels," he'd lecture me. "Besides, you've been too sick. I don't know if you're over the toxemia." Toxemia—a condition in which one's blood carries a dangerous level of toxins—was what they'd decided had gone wrong with Leah's birth. "You may get it again if you get pregnant. The doctor said for you to wait at least a year. You know we can't practice birth control. That's a sin second only to murder! So we'll just have to abstain. Please be patient, Irene. I wish you'd believe I love you."

I felt such a loss without my baby. I longed to hold another child in my arms. At the same time, I needed a little physical love before I conceived again. I prayed God would understand. One January night, in complete despair, I demanded that Verlan make love to me.

"I think you bring suffering upon yourself, Irene," he retorted. "You have too much sex on your mind. You must overcome it, or you'll never be happy."

"Please, Verlan. Please!" I begged.

"Well, let's pray about it first," he said. So we got down on our knees and held hands by the side of the bed while Verlan prayed yet again about having intercourse with me. I wondered if God really wanted to hear such prayers. Since he'd given us our free agency, why did we have to get his permission for every little move we made? Besides, if God by chance gave us the okay to proceed, I didn't want to have to think about him peeking in on us again.

We got back into bed, and I waited. And I waited some more. I wondered if perhaps God spoke, but Verlan just never heard. Impatient, I finally asked, "Well, are we going to do it?"

"No. I have to wait until I feel good about it," he said matter-of-factly and turned over to go to sleep.

Hours later, I awoke to Verlan's advances. He whispered, "Irene, I dreamed we had a beautiful, dark-haired baby. Now I feel good about this."

I was perplexed. Why were Verlan's dreams from God, but mine were not? I'd dreamt hundreds of times that we were making love, and Verlan had never once thought those dreams were inspired. Still, I was overjoyed about his change of heart.

WE KNEW NOTHING ABOUT ovulation. My periods were supremely reliable; I had one every twenty-six days.

After the night Verlan had his glorious dream and we'd finally made love again, my very next period went missing in action. I couldn't believe it. Why, I would even repent and be willing to wash out my dirty rags if God would just let me have fun and try a few more times before I actually conceived the "beautiful, dark-haired baby" Verlan saw in his dream. I wondered if God loved me at all, since he never let me do a thing I wanted.

This is how it went for me throughout my childbearing years. During many of them, Verlan worked in the States and wrote me between visits home. I was so fertile, I once warned him not to write me anymore because I thought I might just be able to get pregnant through the mail.

CHAPTER FIFTEEN

Verlan's cheese-making business at Terrenates was short-lived. In case I had any problems with my second pregnancy, he decided to move his family back to the LeBaron ranch, where I would be closer to Dr. Hatch. So Charlotte and I moved back into our three-room house.

We resumed our Sunday visits to Spencerville. I just knew Verlan was trying to kill two birds with one stone by taking us over there. Yes, one bird was Sunday worship, but the other bird was Lucy Spencer— now eighteen, attractive, and getting very serious about Verlan. I was five months pregnant, unfulfilled, and overwhelmed with loneliness. And I could see the inevitable unfolding before my eyes.

The thought of sharing Verlan with Lucy sexually tore me to pieces. Her testimony of the gospel and her sweet attitude didn't change my feelings one bit. Nor did the horrible fate that had befallen jealous Lucinda have an impact on me anymore. I was coming unglued.

Lucy bragged that she had loved Verlan since she was twelve, and I feared this might give him reason to love her more than he loved me. Such thoughts were driving me mad. I cried to God that it wasn't fair. She'd get the sex I was starving for. I even tried to change Verlan's mind. "Can't we settle on just two wives?" I'd ask. "Isn't that living the Principle?"

"Heavens, no!" he said. "The LDS apostle Heber C. Kimball had forty-five wives! Think of the glory he's going to have!"

I tried to count my blessings. Maybe three wives wouldn't be all that bad, especially considering we had an eternal kingdom to build. I supposed I would have to give in on that score alone. Besides, I couldn't let Lucy be counted worthier than me. I would obey.

Still, I felt insulted by the whole affair. In addition to inspiring such animal jealousy in me, Verlan's desire to marry Lucy hurt my pride. I hoped, and dared to assume, I'd be the one to fully satisfy him, the woman he would not be able to live without. Why did he need anyone else with me around? But Verlan never even seemed to consider that possibility. He was always aimed at glory, and glory required lots of wives.

I felt like I had love to give, but no one to give it to. So I set my sights on my baby. It would love me unconditionally. I'd be able to hug, caress, and lavish kisses on it. I couldn't wait to have it.

At around this time, by the way, I began to see Charlotte in a very different light. How had she been able to let me marry her husband? Was she more converted than I? As difficult as Charlotte was at times, I knew I'd never felt the same kind and intensity of jealousy toward her I now felt toward Lucy. It didn't seem I had a right to. Now I began to compare the way Charlotte treated me with the way I would treat my rival. Though I'd felt her vibes of resentment many times, Charlotte never said a mean word to me. In fact, she'd often been supportive of me. As I looked back on it, I especially marveled at her ability to make me that new nightgown and send it off with Verlan for my wedding night. If I knew anything at all, I knew I'd never make Lucy a nightgown in which to sleep with my husband.

On the other hand, maybe I should. Then I could put a ten-pound padlock on the bottom of it.

IT WAS MY WEEK to do the cooking. Verlan put his arm lovingly around me while he watched me at the woodstove. I was frying up some beans with a little onion and oil in them to give them a better flavor. "Mash them good before you add the cheese," he said. "I'm starved."

A warm May sun shone through our ragged screen door. He held me close, kissing my neck and face. We would have a few more stolen minutes alone before Charlotte would be back from Delfina's to eat lunch.

"Knock, knock." At the sound of Lucy's voice, Verlan spun around like he'd been caught doing something naughty. I could tell Lucy had something up her sleeve by the way she approached us. She looked uneasily at me; then she said directly to Verlan, "Can I speak to you in private?"

"Yes," he said, waving her toward Charlotte's bedroom.

My foot was in the door before he could close it. "Oh, no you don't," I said, boiling with anger. I looked Lucy straight in the eyes. "If you have something to say to *my* husband, say it right here in front of me."

Verlan laughed, embarrassed by my uncomely reaction. He glared at me, hoping to prevent a scene. "Please, Irene, she only wants to talk to me for a minute." He pushed the door against my foot, hoping I would leave them alone.

But I shoved the door almost open, looking defiantly at Lucy. "Whatever it is, say it!" I commanded her. Lucy looked helplessly at Verlan. "Go ahead," I said. "If it's that important, let's hear it."

"Well . . ." She looked at me and shrugged her shoulders. "If you want it this way . . . twenty-eight of our fundamentalist friends from Utah arrived at our home early this morning." She paused and glanced over at me, seeming to question whether I really wanted to hear the rest. When I didn't stop her, she turned back to Verlan and continued. "There are six carloads of them. They're all on their way to a conference in Ozumba. Mother and I talked to Uncle Rulon. He consented to perform our marriage at 3 o'clock this afternoon. I just wanted to make sure you'd be there."

This bombshell rendered me speechless. Tears blinded my eyes. Wanting it not to be true, wanting to step out of this scene and forget it happened, I went back to the stove and took my rage out on the beans. I mashed them like I'd never mashed beans before, crying all the while.

I knew Verlan was as surprised as I, but he still managed to walk her back to the door and promise, "We'll be there." Lucy hesitated and then wisely chose not to tell me good-bye.

Not caring if Lucy overheard me, I screamed at Verlan the moment she walked away. "You may be there, but I'll never go to your damn wedding!" I threw the masher on the cement floor, splattering beans in all directions, and then ran into my room. I slammed the door behind me and fell facedown onto the bed. Verlan followed, trying to pull me close, to comfort me, but I fought him off. "Don't you touch me!" I ordered. "If you marry your true love, you'll never see me again!"

"Please don't be upset with me!" he pleaded. "I didn't know this was going to happen today."

"I won't go, Verlan. I won't ever give you another wife! God will have to send me to Hell. I won't do it! I promise." I sobbed hysterically.

"Irene, this is a part of the gospel. God requires it. It's securing your salvation. Please, if you won't do it for that reason, then do it for me. Please, Irene. You should be glad she wants to be a part of our family. It's a sacrifice for Lucy, too."

"Oh, yes!" I blurted out. "It'll be a big sacrifice for her to make love to my husband!"

"Shh-shh," he whispered, trying to quiet me down. We could now hear Charlotte moving around out in the kitchen.

"Get out of my room," I ordered.

Verlan was distraught. He grabbed me tighter. I stopped fighting him when I realized he was crying, too. We clung together, sobbing in each other's arms. Finally he spoke. "Irene, this is hard on me, too. Don't think it doesn't tear me up to see you unhappy. I'd never do it if God hadn't commanded it." He sighed. "I can't even keep two wives content, let alone three." He looked at his watch. He'd have to be at Lucy's in less than two hours, and he still had to break the news to Charlotte.

I heard a car stop near the house, and I suspected it was probably someone I knew from Utah. I was mortified. I couldn't let one of those faithful saints see me crying, not for the reason I was crying.

I had to be strong. If any of them saw how upset I was, they might think I wasn't celestial material. Aunt Athlene knocked on the outside door to my bedroom. "Irene, can I talk to you?" she called in through the screen.

Aunt Athlene was one of Uncle Rulon's wives. Maybe she would understand how I felt. I begged her to forgive me for the condition she'd found me in. She put her arms around my pregnant body, holding me like a child while I wept unashamedly.

Eventually Aunt Athlene said to me, "The Bible says that obedience is better than sacrifice. Go, Irene. Be brave. Minister unto your husband. He'll love you more if you willingly give Lucy to him. Sure, it's hard, but be strong. By doing it, you'll receive a celestial glory." She kissed me lovingly, moving my rumpled golden hair out of my face. "He can't help but love you more," she promised. "Don't let him down!" She hugged me again. "I'm depending on you being ready to go in an hour, okay?"

I politely heard her out; then I watched her drive off. I respected her too much to let her know I was filled with the Devil. As soon as I was certain she'd gone, I threw myself back onto my bed and rolled back and forth, weeping uncontrollably. Out loud, I said, "I won't go . . . I won't go . . . I won't go! If I do, then the hosts of Heaven will have to drag me there!" By now I was trembling and weak from all the crying.

When Aunt Athlene returned to take us to Lucy's wedding, Charlotte obediently got in the car. Verlan rushed into my bedroom one final time and begged me, "Please, Irene, let's go! Do it for me."

I wanted to hurt him like he'd hurt me. "I won't be a part of it. You can't pay me to go," I said. Verlan knew I meant it. He walked out, subdued.

I listened to make sure they'd driven away. Then I screamed and beat the bed. I could imagine what people would say about me. "Irene doesn't have it in her." "She's too jealous, no spirit of the Lord in her." I would be condemned all around. Uncle Rulon might even think I'd reneged on my promise. These thoughts were interrupted by a knock at the door. A man's voice asked, "May I come in?"

"If you want to," I said, humiliated that a stranger overheard my tantrum.

The man came in and sat on the bed next to my heaving body. He patted my back and said, "Irene, you don't know me. I'm Wayne, a friend of the Spencers' from Utah. I was on my way to your ranch when I ran into Verlan. He sent me back to get you. Please come. You'll always regret it if you don't."

This was surely my last chance to obey God. If I refused now, I might as well forget about godhood. At best, I'd end up an angel. The thought of serving Verlan, Charlotte, and Lucy for eternity disgraced me more than showing up at the wedding red-faced and swollen-eyed.

I grabbed a washcloth, wetting it in cold water from the pump. Then I climbed into Wayne's car and leaned back in the front seat beside him, covering my swollen eyes. I would attend my husband's wedding, but when it was over, he would still have only two wives, because he could count me out. At least this is the thought that got me to the Spencers' without further tears.

As soon as we drove up, Verlan snatched open the car door and practically sang to me in his relief, "Irene, I love you so much for this. I knew you'd come through for me." He rushed me over a wooden bridge and past a grape arbor as he prompted, "Hurry, they're waiting for us."

We ducked to avoid hitting our heads on a door frame as we entered a cubical where a small group impatiently awaited us. Uncle Rulon nodded, and then he folded his hands in front of him. Looking very dignified, he spoke with caution. "We are keeping this marriage a secret. Only Wayne and these few people here in this room know that such a sacred covenant is taking place." He nodded toward Athlene. "I've allowed my wife and Lucy's mother to be here." He looked at Verlan for approval. "So, with the consent of you four (meaning Verlan, Charlotte, Lucy, and me), we'll proceed."

Uncle Rulon told Verlan to step forward. He placed Charlotte on Verlan's left, me on Charlotte's left, and Lucy next to me. I kept my face pointed toward the floor. Everyone there knew how upset I was.

Uncle Rulon began, looking right at me: "Sister LeBaron, do you take Lucy by the right hand and give her unto your husband?"

Screaming inside, I blocked out the words. The silence grew embarrassing. Charlotte nudged me softly with her elbow. Unwilling to answer, I nudged her back.

Uncle Rulon cleared his throat and asked firmly a second time, "Sister LeBaron, do you take Lucy by the right hand and give her unto your husband?"

Nothing came out of my mouth. If I placed her hand in his, I knew, I'd be giving them permission to . . .

Annoyed, Verlan whispered, "Irene, it's you he's talking to."

Uncle Rulon was perturbed. He tried again, and this time he got personal. "Sister Irene, do you take Lucy by the right hand . . ."

I reached over, grabbed her hand, and threw it in his. Everyone but me relaxed then, and the ceremony proceeded. I couldn't hear anything being said. An avalanche of tears fell again as my mind went wild.

"Before God, angels, and these witnesses . . ." said Uncle Rulon. I caught that word "angels." Like all Mormon weddings, this one was taking place before a captive host of enslaved, eternally lonely angels. That prospect certainly got my attention. ". . . I pronounce you legally and lawfully husband and wife." He paused and flashed Verlan a satisfied smile. "You may now kiss the bride."

Verlan kissed Lucy (it's a good thing I didn't have a baseball bat). Then he kissed Charlotte. I flew out the door before he could even think of kissing me. I ran to the small orchard south of the house, tears blinding my way. I sat in the low branches of a small pear tree and wept as never before. I didn't have my family. I was only eighteen. I'd lost my baby. Verlan was all I had, and now Lucy was taking him away from me, too. Hoping to find some comfort, I lay back in the branches of the tree. When the fetus moved within me, I wondered if it was feeling my sorrow.

I watched as Verlan hunted for me in the goat pen. Next he checked the chicken coop. Then he opened the door to the adobe room where Aunt Sylvia kept her canning jars filled with treasured fruits and vegetables. I could tell he was getting concerned. But he finally glanced toward the orchard and saw my sobbing body prostrate in the branches of the pear tree. Without a word, he lifted me out and walked me to the car. I didn't speak to him or to Charlotte the whole five miles home. I wasn't speaking to God, either. I was mad at him, too.

Verlan tried in vain to console me. "I left Lucy at her mother's. I'm not even going to sleep with her tonight." He said it like it was a great sacrifice he was making just for me. "And tomorrow we'll be traveling in separate cars. We'll meet in Chihuahua so no one will suspect our marriage."

I was too angry to answer. Whether he slept with her tonight or tomorrow night wasn't the point. I didn't want him sleeping with her ever. Period.

"Irene, Lucy has to sacrifice, too. She feels bad. Try to understand. This is her wedding day, and she can't even share it with me."

I was glad it was Charlotte's night to have Verlan. I was too full of rage not to take it out on him. He tried kissing me good night before he retired to her room, but I flipped my face around. "Your lips will never touch mine again. Ever!" I informed him.

He shook his head and sighed. "I can't figure you out. Why are you so upset? I'm just building up my kingdom. Women born under the Principle shouldn't act like this." He left, bewildered.

A short time later, I felt him slip into bed beside me. "Charlotte figured you needed me worse, so I'm here to spend the night with you," he said. "See, when you do what's right, you get a little extra."

That did it. I tried to get out of the bed, but Verlan grabbed me and forced me to lie back down. "Please, Irene, listen to me."

"I mean it, Verlan," I raved between sobs. "If you sleep with Lucy, I promise, I'll leave you! You'll never see me again." I knew I wasn't playing the game right, and Verlan didn't know how to handle a hysterical wife. Furthermore, he felt guilty for not sleeping with Lucy on her wedding night. Would she ever forgive him? Would she cause him even more problems than he already had? He took me in his arms, and we spent Lucy's wedding night crying ourselves to sleep.

Across the way, by the light of a dim lamp, Charlotte quietly packed several changes of her own clothing so that Lucy would look appropriate for her honeymoon. The Spencers had lived in dire poverty since their arrival in Mexico. Verlan couldn't tell Lucy her navy satin dress with the bustle was outdated and ugly.

The next morning, I watched with bitterness as Verlan packed his suitcase. He folded two shirts and then tucked clean underwear beneath them. He had to go to Charlotte's room for his blue slacks and clean socks. He brought these back and silently placed each article into his bag.

At one point he paused and looked at me questioningly. Then he reached under my pillow for his pajamas. "Oh, no you don't!" I snapped, jerking them out of his hands. "These are my pajamas!"

"Loan them to me," he implored. "They're really mine anyway. I just let you keep them in your room."

"You'll never sleep with another woman with these on," I said, clutching them to my breast.

Looking just as spitefully at me as I looked at him, he said, "Then I'll just sleep without them!"

AT AROUND NOON three days later, I was busy hanging clothes on the outside line to dry when I spied Verlan cutting through the mesquites, his suitcase in hand, returning from his honeymoon. I quickly took the enamel pan of wet clothes back into the house. Without saying a word to Charlotte, I locked myself in my bedroom. I heard Verlan greet Charlotte when he came in. "How did Irene take things?" he asked her.

"Better than expected," she replied.

I was furious. Charlotte and I never discussed the matter the whole time Verlan was gone. Now, here they both were trying to figure me out. If Verlan wanted to know how I was doing, he should just ask me. Of course, he'd have to be prepared to catch hell if he did.

I could see a butter knife moving under the wire latch on the door. Verlan was trying to get into my room. For several minutes, I kept him from it. It was only for fear of driving him back into Lucy's arms that I relented in the end. As I flipped the latch open, he took me in his arms and said, "I love you. You're so beautiful. Nobody could ever take your place."

"How could you say that? You just got off your honeymoon!"

"I left Lucy at her mother's," he said sheepishly, "just for you. She wanted to come home with me and move right in to be a part of the family, but I decided to wait until you feel good about it first."

He'd thrown open the door to my indignation. "I'll never feel good about it, Verlan." I said. "Don't you dare bring her here. Ever! You hear? Never!"

Verlan cringed. "Oh, no. You'll never make it to Heaven with that attitude."

"Good. I don't want her around now, let alone throughout eternity! Don't you ever mention her name to me again. She may be your wife, but she certainly isn't mine!"

I watched him closely for the next three days, following him everywhere—to see his brothers, to the fields. I was determined not to give him a chance to sneak off to the Spencers' to see Lucy again. I lived in dread of that fateful moment.

On the third day, I came upon him shaving at the washstand in the kitchen. I watched as he held his mouth open, cutting his whiskers away. He saw me watching, but he didn't want any trouble, so he shaved on in silence. I was sick inside. I knew what he was up to, but I asked the question anyway. "Who are you getting all cleaned up for?"

"I'm going to catch a ride to go see Lucy," he said matter-of-factly.

I couldn't hold in the tears. "You didn't see me for a week after we got married. It's only been three days since you married Lucy! Can't you live without her?" I stomped my feet in a rage.

Then he had the nerve to say, "You don't want me to treat her like

I did you, do you? Besides, the circumstances are different. I feel she needs me."

"I need you, too!" I screamed out. "I'm four months pregnant. It's not fair! Please don't go!"

He changed his shirt, ignoring my pleas. Then he darted through the mesquites to the main road, where he could thumb a ride to Spencerville.

CHAPTER SIXTEEN

Three or four weeks after Verlan married Lucy, he announced that he and Charlotte were going to the States for two weeks to visit Aunt Rhea. He wanted me to tend her kids, Verlan Jr. And fifteen-month-old Rhea. I agreed willingly until he told me he wanted Lucy to come and stay with me so I wouldn't be alone. I flatly refused to let her into my house.

"Please, do it for me. I'll love you! She feels bad 'cause you don't like her anymore. It's even worse now that you've quit going up to her mother's for Sunday meetings. I worry about you being here all alone. Please, Irene, do it for me."

I tried to fight my jealousy, but it was no use. "No! That woman will never live one day with me," I said.

Still, after Verlan told me how he needed and depended on me, I just couldn't let him down. "Please, do it for me," he said again and again. He knew just how to get to me. I finally gave in, but I made sure he knew I wasn't accepting her. She was his, not mine. I still hated her.

By the time Lucy showed up, Verlan had thoroughly warned her about my temper and coached her on exactly what she shouldn't say to me. He'd told her not to mention their marriage, their honeymoon, and for heaven's sake, she should never admit to being pregnant. He had a hard enough time getting this far with me. He accomplished it only because I loved him. Since I had no love at all for her, he thought that if I knew she was having his baby, I just might give in to the Devil's tempting and beat her up.

Lucy spent the first day with me in silence—cleaning beans and doing other household chores, but mostly just staying out of my way. As I observed her walking around my house, my anger boiled. Still, I had to admit that she was a nice girl. I also concluded that I stacked up well against her. Even if she had loved Verlan since she was twelve, I was eleven months her junior. That made me Verlan's youngest wife.

I was plenty nervous about sleeping alone, with no man in the house to protect us, but I wasn't about to let Lucy into my bed. That was the only private thing I had. I'd been forced to share my husband and even his pajamas, but I'd be damned before I'd ever let another wife into my bed. So Lucy slept in Charlotte's bedroom and tended her two young children.

On the second morning, I decided to be up front with Lucy. She knew I was mad, so why not tell her exactly how I felt? Maybe if she knew how bad I really hurt, she'd forget any ideas she might have about moving in with me. I started in on her, but before I could get very far, I broke down and cried. Oddly, this freed us to talk about almost everything I was struggling with regarding her—everything except sex. I couldn't deal with that. I would never accept her and Verlan having sex, and I certainly didn't want to hear about it. I just wanted to know one thing: was she keeping the *rules*?

During the two weeks she spent with me, Lucy taught me to sew. We tore apart pants once belonging to our late father-in-law, whom I'd never met. She helped me cut out and sew overalls for little Verlan Jr. I made him five pair, improving on each one. We cut all the cloth scraps into small pieces for the outhouse, since toilet paper was a luxury we'd never been able to afford. Before long, I realized we'd developed a bit of a friendship. And once she went back to her mother's house, I was certain we would become better friends.

VERLAN AND CHARLOTTE ARRIVED unexpectedly at four in the morning, so Charlotte crawled into her bed with Lucy. Verlan slipped

into my bed beside me. He was too excited to sleep, so we talked for
the two hours till sunup. He couldn't have been nicer and more understanding. He let me know I was his main concern, that my happiness came first. But he was going to have to ask a big favor of me:
"Just say yes, and I'll love you forever," he said.

"Okay, as long as it doesn't concern Lucy."

There was dead silence. Then he tried again. "Irene, please let
Lucy stay here and live with us. I'm her husband, too, and she needs
to feel accepted."

"No," I said firmly. "You're just getting her in here little by little,
thinking that I'll go along with it. I will not live with her! And if you
can't live without her, then find me one room by itself somewhere,
and I'll gladly move out!"

He shook his head. "Our family needs to become united. Can't
you just start by liking her? You don't need to love her. Will you let
her stay if she promises never to come into your bedroom?"

"Hell! Where are you going to put her? Damn it! It's not fair!"

"Don't you swear at me, young lady!" he warned.

I continued. "We only have three rooms. Charlotte has her bedroom; I have mine. Do you want to put her in the kitchen? Verlan,
you know that we use that room to sew, make quilts, shuck corn, and
clean beans. On cold days, we scrub our dirty clothes in there."

"Please, Irene, I'll love you forever." He lavished kisses on me, as
usual, hoping his affection would change my feelings. It didn't, but I
gave in anyway. The polygamous gospel demanded my strict obedience. Still, I made it clear I was only doing this for him. He was never
to bring her into my room, or they would both be sorry.

Verlan knew he'd have hell to pay if he called those two hours
he'd spent with me "my night." So early that morning he announced
that he'd spend that night with me, the next night with Lucy, and
the third night with Charlotte. After that, each of us would have
every third night. He'd be fair, show no favoritism. Of course, favoritism was exactly what each of us wanted, but we went along for the
sake of "unity" and so Verlan would love us better and we might win
some favoritism from him after all. As angry as they'd made me, I

remembered his recent words to me: "See, when you do what's right, you get a little extra."

IGNORING OUR DEAL, VERLAN tried to persuade me to sleep with Charlotte so he and Lucy could use my bed on her night with him. I couldn't believe it. I broke into tears at such a contemptible idea. "You won't desecrate my bed with that woman in it," I yelled.

"Shh-shh," he said. He knew he'd pushed me too far. "Then will you let Charlotte sleep with you?" he asked.

We had no sofa, and we used the kitchen as our main living quarters. Just as I'd said, there was nowhere else for them to go. I truly wanted to be a good wife, so after I told Verlan exactly how I felt about it, I gave in as I always did. It was certainly the lesser of the two evils Verlan gave me to choose between. It was settled. Charlotte would sleep with me on Lucy's night, and Lucy would sleep with me on Charlotte's.

A WEEK BEFORE LEAH'S first birthday, Verlan surprised me with a sack of cement. He took an oblong wooden soapbox, lined it with heavy paper, and placed two empty, quart-sized juice cans in the upper corners to create a sculptured design. Then he poured in the wet cement and wrote LEAH LEBARON—BORN AUGUST 7, 1954 AND DIED AUGUST 7, 1954. When it dried solid, he removed the box and the cans. We now had a headstone for her grave.

On the anniversary of her birth, Verlan took me to the grave I'd never seen. We carefully measured the distance from each wall to make sure we marked the right one, but we felt pretty confident, since all those nearby already had Catholic crosses on them.

While Verlan dug into the mound and planted the marker halfway into the dirt, I recalled the surprise and horror of losing our first child, our precious baby girl. Grief surged through me as the tears streaked my cheeks. Verlan pulled me to him. "Irene, I know how bad you feel. I'd have given anything to be able to raise her, too." He patted my big, seven-months pregnant stomach. "Cheer up, honey. Maybe God will give us another little girl."

Over the years, whenever he was away from us on Leah's birthday, Verlan always sent me a sweet note expressing his regrets. She was the first of five babies he lost, and I don't believe he ever completely recovered from the trauma of her death.

ON OCTOBER 6, 1955, I awoke with such violent pain, Verlan had to help me out of bed. I felt like bearing down, but I was frantic to get some medical attention first. Because of the potholes in the dirt roads, it would take at least two hours for someone to go get the doctor from El Valle and bring him back to the ranch. Verlan told Lucy, who was three months pregnant by this point, to hurry but not run for help. She rushed a half-mile through the mesquites and across the gravel highway to Homer Babbitt's house. Since Alma was away in his truck at the time, Homer had the only available transportation in the vicinity. He drove Lucy into town to fetch the doctor.

I stood crying at Charlotte's bedroom door. "Help me, Charlotte. I can't take this for twelve hours again!" The memories of my first delivery still frightened me terribly.

"Come on in," she said. "Don't worry. It will soon be over." Taking one look at me, she added, "My goodness, you look like you're in the last stages." She quickly threw a plastic cover over the mattress and tucked clean sheets into place to prepare the bed for delivery.

But Charlotte was also pregnant; she was due in just three weeks. Verlan was worried that she might start premature labor if she helped me with my birth, so he sent her to wait it out at a neighbor's house.

We asked Verlan's Aunt Annie to be the midwife in case I delivered before the doctor arrived, and she just happened to be at the ranch that night, visiting. Aunt Annie had never actually delivered a baby before. When she got there, she went around wringing her hands and wiping them on her apron, looking more upset than I was as I lay there on the bed, bearing down every few minutes. Aunt Annie kept me covered with the sheet. Each time I bore down, she cried out and moaned as if she felt the pains herself. I grabbed her hand with one of mine and Verlan's with the other. I bore down again and again. Each time, she'd turn her head to one side and grimace.

Verlan asked her, "How're we doing?" She could hardly bear to look but forced herself to peek under the sheet. He was getting exasperated. "Here, let me do it," he said. He took one look, exclaimed, "My golly, it's here!" and jerked the sheet to one side.

Looking as if she was about to faint, Aunt Annie freed herself from my grasp. She pushed her glasses back onto her nose, then mopped up her sweating brow with her apron. "Irene, don't have it yet. Wait for the doctor. Please . . . oh, heavens, it's coming out!" she sputtered.

Verlan took both my hands, and I pushed again. My water broke. Covering her face now, Aunt Annie peered out through her fingers and saw the baby's head beginning to crown. She screamed out, "Wait, Irene, wait! The baby is too big! Oh, please God, do something, quick!" she wailed, flopping down on the bed next to me.

Verlan could see she was too upset to be of any help. And he knew the doctor would never make it, either. Since he had been present at both of Charlotte's deliveries, he figured he could handle things himself in a pinch. He ordered Aunt Annie to get up and get down to the foot of the bed. Then he handed her an open bottle of olive oil. He shoved two pillows under my shoulders so that I was almost sitting up. I bore down again, and the head really did begin to crown this time. Verlan yelled at Aunt Annie to pour the oil freely on the bulging head so I wouldn't tear.

I panted, and Aunt Annie shrieked, "Stop it! Stop it!"

Verlan took me in his arms. "Don't listen to her," he whispered. "You push, and I'll push, okay?" He quickly shoved his folded hankie between my teeth. "Bite this, and give one big push!"

Well, I went wild. I spit out the hankie and bit Verlan on the shoulder. He screamed, and out popped the baby's head! One more push, and it was all over. I now had a beautiful baby girl.

When Verlan saw her dark hair, he teased, "I guess I'll have to fire Pancho [the young Mexican who chopped our wood]."

Aunt Annie's nerves were shot. She sat in the rocking chair and cried, "You take over, Verlan. I can't cut the cord. Oh my." She held her head in her hands. "Stop that little thing from crying!" She slumped down in the chair with her head on the back of the rocker. "Irene, you had no right to do this to me," she whimpered.

I looked at the precious baby on my tummy. I asked Verlan to show me his watch. I delivered her fifty minutes after my very first pain. Maybe having babies wasn't too horrible after all.

Verlan looked at the time. "Too bad you didn't wait five more minutes. She'd have been born on your sister Donna's birthday."

"I'm naming her Donna anyway," I said. "She'll be glad to have a namesake."

Verlan left me with Auntie Annie just long enough to run next door to get Charlotte. He needed her help now. The two of them cleaned and dressed the baby.

Lucy came in about that time with the town doctor. They'd missed the delivery by twenty minutes. I still couldn't understand much Spanish, but I caught the gist of what was being said. Doctor Ramirez was amazed to see Verlan with three wives living in the same house. Why, his wife would not only kill him, she'd kill the other women as well. She had almost gone out of her mind when she recently surmised he had a mistress. Before he left, Verlan paid him ten dollars for checking the afterbirth and seeing that I was okay.

After the doctor left, Verlan offered to pay Aunt Annie as well. But she gestured no with her hands. "However, I do think you should pay Irene. Anyone that brave deserves twenty dollars."

I had to agree, except I thought my bravery was worth lots more than twenty bucks.

CHAPTER SEVENTEEN

Verlan's mother, Maud, gave him her three small adobe houses at the LeBaron ranch for an early inheritance. She was thrilled Verlan was so courageous and diligent in his pursuit of polygamy, and she was willing to rankle older brothers Alma and Ervil in order to demonstrate her approval. She also figured that since Verlan's family was growing so fast, we needed all the help we could get.

Since the cold winter months were almost upon us, Verlan insisted on moving us immediately. Donna was only two weeks old. He had to get all three wives settled into the first house fast. We could keep warmer together, using Charlotte's wood cooking stove for heat. The house only had two bedrooms, so I agreed with great reluctance that Lucy could share my bedroom, but only because I had Verlan's promise that I could live alone in the second house as soon as he could afford to fix it up.

On one of our first days there, the wind blew so steadily and strong, the stovepipes flew off the house and out across the yard. After it happened the second time, Verlan tied them to the corner of the roof with bailing wire. The storm raged on. During the night, I was huddled next to Lucy with little Donna tucked in between us. I had no crib, so I had to sleep lightly, on constant guard so I didn't roll over on her.

The wind moaned for hours, making sleep almost impossible. Earlier in the evening I secured gunnysacks as tightly as I could over the window frames. We had no glass in the windows at all. The wind blew so violently, the bailing wire could not keep the metal stove-pipes from coming loose and flying off the roof again. The gusts also loosened the sacks covering the window frames. The room was un-bearably cold. I could hear the sacks flapping as they beat time in the wind. I got up and tried to light the coal oil lamp, but the matches blew out faster than I could strike them.

The chill went throughout my whole body, causing my teeth to chatter uncontrollably. I slipped on my shoes and felt my way down the dark hall, gliding my hand along the cold adobe wall until I felt Charlotte's bedroom door. "Verlan!" I called, sorry I had to interrupt Charlotte's night. "Please come and help me. I need you! Hurry!"

He jumped up and followed me back to my room in his pajamas. "Boy, this weather is terrible!" he exclaimed. "Get back into bed be-fore you catch a cold." He felt for his coat in the hall. Taking a woven rug off the floor in the hall, he went out and nailed it onto the win-dow frame next to our bed. He came back into our room, stomping his feet. When he finally got the coal oil lamp lit, we were shocked to see that the foot of the bed was covered with snow. He pulled the blanket off and shook the snow into the hall; then he threw it back over our shivering bodies.

I moved my twenty-four-day-old baby to the outside of the bed, where I could hold up the edge of the heavy covers so she could breathe while we attempted to keep warm throughout the bitter cold night. Somehow, pregnant Lucy and I managed to drift off into a deep sleep.

Incredibly, without Lucy or me knowing a thing about it, Char-lotte quietly gave birth to her third child, Laura, sometime before daybreak. Following Charlotte's wishes, Verlan secretly sent for Lucy's mother, Sylvia, to attend the delivery. After Charlotte's par-ticipation in my babies' births, I was shocked not to be included in this birth of hers. So was Lucy. But it was a practice Charlotte would maintain throughout our lives together. She helped out with our confinements, but we were never included in the delivery of any of her nine children.

· · ·

THROUGHOUT DECEMBER, the cold made it almost impossible to keep warm in our house. We wore thick sweaters day and night. I slept lightly, always worried Donna would either freeze or smother under my covers. I longed to have a crib and other minimal comforts of life.

Aunt Rhea came at Christmastime. Though she couldn't afford to do it, she was so shocked at our living conditions, she contributed a hundred dollars to buy windows for the house. Verlan quickly measured the frames and ordered the windows. (When he went to pick them up, he ordered a table and six chairs for me, on credit.) I'll never forget those beautiful, wood-framed windows with real glass in them. What a joy it was to raise them up and down just to see how they worked.

One thing led to another, and pretty soon Verlan was entirely carried away. He bought plaster for the living room walls so we'd have at least one nice room. Then he splurged and bought some bright, rose-colored paint he applied to the walls himself. On the next trip to town, he brought back some loud, pink-flowered drapery material for curtains. I didn't mind him exploring his artistic side, but after seeing how that colorful room turned out, I told him I thought his creativity should be restricted to creating babies.

When Aunt Rhea returned again in the summertime, she was thrilled to see the improvements we made on the house. She approved of the new windows and seemed to think things were progressing nicely. Verlan's ingenuity especially impressed her. He set up a metal tank on the roof of the house. He would carry three five-gallon buckets of water up a ladder and pour the water into the tank, where the sun would warm it for our showers. Because the tank was small and a chore to fill, we were instructed to follow careful procedures whenever we used it. We were to get in the shower, wet ourselves down, turn the water off until we'd soaped up, and then rinse off.

Aunt Rhea did exactly as instructed. She hollered out that the water was nice and warm. In fact, it felt wonderful. I heard her turn the water off to lather up, just as she was supposed to. But a few seconds later, she was shouting in exasperation, "Somebody help me! The water's all gone. I can't rinse off!"

I called Verlan, who rushed out and drew up water from the well. Then he climbed up the ladder and poured the five gallons of cold water into the tank. "It's okay, you can shower now," he shouted. I'll never forget Aunt Rhea's screams as she jumped to one side when the cold water hit her. In an attempt to take the chill off, Verlan added a teakettle of boiling water so she could finish her shower more comfortably.

Even these little luxuries were short-lived. The original four-room house was far too crowded with Verlan, all three wives, four children (two of them small babies), and Lucy's baby on its way in April. So Verlan consented to let me move into the second, unfinished house.

He put glass in the windows, and I was elated as I cleaned the old place out. Donna and I would have three rooms all to ourselves. When my new table and chairs arrived, Verlan finished them beautifully with white paint. He had enough left over to paint the small, rundown cupboard we inherited from his mother. With the addition of a few nails to strengthen it, the cupboard now looked shiny and new. I filled it with the pots and pans Verlan's mother gave us permission to use.

Next, Verlan cut the handle off an old broom and used bailing wire to hang it from the wood beams in the ceiling to serve as a closet for my meager wardrobe. I wasn't too happy with the stove he gave me, because it smoked up the kitchen. It also had no oven, but I could walk twenty feet over to Charlotte's house and use her oven for baking.

The inside walls of the house were plain adobe. No plaster. No paint. I owned no pictures or knickknacks, not even a mirror or a clock. I had no kitchen sink or running water. But I would finally be alone. And I'd be free. For the first time in two years of married life, I'd have my husband all to myself. Now I could hug him and say what I thought without fear of being overheard. No more whispering. I didn't have to be continually on guard. I could laugh and joke and be myself. But best of all, I wouldn't have to share my bed with any other wives.

I spent five days in heaven, then Verlan came in and told me he'd been thinking about things. I knew that meant trouble. It meant the other wives were voicing wants, and I was going to end up with less. "It's not fair for you to live alone. Charlotte should have that privilege first—"

"Hell," I interrupted. "She lived alone with you for two years before I married you. I've never had any time alone! It's my turn. I don't even know you yet!"

"Oh, come on now. It's not right that six of us should be crammed into those tight quarters, while just you and little Donna live over here by yourselves. Besides, Lucy says she prefers living with you."

I blew up. "What more do you want? I was forced against my will to let Lucy marry you. Then you begged me to let you bring her home. You managed to get her into my bed. And now you want her to move in permanently—to live with me for the rest of my life! I refuse, Verlan. She's not my wife; she's yours. So you figure it out."

He couldn't help laughing at that, and he tried to tease me into laughing with him. "You're the one who placed her hand in mine. Now she has the right to go where I go."

"Well, you can both go to Hell!" I shouted. "Every decision you and I make revolves around another wife."

Urging me to comply, he said, "I could put more clay on the roof of that back storeroom, and Lucy could use it for her bedroom. How would that be?"

"Just give me one room of my own! I'll be glad to get by in it if it can be mine alone. I'm sick and tired of all your damn promises!"

"Irene, I can't afford to separate you right now. Please realize I'm doing the best I can. All three of you want your own home. Just don't be so selfish."

I knew what he was saying was true. I had to give in. But it seemed every time I got my hands on something I dreamt of having, it was immediately snatched away. Charlotte and her three children stayed in the original house we all lived in together, and Lucy moved with me into the house Verlan promised I could have to myself.

. . .

DR. RAMIREZ ACTUALLY MADE it on time to Lucy's delivery. She went for hours in hard labor while the four of us—Dr. Ramirez, Verlan, Charlotte, and me—attended her. When her baby finally arrived, Verlan was jubilant. "It's a boy! Can you imagine that? God has given me another boy!" Hearing him sound so proud and surprised, I suddenly fixated on the fact that God had not yet given Verlan that particular gift through me. The germ of a new fear and a new jealousy infected me. Meanwhile, Lucy and Verlan named their boy Chad.

A few days later, at Lucy's insistence, Verlan cleaned up the third, two-room adobe house that had been the old LeBaron toolshed, and Lucy moved into it. I was as thrilled as she was. At long last, we all had places of our own.

We held a family council at which each wife gave her opinion about the fairest way for Verlan to distribute his time and attention among the three separate households. Charlotte, Lucy, and I were already on a continual rotation for sleeping with him. As for meals, we decided he could eat two days a week with each wife. Then, on Sundays, he'd eat breakfast with me, lunch with Charlotte, and supper with Lucy. I had Verlan all to myself on Wednesdays and Saturdays. Those two days were mine and no one else's. When he went to the fields or took a rare trip to town on one of my days, I could go with him. I would respect Charlotte's and Lucy's days with Verlan, just as they would respect mine. It was exciting. I would often save my allotments of sugar and other supplies so I could make special meals for him when he came to my house. Soon I noticed he ate like a king wherever he went. Always vying to be his favorite, we all sacrificed to treat him extra special.

Now that I had my own house, Verlan couldn't understand why I still spent so many nights crying. I wanted to be strong and live up to his expectations, but jealousy drove me into tearful fits of anger. I'd cover my face with my pillow, sobbing and screaming as my mind flooded with images of him and Lucy breaking all the rules, manufacturing baby boy after baby boy. Even if she was his wife, and even if God had commanded us to live plural marriage, I still hated every minute of it. I spent almost the entire first year of Lucy's marriage weeping and imagining she'd taken my place in Verlan's heart.

When I admitted to him how I continued to struggle with jealousy toward Lucy, he reprimanded me and prayed I would overcome such irrational, unrighteous reactions. He wanted his wives to be humble and submissive. Apparently Lucy complied, but my compliance clearly was still not up to par.

ONCE WE WIVES spread out and came up with a Verlan-rotation everyone agreed to honor, I did find life a little easier in certain ways. Finally I had a few things I could count on. I could count on no one being in my bed whom I didn't want there. I could count on no one overhearing me when I voiced my thoughts or feelings aloud in my own house. And I could count on enjoying Wednesdays and Saturdays all alone with my husband. These meager little things were my lifeline.

Late on one particular Wednesday afternoon, Verlan opened my screen door and said, "Irene, do you want to go for a walk with me to the wheat fields?"

"I sure do," I said excitedly.

He hugged me and said, "Then wait a minute. I've got to go to the john. It'll give you time to get ready."

This was perfect. My baby was sleeping, so I'd have a couple of free hours if Lucy would just peek in on her a time or two. I rushed off to my bedroom, where I brushed out my hair, put it in a ponytail, and slipped into a clean dress for our date. Almost the only place I ever got to go was to the Spencers'. I was thrilled that Verlan went to the trouble of thinking up something fun for us to do. I really felt privileged as I fantasized about how romantic it was going to be, just the two of us walking through the golden grain.

When Verlan didn't come back after several minutes, I started to wonder why he was taking so long. He said he'd only be a minute. I decided to meet him outside, but he wasn't in the yard. So I walked past Lucy's house to the outhouse. He wasn't in there either. I couldn't imagine where he'd gone. I opened Lucy's door and called. No one was there. How strange; I'd seen her haul a bucket of water from the well to her house just a few minutes earlier.

It must have been instinct, or perhaps just that irrational, unrighteous jealousy of mine. I gazed out over the yellow wheat field and saw something that extinguished my good mood and my newfound sense of security like a pail of ice-cold water. There went Lucy and Verlan, arm in arm, like the proverbial lovers heading off into the sunset. I wished they'd change course and head straight for Hell.

That proved it—Lucy was Verlan's favorite. It was my day, and he invited me, but he took her. If she was going to steal him away from me in broad daylight, she could just have him. But boy, would they both be sorry.

I'd have to hurry if I didn't want them to catch me. One by one, I carried three dresser drawers from my house over to hers. Two of them were full of Verlan's socks, jeans, underclothes, and belts. The third contained all sorts of his other things, including pens and pencils, erasers, writing paper, books, and various important documents. I dumped all of it onto Lucy's bed and hurried back for Verlan's shirts, coats, and sweaters. Holding these by their hangers, I swung them high and landed them on top of his other stuff. Then I grabbed a wooden crate by Lucy's door, ran back to my house, and filled it with Verlan's shoes, slippers, and rubber watering boots. I piled three old caps and his straw hat on top and lugged the crate back over to Lucy's. Some things dribbled across her floor as I dumped the contents of the crate on her bed along with everything else. She knew darn well it wasn't her day.

I ignored Verlan when he came in. I wasn't even going to look at him, but he pulled me around to face him and said, "Irene, how can you be so mean? You've got Lucy crying over there! You know she doesn't have room in her small house for all my things."

I started to cry. "Well, let her make room! If you're going to give her my time, I'll give her your other things, too. She can just keep them. In fact, she can keep you!" I sobbed.

"Honey, don't be so mad. She followed me out to the john and asked what I was doing."

"You should have told her you were taking a dump!" I interrupted. "How can she be so stupid?"

He tried not to laugh. "Really, honey, I told her I was going out to the wheat field, and she begged to go with me. If I'd refused her, she would have felt bad for a week. But I know you; you blow up, and then it's all over in five minutes. I decided I'd rather deal with you and save myself from a week's worth of trouble. I'll take you next time. I promise."

That was Verlan all over. At least he always felt as comfortable telling me what he was really thinking (selfish as it might be) as I felt telling him. Still, I rejected his hugs. He finally left because he could see I wasn't going to give in.

All sorts of nasty thoughts ran through my mind about Lucy when I saw her a few minutes later at her kitchen door. When she picked up the wooden crate, supposedly to start packing away some of Verlan's stuff, he tried to comfort her by giving her a big kiss. Boy, did the Devil ever whip out his pitchfork and stab me with it when I saw that! I hollered out, "How do you like kissing her big nose?" Lucy went into the house crying, and I backed off, knowing I was in big trouble . . . again.

Two nights later, as was his practice on the evenings he spent elsewhere, Verlan came by to tell me good night. It was his turn to sleep with Lucy. How I hated those damned turns. I wanted to sleep with Verlan when I wanted to, not just when it was my night. We were on the bed kissing, and my body forgot that it wasn't my night. It almost went wild. Verlan tried to leave, saying as he pulled away, "I'd really love to stay here tonight, but I can't."

"You could if you really loved me," I challenged.

"I do love you, but I've got to do what's right. Do you think it would be fair if I stayed at Lucy's all the time? What would you think then?"

I tried pulling him back onto the bed. "If you really love me, prove it!"

"I do love you, but I can't ruin Lucy's night!"

"I want you to stay here when I want you to. Besides, my body doesn't know a damn thing about turns!"

He left in a huff. He was tired of my ungodly innuendos. I knew I'd pushed him farther than I should have, but I just couldn't help it. Now I might as well push him a little farther.

I peered out the window, and as soon as Verlan closed Lucy's old wooden door, I rushed outside and grabbed a rock as big as a grapefruit from the flower garden next to my house. I ran halfway to Lucy's and heaved that rock for all it was worth against her kitchen door. I knew I should skedaddle then, but my anger made time for one more assault. I flung a second rock good and hard, bouncing it off her door, and then I ran for dear life. Safe inside my own house, I locked the door behind me and fell across my bed in tears.

A minute or two later, Verlan almost knocked my door in with his violent banging. "Open this door," he ordered.

I made no response.

"You'll be sorry!" he threatened.

I didn't answer.

"You've gone too far! I can't believe you'd treat Lucy like this! Open up."

My heart was pounding so loud, I was afraid he could hear it. Other than that, I didn't make a peep.

"Okay, you'll be sorry."

Still, I didn't budge. I listened until I heard Lucy's door open and close again. I would just have to make up with him the next day, after he'd calmed down some. It would be my turn to feed him anyway.

But the next day, Verlan didn't come for breakfast like he was supposed to. I watched him working in the fields. At lunchtime, I noticed that he ate at Charlotte's. He passed my place several times throughout the day, but he never stopped in to see me. At dusk, he milked the cows. I knew he'd head over after that to tell Lucy good night before he went to spend the night with Charlotte. He hadn't even told *me* good morning yet. I stood looking out my screen door, hoping that the next time he passed by, we could reconcile. After all, the Bible said not to let the sun go down upon your wrath. I'd suffered enough that day; I didn't want to go on suffering the next. I watched Verlan

approaching, and when he didn't stop, I stepped out in front of him.
"Hey, can't you even say hello?" I asked.

"Do you want me to?" Seeing he was still mad, I didn't know if I
wanted him to or not. "Suit yourself, but you can come in if you want
to," I said. He followed me in, but he didn't touch me. I was actually
relieved. Although he'd never more than raised his voice to scold me,
I'd been a little scared he might hit me on this particular occasion.

"You ruined Lucy's night. She feels terrible. Why would you ever
treat her like that?"

I remained silent.

"I've got to put a stop to this kind of mischief," he said, repri-
mandling me more severely than usual. "You have to learn to respect
Lucy's rights. I'm not sleeping with you for three of your nights. They'll
be given to Lucy." He'd pulled out the big stick—the last resort for
polygamous husbands desperate to keep their plural wives in check.

"That's not fair!" I shouted. "That's nine nights. I only threw two
rocks!"

"I don't care. I already told Lucy, and that's how it's going to be."
And off he went.

Verlan was sincerely shocked and disappointed that a girl like me,
who'd been raised in a staunch, fourth-generation polygamous family, would behave in a manner so counter to that whole way of life. I
was too angry to bother about such expectations.

I started thinking Charlotte might wish I would throw a few rocks
at her house so she could get some extra nights, too. Other devilish
thoughts crowded out my higher reasoning as I screamed and kicked
the bed. Maybe I shouldn't have done what I did; that was true. But if
I ever did it again, I'd be sure to do it better. I'd rock that Lucy right
to sleep. Forever.

ONE DAY BETWEEN THE rock-throwing incident and the birth of
my third child, I was out pinning laundry on the clothesline, thinking
some of my favorite thoughts—how much I hated Lucy for stealing
Verlan's attention from me and for giving him a son before I did. My

delicious jealousy toward her became such second nature to me, I hardly even felt guilty about it anymore. When I realized that, I knew things had to change. It wasn't for Verlan's sake or Lucy's sake or even God's sake but for my own that I finally chose not to dwell on my resentment of her for a single minute longer. When that dark filter finally fell from my eyes, I discovered a sister wife who was gentle and compassionate and ready to be my friend. She always had been.

CHAPTER EIGHTEEN

D ue to Verlan's hard work, the ranch was now fairly productive. (The United Order between the LeBaron brothers went by the wayside, because none of the others had Verlan's stamina or strong work ethic.) In our fields, we grew tomatoes, beans, green chilies, alfalfa, and occasionally even cotton. With our husband's permission, we picked tomatoes and green chilies from his field, and we were allowed to sell a few kilos to our friends and neighbors. For the first time in my marriage, I had a little spending money. Since I now had another baby very much on the way, I saved up every *centavo,* determined to buy a crib. I took my savings to the mercantile in El Valle and secured one on a layaway plan. I chose a blue crib, hoping for a boy this time. As soon as I possibly could, I paid off the balance and brought the crib home. In a matter of a few weeks, I also made a down payment on a dresser. Actually getting to purchase the things I needed was a new experience. I felt so blessed.

VERLAN DESPERATELY NEEDED my help to get a shipment of tomatoes off to Ciudad Juárez. The truck would arrive for the shipment in three days, so we had to rush like mad to sort and pack them. While I worked, I sat on a rough wooden crate with nothing to shield me from the hot July sun. My baby was due in a week, and my huge tummy interfered with the strenuous job I was doing. I worked with

Verlan and some hired men for twelve to fourteen hours a day. Long after dark on the third day, the truck finally left with its full load.

That night, I flopped into bed, exhausted, but my aching back made sleep impossible. I turned from side to side, with no relief. Then, quite oddly I thought, the pain began to come and go. At 1 A.M., it hurt so bad, I couldn't take it any longer. Although it wasn't right for me to bother my husband when he was with another wife (unless it was some great emergency), I figured I felt worse than I could ever make Charlotte feel just by intruding on her rights. So I slipped on my shoes and walked the twenty feet over to her house to get Verlan.

I knocked tentatively on their bedroom window. "Verlan," I called out.

"What's the matter?" he asked groggily.

"Please come and help me. My back is killing me!"

I'd barely gotten back to my house when Verlan and Charlotte came in all excited. "Well, sis, be thankful," she said. "It'll soon be over."

"I'm not in labor, Charlotte. It's only a backache."

"That's what you think." She put a few dry corncobs in the stove and poured some coal oil over them to start the fire. Adding a few small chips of wood, she had the water boiling in practically no time. "What do you have to tie the baby's cord with?" she asked as she started prepping my bed.

"We'll have to use a string out of a flour sack. There's a clean sack in that top drawer," I said. I figured I might as well go along with them in case they knew what they were talking about.

Charlotte pulled the string free from the sack and handed it to Verlan, with orders. "Stand back and let's make it stronger. You twist in one direction, and I'll twist in the other. That's enough, now hand your end to me so we can double it, and then we'll do it again." The string wound together perfectly. She placed it in a saucer, pouring alcohol on it.

I asked her to get my pillowcase from the closet. It was full of white rags I'd sterilized in the oven to be used during my delivery. Then I placed a clean set of used baby clothes and a receiving blanket on the chair beside the bed.

Feeling rather silly about all these preparations, I voiced my opinion one more time. "You're all excited over nothing. I'm sure I've just thrown my back out from all that work packing tomatoes. I ought to know whether I'm in labor or not. With both Leah and Donna, it was just one solid, excruciating pain that never let up."

"No, honey, this is it," Verlan assured me as he rushed out to get his brother, Alma. He asked Alma to drive up to Spencerville and bring Aunt Sylvia back as fast as he could. Verlan and Charlotte then did their best to comfort me, taking turns rubbing my back and joking around until the midwife arrived at 5 A.M. She proceeded to examine me.

"I apologize for all the inconvenience, Aunt Sylvia. I don't think I'm really in labor," I said.

"Oh, yes you are! You're dilating alright, and this should all be over in a few hours."

That settled it; I was in labor. More immediately, though, I was famished. I'd been too tired to eat supper. So, while Charlotte went next door to check on her three kids, I sent Verlan to the kitchen to get me something to eat. He returned with half a cantaloupe with a spoon protruding from its center. Before he could hand it to me, I bore down with a hard labor pain. From his expression, I could tell he thought I was really suffering. He started to put the cantaloupe on the nightstand out of the way, but the pain subsided, so I relaxed and said, "It's okay, Verlan, hand it to me. I want to eat a bite before another pain comes."

He sat down on the chair next to me, and I started to eat. When another pain hit, I quickly gave it back to him. Just then Charlotte walked in with Lucy, whom I was glad to see despite my pain, since I knew she'd feel bad if we left her out. Seeing Verlan sitting there by me with the cantaloupe in his hands, Charlotte lit into him. "I don't believe this! How can you sit there eating while Irene's suffering? You should be ashamed of yourself."

She and Lucy wondered why Verlan and I burst out laughing. He handed it back to me, shaking his head. "I haven't had a bite," he said to Charlotte. "Honestly, it's hers."

She turned to me. "You mean you're actually eating during labor?"

"You know me; I'd have to be dead not to eat when I'm hungry!"

Aunt Sylvia checked me again and shook her head. "Considering how hard your pains are, you're still not making much progress."

I was getting exasperated. I got off the bed and paced the floor. Bending over the dresser for support, I'd brace myself for each pain. I'd rub my protruding stomach and aching back. Then I'd breathe deeply and blow the air out through pursed lips. Eventually, the unbearable pains forced me to lie down again.

At eight o'clock, Aunt Sylvia motioned for Verlan to follow her outside for a private conference. In a few minutes, I heard Alma's truck drive away. Naturally, I got upset, wondering what was wrong. What were they keeping from me?

When they returned, I demanded angrily, "What's going on?"

"Don't worry," Verlan tried calming me. "We've decided to send for Dr. Ramirez so you won't have to keep suffering."

That did it. After what happened with Leah, I wasn't having that man look at me ever again. Hoping to force my body into compliance, I jumped off the bed, and as I did, my water broke.

Verlan and Charlotte helped me back onto the bed. Lucy held the pan of hot Lysol water for her mother to disinfect her hands. When Sylvia was finished, Lucy put the pan down and said, "Alright Irene, this is it!"

With Lucy on one side and Charlotte on the other, I grabbed their hands and bore down while Verlan urged me on. When he saw the baby's head appearing, he said, "Come on, Irene. It'll all come out all right."

"That's what I'm afraid of!" I yelled back. But in the next moment, the violent pain became too excruciating for joking. "I can't. I can't!" I screamed.

Verlan tried to calm me. "Irene, you've got to think positive."

Hell, what did he know about it? I felt like swatting him. I gritted my teeth, looked right at him, and said, "I *positively think I can't!*" But I knew it was up to me now. I pushed one more time . . . and then, thank God, it was all over.

"It's a boy! It's a boy!" Verlan exclaimed. "He's born on our anniversary! Don't ever say I didn't give you a present." He kissed me gratefully.

André was a darling baby. His reddish blond hair was adorable. It felt like peach fuzz.

As thrilled as Verlan was, he was a bit perturbed when Alma showed up with the doctor. He wished he'd waited a few more minutes before sending for him. All the money we had to pay Dr. Ramirez we could have used to feed the kids.

Verlan now had eight children. Charlotte's baby, Mark, was born six weeks before André. And Lucy was pregnant again; that would soon make nine.

ONE MORNING, AROUND 3 A.M, I awoke to Verlan's hired hand, Pancho Ponce, shouting for help. My Spanish still wasn't too good, but I caught enough of what he said to surmise his wife, Cuca, was in labor. He kept saying excitedly, "Pronto, Irene! *Ándale,* pronto!" In my broken Spanish, I tried to make excuses, explaining I wasn't qualified to deliver his wife's baby.

I rushed him over to Lucy, who knew Spanish, so she could tell him I couldn't do it. After they talked a moment, Lucy told me Cuca's labor pains were already less than five minutes apart. There was no car available to rush her to Dr. Ramirez in El Valle. Pancho was begging me, as a friend, to please get into his wooden wagon right now and go with him before Cuca had the baby all by herself.

I grabbed a few clean white rags, some Lysol, and a couple of aspirin. Lucy assured me I could do it and told me not to worry about my two kids, because she would tend them. I dreaded having to leave little André, because it was almost time for him to wake up and nurse. But Lucy promised to take him over to Charlotte so she could nurse him until I returned.

The team of horses raced through the darkness. We could hear Cuca's screams as the wagon approached their one-room adobe shack. Pancho whipped the horses harder to make them sprint right up to the door. Then he jumped out and helped me down. Offering a quick prayer, I followed him into the house.

Cuca's suffering during delivery was pretty obvious, but nobody would ever know the turmoil I endured. What if something went wrong? Would I be blamed? I kept my composure only because I had to look every bit the part of the calm, knowledgeable midwife Cuca thought I was. I'd had an incompetent midwife myself, and it was nothing I meant to subject anyone else to (even if it was true of me at the time). Thank God, it came out all right for Cuca and me.

I was still just eighteen. This was the first of about a dozen babies I was able to help bring squalling into the world.

CHAPTER NINETEEN

By the time I was twenty, I knew all the religion in the world wasn't going to transform me into celestial material. No matter how hard I worked toward perfection, all the rules about self-sacrifice and submissiveness just weren't purifying me. I was worn out and discouraged. Though I knew I'd risk Hell for even considering it, I did the unheard of. I asked for a divorce.

Verlan was distraught. "I thought we'd made covenants to endure to the end."

"I know, and I have! It's just that my end comes every other weekend!"

Verlan actually wept because he feared so for my soul. Knowing my main grievance was still of a physical nature, he didn't feel God would accept my alleged grounds for divorce.

"I've been good to you. I've been more than fair. I love you more than life itself!" he said as his tears flowed. "I feel you don't have any room for complaints. Even if it's true that I've only made love to you seven times, that's no reason at all for you to leave me. Irene, please pray about this before you make the biggest mistake of your life. Please reconsider."

"I'm twenty years old," I noted. "Life is passing me by! I want to be loved. I don't feel we've even had a marriage. We haven't had time together to build up a relationship."

He looked at me pleadingly. "You love me, Irene. I know you do. Please don't do this to me. Please!"

"Don't take it so hard, Verlan. I do love you, and we'll always be friends. But can't you understand? I'm not being fulfilled. I don't want this kind of life anymore."

Verlan went on a five-day spiritual fast. He drank nothing but water, hoping to receive divine guidance concerning my rebellious spirit. He figured God was just testing him, but when I demanded he take me back home to my mother, he fell apart. "Irene, this law of purity is God's law. I never made the rules. God did. I'm just trying to do his will."

I cut in. "Show me in black and white where God said it."

"Well, his servants said it, and that's the same thing. I really don't know where I can scripturally prove it to you, but I know my father taught and lived the law."

Living "the law" was like torture to me. It seemed to be designed for cruelty or punishment. Completely unnatural, it went beyond self-sacrifice to the point of totally rejecting self. One time each month, during the very few months I was not pregnant or nursing, Verlan and I would have sexual relations. The rest of the time, I either had to sleep next to my husband without touching him or suffer alone, believing he was having sex next door with Lucy or Charlotte. These suspicions may have been as off base as theirs were if they were having them about Verlan and me, but I was still plagued by my conjectures. I often thought I would lose my mind.

Finally, after endless arguments, Verlan began to soften just a little. We would ramp up our sex life on one condition. "I know you can't find it, but if the scriptures allow sex for any purpose other than procreation, I'll accept it," he said.

I fervently searched through everything I could get my hands on. Then I found it. Parley P. Pratt, an early apostle of the Mormon Church, wrote an important book titled *A Key to the Science of Theology.* And lo and behold, there before my eyes was a chapter on "The Union of the Sexes." I marveled that a servant of God would stretch his mind so far. He listed not one, but five different reasons for which God allowed sexual intimacy.

I was jubilant. I studied it carefully to be sure I'd found irrefutable proof that God was not as mean as Verlan thought he was. Ha, ha. Now, after four years, we could finally get to the bottom of things. Verlan would have to accept this. An apostle had taught it, and it would be right there in black and white before Verlan's very eyes. I hid the book behind my back as I raced into the field where Verlan was bailing hay. "Verlan, do you believe that Parley P. Pratt was a man of God?" I began.

He nodded.

"Would you take his word on sex?"

Verlan laughed. "I will if you just take it for what it says and not try to impose your interpretation on it."

I confidently read to him that sex was, number 1, for mutual love and affection. "See," I said, "that's what I want!" Number 2, sex is for procreation. "I'll have all the kids you want." Number 3, sex is for times of sadness and sorrow. "That's every other day for me!" I hesitated. I knew I didn't have to read any further, because I'd qualified in all three of the first three departments.

"Let me see that," he said, grabbing the book out of my hands. He read it over and over. "I'll still have to study and pray about this." As good as his word, Verlan spent days in the mountains fasting and praying about it.

Despite having been programmed for twenty-seven years to believe God forbids sex except to procreate, Verlan finally agreed to take a step back from his legalism. "To keep our marriage intact and to keep you happy, I'll give in," he said. "But don't get too many big ideas and get carried away."

On his next night at my house, Verlan said he still felt we were taking the lower road and possibly even offending God by giving in on this matter. He wanted it plainly understood, furthermore, that if God ever got on our case about it, I'd have to tell God it was all my fault. So, after four years of marriage and just a handful of purely procreative sexual encounters, we at last had a night of sex for its own sake—the sake of enjoyment.

· · ·

IT HAD BEEN about a year since Verlan's brother Joel proclaimed himself the long-awaited LeBaron prophet, called The One Mighty and Strong, who would initiate the great religious work in Mexico their father foretold. Alma, Ervil, and Floren accepted him as that prophet, but Verlan remained skeptical for some time. During that year, Joel went on a pilgrimage throughout the western United States, teaching that Jesus would soon return to earth and destroy America. Everyone who wanted to save himself should flee to Mexico and take up with Joel and his new church, The Church of the Firstborn of the Fullness of Times. A few families were actually showing up. The LeBaron ranch became the LeBaron colony. Its official Spanish name became Colonia LeBaron.

In the meantime, Verlan began working for his cousin's painting business in Nevada. He'd be gone for two or three months, then come home and spend a little time with us before heading back north to his job. His affection and attention became ever rarer and more treasured by his wives.

Verlan spent some extra time at the colony trying to get the farm back into shape. We hated to spend our money, but our tractor had broken down, so Verlan hired our neighbor, Grant, to come plow our fields, and I was asked to feed him.

One morning, it was especially hot and windy. Poor Grant worked on in the inclement weather. I'd been extra busy all morning, as it was my turn to herd the cows in and out of the green alfalfa field so they wouldn't bloat. I also had to feed two other hired hands, plus care for my little kids. I was so busy, I hardly had time to think.

I ran into Grant walking toward my house. I was shocked to see his red hair so full of dust. On the other hand, his fair complexion was a bright red, and his lips, too, were blistered and swollen from the relentless sun. "Excuse me," he said, "is there any place where I can lay down and rest for a few minutes? I've got a terrible head-ache."

"Sure," I said. "Just go on in and lie on my bed and make yourself at home. I'll call you when lunch is ready."

I continued to rush around from one thing to another. I had to feed the kids early, before the men came in to eat lunch. My baby wasn't feeling well. I packed him in one arm and bounced him while I worked. He finally went to sleep. I fed Donna and then put them in their room for a nap. It would still be a while before the men came for lunch.

I went into my bedroom to get something. To my pleasant surprise, there was Verlan, lying facedown on the bed. I wasn't going to waste any time. We hadn't made love for days. Here was a perfect chance.

I quickly locked the bedroom door, kicked my panties under the bed, and threw myself down beside him, slapping him on the butt and running my fingers through his hair. "Hey, lover, wake up!" I said in my sexy voice.

To my utter shock, a big, sunburned face that wasn't Verlan's looked up at me. "Huh?" Grant said.

It scared me so bad, I started to cry. Embarrassed and bare-assed, I flew out of the room so fast, I almost went through the locked door.

Verlan was just coming into my kitchen. Seeing me straightening my skirt and noticing my horror and streaming tears, he exclaimed, "What's the matter?"

"Oh, I could absolutely die! I'm so embarrassed."

"What's wrong?"

"Oh, Verlan, I just made the biggest mistake of my life."

"Well, what is it?"

"You have on the same color shirt as Grant has on. It looked like you on my bed. I snuck in there and thought I'd"—I covered my face—"make love to you."

"You didn't." He shook his head in disbelief. "I wonder if marrying you so young has been to my advantage. I don't think I'll ever train you right!"

I quickly set the table, putting the hot food out, ready to serve. I told Verlan he'd have to face the men. I didn't want anybody to see me, so I got lost.

Later Verlan demanded, "As soon as you get the chance, make sure you apologize to Grant."

I rehearsed apologies over and over in my mind. Nothing I came up with sounded right, so I never did apologize.

IN MAY OF 1957, I dropped by Lucy's house to ask her to keep an eye on my ten-month-old baby, André, while I went to see my girl-friend Betty Tippetts. Betty and her husband, Harold, were the first family to move down from Salt Lake City and join Joel's church. "André's on my bed and should sleep soundly for at least an hour," I told Lucy.

"He'll be just fine," Lucy said. "Don't worry."

I took two-and-a-half-year-old Donna, and we cut through the corner of our lot (we'd divided up the upper fourth of the ranch to make room for settlers). I crawled through the fence first and then held the barbed wire up so Donna could duck under it. We walked on about a half block to Betty's new cinderblock house—the first home in Colonia LeBaron that wasn't adobe.

Betty and I became inseparable. We'd felt a deep kinship from the first time we'd met. She was a very giving person and an accomplished seamstress. I'll never forget the six beautiful dresses she gave me within a few days of her arrival. Our measurements were the same, except she was a couple of inches taller. She'd made all the dresses herself, and they were gorgeous. I'd never had anything so nice, even back in Utah before I got married.

And she gave me more than just dresses. We always shared whatever we could—garden produce, canned fruit, and so forth. The bond between us was more than friendship; we felt like real sisters. And, since both of our husbands now worked in the States, we got to spend many wonderful times together.

On this particular day, Betty and I settled down to make fudge. "Too bad we're not rich enough to afford nuts," she said regretfully. I watched as she poured the fudge onto a buttered plate. "Sit down," she said. "Take the load off your feet. I don't see how you can be on them so much when you're four months pregnant."

We didn't wait any longer than we had to before cutting the candy.

I was on my third piece when Lucy walked in the door. She assured me André was fast asleep; she peeked in to make sure he was snoozing on the bed before she decided to join us.

Betty shoved the plate of fudge toward Lucy. "You better dive in if you want your fair share."

After about fifteen minutes, right in the middle of Betty's sentence, I jumped up screaming, "It's André. Something is wrong with André!" I dashed out the door, racing in terror down the dusty road, tearing my dress as I crossed the barbed-wire fence.

Lucy and Betty jogged along behind me with Donna, trying to calm me with their shouts. "He's okay, Irene. He's okay!"

I dashed past the corner of Lucy's house, certain I could hear frantic baby screams. Realizing instantly that André was in the irrigation ditch, I almost stumbled as I ran toward the ditch. The swift current was pulling him away about thirty yards in front of me. I raced along the bank, watching him appear, then disappear in the cold water.

I jumped in, shoes and all, trying to grab him, but I missed as the current pulled him a few feet farther away. Again I lunged forward, and with every ounce of my strength I snatched his near-lifeless body out of the threatening water. I had no time to cry, thinking only of reviving him. He spit and sputtered as I laid him over my arm and pounded frantically on his back. His pudgy little body was blue from the cold water and lack of oxygen. I put his head down and shook him. He began vomiting up water, then hoarsely gasped for breath.

Betty took him from my arms, and Lucy supported my trembling body while we thanked God for sparing his life. Sobbing with relief, I could hear the squish from the water in my shoes as we made our way to the house. Betty helped me into bed. I was chilled and soon went into shock.

I vaguely remember wondering how I was ever going to handle eternity. In Heaven, I was supposed to have billions of kids to populate future worlds. Yet here on Earth, I could hardly cope with two.

CHAPTER TWENTY

On October 4, 1958, my fourth child was born—
a baby boy. I named him Steven. He was a lovely
towhead baby. He should have made my life
complete, but inside, I felt like I was dying. I was twenty-one, and I
wanted more of a life than just work, work, work. I wanted things
beyond the barest of necessities. Most of all, I yearned constantly to
have a man of my own. I pled with God to forgive me and take away
my selfish desires, but day after day they persisted.

Cooking, scrubbing on the washboard, changing diapers, working in the fields—these things might have been tolerable if I'd ever
had any sort of recreation to break up the wearying monotony of it
all. Without a radio or record player, I had no music to brighten up
the long, tedious days. Nor did I have a dime to spare on any sort of
hobby. And my social world did not extend beyond Spencerville.
The few times in four years we had visitors from the States had only
been enough to whet my appetite for company. Like lots of American
girls my age, I thought it might be exciting to go to school, get a job,
and be independent.

Verlan was good to me when he was home, but he was off working in the States a great deal, usually for three months at a time. And
when he was around, I still only got a third of him. I wanted romance
and some passion in my life I knew he'd never be able to give me.
Frankly, although I loved Verlan, I'd never been in love with him—
not the way I'd been in love with Glen. That one thing alone might

have crippled any marriage, especially one cursed with our kind of poverty. But of course, the poverty resulted from the polygamy, and the polygamy added immeasurably to my heartache and oppression. I still yearned for Glen, but I thought I could even have been satisfied with Verlan if I could only have had him all to myself.

God's plan just didn't seem to be the best one for me. I'd been promised that submission to his rules would be its own reward, that it would bring me a little joy, even in the here and now. But in reality, I was joyless, merely existing. My longing to be loved became an obsession.

IN NOVEMBER, when Steven was six weeks old, Verlan employed a handsome, twenty-three-year-old Mexican as a hired hand. Oreliano was the man's name. He slept away from the house in a wooden shed by my fruit room. Verlan arranged for me to wash his clothes and feed him his three meals a day. My husband was such an earnest and devout man, he never supposed any of his wives could be tempted into flagrant sin.

Oreliano was different from any man I'd ever met. Not once did he allow me to carry the heavy, five-gallon buckets of water into the kitchen from the well. In the evenings, when I went to the woodpile to fill my arms with firewood, Oreliano would rush over and grab the load himself, insisting that this was not a chore for women. After supper, he'd play with the kids. More often than not, when the new baby cried, Oreliano would be the one to bounce him. And when we finished eating, he would automatically clear up the table because he saw I was overworked.

I usually retired early on chilly fall nights, but Oreliano soon changed my habit. He brought in a set of dominos, inviting me to play with him.

Soon, I found myself prettying up and waiting for him to appear for his evening meals. We'd hurry with the supper dishes, me washing and him drying, and then the dominos came out. It became our evening ritual. Often, my kerosene lamp burned into the late-night hours, sometimes past midnight.

Oreliano thought me the most organized person on Earth. And he clearly loved my cooking and my company. For my part, I basked in his approval and devotion. One day I realized I was actually content.

One night, Oreliano and I went to make sure the pasture gate was locked so the cows wouldn't wander into the alfalfa and bloat. We walked back under a full moon; I could see quite well the way Oreliano's dark eyes flashed. Grabbing me and imprisoning me in his arms, he surprised me with passionate, forbidden kisses.

I say I was surprised, but I'd been waiting for this night with both thrill and trepidation. For over a month, I'd been pleading with God to douse my own raging desire for Oreliano. Unless God intervened, I knew I would succumb to him when the time came. Well, the time came, and God had not intervened.

It felt so exhilarating being with Oreliano. He was incredibly sensual. The way his tongue explored my mouth when he kissed me was an entirely new sensation for me. No one had ever done that before. I adored it. At the same time, I was torn by loyalty to Verlan. When I was with Oreliano, even when I wasn't with him but was busy thinking about him, guilt wracked my soul.

We spent a week of secret bliss. My evenings in his arms were heaven, but the nights of sleepless guilt afterward were pure hell. Hoping God might understand, I searched the scriptures for solace, but I found only condemnation. This one in particular alarmed me: "But if one or either of the ten virgins, after she is espoused, shall be with another man, she has committed adultery, and shall be destroyed" (Doctrine and Covenants, 132:63). I'd heard that in some polygamist clans, especially in earlier times, this law was taken very seriously; a husband was duty-bound to destroy an adulterous wife. I didn't believe God would destroy me (since, for one thing, we hadn't actually committed adultery), but I wondered what Verlan would do if he found out how far I'd gone. I was plenty nervous.

One evening, Oreliano begged me to run away with him, to take the kids and start a new life with him somewhere far away. More fervently, he pled for me to let him make love to me. He said I should give in so we could be one. Then together, we would fight whatever problems we'd have to face.

I resisted, but I was sick and disgusted with myself because in my heart, I wanted to comply. Only the threat of destruction and the promise of a fiery Hell restrained me. I cried a torrent of tears when I refused his hot advances. That night, as I slept alone still wanting Oreliano, I sent fervent petitions to Heaven. What should I do? Now that he'd declared such serious intentions, I couldn't play games with him anymore. I would not break another man's heart the way I'd broken Glen's.

If I left with Oreliano, not only would I face eternal destruction, but Verlan would demand that I forfeit my children. (Plural wives were free to leave any time they wanted, but if they left, they went alone, with the clothes on their backs. That was another law of our fundamentalist faith. Polygamous husbands could always fall back on it to help control their disgruntled wives.) If I didn't leave, my life would go on as it had, with the twin plagues of polygamy and poverty slowly and steadily breaking my spirit.

Late Sunday evening after supper and after the kids were asleep, Oreliano went out and sat down on my back step. Seeing no lights on at Charlotte's or Lucy's, I quietly opened my screen door and sat beside him. He put his arms around me and pulled me close as I placed my head on his shoulder.

Speaking to me in Spanish, he said, "Irene, I'm poor, but I can give you lots more than you have right now. I know how you feel, but you must take the risk with me, or you'll never be happy. Don't feel so bad. It's not as though Verlan is losing all he has. He'll still have two other wives."

For over an hour, I quietly wept in his arms as he consoled and tempted me. "Tomorrow let's tell Verlan how we feel. I'll stand by you. Let's tell him the truth and face the consequences. No matter what he says, we'll take the children with us. Don't worry about that. I can't offer you the world, Irene, but I beg of you to say yes, and I'll fight like hell for you! I love you too much to see you with another man. If you won't go with me, I'll have to leave here without you. I mean it. It will hurt too much to stay." We thought only the moon was watching as he passionately kissed me good night.

Verlan had returned from the States a couple of days before, and the next morning it was my turn to serve him breakfast. He took his usual place across from Oreliano. Insisting on complete silence, he then blessed the food. I paid no attention to what he said. I wanted to hide from God. I imagined him watching me sit there, vacillating between the two men I loved. Couldn't God see my dilemma? One man had my promises; the other had my heart.

Later, when I was returning from the well with two large pails of water, I noticed my neighbor, Mauro, walking through the fields out to where Verlan and Oreliano were working. As I entered the house, a bolt of fear went through me. Setting the buckets on the counter, I peered out the window and saw Mauro and Verlan crouched down with their heads together. Mauro pointed his finger across the field at Oreliano, and I knew. He was tattling on me.

I'd just finished nursing Steven, and I laid him on my bed for a nap next to my other sleeping children. Without warning, Verlan burst into the house with Oreliano right behind him. The anguish on Oreliano's face told me we were in deep trouble.

Verlan looked me dead in the eye. He spoke to me in Spanish for Oreliano's benefit. "Tell me the truth." He shoved Oreliano toward me accusingly. "Did you kiss him?"

I may have been a traitor, but I couldn't lie to him. "Yes, I did," I said defiantly. "But that's all we did."

He could see the betrayal in my eyes. "Why the hell did you do it?" I stood in silent shame as Oreliano waited for me to defend him. "Answer me. Now!" Verlan thundered.

I brushed my fear aside. Maybe if I told the truth, Verlan would throw me out. "I did it because I love him!" I declared.

When Oreliano started to explain, Verlan shoved him angrily, pushing him out the door, commanding him to go pack his belongings. He'd pay him, but he wanted him on the bus that night. He was to stay away from me and never enter any of Verlan's homes again. Perhaps wanting to cool off before he did something he'd regret, Verlan then stormed back out to the field.

Oreliano reluctantly obeyed Verlan, but I didn't. While he was packing, I went and knocked on the door of his sleeping quarters. He was shocked to find me there. He seemed afraid, but he let me in and enveloped me in his arms. Dismayed, he said, "Please, Irene, come with me now. Here's your chance for freedom."

"I can't," I sobbed. "I'm afraid I'd crack up from guilt. You don't understand our religion. I'd go to Hell for sure if I gave everything up for a Catholic." I pulled away before he could kiss me again. I handed him my leather-tooled wallet as a good-bye gift. He opened it and saw my recent photo inside. "Look at me once in awhile," I said, opening the door to leave. "Please don't forget me."

"I don't intend to forget you! I'll get a job somewhere. I'll send for you."

Crying, I turned my back. "It'll never work out, Oreliano. My religion has to come first."

He whirled me around to face him again. "I love you, don't you understand?" he said desperately. "I'll write to you. We'll keep in touch. I know in a few days you'll change your mind." Hungrily, he threw me against the wooden wall and pinned his body firmly against mine. I felt his hardness as his burning kisses aroused my own yearnings. He almost brought me to the point of surrender, but terror stopped me. I had never come so close to giving in. I felt I was teetering on the brink of Hell.

Fearing what Verlan would do if he found us there in open defiance, I jerked away. "Be sure to answer my letters," he called softly as I turned to go. "I'll never give you up, Irene."

I hurried back to the house before Verlan could discover I'd disobeyed him yet again. Wanting so badly to change my mind, to pack up my children and flee with Oreliano, I settled for a last peek at him through my window as Verlan ferried him away. He told me later that he bought Oreliano a one-way ticket to Chihuahua and made sure he got on the bus.

Alone again, I suffered a dozen conflicting emotions. I tried to block it all from my mind to erase the temptation. The next minute, I thought how thrilled I'd be to get one of Oreliano's promised letters. I vowed to obey God and Verlan better than I ever had before, to work extra hard for that joy and peace I'd been told would come. On the other hand, maybe I could still find a way to justify my love for Oreliano and eventually get up the courage to go to him. I acted on none of this.

It took six months for Verlan to relinquish his hurt. Except on one occasion months after our flirtation, Verlan never spoke Oreliano's name to me again. In a moment of anger, trying to hurt me as I'd hurt him, Verlan confessed to me that he'd "intercepted," and "read with disgust," then "destroyed" three of Oreliano's "adulterous letters."

If I was to have any hope at all of being satisfied with my husband, or at least of sticking it out with him, I was going to have to quit comparing him to other men. This meant closing my mind and heart to something I'd long hidden there and I'd often gone back to for confidence and escape—Glen. My love for Glen, his love for me, the way we'd been together—these were things Verlan and I would never have in the same way. I had to finally let them go. Six years after I last saw him, I said good-bye to Glen for good.

CHAPTER TWENTY-ONE

Steven was now ten months old, and I'd been enjoying a glorious, unexpected hiatus from my procreative duties. I couldn't explain it, except that Verlan had been working away from home a lot. I just figured God really did know how much we could stand at any one time, and I was extremely grateful.

Still, my skirt had been fitting a little tighter, so I put myself on a diet. I was already behind my opposition on this score. Lucy was a size ten, Charlotte was a twelve, and I was a fourteen. I couldn't risk letting myself get fat.

I was relaxing on my bed one evening, talking to Verlan, when all at once I felt that old familiar flutter in my tummy. I didn't want it to be true, but I knew there was no other reason to have butterflies in my stomach. I told Verlan I thought I might be pregnant again. "I'd better go to Casas tomorrow for a checkup."

"You'll just feel silly," he said, getting up to go. "I think all you felt was gas."

Since I had been delivering babies myself, my attitude toward doctors' examinations had drastically changed. Being more at ease now, I went quite voluntarily to see Dr. Hatch. He asked what he could do for me this time.

"I've gained a little weight. I wonder if it's possible that I could be pregnant."

"When was your last period?" he asked, preparing the examination table.

"I quit nursing five months ago. I haven't had one since my baby was born."

"Get up on the table." He felt around my pelvic bones, pushing hard and kneading my stomach. "I'd say you're about four months along," he announced, helping me down.

Darn. "Then why don't I have morning sickness?" I asked.

"Oh, sometimes you do, and other times you don't. Your baby is due between Christmas and New Year's."

Verlan was elated. This would be his thirteenth child, and he was still a young man. His dream of siring countless descendents to populate his future kingdom was coming true.

I don't know if it was the pregnancy itself or my disappointment about being pregnant, but I woke up the next morning violently sick. Verlan was disgusted when I jumped up grabbing for the pot from under the bed, but missed and puked in all directions.

"Hey, cut that out. It's all in your head," he informed me.

"Well, it may have been all in my head, but it's all over the floor now," I replied.

Being pregnant again rendered my chores more difficult, but I made the best of it. I'd been cooking on a woodstove, which also provided our only heat. At night when my baby cried out for his feeding, I'd light the kerosene lamp, holding the milk in an enamel cup over the flame to warm it. The cup would get all black with soot, but that was easier than making a fire in the stove.

Since we now had windows but no real heat, on cold winter nights I'd wrap blankets around the kids' bodies, pinning them under their arms so they wouldn't kick the covers off and freeze. Every evening, I'd put my round, galvanized tub on the kitchen table to bathe the children. I would put one in at a time, scrubbing them clean. I pulled their foamy hair up into combs like roosters, crowing "Er-er-er-er-er." We loved to play and giggle through it all.

One evening, I finished bathing and rinsing my kids off with fresh water. My three-year-old nephew, Joel Johnson, stood watching the whole process. When he saw I was through with the others, he started to undress himself. So, I thought, what the heck? His mother will be glad if I bathed him, too. I stuck him in the tub and was just rinsing him off with clean, warm water when my six-year-old niece, Sylvia Esther, came in. She looked surprised. "Aunt Irene, how come you're bathing him? He's not your kid," she said defiantly.

I threw a towel around Joel's wet body and stood him on the edge of the table. As I briskly dried him, I answered, "Well, honey, he was so dirty, I had to bathe him so I'd know who to send him home to."

STEVEN WAS FIFTEEN MONTHS OLD when Brent was born on December 28, 1959. Brent was a darling child who came to us with one blue eye and one brown one. Unfortunately, I wasn't in the mood for another child. I was sad enough about it even before my postpartum blues set in. My sadness turned into an ongoing depression. Lucy faithfully came around to comfort me, rubbing my feet and back at night so I could calm down and sleep.

I began to feel a deep gratitude for Lucy. She was a quiet, gentle woman with a servant's heart. She was also humble and unassuming, the least likely of the three of us to demand her fair share. As time went by and Verlan's already thin resources were spread even thinner, this meant she became increasingly neglected.

I remember one time when Verlan was leaving town for three months, and he went around and individually explained to us how very tight things were for him at the moment. Then he asked us each what was the least we could get by on while he was away. He refused to tell any of us what the others had said, but we compared notes afterward. Charlotte had demanded $200, I'd asked for $100, and poor, compliant Lucy had offered to live off nothing at all. Verlan took her up on it. When I found that out, I shared my allowance with her.

Lucy and I spent most of our days together, tending and feeding our kids, sewing clothes, but mostly just helping each other survive. As determined as I'd been not to, I found I even loved her.

Miraculously, she'd forgiven me for all my jealous antics. Sweet and calm, she never tried to outdo any of her sister wives. She tried to teach me to relax and not fight life, but I wasn't the complacent type. I longed to stretch my wings and soar to new heights; instead, I seemed to be bogging down deeper and deeper.

During the six years of my marriage, I'd always been frank with Verlan. I spent hours baring my heart and soul to him. He knew my inner conflict, and he was deeply saddened by what he saw and heard. Using scriptures and husbandly advice, he tried to inspire me to place my hope in my eternal rewards.

"You may not be happy in this situation, but hang in there," he urged. "Be faithful, and when you die, you'll find that peace and eternal love you're aching for."

I wanted love now. "Besides, those promises don't make much sense to me," I said. "If I'm obedient and sacrifice, having all the children I possibly can, if I'm good and patient, you say I'll receive a great reward. In eternity, I can look forward to having even more sister wives, to being pregnant and popping out kids like popcorn forever and ever! You call that a reward? It just doesn't entice me at all anymore. If this is a preview of what I'll have for eternity, they can stop the show now."

"Irene, of course you're not serious. You're just upset. For heaven's sake, you don't mean all this." Verlan looked concerned. "I think all you need is a change. You can go with me on my next trip to the States."

In the next breath, he had to spoil it. He didn't want me getting any ideas about pulling out on him, so he insisted I leave all the children home except the baby. He went on to remind me that if I ever left him, the kids would belong to him.

In May, I accompanied Verlan to Vegas, as promised. From there, I took the bus to Salt Lake City by myself. I had a good, long visit with my mother for two weeks. On the way back to Mexico with friends, however, I became extremely ill. Shortly after my arrival, a burning fever sent me into delirium. Lucy cared for me and for my children as well. She coaxed me to drink herbal teas and to submit to other home remedies, but the days passed, and I grew worse. I kept calling Verlan's name over and over in my mind. Why was he always gone when I needed him?

My dear friend Betty Tippetts had been off on a trip to the States. When she and her husband, Harold, got home and saw my condition, they were so shocked, they immediately took action. Betty held the door open while Harold carried my frail body to the car. They rushed me to the hospital in Casas.

I was badly dehydrated. Worse, I needed a blood transfusion. I was in critical condition with typhoid fever. When the Mexican government sent someone around giving the typhoid vaccines, I'd refused on religious grounds. Consequently, I was the only one at the ranch who contracted it, thank God.

Dr. Hatch drew blood from a sister-in-law of mine for my first blood transfusion, but he ordered Harold to immediately find someone else who could donate more. There was no time to waste.

My neighbor Mauro offered to donate, and to the doctor's relief, his blood was a match. When it was over, Mauro leaned over and whispered to me, "This ain't only gonna save your life, it's gonna give you new life! We Mexicans are hot-blooded. Verlan better watch out!"

Still, despite three blood transfusions, my life seemed to be ebbing away. Charlotte and Lucy sent word to Verlan, who was working in Las Vegas. They told him to cancel his commitments and come home immediately. It was urgent. I was hemorrhaging from the bowels, and they didn't expect me to live.

With apprehensive strides, Verlan entered my hospital room. He was relieved to find me still alive, but so shocked at the havoc the illness inflicted on me, he sat beside my bed and wept. My once-beautiful twenty-three-year-old body was now just a bony frame.

He buried his face in my hands, sobbing. "I lived in fear all the way home, imagining that you'd already be buried (Mexican law required the dead to be buried within twenty-four hours). I promised myself I'd . . ." He hid his face, crying so hard he couldn't finish his sentence. "I'd dig you up to tell you good-bye." I had no idea he felt so deeply about me. I was racked with guilt. He did love me. So why wasn't I happy?

Somehow I fought off death. But the doctor warned Verlan it would be weeks, if not months, before I'd be completely well. He prescribed quiet, bed rest, strained foods, and above all, no stress. After I spent two weeks in the hospital, Verlan took me home, but it was too soon. Two more days of vomiting and high fever convinced them to readmit me for another week.

Dr. Hatch thought maybe I'd lost my will to live. I would need love and encouragement if I was going to pull through. Verlan did his best. When he took me home the second time, it was to a new, two-room house he bought for me a block away from both of the other wives. The kitchen in this house was plastered, and the cement floors in the two rooms were not rough like the ones I'd put up with in my other houses.

Verlan stopped briefly in the kitchen with me in his arms to show me the apartment-size gas range he bought in Casas especially for me and then installed himself. I was so weak and sick, I didn't give him all the praise he deserved, but after five years of cooking on a woodstove with no oven, deep down I was most grateful for the gift.

He allowed me a few minutes with my kids and then put me to bed so I would have complete rest. Typhoid had taken its toll on me; I had lost fifty-three pounds. I was too weak even to care for myself, much less anyone else. For the next month, Lucy took on all my responsibilities. She fed and loved my four children, keeping them at her little two-room house so I could recuperate.

Food was tasteless to me, but Lucy and Verlan coaxed me to eat. The only food I wanted was strained potatoes and carrots. I gained a pound or two, but when I tried to get up, I fainted. After that, I restricted myself to sitting up in bed a little each day. Finally, Lucy helped me out of the bed so I could take a few steps, but to my consternation, I'd forgotten how to walk. My legs wouldn't obey my mind. I would swing them about as I stumbled around.

A week later, bored as I could be of my own four walls, I convinced Verlan to help me walk the block to Lucy's. I was desperate for my children and felt guilty about not being able to care for them. Verlan told me it was too far for me to try to walk, but I insisted. He supported me as my legs flopped in all directions. Slowly, he guided me toward Lucy's house. "If you're too tired to walk the whole block, I'll take you back," he cautioned.

I refused to give up, forcing myself to take more steps. When we finally got to Lucy's gate, Verlan was going to release his hold on me long enough to lift the wire hoop over the post. He steadied me as he tried opening it. When he momentarily let me loose, my legs buckled instantly beneath me. He caught me just before I hit the ground. Then he carried me in his arms all the way back to the house.

BY AUGUST, VERLAN WAS BACK in Vegas and I was improving, though I was not yet back to normal. Still, I felt alive enough that I wanted to celebrate when Verlan came home for a spell. I pleaded with him to make love to me.

"The doctor said you mustn't get pregnant for a year at least, or you may die." Only two months had gone by.

"Well, at least I'll die happy," I joked. I suggested some form of birth control. When Verlan hotly refused, I threatened divorce. I figured if God knew my circumstances, he'd make an allowance for me. Was I to abstain for another whole year? I'd done that once, and heavenly rewards or not, I swore I'd never do it again.

Dr. Hatch emphasized I was to have absolutely no stress. I knew I was causing undue strain on us both with my pleas and threats. Instead of consenting to a divorce, Verlan gave in, very tentatively, just this once. As before, he first made me agree to take responsibility for it before God and man. That night, much to my chagrin, we conceived our sixth child.

CHAPTER TWENTY-TWO

My sister-in-law Flora, who was Alma's second wife, asked me to come to her house to fix the tension on her sewing machine. Now one year old, Brent needed to go down for a nap. When I left, five-year-old Donna was bouncing him on the bed, trying to get him to sleep. I told her she could follow me as soon as he fell asleep. I wasn't half a block down the road when she came running after me. "Go back. Stay with Brent. Don't come until you're sure he's asleep," I said.

"He is, Mama," she insisted. So I waited for her to catch up.

I oiled Flora's machine and cleaned the metal bobbin case with a chicken feather I brought from my coop. In less than fifteen minutes, I adjusted the tension and left it running like a top. She thanked me, and Donna and I headed for home.

When I stopped briefly to get the mail, there was a letter from Verlan. I tore it open and read it as I hurried home. "Dear Irene. I worry about the kids. Please watch them extra careful for me." I quickened my step as I continued reading.

I tiptoed into my room to check on Brent, but he wasn't on the bed. I looked under it, then in the closet. I began to panic, running outside. "Brent," I called. "Brentsie, where are you?"

I ran to Lucy's, but she hadn't seen him. When she saw my concern, she joined in the search. When Charlotte heard my frantic calls, she also got alarmed. He wasn't at her place, either. We searched, called, looked in the corrals and ditches. I ran through the mesquites and down the cow trails to the alfalfa field. Maybe by some slim chance, he'd gotten to the pasture. He hadn't. Our hunt became more intense as most of the town—about twenty adults—had now joined the search team. We looked in every hole, lifted every lid, and scoured the landscape.

I was six months pregnant at the time, and my stomach ached from all the running. After forty-five minutes, I was worn out and breathless. But I couldn't stop. We'd still found no sign of him. Word spread. Mexican neighbors from across the highway joined in the search. Everyone was hunting for my missing toddler, but we had no clue of his whereabouts. I racked my tired mind to think of any place we hadn't checked two or three times already.

The wells! There were three open wells we used for irrigation, each of them fourteen feet in diameter. I didn't want to consider the possibility, but there was nowhere else he could be. I reasoned that if he was in one, his plastic baby bottle should be floating on top of the water. I knew Brent had taken it with him because it was no longer in the house.

I headed for the well that was closest to the highway. Verlan's mentally ill brother, Ben, followed close behind me, saying, "The spirit of the Lord told me you'd find your baby floating in the second well."

I cringed, picking up speed. I knew Ben's revelations were always false. I hoped to God this one was, too. I stopped at the well and forced myself to look in. The water was clear and still. No floating bottle.

A crowd gathered. I was told the men already checked the three wells with long poles several times and found nothing. During all these hours, I cried out to God, "Let me find him, Lord, even if he's dead! Let me find him!"

Nothing showed up. No bottle. No body. Nothing. The exhausting search went on for nine hours before darkness caused most of the crowd to give up and go home. A few close friends milled around, wondering what else they could do as they tried to comfort me.

I was hysterical. I could not allow my darling child to be left alone all night. What if coyotes ate his little body? Then I might not ever find out what happened to him. On my way back home, I tried to search the cow pastures one last time. Weeping with uncontrollable grief, I waddled through the darkness, bumping into mesquites and weeds along the way.

Feeling too faint to walk any longer, I stopped and pled with God. "Heavenly Father, please let me find him." Just then, I thought I heard voices in the distance. I tried to quiet my agitated breathing. Then I held my hand over my pounding heart and listened.

"We found him! We found him!" came the relieved cries through the darkness.

Hope spurred my weary body on. I could see the crowd gathered at the house. Someone was waving a flashlight. "I'm not prepared for this, God!" I said out loud. "Help me endure whatever it is." I approached the crowd, ready to hear they'd found him dead.

"He's okay, Irene! He's okay!" Charlotte yelled. Then she shoved Brent's shivering little body into my arms. I wept without shame. God answered my prayers after nine grueling hours.

As I sobbed, Brent pounded me with his empty baby bottle. "Mok, Mama. Mok." He tried to lift my head. "Horsey, Mama. Horsey."

That's when I saw the two eleven-year-old boys standing alongside us, almost in tears. Both boys were named Kimball. They'd been severely scolded by their parents, then ordered to give me their apologies. "We're sorry," they said in unison.

Angry, I asked, "What happened?"

"We were in our cart. The horse was trotting up the lane toward the main road. We saw Brent going in the same direction. He said, 'Mommy bus,' so we figured you'd gone to town, and he was trying to follow you. We thought he'd have a good time riding around with us, so we took him to El Valle, hoping to find you."

Immediately, I forgave them. Lucy and Charlotte helped me into the house, where I fell exhausted onto the bed. I held Brent in my arms all night, unable to sleep after the prolonged torment of not knowing where he was. Feeling the kick of my unborn child, I hoped I hadn't exhausted him, too.

· · ·

EACH TIME A WIFE was expecting a baby, Verlan would buy two pieces of cloth for maternity outfits. He'd wanted to do something special for me this time because he'd missed my wedding anniversary. Instead of the allotted two, he lovingly bought me three pieces as a belated anniversary gift.

When I saw the cloth, I had to fight back tears, and they wouldn't have been tears of joy or tenderness. To put it simply, the lavender material with huge yellow and purple tulips belonged on a couch, not draped across my protruding stomach. Verlan couldn't imagine I thought it was unsuitable. Why, he'd picked it out himself. "The lovely flowers reminded me of you!" he said. I didn't press the point so he wouldn't think I was ungrateful.

When I finished the maternity dress out of that material, I walked up to my friend Betty's. She stared at me in disbelief, then laughed aloud. "My God, Irene, where did you get that awful dress?"

"Can you believe this?" I said, finally giving in to those tears. "It's my anniversary present." Then I lightened up. "One good thing about being pregnant, Betty, is that I'm gaining my weight back after losing so much from typhoid. You know I have an aversion to maternity clothes. I guess I better get used to them, though, because I'll be having babies throughout all eternity." I laughed. "I've decided instead of maternity clothes, I'll call them eternity clothes."

I'D PROMISED DONNA, WHO was almost six, that our new baby would be a girl. Figuring the odds were very much in favor of my little fib, I told her God never sends more than three kids in a row of the same sex. We talked and planned about her lovely baby sister. I told her about Leah's death and explained how death came upon humanity. I assured her God was good, and that when he gave us another darling girl, it could be hers.

On Saturday, May 14, at 10 A.M., I gave birth in Lucy's two-room adobe house to a baby boy. He was the most beautiful child I'd ever seen. I named him Kaylen Douglas. The other boys—André, Steven, and Brent—joyously passed the tiny new arrival around. Donna sat silently on the edge of the bed with her bottom lip out.

Lucy took the three little boys back to my house. She left Donna with me, where she could finish pouting. "Donna," I began apologetically, "Mommy's so sorry that it wasn't a girl. I really thought it would be."

She didn't move. Her bottom lip stuck farther out. "The baby is so cute," I said. "I'll still give him to you. He can be all yours if you'll just be happy."

"I don't want him!" She burst out crying. "I'm so damn mad at Adam and Eve!"

I was shocked she even remembered who they were. Trying not to laugh, I said, "Why are you mad at them?"

She cried all the harder. "If they hadn't gone to the garden and eaten those damn peaches, we'd still have our baby Leah."

CHAPTER TWENTY-THREE

Once when Verlan came home for a three-day weekend, he brought with him a special treat for the children. "Get your poles ready! Daddy's taking you fishing," he told them.

With Verlan's help, all eleven of the kids (minus the babies) hurriedly got their willow poles ready. Onto each one, he tied a string with a bent nail at the end. I'll never forget their excitement and joy. Each wife washed her children's faces and put their sweaters on them so they wouldn't be cold riding in the back of the pickup on the way to the pond. They jumped into the truck and sat down holding their poles, waving good-bye to us as the truck headed for the dirt highway.

That was our cue. Charlotte, Lucy, and I hurried into my house. I pounded large nails into each side of the doorframe. We hung a blanket there, leaving about two feet of space at the top of the doorway. I pulled the heavy cardboard boxes containing Verlan's surprise over close to me so I could easily reach into each one. Charlotte and Lucy took their places on the other side of the blanket, and we waited for the kids to return.

Verlan only drove up to the end of the lane. He then told the kids the best fishing was right at home, and he turned around. He stopped in front of the house and helped the kids off the truck. He ordered the three older boys—Chad, Verlan Jr., and Mark—to form a line holding their fishing poles and then lead the younger ones single file into the house. They all stood in front of the blanket with their poles, wondering what was going on.

Verlan showed André how to cast his hook up over the top of the blanket. He excitedly said, "Okay, here's André. Where's his fish?"

I tied a toy onto the nail and carefully pushed it back over while Charlotte and Lucy eased it down so it wouldn't hit anyone. As it came over the blanket, André started screaming, "I got a truck! Look, I got a truck!"

The whole group of kids ignited with anticipation, squealing and jumping, wanting to be next. Verlan got the next child ready. "Here comes Mark! Where's his fish?"

I rummaged through the box and tied a metal airplane onto his line. The kids laughed and screamed with excitement. We let each one have a turn. Then Verlan repeated the operation all over again. Realizing that it was taking too long, he finally reached behind the blanket and pulled out the big boxes, letting each child take a turn choosing a toy until every doll, truck, and game was gone.

Verlan brought the secondhand toys from the States. The kids were absolutely elated. These were the first real toys they'd ever played with. Though a few of the toys had broken parts (a bent wheel or a missing eye), it never occurred to our children that they weren't brand new.

Long after the kids were grown, they'd still reminisce about the day they went fishing with Daddy.

THE LONELINESS I FELT during Verlan's three-month absences was often unbearable. I knew he had no choice but to keep on painting so he could support his families and also contribute to the church (we'd thrown in with Joel and his converts by this time). But I thought he could simultaneously meet some of his families' emotional needs if he took one of his wives with him to Vegas each time he went. I begged him to consider this, but he refused, saying he could save more money if he went by himself.

Charlotte, Lucy, and I hated his long absences. When he came home for his three-day visits, we all ended up feeling rejected because we still had to share him. If it wasn't my turn when he arrived, I'd have to wait a day or two to be with him. The pain of his stopping in just to say hello before he went to be with another wife was worse than his being gone altogether.

Still, his homecomings were always joyful in a way. Verlan was very thoughtful. He loved to bring home boxes packed with all sorts of used but useful things he'd been given from the secondhand store or found cheap at yard sales. It always felt like Christmas when he did this. Among the assortment of items he surprised us with were bread tins, eggbeaters, graters, plastic tumblers, odd dishes, and those toys for the kids. He got such a kick out of seeing us all so happy.

Shortly after one of these surprises, Betty dropped by to visit me. "Look Betty, Verlan bought me a new bra. The most uplifting gift I could ask for!" I was so elated. This was my first new bra since I'd married Verlan. Now I wouldn't have to make my own.

Verlan came in just as I was taking my new bra out of the box. Betty couldn't resist the chance to ask, "How do you get the right size bra for each of your wives?"

Before he could answer, I blurted out, "Oh, that's easy. He just tries Lucy's on his elbow, Charlotte's on his knee, and mine on his head!"

VERLAN HAD BEEN GONE a long time, and it was my night to have him first for a change. I was jubilant. It was a pleasure to have him sit at my table again. He always complimented me on my cooking, never failing to express his appreciation for me.

After eating, he played with the kids, giving each a turn riding piggyback. He pranced around with them on his broad shoulders. Then he helped me tuck them into bed.

When he tried to leave to go tell Charlotte and Lucy good night, I clung to him until he promised to hurry back quickly. "Of course I will," he said. "I know it's your turn. I'll be back as soon as I can to spend the night with you."

I quickly took my bath in the round tin tub and then brushed out and braided my golden hair. To set the mood for this special night, I hurriedly sprinkled the few remaining drops of my secondhand perfume onto the flour-sack sheets made for the occasion. A freshly scrubbed pot was in its place under the bed. A quart of fresh well water was on the stand. The kerosene lamp was turned down low.

I waited and waited. I guess idleness really is the Devil's workshop, because he got me to take off my panties and my long nightgown and tuck them under the pillow. I jumped into bed naked, pulling the perfumed sheets up over my bare shoulders. I lay flat on my back with only my head in view. In the dim, romantic lamplight, wearing nothing but my most seductive smile, I awaited Verlan's return. Would he ever be surprised.

As it turned out, the surprise was on the both of us when he barged in a few minutes later with Charlotte and Lucy in tow. They all knelt down beside my bed for prayer. Verlan turned up the dim lamp and motioned for me to join them. All three of them folded their hands and waited for me to get out of the bed and down on my knees. I didn't move.

"Come on, Irene. Get out for prayer," he ordered.

"Ah . . . er . . . I'm not in the mood for prayer," I said.

"Don't waste Charlotte and Lucy's time. Come on now! Cut out this nonsense. Obey me. Kneel down here for prayer." He reached over to grab the sheet, but I was gripping it so tight that my knuckles turned white. When he couldn't budge it, his eyes met mine . . . and he knew! Disgusted, he just bowed his head and said, "Let us pray."

He must have thought it best to walk them both home. Immediately, they all disappeared, and I sprang out of bed. *Oh God, please help me out of this one! If Verlan finds out what I've done, he'll really reprimand me.* In a flash, I'd put on my panties and nightie and was back in the bed, striking what I hoped was an innocent pose.

He walked in and said not a word. He just yanked the sheet off me, throwing it clear across the room.

He almost sputtered in surprise. "You weren't like *that* a few minutes ago!" he said, pointing accusingly.

"You're damn right I wasn't. But did you really want me to jump out of the bed and show them the naked truth?"

LUCY'S HARDEST LABOR STARTED without any warnings. Immediately, her pains were one on top of another. We sent a friend by truck to Spencerville to fetch her mother, Aunt Sylvia, to deliver the baby. In the meantime, I threw a plastic covering and a clean sheet onto Lucy's bed to prepare it for the delivery. Wincing and holding her stomach, she also told me where to get her Lysol, cotton, and sterilized rags. As the final preparation, I set out a freshly washed set of clothes for the new arrival.

I ached inside for Lucy. She needed Verlan to be with her, but he was in Las Vegas, working to support us. He couldn't come home every time he had a child. Still, I felt a powerful foreboding that brought back memories of my own ordeal when Leah was born and died without him there. I didn't think any woman should be asked to lay her life on the line or be subjected to such excruciating pain without her husband there to see her through it. But patient Lucy was never one to complain. She hid her needs and fears very well indeed.

Her cries brought me back to the situation at hand. I rubbed her back as she gripped the dresser. I wanted to cry with her. She didn't deserve to suffer so.

Aunt Sylvia arrived with her shabby black bag, which she placed on the floor at the foot of the bed. She asked for a wash pan full of warm water, and I fetched it from the kitchen. Hurriedly, she washed her hands with soap, instructing me to pour fresh water over them. Then she held her clean hands up in front of her as she turned to Lucy. "Get on the bed as soon as your pain stops. I'll need to check to see how far you're dilated."

Charlotte took Lucy's children over to my house, where they wouldn't be able to hear her painful cries. When Charlotte returned, she rubbed Lucy's back gravely. "Is the pain over enough so we can help you lie down?" she asked. Lucy nodded her head as Charlotte and I held her arms and led her slowly to the bed.

Sitting on the side of the bed, Lucy lifted her long, thin legs onto the sheet as her mother placed a pillow beneath her shoulders. "Quick! I'm having another one!" Lucy cried. Charlotte and I each took a side near the foot of the bed. We held our arms firm, and Lucy clung to us as she bore down.

Aunt Sylvia's fingers probed inside as Lucy arched her neck and let out staccato moans of agony. We could see the worry on Aunt Sylvia's face. I thought how difficult it must be for her to deliver her own daughter's baby. Charlotte and I sent fervent prayers to God asking that this woman our husband chose to love would cease to suffer soon and be delivered of a normal, healthy child.

Lucy begged for sips of water as she perspired in the June heat. Then suddenly her water burst, thrusting a piece of the umbilical cord out first. Charlotte, Aunt Sylvia, and I looked at one another, alarmed. None of us had ever seen this happen. "Bear down, Lucy," her mother commanded. "Bear down long and hard. We must get this baby out as soon as we can."

Lucy grabbed her stomach as the baby squirmed, kicking with tremendous violence. Sylvia touched Lucy's tummy. "This baby wants out, Lucy. Push hard!"

Instinctively, I let go of Lucy's hand and ran to the home of the closest neighbor I knew had a car. Without knocking, I yelled, "Come, Earl! Please come and take Lucy to the hospital. Something is wrong."

"What is it?" he asked as we both jumped into his car and he sped down the gravel road back to the house.

"The cord came out first, and her contractions won't expel the baby."

"Oh God," Earl said, shaking his head. "We have to push that cord back inside before air gets to it, or the baby will start breathing. I'll bet it's too late. Don't say a word," he ordered.

We ran in, hearing unbearable moans from Lucy's room. Aunt Sylvia pushed the cord back in as Earl commanded. "Now move out of the way and let me carry Lucy to the car," he said.

I ran ahead with a thick blanket and a pillow, and I spread them on the backseat for Lucy to lie down on. She cried out in pain as we pushed her frail body into place. Aunt Sylvia, holding her black bag filled with sterilized rags and baby clothes, climbed in beside her. I sat next to Earl, and we frantically started toward Casas.

Earl flew so fast down the narrow paved highway, we skipped right over the potholes. The speedometer rose quickly to 50, 60, 65 miles per hour. I pointed nervously at the gauge. Earl shook his head for me not to worry. The needle climbed to 75, 85, 90. My prayers were just about as loud as Lucy's cries as we raced over the dangerous road to Casas.

When we got there, Earl drove the car to the rear entrance of the clinic, and I ran inside to get a stretcher. But he snatched Lucy right up and carried her directly to the operating room.

Dr. Hatch appraised the situation, then ordered, "Irene, have Earl drive you to the public swimming pool. Find Arturo, the anesthetist. Tell him not to take time to dress. Get him over here immediately."

Earl rushed me over there, and I ran along the side of the pool, scanning the bathers playing ball in the water. Each moment seemed an eternity. Finally I spotted Arturo. How he'd matured since he had administered anesthesia to me years earlier for my appendectomy. "Arturo!" I waved my arms as I ran. "Arturo!"

He spoke perfect English. "Yes, what can I do for you?"

"Dr. Hatch said come as you are! It's a matter of life or death."

He grabbed his towel and dried himself as he ran to a small bath-house and snatched up his clothes.

Please God! I prayed as we dashed along with noisy, hurried steps. *Please let it be over soon for Lucy's sake. Don't let her suffer!*

Arturo and I burst into the delivery room, expecting to hear Lucy's cries. Instead she lay quietly on the table, covered to her shoulders with a green sheet. I realized that a nurse was working with an infant nearby. I looked at Lucy, shocked. "Did you have it?"

Dr. Hatch interrupted my questioning. "I had to go in and pull it out. We couldn't wait for Arturo. It was coming placenta previa [afterbirth before baby]. Lucy could have hemorrhaged if we'd waited any longer. I'm sorry to tell you, but the baby is dead. She had an eight-pound girl, but it suffocated at home when it fought so violently inside its mother."

"Can't you do something? Give it mouth-to-mouth resuscitation? Give it oxygen, artificial respiration? Anything?" I desperately pled.

Dr. Hatch shook his head sadly. "It's no use, Irene. There's nothing we can do."

I was filled with rage. I wanted to scream at God. Lucy had already lost a baby—little Roland, who had lived only fifty-three hours. Why hadn't he and my Leah been enough? Why did it have to happen to poor Lucy again? She opened her arms, and I fell into them, both of us sobbing. No grief in the world compares to the agony of losing a child, especially without your husband there to comfort you and mourn with you. How well I knew it. Wishing I could have shielded Lucy from it, all I could do now was share in her grief. Once I'd thought of her as my enemy, yet here we were now, united in sorrow and desperation.

I held the lifeless baby, placing her one final time in Lucy's arms. She wept as she examined her chubby body. "She's the prettiest child I've had. She's just beautiful. I know I'll have her again in heaven. She breathed inside me; I know it, and I'll have her again. [Brigham Young said unless a child breathes the breath of life, we couldn't claim it in heaven.] She's my little Clara," Lucy declared. "Take her home and prepare her for a decent burial."

Earl and I left Lucy and Aunt Sylvia at the clinic with Dr. Hatch. I carried the lifeless little body out through the back entrance to the car. We hardly spoke during the thirty-five-mile drive home. I sat wondering how I could take this bad news home to the family, especially those expectant kids. I unfolded the receiving blanket and gazed at Clara. She had beautiful dark hair, a perfectly formed mouth, tiny long lashes. I sighed. I dared hope this would be the last heartbreak we'd have to endure.

We dressed the baby for burial in a nicely mended secondhand dress. I laid her out for viewing on top of Charlotte's Singer sewing machine cabinet and raised the window to allow a cross breeze to keep the baby's body cool. Donna, almost seven, wailed uncontrollably.

She went up to where the baby was laid out, patting and kissing her, crying, "Wake up, baby! Wake up!" She was in such despair, I pulled her away and had her lie down on Charlotte's bed, there in the same room. I begged her to settle down, but I finally had to leave her there, crying hysterically, because all the other crying kids needed to be fed in the kitchen. I had to hurry up so I could line the wooden casket Earl was making out in the yard.

I was relieved when it seemed Donna finally quit her crying. I figured she fell asleep, and I went back to check on her. I was flabbergasted to see her sitting in her little rocker with Clara in her arms, rocking her back and forth. Quietly sobbing her little heart out, she was unable to accept the fact that the baby was dead. I found it most difficult to explain to her that Clara had gone to Heaven, while her precious little body would now have to be buried like we'd had to do with Leah.

ON SEPTEMBER 30, 1962, I gave birth to my daughter Barbara. She was such a beauty, with dark hair, green eyes, and a smile that told you she was up to something. I delivered her at home with a neighbor's assistance. We all felt she was a special blessing from Heaven, but Donna especially did. It had been seven years since I'd had a girl. After getting stuck with four brothers in a row, Donna was overjoyed to finally have her own little sister. I didn't have to remind her that she could have the baby. Donna immediately claimed her, carrying her around like a doll. But she just couldn't understand why I wouldn't let her sleep with the baby at night.

"Don't lie, Mom! You gave her to me."

I felt so bad, I let the baby lie next to Donna on a small cot while I watched cautiously until my older daughter fell asleep. A while later, when Donna awoke and realized I'd snatched her little sister, she happily joined me and three other sleeping kids in my bed.

Though I always put the children to sleep in their own beds, they would all somehow manage to wake up in mine. They loved to listen to me sing and tell stories at night, especially when the wind was howling. Thunder and lightning would also bring them rushing into my room. My bed was a safe haven; there were always more kids than covers. Sometimes I didn't realize any of them had snuck in until I felt the wet spots in my bed.

The children were none too happy when Verlan came to sleep with me on the occasional coveted night when he was in town and I popped up on his rotation list. Sometimes, neither was Verlan. Once, when he and I had just gotten in bed and covered ourselves with a light blanket, my son André's kitten jumped onto the bed and frightened Verlan. He immediately tossed the kitten to the floor. The poor thing meowed and jumped right back up. No matter how many times Verlan threw it out of the bed, it came right back, insistent on sleeping with us. Finally, Verlan thought he'd made his point. The kitten disappeared. Much as I disliked cats, I commiserated with its desperation for a little love.

After a sound sleep, I awoke early in the morning and put my arm around Verlan, hoping for a little extra attention before my turn was over. He rose up, intending to turn toward me. I cupped my hand under his side in order to pull him into an embrace, but instead of pajamas, I felt fur. Without our knowing it, the kitten had quietly snuck back into the bed. In his sleep, Verlan had accidentally rolled over on it, squishing the life out of the poor little thing. Verlan felt bad, but not as bad as André and the other kids felt. They cried buckets of tears as they prepared their kitty for burial in a cardboard box. To console them, Verlan dug the hole, buried the cat, and for the kids' sake, put a wooden marker on the grave. Knowing our neighbor had an abundance of kittens, we let André pick out another one the next day.

CHAPTER TWENTY-FOUR

The spirit of expansion seemed to be contagious. Not only were the LeBaron brothers busy multiplying their wives and children for the sake of their heavenly kingdoms, but Joel (our prophet) decided it was time to start expanding the earthly kingdom as well.

The scriptural prophecy in Doctrine and Covenants, Section 85, claimed that "the One mighty and strong" would set the house of God in order and arrange by lot the inheritances of the saints whose names were listed in the book of the law of God. These lots were to be our "eternal stewardships," deeded only to those faithful saints who complied with the rules. For this purpose, property was purchased in the midst of the beautiful Sierra Madre, west of Colonia LeBaron in the town of Nicolás Bravo (or just Bravo). This was to be the next step toward fulfilling Joel's dream of world domination.

Joel directed the new enterprise, selecting several dedicated brethren to help launch it. These men left Colonia LeBaron with their families, honored and excited that God found them worthy of such an undertaking. In less than a year, a dairy farm, lumber mill, cheese factory, and mechanic shop had been set up as preliminary stewardships. The participants were elated to work directly under the guidance of their prophet.

Common sense rather than God convinced Joel that Verlan and a few other good men needed to work in the States so they could make money to pour into these projects. I was thrilled when Joel asked Verlan to move his families from the colony to the mountains. Anything had to be better than what we had. But I was deeply saddened when I learned Verlan would again be gone for two or three months at a time, leaving us all behind so he could minimize expenses. Verlan seemed determined to sacrifice all he could for the cause.

I prayed to God repeatedly, telling him I wasn't cut out for all this. I wanted to do his will, but I needed a man whose loyalties weren't so divided. It was too heartrending to share Verlan with other women. I also resented his submission to Joel. Except in a crisis, such as the loss of Leah or my own near death from typhoid, my rights and needs rarely made it onto Verlan's radar.

Somehow, Charlotte managed to talk Verlan into moving her to Las Vegas to live with him for the school year. Because Lucy had just lost a second baby, I insisted that he take her for a short trip also. She needed his love and comfort at this time.

I was bogged down at home with my six little kids, plus Lucy's four. The oldest was my eight-year-old, Donna. With what little help she could give me, I figured I could bear the extra responsibility for two weeks while Lucy was gone.

After only one of those two weeks, I received a letter from Verlan instructing me to pack Lucy's and my belongings and move to the mountains. He wanted me all settled in when Lucy returned.

The day before leaving, I canned a hundred quarts of peaches to take with me. I cooked twenty-five bottles at a time in a galvanized tub of water over an open bonfire in the backyard. I packed the jars in wooden crates to be shipped on the train with all our other belongings.

I packed clothes, diapers, baby bottles, and lunch for our eight-hour train ride into the mountains. The next morning at 6 A.M., we loaded everything onto Harold Tippetts' old flatbed truck and left for Casas. There, the load was transferred onto the freight train as the children and I settled down in the passenger car.

Although we were all excited because this was our first train trip, I was exhausted before it even began. I ached from lifting stoves, beds, dressers, butane tanks, and all our other worldly possessions. I was beat as soon as I sat down, but we had many, many miles to go before I could rest.

The kids were having a grand time, especially when the train passed through several tunnels. I held four-year-old Brent close to me, telling him not to be afraid as we went through the longest one. There were no lights on the train. It seemed like we'd never reach the end. When we did, little Brent's face lit up as he exclaimed, "Mommy, we just came out of a gopher hole."

Early on, one of the children dropped the two-quart bottle of milk I had brought, splattering it all over the floor of our car. I had two hungry, crying babies on my hands for the remaining six hours.

Dan Jordan, one of our new converts, met us at the station with his big truck. I helped him load it with our heavy furniture and boxes while the babies screamed, crying to be changed and fed. I took the youngest four in the cab of the truck with Dan and me; the other six kids crowded together in the back with our furniture.

Reassuring the children we'd soon be to our new home, I asked them to be patient for the remaining thirty miles. Dan announced that his two wives were preparing a hot supper for us to enjoy on our arrival. He instructed the kids to sit back and enjoy the ride.

Leaving the train station, we traveled for about twenty miles on a terrible muddy dirt road through cornfields as far as the eye could see. It was the rainy season in the mountains. The roads were gooey with soft mud. Three times, we got stuck. Each time, we had to pull up a couple of fence posts and wedge them under the dual tires to give us enough traction to drive out of the deep trenches we made.

While we went along this way in muddy fits and starts, the sun went down, and black clouds moved in to cover our sky. It was evident we were in for another hard rain. As the dusk settled in, many large, hungry mosquitoes buzzed in through the broken window of the truck. It was a nightmare just trying to keep them from biting the children.

Dan slowed the truck down, coming to a near stop before a huge mud puddle, unsure if we could make it through. The water along the fence line covered the road for several yards in front of us. Deciding to make a run for it, Dan floored the gas pedal, and the truck charged into the sea of mud. We swerved, swaying back and forth. Then we sank as the wheels sprayed mud and water in all directions. The truck was hopelessly bogged down.

"Well, we're here for the duration," Dan said matter-of-factly. "Irene, you'll have to stay here while I walk into town for help. I'll have Joel bring back his car, and I'll bring a tractor to pull us out. The wheels are buried up to the axles. I'll have to walk eight or ten miles, so be patient. I'll be back as soon as I can."

It grew darker, and armies of mosquitoes now feasted on us. I had Dan's big metal toolbox and a couple of long, thick chains under my feet. I tried to keep the two wailing, fourteen-month-old babies soothed by bouncing them both in my arms, singing to them.

The first loud clap of thunder sent the six kids in the back into hysterics. I went outside, stepping into mud as I searched around for the oil cloth I used to cover my kitchen table. I found it packed in a cardboard box. Then I ordered the children to crouch down and hold the oil cloth over their heads. When it started sprinkling, they all laughed, enjoying the feel of the cool rain. But the sky soon exploded in torrents, and a gust of wind tore their covering off, blowing it into the muddy weeds.

This time, I left the four screaming babies inside the truck just long enough to help the soaked and frightened children into the cab. Talk about misery. All eleven of us were sandwiched together, kids stacked on top of each other, hurting and complaining as the rain blew in through the broken window. With all the commotion and wailing, we sounded like a raucous mob at a wrestling match.

I knew I had to remain calm. Somehow we endured the stench of dirty diapers and the constant readjusting of pinched and numb body parts until all of us were completely worn out. The kids cried and complained until sleep finally subdued them.

Hoping this trip was not a preview of things to come, I listened and watched for what seemed like an eternity. Finally, I spotted lights coming toward us through the cornfields. I heard the sound of a tractor approaching.

It took great effort on Dan's part to walk clear into town through the rain and mud. Now he'd finally returned with Joel, plus a hired Mexican man, to rescue us. Dan was steering the car while Joel towed it with a tractor.

Joel began carrying the sleeping children from the truck cab to his car. "Good grief! How many kids you got in there?" he asked as he grabbed up the third or fourth one.

"Just ten," I told him.

Dan left the hired man sleeping in the truck to wait for daylight, when Dan meant to return to pull the truck home and salvage our drenched belongings. The eight-hour train ride, the first twenty stop-and-start miles from the train station, and the four-hour wait for Dan to return with Joel was grueling enough. It then took us an hour and a half to travel the last eight miles. We repeatedly got stuck in the muddy roadway and had to be pulled out with the tractor. Finally, at around midnight, we arrived.

Lucy came to the mountains from Vegas two weeks later. We settled down together in the same house. For the first time in our married lives, we had electricity.

At first, I was back to scrubbing on a washboard. It was three months before Verlan bought a used wringer-washer for Lucy and me to share. Now that we had electricity and the appliance, it was a breeze to wash. No more fighting to keep the gasoline motor of the old washer running. It was also wonderful to have electric lights after using coal oil lamps for eleven years. I didn't have to worry about buying coal oil or keeping the blackened chimneys clean. But it was still no life of ease. We drew water from a well and used an old outhouse.

Verlan was slaving away in the Las Vegas heat, painting to pay off the debt he'd incurred for the dairy cows, plus the big barn that was being built on the flats outside of town. From this project, Lucy and I were allowed to sell milk and cheese to provide for our daily needs. The poverty of those around us sickened me. We were rich compared to our Mexican neighbors. To them, even milk was a luxury. I was soon giving away more than I could afford.

On cold winter days, Lucy and I sewed quilt tops from the used clothing provided by the Vegas secondhand stores. That first winter, we made forty quilts, which we gave to our appreciative neighbors. We were loved and esteemed by everyone. We formed bonds of friendship there in the mountains that have lasted ever since.

I CONTRACTED GERMAN MEASLES while pregnant with my eighth child. When it got close to the time I would have the baby, I insisted on going to the nearby town of Gómez Farías to deliver it in a clinic because I was alarmed at how small my stomach was. At nearly nine months, I was still the size I usually was at five. I'd never been able to afford prenatal vitamins during any of my pregnancies, and I was worried that maybe I hadn't eaten well enough to sustain this baby. I had no transportation of my own, so about a week before my due date, I went and stayed at the home of Joel's first wife, Magdalena, who lived near the hospital.

When my labor started at 5 A.M. on December 20, 1964, Magdalena woke up her two oldest boys, who were six and eight at the time, to run and get Dr. Bringes. He returned with the boys in his pickup and then took Magdalena and me back to his clinic.

With each of my prior childbirths, I'd resigned myself to being strong and just seeing it through, but this seemed like the four worst hours of my life. The baby was positioned to come out face-first. Furthermore, it was so firmly lodged, the doctor had to use forceps.

As I bore down, Magdalena joined in my screaming. The doctor tried to make her leave, but I begged him to let her stay. I needed someone I knew to be with me. With the help of our unified screaming, I finally delivered a tiny, six-pound baby girl at 9 A.M. I thanked God the measles hadn't harmed her in any way.

Verlan promised he'd be home a week early to be with me, but he arrived the day after she was born. Like every other time I had a girl, he wanted to name her Olive after my mother. I loved my mother dearly, but I thought nobody deserved to go through life with a name like that. I jokingly told Verlan to name her Olive Irene LeBaron.

Then her initials would be O.I.L., and we could call her Olive Oil.
Instead, he named her Margaret.

LUCY WAS PREGNANT with her seventh child and was in constant
danger of miscarrying. I hired a sixteen-year-old Mexican girl, Clara,
to be my housekeeper because I knew Lucy couldn't shoulder her
part of the burden without this assistance. Clara more than earned
the sixty pesos a week she charged me. I gave her extra milk, used
clothes, and wheat to keep her animated.

Clara arrived for work after the children left for school. Once,
while gathering up the breakfast dishes to be washed, she asked me,
"Do you think you could love a Mexican baby?" I wondered if she
was testing me, wanting to know if I was prejudiced.

"I would love one!" I answered. "I think Mexican babies are all
beautiful, with their dark hair and lovely brown eyes. But my husband would kill me if I had one," I laughed.

Clara answered me with a broad smile. "I'm so glad you said that.
Yesterday, a pregnant woman came to our house, soliciting my mother
to take her unborn child. My mother refused because we have eight
of us in two rooms. My father's earnings of a dollar a day don't even
begin to provide for us. Then"—Clara paused—"I thought about
you. You are rich compared to us! You are such a good mother. I
think maybe you should consider taking it."

There was not even a chance. I had seven lively children already.
Plus Lucy and I were living together—all thirteen of us in a three-
bedroom house with no bathroom or running water. I'd always had a
soft spot in my heart for those less fortunate. I'd even rescued a puppy
now and then. But a stray child when I knew I'd probably have to
have several more of my own? Absolutely not.

Clara told me this desperate woman's plight while she cleaned the
house and I cooked lunch for the kids, who would soon come in from
school. Six months pregnant, she already had five small children, all on
the verge of starvation. In a drunken stupor one night, her husband
beat her almost beyond recognition. As Clara spun Juana's tragic tale,

I hurt for her more and more. So I finally went to see her at her home in Gómez Farías, about forty-five minutes from where I lived.

After meeting Juana and seeing the severity of her pathetic living conditions, I knew I'd be the answer to her prayers. She admitted to me the baby's father was an American from Casas. Her furious husband wouldn't support her or any of their children unless she gave the unborn baby away. I left money for her to send a telegram to me in Bravo to notify me of the baby's birth. Twelve weeks later, on June 19, 1965, I adopted the beautiful, dark-haired baby girl and named her Sandra. The next day, Margaret turned six months old, so it seemed as though I had twins. Verlan was as delighted as the rest of us because Sandra would be his child in his future kingdom.

LATER THAT SPRING, VERLAN surprised me by sending money for me to build my own house. After eleven years, I was supposedly going to have a home of my own design, with a bathroom and electricity. I chose a plan from a magazine Verlan brought home, and I immediately hired some local laborers. The adobe walls went up fast, and it was soon roofed.

Charlotte was coming home from Vegas as soon as school let out. I wasn't about to endure all three of us living in the same cramped quarters, so while my home was being finished, I rented a two-room adobe house for myself and my children. It only had one window, in the bedroom, which meant the kitchen door had to be left open to let light in. I ordered three windows from the carpenter and had them installed before I moved in. The kitchen in my rental house had a cement floor, but the bedroom did not. I had to sprinkle water on the dirt floor in that room to keep the dust down. I often thanked God my mother didn't know how I lived.

With no electricity or water in this house, I had to resort to kerosene lamps again, and I carried fresh water half a block from my neighbor's well. I was also back to scrubbing on the washboard because I'd left the Maytag wringer-washer with Lucy. Still, I had my own place.

That first night in the rental house was something to remember. All seven kids were sleeping soundly as I finished my unpacking. I cut the handle off a worn-out broom like I'd seen Verlan do in my other homes. Then I tied bailing wire onto the pole and nailed it into the rafters for a closet.

I was hanging up a few of Verlan's shirts when I happened to smell a light blue one I'd forgotten to wash. His familiar scent brought on rushes of tears as a wonderful emotion surged through me. I crawled into bed crying, hugging that shirt to my breast, savoring it as though I actually held a part of him.

After months of being without Verlan, I would have to share him when he got home. Lucy was as desperate as I was to have him back. And, though Charlotte was having a prolonged turn with him now, she'd soon be back to compete for his attention whenever he came home. I didn't know which was worse—all of us having to do without him or having to share him. At least when he was gone by himself, Charlotte, Lucy, and I didn't have to resent each other.

I'D ONLY BEEN IN my small rental house for about a week when Charlotte's two oldest girls, Rhea and Laura, came running down with Lucy's daughter, Verla, to see where I lived. They let me know their father and Charlotte had arrived from the States. Verlan wanted me to come greet them at Lucy's. The three girls left immediately to help Verlan unload the truck. He'd brought some used bikes for them.

I wanted to see Verlan alone, so I waited impatiently for him to come to me. Sure enough, he rushed in all excited. "Look, Irene. Look what Betty sent you!" Knowing it was a gift I'd waited years for, his face was all lit up as he handed me the box. I opened it and started to cry. I pulled out the most beautiful, gold-colored radio I'd ever seen. And it was mine.

Verlan handed me four extra batteries. "It runs on these as well as electricity. Betty sent her love and knows that you'll like it."

For the first time in eleven years, I had music at the turn of a knob. I listened to it all day, and many times long into the night. XTRA, a music station in California, came in loud and clear in English. Of all the gifts I'd been given, that special radio was a heavenly blessing. I now had contact with the real world.

CHAPTER TWENTY-FIVE

Irene, I love to come home to you. I've missed you. Your humor always makes me feel needed," Verlan told me. "The new house is really looking great so far. I brought more money for the cement floors and windows. Pretty soon you'll be in it, and then we'll plaster the walls and paint later. You sure made up a good floor plan. It looks like it'll be the best house in town."

"I will appreciate it, Verlan, but it will never be a home without you in it. I'd live in a tent if I just had someone to love me," I sniffled.

He stroked my hair away from my face. "Please don't cry! I'm here now, so enjoy it."

"This has been the loneliest year of my life. I can't take being abandoned all the time. Verlan, I love you, but life isn't worth living if you're not at home to be a husband and a father to our kids. I need you. I won't be left for month after month like this."

He held me, soothing my frustrations with his kisses. I thought it was because he missed me as much as I missed him. But he was merely preparing me for another blow.

"Irene, God works in mysterious ways his wonders to perform. Right at this moment, he is offering us a blessing. You can be a part of it. I'm depending on you to uphold me."

My mind raced ahead of each sentence. Is he going on a long-term mission for the church? Will he separate himself from us for

Above: Holding Connie, 1968. *Below:* My brother Douglas with many of the children. On the right is Donna, holding towels, ready for the beach; 1968.

Right: In front of the Big Brown House in Ensenada, Mexico; 1968. *Below:* Eight of Verlan's wives in order of marriage. *Bottom, left:* Working in the tomato fields while Verlan is courting Priscilla. *Bottom, right:* Verlan's children working in the family garden in Nicaragua.

Above: A family picture, with twelve of our thirteen children. *Below:* Our twenty-fifth wedding anniversary. Taken upon my return from Europe in 1978.

Above: Verlan surrounded by more than forty of his children, in July 1979.
Below: At Verlan's funeral in August 1981.

Above: He is buried in Chihuahua, Mexico. *Below:* LeBaron Colony in Chihuahua, Mexico.

Above: My thirteen children in the spring of 1982. *Below:* With Geraldo Rivera and my daughter Donna in November 1991.

Above: With Hector J. Spencer, my current husband of nineteen years. *Below:* Thirty-seven of Verlan's children gathered at the funeral of their sister Sandra in July 2000.

Above: Twenty-six sisters on their "Sisters Sailebration" cruise in September 2003. *Below:* With all thirteen of my children in February 1993.

even longer periods? Is he going to finish my house and then ask me to sell it?

"You're not listening, are you?" he asked.

"Yes, I am. But I have a gut feeling that I don't want to hear the rest."

He sat in silence. I could see he didn't have the heart to tell me whatever it was. I knew it couldn't be, there was no way it was possible, but I figured I'd say the craziest thing first, getting it over with. "You're not getting married again, are you?"

"See?" He grabbed me excitedly in his arms. "I knew the Lord would make it known to you! He does whisper his secrets to his faithful! Irene, I haven't told Lucy or Charlotte yet. I need you to back me up. Please." He threw me back on the bed, pinned me down with his body, and moved around as if he were making love to me. "Irene, I'll love you forever!"

I was crying too hard even to think. I didn't want to know who it was, but I guessed I'd better ask. "Who is she?"

"It's Beverly Paisano. Her father already gave me permission to marry her." Beverly's father was one of the first Mexican converts into Joel's church, and she'd consequently grown up at Colonia LeBaron. "Irene, she's seventeen, and she could raise up some beautiful children for us. But don't worry," he quickly added, as though this would make it all okay. "She's willing to stay down there on the LeBaron ranch. You won't have to live with her. You've already sacrificed enough. I'm not even asking you to go to our wedding."

"Damn you, Verlan. Every time I almost get a home, thinking I can have you, my dream crumbles. Here I am on dirt floors and dying inside."

"God says he'll never ask us to do anything unless he gives us the strength to do it," Verlan reminded me.

I screamed, "You can only get so much blood out of a turnip, and mine's all gone! Every damn drop of it. Do ya hear?"

When things calmed down, Verlan decided to take Lucy with him to give him his new bride. I dutifully tended Lucy's children while she accompanied him to Colonia LeBaron. There, in May of 1965, she faithfully placed Beverly's hand in his.

I WAS SHOCKED to see Verlan coming through the backyard in the early morning, returning from his honeymoon. He sauntered in, kissing the kids and looking a little sheepish. I refused to let him kiss me.

"How's my little darling?" He followed me into the bedroom.

"Not as well as you!" I snapped.

"Oh, come on now. Don't let a little thing like Beverly bother you!"

"It's not her thing I'm worried about," I said bitterly. "It's yours!"

"Please don't ruin things again, Irene. It seems like every time I'm here, you find something to feel bad about."

I didn't comment, so he continued, talking to me as if I were one of his brothers rather than his wife. "Beverly did look beautiful in her white dress. And her black hair was in a gorgeous French braid."

I started beating on his chest, hysterically out of control. He threw me onto the bed, trying to hold me down. "Don't tell me another thing about your damn wedding!"

He laid his head on me. "Irene, I'm just trying to carry on a conversation with you. Besides, nobody's as beautiful as you. She'll never be able to take your place. And once I get my quorum of seven wives, our love will be secure for eternity." He sounded perplexed as he continued. "You ought to be used to plural marriage by now. You've lived it for eleven years. Time is passing, and we've got to do our duty by building up God's kingdom. Believe me, it's harder on me than it is on you."

I fought him off me. "Like hell it is!" I felt so miserable, I wanted to fade into oblivion.

"Irene, I have to trust God to touch your heart so you can be more understanding of our privileges and responsibilities. I think you're looking at this negatively, when it's not. You say it's a curse, but it's actually a blessing. In fact, we're going to have a double blessing." He paused. "Esther Castro is also marrying me in seven more weeks!"

I went completely berserk. I called him all the names I could think of. I beat him on the chest and surprised us both by smacking his face. I lay on my bed, kicking the adobe walls, and then I wept and screamed until I was too worn out and hoarse even to speak. Verlan decided it was time to leave. He still had to share the glorious news with Charlotte and Lucy.

I turned on the radio to soft music. The song "For All We Know" was playing. "Love, look at the two of us, strangers in many ways . . ." I wept. We were strangers all right. And after how I acted—as if I hated the Principle and held Verlan personally responsible for roping me into it—I doubted we were even friends.

Esther's wedding, in July 1965, was also performed at Colonia LeBaron. Beverly was there to place Esther's hand in Verlan's. A few days after the honeymoon, Verlan returned to the mountains. Even though it was 2 A.M. And it was Lucy's night to sleep with him, he came in to report to me what he thought was good news.

He told me what a great event Esther's wedding had been. Then he went on and on about a prophecy of Joseph Smith's implying that American Indians would be saved by being joined in plural marriages with "pure" Mormons, meaning Caucasians. Verlan was tickled to be able to help the cause. "You know that both Beverly and Esther's fathers and families were among the first Mexicans to convert, and they've gathered in Colonia LeBaron to help us build up the kingdom of God. The least we can do is to embrace them in plural marriage. We're helping their race to become white and delightsome, just as the scriptures prophesy."

I'd heard enough. "Don't you ever wake me up again to tell me something like that!" I scolded as I turned my back to him. This time I didn't rant or lash out, because I was just plain numb. I guess I didn't give a damn.

Thinking he'd won me over, Verlan got up to leave. "I'm glad you're taking my marriage to Esther so well. I see you've finally accepted the Principle. Thanks for being so patient with me. I'll be seeing you!" And off he went to sleep with Lucy.

. . .

I PUSHED THE WORKERS to finish my new home quickly so I could get out of the tiny rental house with the dirt floors. Our financial circumstances did not make it possible to install a bathtub or toilet in the house, nor did I wait for the walls to be plastered or painted. I moved in as soon as the cement floors were dry. At least I had electricity again.

Lucy rented a two-room adobe house just two blocks away, where she had no electricity. She had to bring her clothes to my house to wash, which was a great inconvenience because she was pregnant again. I couldn't bear to see her living like that when I had it so good, so I invited her to move into my big playroom. We took turns cooking and cleaning. I may not have had a husband at home, but I certainly had a faithful sister wife.

CHAPTER TWENTY-SIX

Our enjoyment of my wonderful new house in Colonia Nicolás Bravo was, as usual, short-lived. We were on the move again. Joel's entire "mountain utopia" turned out to be a monstrous fiasco. Within a couple of years, all the projects failed; even our cows were fed so poorly that some had to be held up in slings in order to eat the dry grass and old beans on which we forced them to survive.

After just five months in my new house, Verlan sold it, along with Charlotte's three-bedroom adobe home. I sold a few of my other prized possessions to obtain what little cash we took with us. I left my precious washer and furniture with a friend from church, trusting her to send me cash as soon as she returned to the States. As it turned out, her husband forbade her to pay me because Verlan still owed him for an old debt the rest of us had all forgotten. So, I basically lost everything and had to start over from scratch.

Although the men failed at their enterprises, we took many good memories away from the mountains with us. I made wonderful friends among the Mexican people. Many of them lamented with us, expressing their grief to see us leave. While we'd been with them, we were able to help them in so many ways. I'd often shared my food and clothing, counseling them as needed. And my Spanish improved tremendously.

The already strange and depressing circumstances of my family life, however, became ever more absurd. I now had eight living children

and shared Verlan with four other wives. As if all that wasn't challenge enough, Verlan's growing loyalty to the Church of the Firstborn
of the Fullness of Times now seemed to dictate our every movement
and decision.

I simply had no idea how good I'd had it up till now.

JOEL FELT INSPIRED by God to form a new colony. So Verlan gave
us orders to pick up and move to Baja California, Mexico. Land was
purchased, some of which was beachfront property, and those involved hoped this would be a place of refuge for our church members. The five LeBaron brothers who participated in the venture
considered the new Baja colony to be an ideal location, where each
family could have a self-sustaining little place of its own.

Joel proclaimed the climate to be exactly what we needed. "Plants
practically grow by themselves from the moisture of the ocean
breezes. Goats and bees thrive there; it's a land of milk and honey.
Each man can sit under his own vine and fig tree as the ancient
prophet Isaiah predicted." Like most of his dreams, Joel's big plans for
the Baja colony were never fully realized, but at first, as always, we all
tried our best to believe and be excited.

Joel set an example by immediately digging several wells on the
property. He set up small pumps powered by monstrous, plywood,
fanlike windmills. In Spanish, they were called *molinos,* so the new
colony was soon known as Los Molinos.

In Las Vegas, Verlan purchased used trailer homes he and Joel
hauled to Baja and put on our designated lots. Many other families
purchased used tents from the army surplus store to live in until their
homes could be built.

As compensation for having to move from my new home in the
mountains, I noted that Baja was only a five-hour drive from San
Diego. We were in a "free zone" in which U.S. products could be
imported without any problems or duty expenses. It was also close
enough so the men could work in the States during the week and
then come home to be with their families on weekends. With these

incentives to spur me on, I dared to hope for a better life and an improvement in our economic circumstances.

Charlotte was again living with Verlan in Las Vegas when Lucy and I made the move. Our trip from the mountains to Baja was even more miserable than my move to the mountains from Colonia LeBaron. Naturally, Verlan was too busy to take us himself. He asked a friend, Joe Martson, to move us, along with his own wife and teenage son, in his six-passenger van.

Seventeen of us traveled for over twenty hours, jammed into this van with our scant belongings. For my bunch, I got to take a basket of dishes, a few quilts, two changes of clothes per person, and my precious radio. I was sick about having to leave behind my crib, dresser, and the gas stove Verlan gave me when I had typhoid fever.

Just keeping everyone alive in that van was a miracle. Realizing the incredible stress we were all under, Joe drove as fast as he safely could, up and down and around the hills and across the bumpy roads. People started getting car sick almost as soon as we started. We had to stop every few miles to take a breather and get up enough courage to continue. I'll never forget how ten-year-old Donna, sick from vomiting, lay down on the road beside the van during one stop and begged me to not force her back inside.

Twenty hours stretched into twenty-six. By the time we arrived, my fear of Hell vanished. We found our "land of promise" to be a flea-infested desert with undeveloped sand dunes and salt flats close to the ocean. After our ordeal in the van, however, the dilapidated trailer house that would be my new home looked like a little piece of heaven.

Joel's second wife, Jeannine, sent bread and honey over to feed us all when we arrived. I changed wet diapers, put blankets on the double bed in my room, bundled all the kids up in sweaters, and put five of them to sleep in one bed. I put my three boys on a box spring with no mattress off the hall. Immediately I was summoned to deliver Jeannine's baby. After two hours of trying to keep my composure, I delivered her baby girl and returned to my trailer. Then, wrapping myself up in a blanket, I flopped onto the bumpy, broken-down couch and let tears wash away all the exhaustion, stress, and disappointment I'd kept inside.

With no heat in the trailer, I awoke several times during the night to cover chilling kids. Until summer rolled back around, we had to wear sweaters night and day in order to keep warm. We also had a tough time adjusting to the confined quarters; the moist, salty air; and the constant fog blowing in from the ocean two miles away.

The rains may have been what made our lives the most miserable. Mud was tracked in constantly. My nephew Joseph and his wife, Margarita, lived in a tent next to two Mexican friends, Eulogio and Lola, just a few yards outside my front door. During one violent storm, severe winds loosened the stakes and collapsed the tents, leaving canvas and ropes flapping about. All four of the occupants ran to my already overcrowded trailer for cover. With thirteen of us now, Lola and Margarita slept on the sofa, while the two men slept on the floor next to the kitchen table.

Two nights later, I awoke from a deep sleep to find Lola in labor. I put Joseph and Margarita to sleep on the floor in the hall next to my frightened kids while Lola screamed through the rainy night. At 5 A.M., on my ramshackle sofa, I delivered Lola's baby girl.

These people lived with us for six weeks, until they could afford to get a trailer of their own. Sleeping with my five kids in the double bed, my legs would get so numb, I could hardly move them. I'd put a small chair beside the bed and stretch my legs out on it until they got so cold, I'd have to pull them back in.

With no high chair, I had to sit five-month-old Sandra and eleven-month-old Margaret on the small Formica kitchen table to eat. The older kids had to stand beside them to keep them from falling to the floor. With so much mud and dirt constantly being tracked in, the linoleum floor was next to impossible to keep clean.

My first big thrill in Baja was the day Verlan brought home a brand-new Maytag washer with a gasoline motor for his five wives to share. Joel got wind of it, and before long we were sharing it with several members of his family as well. That washer ran from morning till night, with everyone wrangling constantly about who should get it next. Once, on my turn to wash, I drew water from the well, carried it over, and filled the washer plus the two rinse tubs. While I sorted out my clothes in my trailer house, another woman started her wash in my water, without so much as a "Do you mind?" Being used so much, the wringer on the washer soon broke. My wrists ached from constantly wringing out the clothes by hand. Then the motor died completely.

It was terrible having to wash out my two babies' diapers, plus all my other laundry, by hand. Then several of the women who helped wear out my washer each got their own, but they refused to share. So much for a United Order.

I HADN'T SLEPT WITH or written to Verlan for five months. I was mad at him for making me move and for selling my wonderful (if unfinished) house in the mountains. I fumed further when he told me he felt that Beverly and Esther, his two Mexican wives, needed "extra time" with him. He defended this by reminding me they were new brides and each only seventeen. To my chagrin, he moved both new wives to live by me in Baja. To make matters worse, he put me on a budget of only $20 a week, saying we should be grateful for that much, since he had to help support the church.

Somehow we managed. My two older boys spent hours fishing for our dinners. When the grunions were running, we all went out and scooped up buckets full of fish as they washed up on the beach in the waves to lay their eggs. Finally we had some tasty animal protein in our diet.

We scrounged around as best we could to make ends meet. All five wives used one old pickup truck to go everywhere we had to go. I'd drive to nearby farms that shipped their crops to the United States so I could get their leftovers—imperfect and unwanted olives, tomatoes, potatoes, and all kinds of vegetables. I often distributed my loads to everyone in the colony.

Emotionally, I was falling apart. I knew I couldn't go on this way much longer. I told Verlan I needed a better way of life. I begged him to take me to Las Vegas to live with him like he did with Charlotte. He refused. He claimed he was saving money by doing it his way, but I knew the truth. All along, he'd favored Charlotte in a number of ways.

I was sick at heart. I went on begging for a little attention, pleading for my needs to be fulfilled, but Verlan couldn't do a single thing for me because, as he said, "It would be unfair." I got that response whenever I asked for what I felt I really needed. Each time, it spelled nothing but more sacrifice for me.

I was now twenty-eight years old, and I could see my life was going nowhere. Although the prospect was traumatic, I thought a lot about divorce. According to our religion, I would lose my blessings if I left my husband for no other reason than that he was faithfully living the Principle. Even the natural consequences of a polygamous life—the poverty, loneliness, and insecurity I'd come to know so well—were not valid reasons to divorce a husband. Besides, I had no way to support myself. Even emotionally, I wasn't prepared to go out into the world alone. Nevertheless, I went many times to Joel, who convinced us all he was a prophet and our ultimate earthly authority, and I asked him to exempt me from the rules. Instead, he changed them.

In order to get an official divorce, Joel decreed a wife had to physically and emotionally separate from her husband for at least six months. After that, she could marry someone else, but he would have to be of our church in order for her to keep her blessings. In one more month, I would satisfy the time limit, but I begged Joel to give me a divorce immediately. Instead, he took me to Las Vegas himself, hoping to get us reconciled.

I held out for five days after seeing Verlan because I wanted a few concrete promises from him before I gave in. I demanded more money, my own washer, a high chair, and at least a front step for my trailer. He swore he'd do as I asked, but I knew deep down that we'd soon be back in the same rut. I returned home still distraught and pregnant once again.

CHAPTER TWENTY-SEVEN

I looked forward to driving all the kids to school in Guerrero each day. It was my chance to get away and associate with other people while in town. Linda Stanley, who previously lived in Bravo, moved with us out of the mountains and now lived near the new Baja colony. I helped Linda with a difficult delivery in the mountains a year earlier. We now loved each other like sisters.

Almost every day, she'd wave me down as I drove by her house, taking the truckload of children to or from school. She would insist that I drop whatever I was doing to spend some time with her. I knew she was lonely, with her husband working in San Diego except when he came home on sporadic weekends, and no one but her two-month-old and one-year-old daughters to keep her company most of the time.

I was most appreciative of the fudge, brownies, and hot meals she served me whenever I stopped in. I knew no such luxuries. Invariably, though, I had to cut short those visits in order to get home and get to my housework. I also hesitated to impose on Lucy for a minute longer than necessary, since she tended my little ones each day until I returned from town.

One morning, after dropping the kids off at school, I was making a mad dash to go to the outskirts of town to fill four butane tanks to take back to Los Molinos. The wives needed the gas to heat water and start their meals.

As I passed her place, Linda waved, trying to stop me. If I stopped, I knew it would be at least a half hour before I could pull away from her, so I just waved and drove right on by. In my side mirror after I passed, I could see that she'd started crying and yelling, waving her arms in despair. Something was wrong. I swung around and drove on the shoulder of the dirt road into her yard. I'd never seen anyone look quite so pathetic. She put her arms around my neck, clinging to me, sobbing, unable to talk.

"What's the matter, Linda?" I asked, thinking she might just be feeling lonely or rejected because I'd failed to stop.

"I need to talk to you," she said gravely. "It's really important."

I followed her into the kitchen and took a chair by the cluttered table of breakfast dishes. "Irene, you're the best friend I've ever had. I feel I can confide in you." She sobbed between words. "I'm going to die," she wailed. She picked up a notebook, handing it to me. "In here I've written down all my funeral arrangements, my wishes concerning my burial. I want you to promise me you'll carry them out."

"Oh come on, Linda. I think it's just those postpartum blues. Come on, get your kids ready. Get some diapers and a couple of changes of clothes. When I pick up the kids after school, I'll drop by and take you home with me. All you need is a change of scenery."

She hung onto me and sobbed. "Irene, it's not the baby blues. I've had a premonition that I'm going to die."

I shook my head. But not wanting to offend her, I asked, "What's wrong with you? Are you sick? Do you have any symptoms?"

"No. I just woke up at 2 A.M. with this premonition that I should write things down in a book and make funeral preparations!"

I assured her I'd be back after school was out. My heart ached for her. I'd had the baby blues many times, feeling as if I were going to die. But I knew it would soon pass.

Promising to return for her, I left to make preparations for her visit. There was no way I could repay Linda for her all special kindnesses to me, but at least I would try. I baked a German chocolate cake from a mix she'd given me the day before. I also made a big potato salad; then I hurried like mad to finish my wash. After completing my errands, I picked up Linda and her babies when I went to collect the children at school.

"You had time to make that cake for me?" she asked me, clearly touched. She seemed excited to be with us for supper, and I could tell she looked forward to the opportunity to chat alone with me later that night.

We threw clean sheets on the old, outstretched sofa. Soon Linda's two little girls and my own eight kids were settled down for the night.

Linda talked long into the night about her teenage years in Florida and her marriage to Chuck. She told me all about meeting him, painting quite an interesting love story. Then she got around to the premonition she had the night before. I was exhausted, but she begged me to stay up with her. She needed me to console her, but mostly she wanted to tell me the intimate details of her life, which she insisted was coming to an end.

I confided in her that I was expecting again. I hadn't even told Verlan, but I wanted her to know. She told me I could have all her maternity clothes.

At 4 A.M., I made her lie down and try to rest because I desperately needed sleep before my kids got up. I'd have to fix them breakfast and then take them along with the rest of Verlan's kids into town for school. I eased myself onto a sliver of my bed alongside five of my sleeping children, and I pulled the chair into place for my feet. I was instantly out.

"Irene! Irene!" Linda's cries awoke me. I made my way groggily down the dark hall, lighting a kerosene lamp on the table beside her. I could tell by her cries that she was in real pain. It was only a quarter to five. How could something have happened so quickly? Linda was holding her hand over her left breast, sobbing. "Irene, I've never had such a pain in all my life."

"Maybe your breast is caked," I said. "Are you sure you've been nursing your baby on that side?"

"Yes, I'm sure. It's never been sore like this. I know the baby has nursed just fine."

Holding the lamp up close to her breast, I could see that it was inflamed. I heated water on the gas stove, then dipped a washcloth in hot water, wrung it out, and gently fanned it in the air until it cooled enough to be put on her breast. "This should make it feel better."

She got some relief and quit her moaning as I continued the hot packing, but neither of us slept anymore. I promised to take her with me to see the doctor as soon as the kids were up and ready for school.

DR. CORTEZ SHOOK his head. "We need to give her antibiotics every four hours. Can you continue the hot packs?" he asked. "An abscess is forming. The heat will help draw out the inflammation. Do you have someone who can give her the shots if I let her go home with you?"

"I will!" I promised. "I'll make sure she gets them on time."

We later dropped by Linda's house, and I picked up all her dirty clothes. I offered to do her wash for her so her kids would have enough changes of clothes to last for three or four days.

"Irene, you're like a mother to me. I love you so much. I hope I'm not being too big a burden."

"Of course not; that's what friends are for. I'm happy to help you. Just lie down and relax. I'll take care of your babies so you can have complete rest."

The next morning, Linda's breast was swollen even worse. The pain was becoming unbearable. I kept Donna out of school to stay with Linda and the small children while I drove to town, dropped the kids off, and then went to persuade Dr. Cortez to come to my trailer house to check on my friend. At the hospital, I watched as he rummaged through his cache of medicines. He brought six more shots, plus some strong painkillers, hoping that things weren't quite as bad as I'd described.

As soon as Dr. Cortez saw Linda, he administered the painkiller. He said he'd never seen an abscess so large, and then he added, "Her breast is filling with pus. You must continue to give her these shots and painkillers. Bring her to the hospital tomorrow afternoon. If it's not improving, I'll have to operate. A lancing should correct the problem."

The following day, Linda was in too much pain to ride along with a truckload of kids, so I brought them all home from school first. I left Donna in charge of the children until we returned.

Dr. Cortez took one look and said, "I'm very concerned. We'll have to operate immediately. I'll go get the room ready."

Linda put her head down on his desk and started sobbing. "Irene, I want you to tell the doctor that the only way I'll consent to do this is if he'll let you be with me every minute. I don't want to die alone."

I put my arms around her shoulders. "Linda, if you're really that worried, let's get you out to San Diego, where you can be with your husband and go to a hospital that can give you the best of care."

"No. I just want to get the operation over with. I can't impose on Chuck now. My only regret is that he doesn't have another wife to comfort him when I'm gone."

The doctor returned while Linda was crying. He asked me in Spanish why she was so upset. I was embarrassed to answer him because I thought Linda was just paranoid and overreacting. Still, I explained to him that she wanted me to be with her for the operation because she thought she was going to die, and she didn't want to die alone.

"You can be with her, but tell her it's a simple operation. It'll be over with in no time." He then led us both into the operating room. I helped Linda remove her clothes and put on a white gown that tied in the front.

The doctor had me put on some green pants, a shirt, coverings for my shoes, and a green cap; then he tied a gauze mask around my nose and mouth. We helped Linda onto the operating table, and a Mexican nurse untied the strings on her gown, letting it fall down at her sides. Then the nurse painted Linda's whole breast area clear down to her navel with disinfectant.

Tearfully, Linda grabbed onto my hand. "Irene, promise me you won't leave me. Promise?"

I patted her hand, holding it firmly, hoping to put her at ease. "Don't worry. I'll be here every minute. I promise I won't leave you. You'll soon wake up, and I'll be holding your hand."

The doctor motioned for silence as the nurse prepared to administer the anesthesia. Wanting to say one more thing, Linda wouldn't let the nurse cover her nose and mouth. "Oh, Irene, it's so comforting to die with your best friend by your side. Tell Chuck I love him."

In the next moment, I felt her grip loosen as her body relaxed. The nurse turned up the fumes as she monitored the flow through the gauge, nodding her approval that all was well.

The doctor began the operation. I swallowed hard, gritting my teeth as I watched him cut Linda's left breast from the base halfway to her nipple. Immediately, he and the nurse were mopping up thick, yellow pus. Dr. Cortez's gaze met mine as he checked for my reaction. He pressed gently on her breast again, forcing more of the nasty gook into a special container. He must have extracted at least a pint.

Linda thrashed around. One leg almost fell off the table. I quickly pushed it back, holding it in place as the doctor proceeded. She moaned and then thrashed around again. The doctor paused as we watched, waiting for her to calm down. Her chest rose and fell, up and down, then up and . . . stopped.

"Doctor, she's dead!" I exclaimed. "Do something quick. Oh, she's dead!"

The young nurse removed the mask from Linda's face as the doctor forced her chest up and down with his strong hands. With a telltale frantic look in his eyes, he kept trying again and again, all in vain.

I begged him, "Can't you give her a shot in the heart? I've heard of that saving people. Anything, Doctor! Please!"

I watched with frozen anxiety as he tried one final time. He injected some liquid into her heart with an extra-long needle. I stood by helplessly, watching in silence. I was praying to God that what I was witnessing wasn't really true.

"I'm sorry," the doctor said. "There's nothing more I can do. She's dead."

I fought back emotion as tears welled up in my eyes. I had to carry on. I found the nearest phone and called San Diego. Chuck wasn't available, so I left a message with his friend. Then I forced myself to drive to Linda's house to get her clothes so I could return to the hospital and dress her for burial.

The notebook Linda showed me three days earlier was still lying there on her kitchen table. I opened it and read the instructions for her funeral. I went down the list and found every article, even her favorite beads, nylons, and best dress shoes. When I got back to the hospital, her body was still on the operating table. The nurse helped me dress it. She was only in her early twenties.

I finally made it back to my crowded trailer house to find that Linda's infant was refusing to take a bottle. She was crying her head off, expecting her mother to come nurse her. That was more than I could stand. I toted both her little babies around in my arms, sobbing my heart out. Life was hard enough, but being without a mother was the saddest thing I could imagine. After much coaxing and cuddling, the baby took a bottle and fell asleep.

I left Donna in charge of all nine kids again, and I drove back to the hospital to be by Linda until someone could arrive with a casket so we could take her home. Everyone had left the hospital except for the doctor and the nurse, who waited for me to return. They now took their leave. I began my lonely wake.

The generator automatically shut off at 11 P.M. sharp, which soon left me in the dark. I lit the kerosene lamp and turned it down low as I nervously reclined on the nurse's cot in a small room adjacent to the operating room. I could still see the remains of my friend through the open door.

Nervous and alone, I couldn't sleep. The whole past few days seemed so unreal. Linda never knew I secretly envied her life. Although she and Chuck planned on entering into the Principle at some point in the future, at the time of her death, she had a husband to herself and a cozy house for just them and their girls. She was the first woman I knew who actually had a checkbook. She used her own judgment, spending her money freely on things she considered necessities. To me, many of them were luxuries. She'd buy cold cereal,

lunchmeat, crackers, mayonnaise, tuna, and chocolate. I could go on
forever with the list. I tried not to compare, but my children ate boiled
wheat and ground corn for breakfast. Every day, my boys used a hand-
turned grinder to turn whole kernels of wheat into flour and hot cereal. Pinto beans and bread were our main staples. I was lucky when I
could afford rice or potatoes to serve along with the beans. Occasionally, I splurged and bought margarine.

The flickering lamp released fumes from the kerosene into the
eerie partial darkness. It brought back memories of my night with
little Leah. She'd been just as cold, stiff, and lifeless as Linda was now.
During those six hours of contemplation, I think I surrendered my
desires for worldly comforts. What I really envied was Linda's departure. Wherever she'd gone, it was far away from this harsh world. Here
was a woman who'd been granted an easy out. I became convinced
that the only way to freedom was death.

CHAPTER TWENTY-EIGHT

L ife was chaotic for all of us. Verlan managed to come home on a few weekends and some holidays. When he did, he was lucky if he spent two nights home, and all five of us wives were upset. We were all dying for love and companionship, but only two of us got his attention, while the other three waited for their turn to come around next time. We were lucky if we each spent two nights with him a month.

Verlan soon realized his troubles had compounded, so he decided to move Beverly and Esther to the States and set them up as live-in maids earning enough to support themselves. He moved Charlotte, Lucy, and me to Ensenada, which was halfway between Los Molinos and San Diego. He found a big, green, two-story house that had been part of a motel complex. Charlotte and Lucy got the place by themselves until I recuperated from my recent confinement after delivering Connie. My ninth child, Connie was born on June 14, 1966, in the same Guerrero clinic where my friend Linda died. When my baby was two weeks old, I moved into that overcrowded house in Ensenada, making a total of twenty-five people living under one roof. Understanding this was to be a temporary arrangement until we could afford separate homes, we all tried to love one another and do the best we could under such crowded circumstances.

Verlan's paychecks not only went to support us, but they had to cover his rent and living expenses in San Diego, monthly payments on a truck, and the assistance he gave Joel on the newly acquired land in Baja. As always, his earnings fell short.

When Verlan arrived on December 23, he was determined to make this the best Christmas ever. He told me how he showered praises on Beverly for sacrificing $15.00 of her hard-earned money so he could buy presents for his kids. Our spirits were high—we could really surprise the unsuspecting brood. The oldest child was only fifteen. We knew we'd really have to stretch that money to get something for each of the twenty-one kids, but somehow we'd succeed.

I was the lucky one who accompanied Verlan into town, and he warned me several times to be certain to not forget any of Charlotte's little girls. "Make sure we don't forget anyone," he commanded. I looked longingly at all the boxes of games, beautiful dolls, tea sets, and other expensive toys, dreaming that we were rich enough to afford them. I realized that they were all out of question when Verlan called me to come down the next aisle. I joined him in the party favor section, where the small toys and balls were.

Verlan excitedly grabbed several different small, rubber, colored balls. He put them in the cart. I got three sets of jacks for the three older girls. Verlan mentally summed up the prices as I continued carefully choosing each child's gift. "Let's see now," he began checking it out. "We have three sets of jacks, eight balls, and these lovely dominoes for the three older boys to share. I wonder if there will be too many fights?" he questioned. "But at their age they deserve something nice. That will do for fifteen of them. Hey, these plastic whistles are on sale!" he said excitedly as he grabbed five different colors, examining their quality.

"Put those back! Please, Verlan, it's bad enough having twenty-five of us in the house when we're all quiet, let alone with children blowing whistles."

"No," he insisted, "they'll love them! That's it. Let's get the rest of the kids balloons!"

We watched the register closely, adding up each item, making sure we didn't go over the designated amount. Verlan was jubilant as he walked out, carrying our treasures. "Boy, will the kids ever be surprised!"

We stopped at a fruit stand on the side of the road. Verlan talked the owner into giving him credit for two weeks. He went wild—his kids would have the best Christmas yet. He got five kilos of peanuts, a box of oranges, plus a crate of bananas. Verlan's eyes danced when he selected three bags of candy. Regretfully, he bought a big bag of colored bubble gum. "God must really be on our side," he smiled. "Look, they even have brown paper bags here. We can put a toy plus some goodies in them so each child will have their own individual present."

When we got home, Lucy kept the excited bunch of kids behind a locked door, just long enough for the gifts to be hid in my bedroom.

The day before Christmas was especially busy with preparations. The children worked in teams doing their chores extra carefully. Along with everything else, I tripled the recipe for bread. Cinnamon rolls were an extravagance, but tomorrow the family would have their fill! By evening, I could see in all those little dancing eyes that it would be a sin to make them wait until tomorrow, so I gave in: they could celebrate tonight, but only *one* frosted cinnamon roll apiece.

The older ones begged me to give them hints. "Please, Auntie, what did Daddy buy for us?" they asked. I insisted they start their baths early and go to bed, so they'd all be ready bright and early for Santa Claus.

After they went to bed, we set to preparing the gifts. Following Verlan's instructions, I took a black marker and wrote the kids' names on the sacks, starting with Charlotte's children. I wrote her name at the top of the first bag, then the name of each of her children on their own bag. There would be a Christmas bag for everyone.

Verlan impatiently grabbed the first ones as he said, "Keep marking more as we fill them up. Charlotte and I will distribute the peanuts and fruit. Lucy, you count out the candy so it will be divided equally." I handed over Lucy's children's sacks, all marked. Verlan checked over each name to make sure the count was right. "That's great! Now, hurry up with yours, Irene. Mark them and start helping us."

When mine were all done, I opened them up myself and started filling them with peanuts and the allotted fruit, one orange and one banana each. I'll never forget how happy we were all together, switching a toy from one sack to another, each wife making sure her kids got their fair share. Verlan had the final say on what he thought was best for each child. "How nice," he commented with satisfaction. "Everyone has a gift in their sack except for us adults."

We carried the bags into my bedroom, pushing them close together to form two long lines, all ready to be distributed tomorrow. We were jubilant; it seemed God had worked things out. There were even enough goodies for the adults.

On Christmas morning, I could hear little children giggling and whispering at my bedroom door. "Go get dressed," I commanded. "Tell your mommies to get your hair done, then we'll have our Christmas." Was there ever commotion in the house! Kids hunting shoes, older ones dressing their younger brothers and sisters. Verlan was doing final details. He washed little faces and wiped a few runny noses.

With all the eager anticipation it was no easy task. We finally got all twenty-one kids quietly kneeling in a circle for prayer. Verlan thanked God for the occasion we were celebrating, for his wonderful family, and for the many blessings we enjoyed. The "amen" seemed to zap little bodies into a jumping, scampering beeline to the presents.

Verlan calmed the children down. "Just be quiet and stand in line." He looked pleased to see them so excited. "Now, when Daddy calls your name, come and get your sack. Be quiet until your name is called. Understand?"

Charlotte and I passed sacks to Lucy, who in turn handed them to Verlan. The names weren't in any particular order, but he began, "Loretta ... Pierre ... Beth ... Verla ... Norman ... Connie." He turned to me, "Irene, this is for your baby Connie. Make sure she doesn't choke on the peanuts."

My little five-year-old, Kaylen, couldn't stand the suspense a minute longer. "Daddy," he yelled above the commotion. "Where's mine?"

"Be quiet, son. Wait, your turn. It's coming. Mark ... André ... Chad ... Sandra ... Margaret ..."

Kaylen got more upset. "I'm littler than those big kids," he whined. "Where's mine?"

Verlan wanted obedience, so he grabbed Kaylen, shaking him a couple of times. "Now be quiet! Or you won't get one!" He continued handing out the bags. He was having the time of his life! It was fun just to watch him. He got the biggest thrill seeing those little kids' faces light up with joy. He continued, "Verlan M.... Laura ... Donna ... Rhea ... Brent ..."

Kaylen lost his patience. He was more frightened of being left out then of getting punished. "Daddy, you're forgetting me!"

Verlan stopped, looking very firm. He repeated, "Kaylen, I told you, if you don't behave, you won't get one!" He passed out more sacks. "Byron ... Susanna ... Steven ... Barbara ... Norine ..." With each additional sack, Kaylen sank deeper into despair. Seeing tears forming in his eyes, Verlan finally gave in. He turned to me. "Give me Kaylen's sack. He's been a good boy to wait this long."

Before I even read the names, I counted the remaining sacks. 1, 2, 3, 4—I got sicker with each count. There should have been five. I checked each sack, reading the names out loud. "Lucy, Charlotte, Irene, Daddy." I couldn't believe it—I'd left out my own kid!

Verlan was crushed. He'd only wanted to teach Kaylen to be patient and obedient. He didn't want Kaylen to know that he'd really been forgotten, so he grabbed his own sack, hoping Kaylen wouldn't notice. Hugging him close, to make up for the oversight, he thrust his own bag into Kaylen's expecting hands.

Kaylen quickly opened the sack rummaging around to find his toy. He looked up disgustedly at us. "Where's my toy?" he demanded tearfully. He looked accusingly at Verlan, pointing to the writing on the sack that said DADDY. "You know that's not my name!"

We were sick with guilt! Poor little Kaylen was absolutely brokenhearted. I thought we'd succeeded in stretching the $15.00, but we hadn't stretched it quite far enough. Verlan promised Kaylen that, as soon as we could afford it, he'd buy him his own special toy. But many a Christmas has come and gone, and Kaylen swears he's still waiting!

. . .

SOON OUR STAY together in the big green house seemed more per-
manent than temporary. Living conditions became more and more
intolerable with the three of us wives having to deal with each other
as well as our combined twenty-one children, who were constantly
underfoot. School in Ensenada for the older children plus an occasional outing at the beach for all of them were about the only outlets
for the kids' unrelenting energies.

Lucy, Charlotte, and I did well at avoiding major fights, but the air
was thick with feelings. Verlan's absences became the norm. Most
recently, he'd gone off on a three-month mission trip to persuade
polygamists living in Canada to come down and join Joel's church.
He arrived home from that trip with nothing to offer his impover-
ished families. We'd been subsisting on donations from the church
storehouse, but we somehow scrounged up enough to celebrate his
homecoming.

It was Lucy's night to sleep with him. Her bedroom was upstairs,
directly over Charlotte's. Mine was upstairs, too, across and down the
hall from Lucy's. I cunningly cleaned up my room nicely and offered
to let Verlan and Lucy sleep there. I insisted that Lucy let me take her
baby to tend along with mine, and I'd sleep in her room. They were
both pleased that I could be so thoughtful by giving them the night
alone.

I made sure the babies were asleep. Then I lay on my stomach and
rhythmically bounced the bed for all I was worth. I was laughing so
hard, I had to smother my face in the pillow. I waited five minutes,
then continued the rhythmic bouncing, waited, then continued.

The next morning, Charlotte was in the kitchen when Verlan came
downstairs in a chipper mood. He tried to kiss her good morning,
but she flipped her head and refused to accept any of his attentions.

"What's wrong with you?"

"You know darn well what's wrong. I refuse to live another day in
this house!"

Verlan was baffled. "What on earth are you talking about?"

She blurted out in tears. "I heard you! And I can't believe it."

"Heard what?"

"I think it's terrible that I had to listen to you and Lucy making love."

"How could you have heard anything? We didn't even sleep in her room!" he said defensively.

"Don't lie to me! I heard you!" Her sobs grew louder. "I will not tolerate living here another day!"

Verlan rushed upstairs to consult with me. "Boy, does Charlotte have an imagination!" he said. "She's so upset. She says she's moving out for sure. What do you think is her problem?"

I let him talk on and on, fretting about it, until I couldn't restrain myself any longer. I threw myself on Lucy's bed, laughing uncontrollably. Then I bounced that bed up and down, clueing him in on my prank.

He pointed his finger at me in disbelief. "You didn't?"

I was laughing so hard, I could barely squeak it out. "Yes . . . I did!"

"Why on earth would you do this to her?"

Still giggling, I ventured, "I guess I just wanted her to think we were getting more than she was."

FOR A SHORT TIME, we all benefited from my fun. True to her word, Charlotte did move out. She rented a brick house a few blocks away. Verlan decided he couldn't afford the rent on that house and the big green house as well, so Lucy moved into a trailer house nearby in Chapultepec, and I rented a small, four-room cinder-block house next to a winery (called La Vinata) for $35 a month. This was the eleventh time I'd moved in thirteen years.

Because my house had a convenient cement slab for a carport, Verlan moved a small camper trailer onto it for pregnant Beverly. She cooked in my house, but slept in her little trailer. Esther moved back to Los Molinos. Although Beverly and Esther both lost their first babies at birth, the number of Verlan's offspring reached twenty-nine.

He put each wife on a strict budget he supplemented with clothes and shoes from the secondhand stores, most of which was given to him because it was so torn, stained, dirty, or simply out of style, no one would pay for it. We still ground wheat for bread and cereal on a hand grinder. Each wife was more or less left to fend for herself, with rarely more than was needed to cover necessities.

One weekend when Verlan was able to come home from Vegas, he arrived to find my two-year-old, Connie, deathly ill. Her eyes would roll back in her head as she lay clammy and barely moving. My usual home remedies and prayers brought about no marked improvement. I knew if we didn't get professional help immediately, we'd lose her. She was near death when we arrived at the government hospital in Ensenada. Dr. Martinez, the attending physician, diagnosed her as having pneumonia and gave us little hope for her recovery.

Once she was admitted, Verlan was in a hurry to leave because he had only eleven hours to get back to Vegas in time for work. I was frantic. He was about to leave me there alone, and I felt emotionally incapable of dealing with the situation. Not even in an emergency could Verlan find time to be with me. Anxiously, I pled with him to stay longer, at least till we knew she'd be all right. Verlan tried to hush me, ordering me to dry my tears. He left, angry I'd made such a scene in front of the doctor.

In my own desperate way, I tried to understand. Was it utterly unrealistic for him to take off work each time one of his neglected wives or children got sick? I'd endured six of my babies' births without him. *God,* I prayed, *why can't my child's own father be here to comfort us at such an uncertain time?*

I should have been strong, able to bear whatever was necessary, but my heart was wrenched seeing my precious child so ill. I was sick with apprehension lest God decide to snatch her away from me as he'd done with Leah. Tiptoeing into the ward, I found Connie strapped into an iron crib. Despite all the other children in the room who were crying, Connie appeared to be sleeping. I watched the glucose drip into my beautiful child's arm. *Please, God, watch over her. Please let her recover.*

I had no alternative but to leave her in the doctor's care while I caught a bus and sadly returned home to my other duties. It was

Sunday, and there was a great deal to be done before school the next day.

While Connie was in the hospital, I rode six miles into town on the bus every day to check on her. I was only allowed short visits. I'd see her screaming, begging for me. I pleaded with the nurses to let me untie her so I could hold her, but they refused. It was so hard for both of us; the two-week ordeal seemed to last forever. Dr. Martinez cared for my baby and kindly befriended me. I'm sure some of it was pity, especially when he met Lucy and learned Verlan had a string of wives.

My guilt mounted as quickly as the hospital bill increased. I knew we were spending precious money the whole family desperately needed. Everyone had to cut back whenever there was an emergency. Verlan sent $400 of tithing money from the church coffers to make a down payment on the bill, promising he'd pay the balance as soon as he could.

Dr. Martinez called me into his office. He told me to go get the file paper from pediatrics and take it down the corridor to the cashier. I had to settle the bill before he could sign Connie's release so I could take her home.

I watched as the nurse stamped a couple of forms and then handed the original to me. "That will be seventy-five," she said matter-of-factly.

I was shocked. Thinking I misunderstood, I asked, "Seventy-five dollars?"

"No, it's seventy-five pesos." That was six dollars at the time.

I paid her, knowing there'd been some grave mistake. I returned to Dr. Martinez's office, hoping he could rectify the matter. But when I tried to explain, he put his arm around my shoulder and said, "Señora, I worked things out so all you'd have to pay was a minimum that the government hospital requires. All my services are free. Tell your husband to take you on a long, overdue vacation with the money. Tell him it's my prescription for you."

My house was unheated except for what warmth came from the gas range in the kitchen. The doctor refused to let me take Connie back there because he knew the conditions wouldn't be conducive to her recovery. A friend, Juleen Hafen, insisted I stay two weeks with her while Connie regained her weight and the color returned to her cheeks. I don't know what I'd have done without kind friends like Juleen, who seemed to appear in many of my darkest hours.

WE COULD PLAINLY SEE we'd never get ahead financially by paying rent, especially on several houses. So Verlan purchased a lot around the corner from my small house. With the help of his older boys and a couple of wives, he started building a home large enough for several of us to live together. We called it the Big Brown House.

In the meantime, Lucy's heater caught fire and her trailer burned to the ground, destroying everything she owned. No one was hurt, but she had to move into the Big Brown House before it was completely finished. Charlotte had no sooner set up her living quarters with Lucy when Verlan moved me in also. Beverly's trailer was set up behind the house.

We were thrilled to have hot water and never thought to complain that we only had one bathroom. Around the walls of the dining area, Verlan built a one-piece bar that served as a table. He also built long wooden benches so all the kids could sit down at once to eat.

We three wives took turns doing the cooking. For breakfast, the three oldest girls—Rhea, Donna, and Laura—held plates over the stove while I rationed out the food, making sure everyone got his or her share. The girls then served a plate to each child. It was a riot. I often made hotcakes for all thirty of us. I found that it was easier to make each person one large pancake the size of the frying pan. That way, no one came back for seconds, and it kept the confusion down.

Even in these strained circumstances, I believed we needed to "live a little" because, well, we couldn't postpone happiness forever. Once, I got the ice cream vendor who made daily rounds through our neighborhood to give me credit until the weekend. Verlan paid for the twenty-six Popsicles when he returned home, but he was disgusted with me when he found out I was spending money unwisely.

I ignored his reprimand because we didn't have many other joys. The squeals of excitement from all those kids made it worthwhile. I found a way to buy a large pan full of Popsicles at least once a week. They only cost twenty centavos each, so we continued the ritual without mentioning it to Verlan.

With only the one bathroom in the house, Verlan set up the faithful old outhouse in the backyard. There were so many of us using it that he knew it would fill up fast, so he made the hole extra deep. It was already half full when I stepped into it one day, big and pregnant with my tenth child. My little two-year-old, Connie, stepped in beside me. With no warning, the floorboard gave way, and down we went. Before I could grab her, she fell right into the awful cesspool. One of my legs went through also, but my stomach saved the rest of me from flying through the hole in the floor.

I screamed bloody murder. Six of the boys were just outside the outhouse, playing marbles. They came running with Lucy and Charlotte close behind to see what all my screaming was about. They helped me up, but Connie was in up to her armpits. They tipped the toilet house on its side, and before eleven-year-old Chad knew what was happening to him, Charlotte and I shoved him, screaming, headfirst into the hole. We were holding onto his feet, shouting for him to grab Connie before she went completely under. Chad was terrified that we would drop him in there with her. He didn't even want to touch her, but we forced him to reach down through the filthy slush and grab hold of her arms. Within a few seconds, we drew them both out of the stinky hole.

I sprayed both Connie and me off with a hose. Then I put her in a tub of water and scrubbed her with soap, vinegar, Pine-Sol, and even Purex. Nothing seemed to eliminate the awful odor. I finally had to cut her hair off. That was the only way I could get the nauseous smell off her. She'd been a world-class thumb sucker before our outhouse incident, but now she would smell her thumb and just cry. She gave that habit up real quick.

We made sure not to dig a toilet hole that deep again, but Connie's continual fear of falling in drove her to use the inside bathroom faithfully. I told her that whether or not any of the other kids wanted to believe it, she really was the cutest little stinker I ever had!

CHARLOTTE GOT A JOB teaching school in San Diego. Lucy and I were left to tend all the children, including Charlotte's eight, in the Big Brown House. One day while washing clothes outside, I suddenly heard screaming coming from the house.

I opened the door and saw Lucy whipping Mark with a belt. Not wanting to question her authority over the kids, I said nothing. I couldn't imagine what they'd done to deserve it, but from what I could tell, everyone in eyesight was going to get it before Lucy was finished.

Twelve-year-old Susanna was Lucy's next victim. Charlotte's daughter Susanna was the sweetest and most timid of all the kids. I couldn't stand there and watch Lucy whip her. Not wanting any trouble between us, I grabbed Susanna away from Lucy, stating, "If she deserves to be whipped, then I'll do it and I'll do it good."

I pulled the frightened girl into the closest bedroom and locked the door. Susanna started to cry. I whispered to her, "Keep it up. Scream loud, and carry on each time this belt hits the bed." I lashed the bed and yelled out, "Don't you ever do it again." Then I motioned for Susanna to scream louder.

That's how she got the whipping of her life. My pretend violence scared Lucy so bad, she either forgot or decided not to punish the three remaining culprits for whatever they'd done. Years later, Susanna admitted to her mother that I hadn't really whipped her. She loved me even more because I came to her rescue.

BEFORE LONG, Lucy also got a job as a nanny in the States. She and Charlotte were only home occasionally, for a few days here and there, usually just for a weekend. During this time, Verlan added on to the Big Brown House so Beverly could move out of her trailer. Esther was still in Los Molinas. Meanwhile, I inherited all the parenting responsibility for Verlan's twenty-five children living in that four-bedroom house.

I had to send fifteen kids off to school every morning. They all wore uniforms I had to keep washed and ironed. Four babies were in diapers, and we couldn't think of buying disposables. I prewashed all the stinky diapers by hand so they could be washed a second time in the Maytag wringer-washer, which ran continually. The older boys always filled the washer and the rinse tubs with water before they left for school. The older girls made beds, swept floors, and dressed the younger kids while I made breakfast and braided nine heads of hair. It was pandemonium getting them all out of the house on time.

I had to bake twelve loaves of whole wheat bread every other day. I cleaned, served, washed dishes, ironed, and cooked for the whole crowd, plus the many visitors who always seemed to be on hand. (Church members dropped in unannounced several times a week on their way to Los Molinos, because our house was the halfway point from San Diego.) The little kids and babies cried for their own mothers. I cried with them at night from sheer exhaustion.

I tried hard not to complain about my job. I told myself God required it of me and would bless me for it. For his glory and for our future kingdom, I was raising these children born under the covenant. My reward would surely be great.

To that end, and with Dr. Cortez's help, the stork brought me a ten-pound baby on November 7, 1967. Verlan named him LaSalle after an old friend of his. It all happened so fast, I barely had time to summon the doctor. There went another $35, and still no vacation from my dormitory duties. Now I had a newborn to care for, too.

My heart longed for Verlan, especially when I'd get the blues. But I'd remind myself how hard he was slaving away with a paintbrush in the 90- to 100-degree Las Vegas heat just to clothe and feed his kids and contribute to the Lord's great cause. The burden was too great for him to bear alone. Like my Mormon pioneer ancestors, I squared my shoulders and pushed onward.

Verlan didn't have much to give me physically or emotionally, but he did praise me. And he needed me; I could see that. I was gifted

with being fast, organized, and able to multitask. I knew we were living through the toughest years. The boys would soon be old enough
to go to work and help support their brothers and sisters. Until then,
I just couldn't let Verlan down. I, too, would work for the cause and
strive for heavenly glory. There was certainly none to be had on
Earth.

I also worked hard so Verlan would love me more, as he frequently
promised to do. As much as ever, I wanted to be his favorite.

IN JUNE 1967, my brother Douglas, who lived in Victor, Montana,
decided to surprise me. He brought Mother, along with his wife and
ten kids, to pay us a visit. All he had with which to locate us was a
post office box number in Ensenada. When he inquired there, the
postal clerk didn't know any more about us than Douglas did, so
Douglas set out to find us on his own. He knew we lived about six
miles outside of Ensenada, so he searched every beach and housing
area within that distance, hoping to locate us.

This was only Mother's second trip to Mexico to see me in fourteen years. They were disappointed when they couldn't find us after
driving all the way from Montana. But even after two days of looking, Doug wasn't ready to give up. He traveled south out of Ensenada
to the Chapultepec area, asking everyone who could understand
English if they'd heard of us or knew our whereabouts. At 5 P.M. on
the third day, he decided to give up the search and go home. Mother
broke down crying, so Doug drove west to check one final beach.

As they passed a big winery, Doug spotted two blond-headed boys
trying to ride a burro. He stopped the van and yelled, "Do you boys
speak English?"

"Yes," they answered, jumping off and leading the burro toward
the van.

As they approached, Doug turned to Mother and pointed to the
tallest boy. "That's got to be Irene's kid. He looks just like I did when
I was growing up." Then he asked them, "Do you kids know an
Irene LeBaron?"

André, the taller one, answered shyly, "Sure, she's my mother."

"Well, I'm your uncle Doug, your mom's brother. Get in with us and show us where you live."

A few minutes later, the blue van pulled into the yard. André jumped out ahead of everyone, shouting into the house, "Mom, Grandma's here!"

When I looked out the open door and saw my mother's now-frail form, I was astonished and grieved. She was an old woman. Her once-beautiful features were faded and wrinkled. She'd changed drastically in the seven years since I'd seen her last. But in a few moments, we were in each other's arms, weeping and rejoicing that we were together again.

I was so very glad to finally see a part of my family again. I'd longed for them deeply throughout the years, but my circumstances made it impossible for me to see them except on rare occasions. Even when I got to, there was so much I couldn't tell them. On this visit, we spent five wonderful days trying to catch up on years of experiences.

At one point, when Mother and I were alone, she launched onto the topic I'd so long dreaded discussing with her. "I'm glad you at least have electricity," she said sadly. "I was worried that you'd be scrubbing on a board."

How thankful I was that I now had a Maytag washer.

"How do you stand the constant noise from all the children? Irene, how have you been able to make it through all of this?" The grief on her face made her look even older.

I told her the sort of lie all good daughters tell their mothers about their most egregious mistakes. "Don't worry, Mom," I assured her. "It's only made me stronger."

CHAPTER TWENTY-NINE

In April 1968, at the age of thirty-eight, Verlan came home from a church conference held in Colonia LeBaron. He had that certain glint in his eye. "I have wonderful news to tell you!" he said. "After the final meeting at conference, Brother Ray asked to talk privately with me. His fourteen-year-old daughter, Susan, wants to marry me. What do you think about it, Irene?"

I was stunned. "Verlan, she's too young. Why, she's only two years older than our own daughter Donna!"

He'd thought of that and had a quick answer. "So it's got to be from God, Irene. Who else at that age would even consider me? This is a blessing straight from Heaven! Susan will be such an asset to our kingdom. Ah, come on, Irene. Please don't cry."

How could I help it? I was now thirty-one and my looks were fading. Whether he thought so or not, Susan was a tremendous threat to me—her beauty, her youth. Mostly, I was sick and tired of sharing the one and only man for whom I'd given up my whole life. I felt jealous, hateful, and thoroughly uncooperative. I'd coped all these years, struggling just to survive, and now he was marrying one of Donna's friends for me to compete with.

Verlan grew more concerned because he could see my depression deepening. "Please don't look so sad. You know I've never courted anyone, have I? Somehow, God just sent each of you to me. Please don't give me problems, Irene. I've got to have you stand behind me."

He wrapped my sobbing body in his arms. "Oh, honey, don't get silly ideas. This won't change the way I feel about you one bit. Please, give me your permission."

Our circumstances were worse than ever. But I'd sworn to take this man for better or for worse. What else could I say? "It's up to you, Verlan," I said halfheartedly.

During the following months, though I was reluctant, it was gratifying to be doing my duty and seeing Verlan happy. Susan came from Chihuahua to visit. At least she got to see what she was getting herself into. And, for some unknown reason, I found I liked her.

They'd decided to be married in October at our church's next general conference in Colonia LeBaron. By then, she'd be fifteen. When the time approached, Verlan began making the required arrangements. Which wife would get the traditional privilege of placing Susan's right hand in his? Esther was still in Los Molinos. Charlotte and Lucy were off at their jobs in San Diego. It was easy for his fourth wife, Beverly, to make her choice. She had just moved into the new addition Verlan made for her. She would rather tend all the kids by herself than give Verlan a new wife. She wanted no part of it.

I'd been begging for a vacation ever since Dr. Martinez prescribed it. This would be my chance. I desperately needed a few days' rest. My need was so urgent, I decided to attend my own husband's wedding to get it met.

Verlan planned to go straight there from San Diego. Harold Tippetts gladly offered to drive me in his big green commercial truck, but he explained, "You'll have to ride the twenty hours in the back with all the other members who are going to the conference."

I fought morning sickness as the truck jolted along the dirt roads. With eighteen others all crowded together, I kept to the very back to relieve my claustrophobia and be where I could throw up. I was so glad when that trip was over. I gratefully showered at my mother-in-law's house once we got to Colonia LeBaron. Then I flopped wearily into bed. Verlan arrived the following morning, as planned. Preparations were made for him to marry Susan two days later, right after the last service of Sunday conference.

In the meantime, I didn't get to see much of him because he had to attend so many meetings. Though he slept with me, he was up by 6 A.M. And didn't get back in bed till past midnight. I'd looked forward to spending time with him, but if I wanted to see him, it was either at conference meetings or after he'd fallen asleep. So at night I'd lie quietly and watch him sleep, as I'd done so many other times over the years. It was a sad ritual only a plural wife can really comprehend.

Early Sunday morning, Verlan told me to wash out two changes of his clothes and repack his suitcase. With his briefcase in hand, he came back to where I was still in bed. "I want to leave tonight, immediately after the wedding. Irene, I sure love and appreciate you. I'll see you tonight." And out the door he went.

I heard Susan would be wearing a traditional white wedding gown she had borrowed from someone. Verlan had his usual gray suit. I only had one good dress that still fit at all—a red and black checkered cotton sack dress I'd selected from the cast-off clothes Verlan hauled home from Vegas. I was pregnant with my eleventh child, and my tummy bulged at the buttons down the front of my dress, but I would try and remember to hold it in during the ceremony.

I tried not to think selfish thoughts. For months, I'd been begging Verlan for some desperately needed maternity clothes. I knew the money Verlan would spend on his honeymoon with Susan could dress me like a queen. I felt sick and out of place in my cheap, ill-fitting outfit. Imagine, not having a decent thing to wear to my own husband's wedding! Under the circumstances, such thoughts hardly even made me smile.

Verlan was now president of the Church of the Firstborn. That's why most of his family and friends at the conference heard about his impending marriage to Susan. Several of them shook my hand, congratulating me on my "sister wife-to-be." Enviously, an elderly brother, Joseph Parson, said to me, "How lucky you are! Why, she'll be a beautiful flower in Verlan's heavenly bouquet."

I thought a cactus might describe her better. But I had to guard Verlan's image; it was required of me. I hung an artificial smile on my face and endeavored to set a good example for the other women.

During the closing hymn of conference, I gave myself a good talking to. "Don't goof things up for him! For heaven's sake, don't cry! And no matter what, stay until the reception is over."

I hadn't given Verlan a wife for fourteen years, since Lucy. And that was a catastrophe. Since that time, he'd married his two Mexican wives, Beverly and Esther. I wasn't present for either of them, though I'd given my consent (after a fashion).

Maybe God would forgive me for the terrible way I acted at Lucy's wedding if I willingly gave Susan to Verlan. Yes, I was sure this would make up for it. Back then, I was devastated and brokenhearted, but I at least had a little comfort knowing Lucy probably wouldn't get any sex except for procreation purposes. I shook my head regretfully. I was the one who convinced Verlan to fulfill my sexual needs. I looked at fifteen-year-old Susan, a mere child, and I shuddered. Was I ready to give her to my husband so he could fulfill hers?

I thanked God. At least Susan was pretty and smart. Every other man in the group would have given his eyeteeth to have her. I tried warming to Verlan's new marriage by recognizing that Susan would put him just one wife away from that quorum of seven he'd always wanted.

I needed someone to hold my hand through this trial, so I went to get my good friend Linda, who was the town midwife. We hurried down the gravel road toward the Wakehams' home, where the wedding was to be held. I was surprised at the large living room. It was about twenty by thirty feet, with an extended area that opened into an even larger kitchen. It would accommodate fifty to seventy guests if we crowded close together.

By this time, it was well known that Colonia LeBaron was a polygamous community, and the LeBarons were openly proclaiming polygamy as a tenet of their religion. No one worried about the law interfering, because the Mexican officials only intervened if a person involved in it made an accusation of wrongdoing. That's why all of Verlan's wives after me got to invite guests to their weddings and otherwise do all the same things any other bride and groom did on their wedding day. None of them had to slink around, looking for a secluded park to be married in or hide her marriage from everyone she loved.

Linda sat down on the first wooden chair of many lining the walls for guests. I was far too nervous to sit, so I stood beside her. Verlan came in and started greeting the approving guests. He peered around the room, searching for me or for Linda (because he knew I'd be with her). As soon as he pinpointed her, he hurried over and sat for one brief moment in the chair next to her. Leaning toward me, he whispered, "Susan is around the back of the house. Her father, Vern, will walk her in on his arm, so you get ready." He held my hand, seeking reassurance. "Please don't let me down with all these people watching. Be strong. Come through for me." He kissed my cheek. "I'll make it up to you. I promise!"

I'd already been to the bathroom twice, but I was very nervous, and being pregnant made it worse. I had to go again. When I was finished, I checked my hair in the mirror. I hadn't worn mascara on purpose, just in case a tear slipped out. I looked at my pretty reflection and then spoke consolingly to myself. "It's okay, Irene. Be good." I took a deep breath; then I turned the doorknob and stepped out into the crowd, prepared to do my religious duty. I held my head high and greeted guests as I obediently walked across the crowded room and took my place beside Verlan in front of the fireplace. He smiled at me approvingly as he nervously shuffled his feet and wrung his hands.

About half the crowd had never witnessed a plural marriage before. The curious and inquisitive guests moved to the sides of the living room, making space for the bride to enter. The air was filled with expectancy. The procession began as the piano intoned "Here Comes the Bride." Susan appeared, holding the arm of her bald, rotund father, who smiled at Verlan with satisfaction, clearly feeling it an honor and privilege to give his daughter to such an important man. Although our church of about a hundred families never grew very large in all the years it limped along dramatically, those who participated thought it was a gift straight from God, and thus their highest priority. As its president, Verlan was highly esteemed.

In unison and in rhythm to the music, Susan and her father took their halting steps toward us. Her two younger sisters held her train while the beautiful virgin glided along. With her short, platinum blonde hair and white dress, she looked every bit an angel.

Joel officiated. "Do you, Sister Irene, take Susan by the right hand and . . ."

I said, "I do." Then I placed Susan's right hand in my husband's and moved to one side so she could take her rightful place beside him. It was my duty to fade into the background now. Here I was, an intruder again. I reminded myself repeatedly that I was no more than an invited guest at my own husband's wedding.

I'd done it all perfectly. In a few minutes, it was over. Verlan kissed the bride, and I quickly disappeared into the kitchen. The occasion belonged to Susan. I kept busy serving cake and punch so I wouldn't have time to think. I joked and smiled with other plural wives and wedding guests, hoping the bride and groom would hurry up and leave so I could, too.

"Come quick if you want a ride," Verlan said, interrupting my internal conversation. "Susan has gone home to change. I need to go to my mother's to get my suitcase." Verlan praised me as we drove the three blocks over there. "Things went well. I appreciate it, Irene. I just hope my other wives will love Susan as you do and make her feel just as much at home."

Verlan checked his suitcase one final time to make sure I'd packed the change of clothes he asked me to wash. "Hey, what's this?" he asked, picking up a white envelope. He knew it was my handwriting, and it clearly annoyed him.

"I just wanted to say good-bye, that's all. Who knows when I'll see you again? Besides, there's no reason for you to be mad."

"Well, I'm glad I found it here. I wouldn't want Susan to see this and think that you're feeling bad. That might have ruined things for her."

The dam inside me broke. "Ruin things for *her*?" I screamed. "Some damn fifteen-year-old . . . punk . . . marries *my* husband, and *I've* ruined things for *her*?"

He left before he had to hear any more. I couldn't believe how

furious I was. Plural marriage was supposed to refine me, help eliminate my envy and jealousies. But it wasn't working out that way at
all. The price of godhood was simply too high. If this was any sort of
preview of the life to come, I wanted out.

A WEEK LATER, Susan and Verlan returned home from their honeymoon. He left her with me at my house in Ensenada until he could
decide where she would live. Having grown up with Verlan's daughters at Colonia LeBaron, she was excited to see Donna, Laura, and
Rhea again. They were her friends. I often felt that part of her decision to marry Verlan was the fact that she would get to be around her
girlfriends permanently.

Donna, on the other hand, was not so thrilled with the situation.
She confided in me that it seemed weird that her daddy married a
close friend who was only two years older than her. "It's almost as if
Daddy has married his own daughter," she said. She didn't understand the male perspective that younger wives could be more easily
trained to a man's liking.

The first few days Susan spent with us went well enough. But
soon I learned that Verlan bought her some new shoes, while my
only pair was all worn out. I was more than jealous; I was downright
mad. Then I saw them.

Susan was old enough and wise enough to sense my feelings.
She almost cried, explaining to me how Verlan insisted she buy the
awful, matronly shoes of his choice rather than some like all the other
young girls were wearing. She felt much better after we joked about
how men like nothing better than keeping their women barefoot and
pregnant.

My heart went out to this child bride because I so powerfully felt
her disappointment. I knew she'd basically made her last free choice
when she chose to marry my husband. Because of her genuine inno-
cence, I felt a protective love for Susan, a motherly bond of concern. I
would never again be jealous of her. She not only won Verlan's heart,
becoming his favorite wife, but she also won mine.

CHAPTER THIRTY

Morning sickness and inflamed varicose veins in my legs made it impossible for me to care for twenty-six kids a single day longer. Not only was I exhausted, at times I thought I was losing my mind. Love or no love, I resigned.

Verlan didn't appreciate this at all. He reprimanded me for even thinking such things. Crushed at this lack of understanding, I demanded he move me back to Los Molinos, even if it was into the old, run-down trailer house again. I needed peace, quiet, and a place to rest before my impending delivery. Lucy quit work in San Diego and moved back into the Big Brown House with her seven children. Charlotte took her nine children to live with her in Tijuana.

Verlan decided the best thing to do was to build me a house in Los Molinos. A truck loaded with lumber, drywall, and other materials left Ensenada two hours before we did. I had nine of my ten kids with me, plus I was big and pregnant. We took the bedding, clothing, and utensils we ended up with after giving Lucy and Charlotte their shares and jammed into our camper for the two-and-a-half-hour drive to the Baja colony.

My friend Betty invited us to move into her home. She insisted I not fret about any inconvenience to her and her own seven children. Verlan assured us all it would be only a few days before he finished the small, three-bedroom home for me and the kids. The cement floor had been poured the week before, so Verlan, Verlan Jr., and a friend, Rodolfo Gaytan, worked on it from sunup till near midnight. In just six days, I moved in.

The bathroom had no fixtures, the floors had no carpet or tile, and the walls still needed to be taped and painted. They wired the house, hoping we'd have electric power down the line. Because the children were so noisy and I didn't want to impose on my friend any longer, I camped in the unfinished house for a week until Verlan returned. He brought a load of used furniture for us he bought at garage sales. A month later, my home was taped and painted on the inside. It had been four and a half years since I had left my new home in the mountains.

I could hardly imagine having three bedrooms for just ten of us. But the flies from the neighbor's goat pens swarmed in through the screenless windows, and the sand fleas kept us all scratching until we had bloody sores. Then there were the chilly ocean breezes that made it so difficult to dry clothes in the damp air. So it ended up feeling like a LeBaron home after all.

Luckily, I was allowed to take another short vacation to San Diego to visit friends. While I was there, they bought me a pair of navy blue maternity pants and a beautiful red and navy blue smock. These were the first store-bought maternity clothes I ever had. It felt so good—like I belonged to the real world.

When I got home, Verlan rebuked me for wearing pants. He proceeded to buy me the usual two pieces of cloth, which I made into the usual two maternity dresses. But I disobeyed him and wore my pants and blouse as my best outfit. One advantage of his being away so much was that he couldn't keep close tabs on me.

A COUPLE OF MONTHS LATER, I left my entire brood in Donna's care while I went to Ensenada to have my eleventh baby. I went a week early, thinking I'd have it in a day or two. Instead, I went thirteen days over my due date. Beverly let me stay with her in the one-bedroom apartment Verlan had built for her as an add-on to the Big Brown

House. I enjoyed peace while resting there, but I was very worried about leaving my children for so long. I wondered if they were warm enough at night. The cold, foggy April weather concerned me.

At 5 A.M. on April 10, 1969, a hard contraction suddenly gripped me. I waited, watching the clock to try and time my next contraction. To my surprise, none came. This was new.

At 8 A.M., I had my friend Juna drive me to my sister-in-law Jeannine's place three blocks away. "Jeannine, would you examine me to see if you think I'll have this baby today?" I said. "I've only had one huge contraction."

After examining me, she warned, "My golly! You better get the doctor here quick. You're fully dilated."

On our way back to the Big Brown House, we stopped at the winery, and Juna ran in to make an emergency call to Dr. Cortez. Before she finished the call, my pains started fast and furious. She told him to come immediately. We rushed back to Beverly's. I gave instructions as Lucy and Beverly helped Juna prepare my bed for the delivery. I'd only been in labor for twenty minutes. Doctor or no doctor, the baby was coming.

Dr. Cortez rushed in just as the head was crowning. He rinsed his hands in a pan of Lysol water Lucy held ready for him and delivered my precious baby girl on the very next pain. I was in labor for exactly twenty-five minutes.

Charlotte had a Verlan Jr., Lucy had a little girl named Verla, and I felt that I should also have the privilege of naming a child after our husband. So I decided to put an "a" on the end of his name and call her Verlana.

Verlan arrived when the baby was a week old and took me back to Los Molinos, where I found my kids all sick with colds and fevers. LaSalle had an abscessed ear, which broke. I'd just delivered our eleventh baby and I had all these sick children, but I couldn't have any extra time with Verlan. It wasn't my turn. He just dropped me off at my house, and then he left to spend the night with Esther, who hadn't seen him in almost a month.

The kids were overjoyed to see me again, especially Donna, who had shouldered all the responsibility while I was away. I put the new baby in the crib and then let the five youngest ones crawl in the foot and sides of my bed to get some comfort and hugs that were long overdue.

Before long, Verlan decided he needed me to help Lucy care for the Big Brown House in Ensenada and the many guests we constantly had there. So I moved back.

VERLAN'S COUSIN, Theron Leany, was like a brother to us. He gave Verlan work in his Las Vegas painting business for over sixteen years. No other member of our church gave more money to it than he did or was more willing to make whatever sacrifices might be necessary to forward the kingdom of God. His first wife, Helen, and nine of their eleven children lived in Los Molinos. They only saw him on the weekends that he and Verlan could make it down.

On May 10, 1969, I was washing clothes out at the wringer-washer when I saw the car of an old friend, Lane Stubbs, come zooming over the dusty road faster than usual. Fear surged through me. Instinctively, I knew he had bad news, and I started running toward him. I wasn't quite to the corner of the house when Lane jumped out of his car. "Come with me, quick! Theron's been in an accident. The ambulance has taken him to the hospital."

Slipping off my wet clothes, I quickly changed, leaving instructions for Donna to hold down the fort. Lane and I rushed to the hospital.

I found Theron unconscious, bound with cords at his feet and wrists, tied securely to an iron cot. I felt relieved to see that he wasn't all black and blue and swollen like other car accident victims I'd seen. I knew that before long, Theron would wake up, and I'd be able to take him home.

He thrashed around, almost expelling the needle that was inserted into the vein in his wrist. I stroked his hands, hoping to calm him as I watched the glucose slowly drip down the tube into his arm.

Nobody worked harder or was more on the go than Theron. I didn't think he ever got enough sleep. Knowing he was unconscious and couldn't hear me, I said, "Theron, you're finally going to get the rest you deserve."

Seven other men were in cots in the same ward. To the left of me was a man burned so badly, I was unable to guess his age. He constantly moaned and cried out in pain. I struck up a conversation with him in Spanish, but then a chubby nurse approached his bed with gauze and bottles of medicine. She asked me to please step out of the room while she treated his burns.

I patted Theron's cold feet and walked out reluctantly, not wanting to leave him alone. I sent Lane to phone Theron's son Terry in Las Vegas to inform him about the accident. We also needed money to bail Theron's sixteen-year-old son, Dale, out of jail. In Mexico, the driver in any serious car accident automatically goes to jail, and he'd been driving. Theron's daughter Debby was also in the accident and was in the woman's ward with a badly gashed foot.

I knew Theron had health insurance, and I wanted to send him by ambulance to San Diego, where he could receive quality care. I talked to Dr. Martinez about it, but he wouldn't even entertain the idea. "He's too badly injured to be moved anywhere. If you'll be the responsible party, we'll take X-rays now and do everything we can for him here."

I signed the release forms. Then we stepped out into the hall as Dr. Martinez started explaining the next procedures. The banging of a gurney drew our attention as two nurses wheeled it out of the men's ward and off down the hall. A sheet concealed a body on the gurney.

"Someone just died," sighed Dr. Martinez. I hoped it wasn't the poor man with all the burns.

We returned to the men's ward, hoping to take Theron for X-rays immediately. To our astonishment, Theron's cot was empty. Turning to the burned man, I asked, "Where did they take him?"

"He died moments after you left," he said.

I ran into the hall, unable to comprehend such a disaster. We needed Theron. The church needed him. How could God take such a vital man? I pounded the wall, weeping as I prayed, *No, God, no! Please don't let it be true!*

Dr. Martinez put his arm around me. "He's gone. Get a hold of yourself. He's now at peace."

My head was spinning. I had to go look for Lane. I waited on the curb in front of the hospital, hoping for Lane's immediate return. Brown-skinned strangers passed by, nodding to me respectfully and saying in Spanish, "Happy Mother's Day."

I choked with emotion. Poor Helen! I dreaded sending her the tragic news of her husband's death, especially on Mother's Day.

I didn't notice Lane until he was right beside me. I threw myself into his arms and wept, "He's dead! Theron's dead!" Lane stood there like a statue. "Lane, you've got to be the one to call Terry back," I said. "Tell him that his father is dead, because I can't bear to do it."

He shook his head. "I can't either! I just called and told him Theron would be okay and that we had things under control. I'm not calling back. You'll have to."

Theron's daughter Sherry answered the phone, surprised we'd call back so soon. "Sherry," I began, "I have bad news . . ." I'll never forget her sobs. I joined her. I was sick that I was dumping my emotions on her, but I loved Theron as family. I, too, was devastated.

Lane got his father-in-law to drive the three hours to Los Molinos to inform Helen and the rest of her children of the sad news. I rushed home to clean house, cook food, and prepare beds for the mourners, who would arrive shortly from the States for the funeral the next day.

That evening, I returned to the hospital to tell Debby her father died. While I was there, Verlan arrived home for the weekend. Our daughter Donna told him the sickening news, and he came and found me at the hospital. Immediately, he insisted I go with him to the mortuary. "I don't think he's dead," he said hopefully. "God needs him too badly here. There must be some mistake."

Verlan cringed when he saw Theron's naked body. He shook his head in disbelief, then said with finality, "He's dead all right. He's dead for sure."

Outside the morgue, we sat in Verlan's car, and he let his tears flow freely. "Theron was the best friend I ever had," he lamented. "He was just too perfect to live. Oh, how I'm going to miss him!"

ON SEPTEMBER 2, 1969, I returned home to the Big Brown House with a renewed spirit. Verlan had taken me to a movie, then out to eat Mexican food. It was a rare occasion when we could celebrate like this alone. For once, I wasn't pregnant. I felt like I was being courted. Verlan was most attentive. We held hands during the movie, just enjoying being together again. His thoughtfulness eased my burdens. I felt for the first time in years that our relationship might improve, in spite of all the problems.

He kissed me before we got out of his truck. Then he hugged me and said, "I could never keep going without you, Irene. I really love you for all you do for this family."

The next morning, Verlan unloaded a large cardboard box from the camper of his truck. It contained thirty or more pairs of used shoes he had purchased from Veteran's Thrift. His throng of excited children grabbed frantically for a couple of pair each as he dumped them onto the living room floor.

Verlan left my $50 weekly allowance (which he'd finally raised from $20 because of the numerous children), then bid us farewell early Sunday evening. He was rushed because he wanted to drop by Charlotte's home in Tijuana and visit with her and her kids before he crossed over into San Diego.

Four hours later, he unexpectedly returned. I knew when I saw him that he was a bearer of bad news. "Who is it, Verlan? Who died?"

"Your mother. She died of a heart attack in Montana."

"No, not my mother. How could it be? She's only fifty-nine!"

"When I arrived at Charlotte's, she told me the news. Your brothers are on their way to Montana now to bring your mother's body back to Salt Lake, where she'll be buried." Verlan hugged me. "I'm so sorry, but I don't think you need to go. They'll probably just have a graveside funeral anyway."

"What do you mean I don't need to go? She's my mother! You won't keep me from going!"

"I can't have Lucy quit work just to tend your kids."

"Well, you can tend them then. They're your kids, and I'm going!" I cried, convulsing between sobs. "You've always gotten to live around your family, have your mother constantly nearby. Why didn't you let me go see mine this summer like I wanted to? Now she's dead!"

Verlan got up to answer the door. Two of Joel's wives, Gaye and Priscilla, were at the door. "Where's Irene?" Gaye asked.

"She's too embarrassed to come out. Her mother died, and she's crying because she can't go to the funeral."

"What do you mean she can't go? Are you crazy?" Gaye asked.

"Well, she's got responsibilities. There's no one else to tend these kids."

Both women rushed in to console me. In a matter of minutes, it was decided. They would both stay and care for my kids until I returned.

Within twenty minutes, Verlan and I were out the door. As we drove to Tijuana, I begged him to accompany me to Salt Lake so we could attend the funeral together. My family was bitter toward the LeBarons, and I wanted him to go with me so I could walk proudly at his side and make a statement to all my relatives that they'd better accept him.

"I can't go; you know I have to work. I'll put you on a Greyhound bus in San Diego. From there you can go to Las Vegas and then ride with your sister Becky and her husband."

We stopped at Charlotte's just long enough for her to try and find me something decent enough to wear to the funeral. She donated a navy blue and white plaid sack dress that was a size too large for her. She also gave me a pair of nylons and a purse and loaned me a pair of her shoes.

When I arrived in Salt Lake, my older brother Richard informed me that Verlan had called. He'd made arrangements to attend the funeral after all, and he was en route to Salt Lake with my daughter Donna and Verlan Jr.

My heart was in my throat as Becky, Richard, and I drove to the funeral home. We tiptoed into the viewing room. Our three other siblings—Douglas, Roger, and Erma—were already locked arm in arm in front of Mother's casket. For the first time since we were children, we were reunited, and it had to be at Mother's funeral. As we viewed her body together, I felt a great wave of homesickness for them.

I was shocked by how pale and old our mother looked. She'd been such a beautiful woman in her youth. I hoped to attain her wisdom and strength one day. Now I wanted to cry out to her, ask her for forgiveness for being so stubborn and make her understand the things life had taught me. I wanted to tell her I knew she suffered alone all those years. In my inadequate way, I wanted to tell her I loved her, but it was too late.

Life seared me with the realities Mother couldn't get across to me back when I wasn't in the mood to listen to her. She gave me a legacy of knowledge and courage. Her wisdom and beauty would stay with me through the years, reminding me of the debt I owed her.

I still choke up whenever I sing her favorite song, "Painting the Clouds with Sunshine." I often hear her lovely voice singing a song I heard no other person sing: "When I pretend I'm gay, I never feel that way. I'm only painting the clouds with sunshine." It was Mother who taught me to laugh at life. And throughout the years, I've had the opportunity to paint countless dark clouds.

CHAPTER THIRTY-ONE

I'm sure Verlan loved us all in a way, but he absolutely flipped over Susan. He didn't have to tell any of us he favored her. He was intensely in love with her, and it showed. She needed him, and he thrived on her attentions. I believe he felt young and virile again with such a young, pretty woman at his side. She was an absolute doll. Any man would have been proud to be seen with her.

Susan experienced the polygamous society while growing up in Colonia LeBaron. Her father had two wives, so in theory it probably seemed like something she should be able to do. But actually practicing it, with five older wives and dozens of children already in the picture, was more than most girls born under the covenant would have been able to endure.

We became friends. Over time, we even began to confide in each other about many things we couldn't share with anyone else. We discussed our desires and our doubts, admitting to each other that the glorious Principle around which our fundamentalist faith was centered wasn't in fact satisfying to either of us. We both wanted a man of our own and a normal life, but God seemed to have other plans.

JOEL'S STEPDAUGHTER, Lillie, was destined to become Verlan's seventh wife, though it took God a while to work it out. Two years before his marriage to Susan, when Lillie was seventeen, she and Verlan were engaged to be married, but she suddenly changed her mind. Time passed, and Lillie was now a beautiful, willowy blond. Still just nineteen, she was under pressure to marry before she became an old maid (in the eyes of our society). To complicate matters, she was in love with a handsome young man her own age, but the brethren counseled her to marry someone with experience instead—someone who could exalt her right now rather than a man who wouldn't exalt her unless and until he leapt into the Principle for himself by adding other wives down the road. Everyone agreed that that someone was Verlan.

With six wives and thirty-three kids already part of his burgeoning heavenly kingdom, Verlan believed he was well positioned to exalt another wife. He certainly wanted to try, especially since Lillie would thereby round out his quorum of seven wives. According to our faith, this would practically guarantee him godhood if he did nothing to mess things up.

I was surprised when Lillie decided to marry him, especially since she knew full well the poverty and loneliness we experienced. I was even more surprised when Verlan told me Lillie preferred that I not attend their wedding. He said she wanted it small and private, meaning I wasn't welcome. I couldn't understand it. When Lillie spent a year going to school in Ensenada with us, I'd been like a mother to her, always looking out for her needs. Why, I'd bought her first bra. She was my daughter Donna's best friend. I was especially crushed when I discovered she invited some of Verlan's other wives.

I finally found out that Lillie's problem with me was jealousy. She told Verlan I was too often the life of the party, and she didn't want me around on her special day to take away her limelight. I was hurt that Verlan allowed Lillie's jealousy to keep me away, but I was more hurt by her rude snub. Now she'd have to contend not only with Susan, who was the youngest and prettiest of Verlan's wives, but with me as well.

Lillie made her own white satin wedding gown. She and Verlan married in San Diego on January 15, 1971, surrounded by her family and friends. The ceremony drew a larger crowd than any of Verlan's previous weddings. Everyone knew that by marrying Lillie, Verlan was securing his heavenly position.

I tried not to dwell on the fact that I'd had such a simple, secretive wedding—under a tree with no guests and no gifts, wearing a borrowed suit of Charlotte's. My only consolation now was that Verlan had finally fulfilled his dream. With his (and our) salvation now secure, Verlan could stop his mad dash to add more wives. Now all he had to do was father seventeen more children, and he'd have accomplished everything in life he'd set out to.

AFTER LILLIE'S WEDDING, Verlan's family multiplied faster than ever. Those were such trying times, I quite resented it when Verlan came home and announced that he felt he had to go on another mission for the Lord. I begged him to stay home. It was bad enough sharing him with six other wives, but if I had to share him with God, too, I'd never make it. Verlan insisted that his God came before any woman or other mere earthly duties.

I knew it was against church rules for a woman to go on a mission trip. A woman's mission was to stay home and indoctrinate the children. Still, while Verlan packed to leave, I teased him just to give him a hard time. I clung playfully to him as he tried to leave. "Please, let me go on this mission with you."

"No," he said, trying to pull away. "You know my companion has to be a man."

"I have more qualifications than any man," I said, throwing out my chest. "See, I could go and be your bosom companion." He laughed, but my qualifications didn't get me anywhere, and he left.

While Verlan was still off doing his duty preaching and trying to bring in new members to the church, I wrote to him: "Lover, if you'd come home and be with your seven wives, we could produce more members than you could ever convert."

. . .

THE BAPTIST WORLD MISSION set up a small clinic just twenty miles south of us in San Quintin. I was back in my house in Los Molinos, pregnant with my twelfth child. I was glad for the new Baptist doctors. EL BUEN PASTOR (The Good Shepherd) was written on the Quonset hut in which the clinic was housed. The small new facility had only three beds, one of which was the delivery table.

It was November 3, 1971, my due date, but since my previous labor lasted all of twenty-five minutes, I decided to go to the clinic before I actually had any pains this time. When I arrived, the doctor didn't have a place to examine me. All the beds were already occupied by women who had just had their babies. Dr. Cano had his assistant drive one of the women to her home, freeing up the delivery table.

The nurse helped lift me onto the table and then prepped me for delivery. Before they proceeded, the doctor and nurse prayed over me for God to guide their hands. Then Dr. Cano dripped a solution into the vein in my arm to induce labor. In exactly forty-five minutes from beginning to end, I gave birth to Seth Michael, who weighed in at nine and a half pounds. Having such a big baby so fast required me to get my first stitches ever.

"Hold still. It'll be over in a few minutes," Dr. Cano said. "I only need to put in three or four stitches." Still groggy from the anesthetic, yet never too drugged for humor, I said, "Doctor, let's really surprise my husband. Just sew the whole thing up."

After Seth's arrival, I was sick in bed for several weeks. I had blood clots in my leg and was in danger of having further complications. My friend Betty took me to her home to care for me. She bought me my first new nightgown and bathrobe since the nightgown Charlotte gave me for my honeymoon. I was elated about the turquoise satin robe.

After I recovered, I went on a two-day trip with Verlan to San Diego. While we were gone, fourteen-year-old André had an attack of appendicitis. Donna rushed him to the Baptist Clinic, where they operated on him. That was a miracle in itself. Only one day a month, doctors flew in from the States to donate their time and perform various operations. It just so happened that André arrived in pain on the designated day. When they saw him doubled over, they took him ahead of the scheduled patients and operated on him immediately.

WHEN SETH WAS ONLY four months old, he was sick for several days with a fever and an earache. It was foggy and cold out—the middle of February. Our only source of heat in the whole house was a gas heater in my bedroom. I rocked my crying baby until I could no longer stay awake.

It was just growing light outside when I crawled into bed between my daughters, Donna and two-year-old Verlana. I needed to snatch at least a few minutes of sleep before it was time to get the kids up for school.

As if in a far-off dream, I heard little Verlana fall off the bed onto the cold cement floor. I was so out of it, I couldn't think of what to do, couldn't figure out that I needed to pick her up and put her back in bed beside me. She didn't cry or try to get up. I seemed to be in a deep sleep when a voice spoke to me: "Irene, get up immediately, or it will be too late." I tried to move, but I couldn't make my body function. Again the voice warned me, "Get up right now!"

Forcing myself to respond, I swung my legs over the side of the bed and weakly stood up. I hollered, "Donna!" Then I passed out on the floor. Donna immediately threw back the covers, saw her sister and me passed out on the floor, and screamed for help, "Steven! Steven!" Then she too crumbled to the ground.

From across the hall, Steven heard our cries. Opening my bedroom door, he saw our bodies sprawled out on the floor and realized we'd all been asphyxiated by the gas. He rushed to turn off the heater and butane lamp, then threw open the windows. He picked up his unconscious little sister and carried her into the living room. By then, André, Brent, and Kaylen were in the room, trying to drag Donna and me out. They also rescued baby Seth from his crib.

When I regained consciousness, I was weak and had a terrific, pounding headache. My fingernails were blue from the lack of oxygen. André drove us to the clinic, where we suffered all day with nausea and ringing in our ears. Still, we were thankful to have survived and to know we'd be okay.

DR. CANO WAS VERY CONCERNED about my health. Several varicose veins were swollen and broken in my legs, causing me a great deal of pain. He explained to me how important it was that I didn't get pregnant again. He insisted I bring Verlan in for my next consultation.

I considered myself fortunate to be able to comply with the doctor's orders by getting Verlan there, but then Verlan embarrassed me with his reaction to what the doctor had to say. "Why do you let this woman become pregnant so often?" Doctor Cano lectured. "Look at her bad veins. She's too young to have so many children. I believe you should go on some form of birth control."

Verlan flared up. "We don't believe in that! Our whole purpose is to multiply and replenish the Earth." Standing up to leave, he added, "It's our private business how many kids we have."

When we reached Verlan's truck, I got in beside him, knowing how upset he was. "That doctor is far too worldly," Verlan said. "I don't want you ever to see him again. Besides, I have a better way to solve this problem. I just won't sleep with you anymore. That way you won't be tempted, and for sure you won't conceive again."

I was frantic, devastated. Here I'd borne him twelve children, allowed him to take five new wives (two of which I'd given him personally), and now, when I was just thirty-three, Verlan was shelving me. In my mind, that signaled the end of our marital relationship.

Only God knew the turmoil this caused me. In the evenings, I'd walk the two miles to the beach, where no one could hear me lying in the sand, crying and calling out to God. All hope was seeping out of me. I felt used and abandoned.

Summertime arrived and while trying to get my mind off my

problems, I borrowed Verlan's truck to solicit nearby farmers to give us more free produce. I brought home loads of cauliflower, brussels sprout, and potatoes. The older children helped cut the spoiled parts off the potatoes, and then we left them in the sun until a scab dried over the cuts. We then put the potatoes in gunnysacks and stored them in our family storehouse.

The only attention Verlan gave me was when he praised my ingenuity. He was grateful that I helped him feed his giant family. Seeing how he relished unity among his wives and wanting desperately to regain his favor, I continued to fend for us all as best I could.

As I fought against depression, I often wondered what the future held for my beautiful Donna. At just seventeen, she'd already been approached by at least ten men, many claiming to have had divine revelations that she should marry them. It was one thing for me to suffer living this life, but it enraged me to think of my precious children having to endure it as well. No reward—here or in the next life—could be worth the disappointment I'd experienced. I'd come full circle to exactly where my mother was when we talked that afternoon in her cellar. The only two differences were that I'd never had the heart to teach my kids the Principle the way I was supposed to, and Donna was already figuring out that she wanted no part of it anyway.

Being president of the church and the head of seven families really put Verlan in a bind, so the squeakiest wheels continued to get all his grease. I finally clued in that he took my being quiet and supportive to mean I was doing just great. Since I knew how to be fairly self-reliant, I found myself getting left out more and more.

Of course, my greatest loss was no longer having the touch and comfort of my husband, even once a month. And while I went completely without, I had to deal with the fact that he was busy enjoying sexual pleasures with his other wives.

I prayed to God every day to let me die. Verlan came to see me and tried to spur me on. He explained that now that our sex life was over, I should just buckle down and find joy in my children. I clung to him, begging him to make love to me. Fifteen months of abstinence was too long. Where was the reassurance that he even wanted me anymore? I lied and told him there was no chance I'd become pregnant. I said that my period was due the next day, so he finally gave in and granted me one sweet moment of bliss.

A torrent of tears followed a few weeks later when I discovered I was pregnant yet again.

VERLAN TRIED to make his bad behavior up to me by inviting me to go to Colonia LeBaron with him. Donna knew I was desperate for a trip, so she insisted I leave the other ten children with her while I went with her father for a week.

The day after we arrived at the colony, my friend Priscilla invited Verlan and me to her pizza party along with two unmarried women, Elizabeth and Helen. I'd been close friends with all three women for years. All three were dedicated to our religious beliefs.

Forty-year-old Helen was widowed, heavyset, and had her eye on my husband. Several times since her husband Theron's death in that terrible car accident, she'd suggested to me the possibility of becoming part of our family. I knew she was lonely. My relationship with her had endured for over twenty years, and I hated to have something like a husband come between us, but Verlan already had his hands way too full. However, our gospel teachings didn't exactly recognize such earthly limits. No good man had a right to turn down a converted woman who wanted to marry him. If he did, God might not give him any more wives. Well, as far as I was concerned, with the seven he already had, Verlan didn't need more wives, even by his own ambitious measure.

Helen was a great cook and a remarkable mother. Her eleven children loved her dearly, but they needed a father also. I felt bad there weren't any more men who were willing to share the responsibility for good women like her, whose husbands left them behind on this Earth without any man to help shepherd them. Still, Verlan's dance card was quite full.

At the party, I eventually managed to relax and put my worries about Helen aside. The five of us were joking, having a great time, when suddenly Verlan became very quiet, obviously deep in thought. Then he asked, "Hey, Priscilla, do you have a piece of paper and a pen I can borrow?"

I wondered what was so important that he had to write it down. Maybe he was starting a new game. We sat in silence, wondering. He scribbled a few words, folded the note, and handed it to me, playfully bumping my knee with his. "Pass this over to Helen, will you?" he asked, seeming to be daring me.

Elizabeth eyed Helen; then her eyes shifted to mine. "What's going on here?"

I obediently handed the note to Helen. "What's this?" she asked, looking surprised.

"Go ahead and read it . . . but not out loud," Verlan said as he nervously stood up.

Helen carefully unfolded the paper. We watched as her mouth opened wider with each word she read. She looked at Verlan in disbelief. "Is this for real?" she asked, almost in a whisper.

"Yes, but don't say anything," he ordered as he walked toward the door.

Helen jumped up squealing. She hugged Elizabeth. Then she almost knocked Priscilla off her chair when she threw her arms around her. Coming toward me, her face red with embarrassment, she exclaimed, "I can't believe this!" She hugged me tentatively, obviously hoping for approval. "Oh, this is so wonderful!"

Verlan had the door open before she could get to him. "Come outside, will you, Helen?" He flipped his head and gestured for her to follow.

After he closed the door, Liz started to laugh. "What on earth is going on?"

I shrugged my shoulders, trying to keep my composure. "Who knows?" But deep down, I knew.

Several minutes later, Helen barged in, with Verlan following close behind. She was waving the note teasingly from side to side in the air. Then she mischievously danced past the other two women and handed the note to me. "He said you can read it out loud."

I could see the joy on her face. I prayed for God to help me remain calm. I began reading, "Dear Helen, Will you marry me tomorrow? I'll take you with me to Nicaragua for a honeymoon. Love, Verlan."

Smothering my rage with a fake smile, I acted like any other noble plural wife. I pretended sacrificial joy while I thought about how much I hated them both. Here was my long-awaited trip with Verlan, and he was taking someone else on a honeymoon instead.

He hugged Helen and said, "Well, it's all settled. We're getting married tomorrow at 9 A.M. so we can leave for Nicaragua by noon." He kissed Helen for the first time. She almost ran the four blocks home.

That night Verlan came to bed uneasy, and rightfully so. "I hope all my other wives will forgive me for this. I really should've notified them first." He talked on, trying to justify himself. "Please forgive me, Irene. I know you wanted this trip, but you've got to realize it's a perfect time to marry Helen, since there are no other wives around to object, and it won't really be taking anybody else's time."

"What about me?" I snapped.

"It won't be your time, either. You knew I was going alone to Nicaragua, so don't count the time as yours."

"I can't believe I deserve this, Verlan," I said angrily. "Every time I get close to a woman and share my intimate secrets, she pulls a fast one on me and marries my husband! What a hell of a way to ruin a good friendship, especially when I see her more than I see you."

Verlan pulled me closer, laughing as he spoke. "I can't help it if you're such a neat wife. You're so good to them, they all want to spend eternity with you." I dug my elbow into his side, afraid to say more for fear I'd cry. When he saw I didn't respond, he said, "Hey, don't get mad. She really loves you. Helen wouldn't even consider marrying me if you weren't part of my wonderful family."

Then, talking more to himself than to me, he said, "Gee, I wish I had time to buy Helen a wedding ring."

"Damn it, Verlan! Why don't you just order a dozen from Sears? Then you'll have them handy when you need one."

He laughed. "I appreciate you being so good about this marriage. It means a lot to me that I can always depend on you to come through."

"I'm not good, and I don't understand! Why in the world do you need any more wives?"

"Irene, are you going to reject a wonderful blessing like this? Isaiah says that in the last days, seven women will take hold of one man."

I angrily interrupted him. "Hell, Verlan, you've already got seven! You've fulfilled that prophecy. I told you years ago I'd leave you if you got more than seven wives. I think I deserve at least one day a week!"

"Honey," he pled, "try and understand."

"How can I? Even if you were home all the time, every day, I'd only see you four nights a month. That's forty-eight days a year. That's only a month and a half out of twelve."

"Hey," he said firmly, cutting me off, "let's not get a bad spirit about this. See, I'm here now, and you're just ruining your precious time. I don't know why you always want to waste it talking about other women. Besides, no one will ever take your place."

"Good hell, Verlan. Tomorrow someone will!"

"Be thankful you are even here. It should be Lillie's turn to give Helen to me, since she's the last wife. But you get the privilege. I think Helen will feel honored because she loves you so much." Yes, it would be the third time I'd have the incredible privilege of giving another woman to my husband in marriage. Imagine how thankful I was.

Verlan kissed my unresponsive lips and said, "Let's go to sleep. I have so much to do, so many responsibilities; I can hardly take time off to get married." Then he rolled over.

I lay in the dark, rubbing my hand over my pregnant stomach, wondering what more God might require of me. I thought about Helen. She really wasn't a threat to me. I even loved her. *But, God, it's so hard to share my husband with so many wives!*

I'd been taught it was better to have a tenth of a good man than a "worldly" man all to myself. Would I trade some failure for the husband I had? Not hardly. I tried to smother the jealousy burning in my chest. Since I'd already hung in there for so many years, I thought it best to be patient. Why, I was right on the edge of glory. This life would be over soon enough, so why give up now?

Verlan woke me up at 6 A.M. to give me his final instructions before he left. "Please iron my shirt and polish my best shoes." I felt pangs of sadness in my heart. How many times had I packed his suitcase for essentially the same journey? "I can spend a whole month with Helen," Verlan continued. "This is a good chance to really get to know her. With so many of you around, this will be the most time Helen will ever have alone with me. I feel she needs it after being widowed so long." He left immediately to get his business done so he wouldn't be late for his own wedding. I heard him call back to me, "Be sure and be there a few minutes early. I'll see you there at nine o'clock sharp."

Six of Verlan's other wives were in Los Molinos. There was no electricity or telephone service in the colony where they lived, so he had no way of contacting them to inform them of his impending marriage. He just had to trust in God, hoping God would touch their hearts with understanding when Verlan returned from his honeymoon with the belated news. I knew he hated to do this to them, but with me backing him up, he could go through with it.

His other wives had every right to be angry, and they certainly would be, not only with him, but with me as well for upholding him in this marriage without their knowledge or consent. I felt comforted knowing I wasn't proving a problem for him. He needed me to play my part in furthering his kingdom, so I suppressed my feelings of rejection. If I would just be obedient and comply with his demands, he promised once again he'd love me even more.

When it came time, I walked the three blocks to my sister-in-law Luz's house. Several cars were parked along the dirt road out front. I was surprised at how many came to celebrate so early in the morning and on such short notice.

I shook hands all around and made sure I kept a smile on my face, knowing how I'd be judged by everyone. I would play the part, giving no one a chance to say I'd shirked my duty or let a good man down. Thank God for Linda. She saved my usual place next to her. When I got over there, she covered her mouth and whispered, "Why didn't you tell me about this yesterday?"

" 'Cause I didn't know."

"Since when did they decide to get married?"

"Last night."

Verlan walked in, apologizing to everyone for being late. He looked handsome in his worn gray suit. Taking a seat beside Helen, he grabbed her hand in more of a handshake than a caress. When he saw me, he smiled and waved mildly, obviously relieved to see I'd come. Then he leaned over and whispered a few words to his brother Alma, who stood up, ready to conduct the meeting.

Alma stoically welcomed everyone. Glancing at his watch, he announced, "We need to get this show on the road. We're running late." He waited for complete silence, then continued. "I appreciate all of you for making an effort to be here so early and on time. It always thrills my soul to see women so valiant who are willing to put aside their selfish wants and enter into this holy Principle of plural marriage." He was overcome with emotion. "Excuse me for crying," he said, sniffing and wiping his tears with his hanky. "I know this takes a woman of conviction." He cleared his throat and nodded toward me. "I'm so glad to see Irene coming through for Verlan again." A smile crossed his worn face, and his blue eyes twinkled. "She's always been outspoken and rebellious. But still she repents at the last minute, always coming through. You women here this morning would do well to follow her example. Being obedient is always what the Lord requires."

Verlan must've been reading my mind, as I was thinking, "Yeah, we have no choice in the matter; it's shape up or go to Hell." He caught Alma's eye, motioning for him to start the ceremony before my repenting subsided and my outspoken rebelliousness again took over.

Alma then invited Verlan and Helen to come forward and take their places beside him. Flipping his head, Verlan motioned for me to take my place next to his bride-to-be. After so many times, I surely ought to have been trusted to take my place without being told.

After a moment of silence, Alma cleared his throat. Looking directly into my eyes, he asked, "Do you, Sister Irene, take Helen by the right hand?"

"I do," I said on cue as my voice cracked. I forced a broad smile and placed her hand in his. My eyelids fluttered frantically to divert the tears welling up in them. Verlan winked approvingly at me as I stepped back into my place.

Alma continued, "Do you, Brother Verlan, take Sister Helen by the right hand and receive her unto yourself?"

I gave myself a silent sermon. *Don't you dare let a tear fall. Please be good. Come on, Irene, God still loves you.*

The next exhortation jarred me quickly out of my self-talk. "Be fruitful. Multiply and replenish the Earth." I hated to have them both admit they would. Besides, Helen had already done that. She had eleven children. She was going through menopause, so her sex life would be short-lived, thank God.

Alma neared the end of the long, divinely revealed ceremony. I knew it almost by heart, though this time it would be worded a little differently. "I now pronounce you legally and lawfully husband and wife, for time only." It usually said, "for time and all eternity." Helen was sealed to her dead husband, Theron. He would have her again in the next life, not Verlan. But that wasn't much consolation to me, because I had to deal with her now.

Alma sighed. "You may now kiss the bride." Verlan obeyed, giving her a brief kiss. Then he pulled her close and hugged her. With Helen still partly in his embrace, he pulled me over and kissed me also. It made me feel so out of place. But I'm sure he meant it as a reward for giving him his eighth wife.

Thank God I had Linda—the one person I could count on in this life. She walked me back to Priscilla's house, promising me along the way she'd never marry Verlan. Never, even if she became a widow. I appreciated such loyalty. I was so proud of her.

She read my mind. "Let it out, Irene. Cry! Just let go of your feelings. You'll feel better."

I tried, but I soon realized I wasn't going to cry. There were no tears. I knew Helen couldn't take away something that never really belonged to me. When we got to Priscilla's, the three of us discussed our husbands' many weddings, laughing about how bad they once made us feel. Soon, Lane Stubbs came knocking on the door for me.

"Verlan sent me to get you. He said to drop whatever you're doing and come now."

I laughed and joked with Lane as we drove to Luz's home. The newlyweds were supposed to leave from there for their honeymoon. "I bet Verlan realized he didn't spend any time with me. I'm sure he wants to tell me how much he appreciates me," I said.

"Yeah, I guess all men forget things like that. I don't tell my three wives that I appreciate them enough, either," he commented. I got out of his truck and walked into the house. Lane left to get Helen because Verlan wanted to talk to her, too.

I walked down the dark hall into a bedroom, where Verlan was impatiently waiting for me. He seldom got angry, but he was hopping mad now. "Damn it, Irene, you knew!" He pointed at me accusingly. "You did this on purpose!"

I couldn't begin to imagine what he was talking about. I stood wide-eyed and speechless. He ranted on. "You knew, and don't you tell me you didn't!"

I was completely baffled. I didn't know whether to laugh or cry. "What on earth are you talking about?" I sputtered.

He grew even angrier. "You knew damn well that today is Charlotte's anniversary. You did this to her! Just because you two don't get along, you let me marry Helen today on purpose!"

It was so ridiculous, I couldn't keep from bursting into laughter. "You're the one who proposed, Verlan. Don't try and blame me. You're over twenty-one. You knew what you were doing, and I didn't do this to you on purpose, either!"

"Irene, I'm absolutely sick about this. Now my problems have really gotten out of hand. Swear to me you'll keep this from Charlotte, no matter what."

Helen's soft knock quieted Verlan down. He shook his head, readying himself to face whatever was ahead with his new wife.

Helen entered, surprised to see me. "Hi." She looked at Verlan. "What's going on?"

"Sit down," he ordered. "We have a little problem that needs to be discussed," he began tactfully. Almost pleadingly, he asked, "Would you be willing to change the date of your marriage? Just move it up two days and have the tenth for your anniversary?"

Helen's look told both Verlan and me she wasn't one to be pushed around. A puzzled expression came over her face. "Why?" she asked, adding stubbornly, "Today's the eighth, and I happen to like the eighth."

Verlan buried his face in his strong hands. "Please, Helen. This is a matter of life or death. Just say yes; do it for me. It's Charlotte's anniversary today, and she'll never forgive me if she finds out!"

Helen shook her head disgustedly and said, "I wonder what I've gotten myself into." I thought it was a little late for her to be wondering that. Besides, she'd already lived polygamy when she was married to Theron. I figured she'd have been accustomed to this sort of nonsense.

"Just do it for me," Verlan said and sighed. "You see, I'll have a hard enough time making Charlotte realize the necessity of marrying you without her permission, let alone marrying you without her permission on her anniversary."

Helen shook her head. "I don't like it! I really don't. But I guess if you say so." She reluctantly agreed.

Poor Helen. My heart went out to her. She hadn't been married thirty minutes and already she was stomping on another wife's rights.

BOOK THREE

NO MORE
TURNS

CHAPTER THIRTY-TWO

I cried until my head was splitting. Repeatedly, I asked God, *What did I ever do to deserve all this?* Things were not going well within the Church of the Firstborn. The craziness among Verlan's siblings spread, and Ervil actually had Joel, our prophet, murdered. Ervil, once the patriarch of the church, was removed from that position after considerable misconduct, and was exacting vengeance on the other church members. Verlan was still president of the church, so Ervil was after him, too. Verlan thought it would be a good time to colonize in some out-of-the-way place like Nicaragua, so naturally he was planning on sending me down to this unknown country to help start the process.

I was pregnant with my thirteenth child, and my health was shot. I was told I could expect more clots in my legs and would probably die if I had another natural birth. On the other hand, if I had a cesarean section, I knew I wouldn't be able to resist letting them tie my tubes while they were in there.

Verlan believed there were still spirits waiting in Heaven for me to be their mortal mother. He assured me that tying my tubes would be a slap in God's face, strictly against his laws, and a recipe for going straight to Hell. Death, apparently being my only righteous option, was looking pretty sweet to me right then. No more heartache or pain or other wives to cope with. I'd have peace and finally be free.

Verlan was in San Diego buying fruit and nut trees to be shipped to Nicaragua. His scheme was to plant orchards that would produce large enough crops to supply the needs of the new colony on a year-round basis. Moving the church into Central America would be a slow process, but going out first and starting a business that could sustain future colonizers would lay the foundation. As a general concept, it was solid enough, but Verlan was never any good at managing such enterprises. Churches and marriages, perhaps, but not businesses.

Verlan's other wives took turns visiting him in San Diego while he was out there searching for trees at the right price. Each time a wife went, I sent a long letter to Verlan explaining my medical predicament and apologizing for wanting the operation to tie my tubes when I had my baby. I felt it was a lifesaving necessity. Verlan felt it was a sin.

He knew I had a deadline. The cesarean had to be performed on or before Saturday, January 20, because the only surgeon would be gone after that. All my letters were pleas for him to come be with me and bring the hundred dollars I needed to help cover the costs of the operation at the Baptist clinic.

On Monday, Lillie returned from San Diego with a short note from Verlan. "Irene, I'm sorry I can't come now. These trees are of great importance. I need to do something on a large scale for the future of the Saints. I promise I'll be home Friday for sure. We'll decide then whether or not to go through with the C-section."

Donna helped me scrub walls, wash windows, and clean the yard. I spent a day mending clothes and scrubbing out the dirty ones on the washboard. We also washed sheets, blankets, and rugs. I wanted everything clean and in order so life wouldn't be so rough on Donna while I was in the hospital for a week. It was a huge responsibility for her to have to manage her ten brothers and sisters all by herself. She didn't even have André's help, now that he'd gone to work to help support the family. I helped her wash buckets of wheat to be used for cereal and bread. To keep the wheat away from the incessant flies, we dried it in pillowcases pinned to the clothesline.

Donna's sweet and willing spirit urged me on. At seventeen, she was not only my daughter but a dear friend and anchor to her

overwrought mother. I turned to her often for comfort and understanding.

On Friday afternoon, Dr. Cano sent a message reminding me he
was going on vacation and wouldn't be back for two weeks. I could
either come sometime this weekend and have him do the cesarean
section, or I could find someone else to deliver the baby naturally in
his absence.

I was nauseous with uncertainty about what to do. All my life,
I'd been taught obedience. My husband was to rule all my decisions.
I was to accept and follow whatever choices he felt best for me. I
struggled with God's unbending rules. How could Verlan know what
was best for me? How could he assess my situation without even
talking to a doctor? How could he ever understand my feelings as
a woman? If tying my tubes gave me my only chance to live and
raise my own children, who had the right to deny me? I desperately
needed Verlan's support and approval not only to have the cesarean
but to have my tubes tied at the same time. Why couldn't he just give
me his permission? Would he even keep his promise and come home
to me that night?

For years I lived on Verlan's broken promises. I didn't think he went
around promising to do things and then simply changed his mind
about doing them. I believed he basically wanted to fulfill his promises, but his responsibilities as a husband and father to so many just
made it impossible. Okay, lots of times he promised me things just to
keep me happy at the moment. He didn't generally concern himself
too much about whether he'd really be able to keep his promises; he
just said what he needed to say and then tried his best to do what he
said he would. Well, his best got less with the addition of each wife
and child.

I turned down the wick of the coal oil lamp, leaving a soft light
barely lighting the room. All the kids were asleep, so I made myself
comfortable on the sofa to wait for Verlan's return. I heard a car stop
outside and got up to open the door. I glanced at the clock; it was
12:30. Though it was late, I felt relieved by Verlan's arrival. I opened

the door with eager anticipation, but my heart fell when I saw it was
only Charlotte.

"Hi. Here's a note from Verlan," she said, handing it to me. "He's
sorry he couldn't make it. Good night."

I closed the door, trembling with rage. Then I turned up the lamp
and tore open the envelope. "Dear Irene, I'm too busy getting the
trees. I think I'll be at least another week. Just do the best you can.
My prayers are with you for the delivery. Enclosed is $100. I love you
dearly. Verlan."

My pitiful cries of anguish woke Donna. She tried to calm me as I
repeated my conviction over and over out loud: "He doesn't love me!
He doesn't love me! After all the wives I've given him, the children
I've borne . . . he has no time for me!" I paid no attention to Donna's
words of comfort. "That man has let me down over and over again!"
I cried.

A pall of grief and indescribable despair enveloped me. My whole
married life seemed to hang before me, and all at once I saw how
much I gave up in order to indulge Verlan's grand illusions. I loved,
served, obeyed, complied, gave and gave and gave some more, always
denying myself. Now nothing was left of me but physical and emotional wreckage. And in exchange for all of this, Verlan was too busy
getting trees. My faith in Verlan was exhausted.

Donna and Lucy accompanied me to the Good Shepherd Clinic
in San Quintin the next day. Gene and Claudia, friends from our
church who were also expecting, followed close behind us. Claudia
was going to have her fifth cesarean. I called her in California to
make sure she came before the doctor went on vacation. Having her
baby in Mexico would be more within their financial means.

Afraid I'd chicken out, I insisted the doctors perform my operation
first. Lucy thought I went to the hospital to induce labor. When they
wheeled me down the hall to the operating room, Donna walked beside me. She whispered words of encouragement and kissed me just
before they pushed me through the swinging doors. Then she said
to Lucy, "Start praying! Mom's having the baby cesarean and getting
her tubes tied."

Forty-five minutes later, the nurse carried an eight-and-a-half-pound baby boy wrapped in a thick receiving blanket out into the chilly hall and presented him to Donna. She and Lucy cuddled the new arrival, waiting for me to come out of the anesthetic.

Meanwhile, in my druggy dream, I was clinging by my bare hands to a high, protruding cliff. My fingers were bleeding, and I felt myself slipping. I tried desperately to hold onto the jagged precipice. I clung tighter, but felt myself still slipping. "I can't hang on anymore," I screamed, plunging into oblivion. Then I woke up.

I should've been happy to wake up and see the darling little boy I'd borne, but I felt like I awoke to the same old nightmare. I had to face the world again, alone. For days, every muscle in my back and shoulders twitched. Insomnia made things worse. The constant depression was snuffing out my life. Verlan came to the clinic three days after the operation to see me. He asked if we could have some privacy. Lucy and the nurse softly closed the door, leaving the two of us alone.

"Who knows that you tied your tubes?" he began.

"Just Lucy, Donna, Claudia, and Gene."

"Don't tell another soul what you've done. Think how it will make me look, being president of the church. If we permitted this to go on, every woman in our group would do it. We must be examples before them and the Lord." He shook his head in disgust. "You've sure goofed up your life. You've made it so we can never have a sexual relationship again. What you've done is the biggest form of birth control I know of. You shouldn't have done it."

Each sentence he spoke drove me deeper into the abyss of despair. He continued, "I'll be back on Saturday to take you home. The doctor said you'd be well enough by then. I hope that my taking you home when you get out of here will make up for the fact that I wasn't here for Lothair's birth."

Circumstances made it impossible for Verlan to keep his promise again. Gene and Claudia took me home, stopping off at Charlotte's house to retrieve my newborn son. I thanked her for caring for him during the time I stayed at the clinic. Gene carried my baby into my house as I slowly followed them inside. He wished me the best; then he left with Claudia and her new baby for the States.

When I entered the house, things had never seemed so bad before. I noted the cold cement floors, bare walls, sagging drapes, and seaside dampness of the January cold. I wondered how my infant son would survive in this unheated house.

Donna helped me into my bedroom, where my brood of lonely, neglected children came scampering to get into bed beside me. I wanted to gather them into my arms and love them one and all, but instead I pushed them aside for fear they'd hit my stomach and hurt my incision.

I felt so overwhelmed. How had I washed, cooked, and worked so steadily and hard for so many children? All my strength seemed to have drained out of me. I knew I couldn't cope with it anymore. I looked in the mirror, but the eyes I saw weren't mine. The eyes in the mirror were empty and hopeless.

Eyes are the windows of your soul, a little voice taunted me while I stared.

"What soul?" said the face in the mirror.

Once there, in my deepest despair, I settled in for a long stay. I cried night and day for six weeks. I constantly woke Donna up at night, begging her to talk to me. My hope for a better earthly life was lost. I'd also forfeited my godhood by having my tubes tied.

Moreover, my secret was out. Everyone seemed to know. Alma, who was now bishop of the Church of the Firstborn, counseled me to go back to the hospital and reverse my operation. "How could you do something so drastic?" he demanded. "There are spirits who are begging to come to Earth to obtain their bodies. There may still be a few you've covenanted to bring forth, and now you've denied them a chance to work out their salvation."

Because of his position, I didn't dare refute him. But to myself, I thought, "My hell! Wasn't thirteen kids enough?"

Another well-meaning friend asked me if it wasn't feasible that I'd sinned against the Holy Ghost and thereby committed an unpardonable sin.

All the interrogating sent me into even more of a tailspin. My mind whipped me, screaming accusingly that I'd turned against the very God I tried so hard to serve. No one could have been more disappointed in me than I was in myself. I hadn't followed Verlan's counsel. I'd tied up the fountain of life. I'd sinned against the Holy Ghost. And if God wasn't mad enough, Verlan made up for it.

At not quite thirty-five, I was alone, saddled with thirteen kids, and certain I could never enjoy sexual intimacy again. I couldn't even love God. Where was he? The only fate I could foresee when I arrived at the pearly gates was a wrathful God thrusting me into the burning pits of Hell forever. If God intended to raise his hand to destroy me, then I'd beat him to it. My only recourse seemed to be suicide.

Incessantly, I cried to the Lord for forgiveness. But how could he forgive me for the unpardonable sin of which I'd been accused? I was emotionally incapable of caring for my children. Once more, Donna had to take on the full responsibility.

Reluctantly, I confided in Verlan that I wanted to kill myself. He was shocked. He immediately informed me that I was possessed by evil spirits. So he instructed me to sit quietly on the bed. Then he solemnly placed his hands on my head, and by the holy priesthood he held and in the name of Jesus Christ, he cast the evil spirits out. But the demons didn't budge.

I felt worse than ever because I knew something Verlan didn't. I wasn't possessed. I was disillusioned, brokenhearted, rejected, and un-loved. No exorcism would cast all that out of me. Now my husband also thought me to be filled with the Devil. There was no end to the agony.

My sister wife Beverly was out of town visiting her parents in Colonia LeBaron at the time. Her vacant house was just a block away. I locked myself in, determined to hide from my distressed children. I prayed for answers, but none came as I spiraled into greater and greater hopelessness. Then insomnia stole the few remaining shreds of peace I knew. I fought my longings for death, but I was losing.

I'd never drunk liquor before, but I sent Donna to my friend Yolanda's in Guerrero for alcohol. Even in my jarred state of mind,

I found momentary solace in Proverbs 31:6–7: "Give strong drink unto him that is ready to perish, and wine unto those that be of heavy heart. Let him drink, and forget his poverty, and remember his misery no more." Every verse pertained to me. Emotionally, I was perishing. My mind was filled with anguish. Oh, how I wanted to forget my poverty. My life was full of misery. So, with the Bible's permission, I eased myself into drunken oblivion.

For over a month, Donna supplied the liquor, sneaking it over to me so no one would discover my whereabouts, especially my children. I couldn't get off my emotional seesaw. First would come the urges to commit suicide; then I drank to knock myself out and keep me from doing it. When I awoke, I wanted to do it all the more, and on and on and on. I hated the stranger in my mirror for constantly tempting me to kill myself. I couldn't go into the kitchen at all. Each time I tried, she'd tell me to grab the butcher knife. I'd have to run out immediately before the woman took my life.

Verlan returned to find me plastered. "Satan has really taken you downhill," he pronounced.

I cried out in the best way I could think of. "I can't survive another minute! Suicide is the only way out. I'm in too much mental pain to live another agonizing day!"

"You ought to count your blessings," he said. "You have the gospel, and you should find joy in it. You should forget about everything except raising your kids. I want you to go back to your own house and ask God to give you strength to do your duty."

"All I need is your love," I answered. "How can I possibly go on without it? Please," I begged, "don't go away and leave me like this." He turned to go. "I promise I'll kill myself! You'll be sorry!" I threatened. I needed an anchor for my soul. I was willing to settle for the love of this man. What I couldn't take was his disdain. Clinging to him, I sobbed, "Help me, Verlan. I can't go on alone!"

He did not pull away, though I could see it was clearly beneath him to hold such a weak and sinful woman. "Please get a hold of yourself, Irene. If you don't, your children will never want to live the gospel. If they refuse because of your actions, God will surely hold you accountable."

In complete frustration, I screamed out, "I hate you! You've ruined my life. When I'm dead, you'll be sorry." I cried such pitiful sobs that he decided he better spend the night with me.

He walked me back to my own home, preaching all the way, trying to console me in his own fashion. Before getting into my bed, he placed his loaded pistol on the dresser. Since Joel's death, it became Verlan's custom to have one handy for his protection.

He patted me wearily. "Well, good night, Irene." And he rolled over. I got no touch; no warm, comforting embrace; and certainly no sex. I'd have been grateful if he'd just talked to me, tried to understand me. His steady breathing from under the sheets was my only consolation.

While on my drinking binge, I lost all sense of time. I didn't know the date or month. My head was in a vice being tightened a little more every day, causing excruciating mental pain. I couldn't take another minute of it, thinking my brain was literally going to rupture. Images flashed across my warped mind, revealing the horrific crimes I'd committed, even some I hadn't. They deceived me into thinking I killed my first baby. They showed me that at times I'd hated my sister wives. What's more, Verlan was right. I had been lustful. I was oversexed. I committed adultery with my own husband. Trapped in this tortuous mental maze, I saw that Verlan knew best. I did deserve punishment.

It was in this state of mind that I made the dreadful decision. Quietly in the dark, I eased myself out of bed. Feeling for Verlan's pistol, I raised it with resolve, knowing that if I hurried, I'd be able to do it. Determined, yet frozen with fear, I held it in my trembling hands. I didn't really want to do it, but I knew I had to. There was nothing left for me in life.

I saw flashes of my casket, with Verlan weeping at its side. In my crazed mind, I was gleeful with a sick satisfaction. I thought if I could not have him, then he wasn't going to have me. I would finally get even with him. I'd lost him somewhere in life's shuffle. Now he could just lose me. He deserved it.

I held the gun to my pulsating temple, placing my finger on the trigger, ready to administer the punishment both Verlan and I deserved. Then, gathering courage, I silently prayed, *God, receive my unworthy soul.*

In that instant, two-month-old Lothair cried out to be fed. For the first time in months, I felt someone needed me. Still shaking, I cautiously placed the pistol back in its place as Verlan stirred a bit in response to the baby's cries, but then went right on sleeping.

Realizing my baby needed me and yearning to raise my children, I vowed to fight through my agonizing nightmare. Not for religion, not for a man, but for the love of my children.

CHAPTER THIRTY-THREE

I now wanted to get better, but I had no idea how to accomplish it. On my own, I couldn't quiet the voices within. Once again, I left my eleven neglected children with Donna. My oldest son, André, now fifteen, was already out of the house, working in San Diego as a drywall finisher to help support the family. I decided I would go there, too. I knew Verlan would be disappointed with me because I was once again taking a significant step without his permission, but I was too distraught to care. I caught a bus in Los Molinos, intending to hide for a few days at my friend Judy's (a church member who moved to San Diego to tap into the California welfare system). I didn't want anyone else to see me in such an unstable condition.

At Judy's, I spent the night praying, begging God to grant me a little sleep so I could rest from my mind's frenetic whipping back and forth from one self-accusation to another, from this lie or half-truth to the next. The mental suffering was excruciating. I longed for somebody, anybody, to help me out of my hellish maze. At 7 A.M., I heard Judy in the bathroom. My heart started beating so fast, it literally felt like it would race out of my chest. The thumping pain took my breath away. Judy heard my frantic cries and rushed me downtown to University Hospital.

After examining me, the doctor informed Judy and me that I was having panic attacks. A psychiatrist came in and asked me probing questions. "Are you married? Where is your husband? Do you have children?" I kept silent. No matter how much agony I was in, I couldn't put Verlan in danger by revealing that information.

As the psychiatrist continued to press me for a response, all the old tapes played faithfully. "No matter what, never, ever betray the brethren!" they told me.

The concerned psychiatrist then gave me a list of words, instructing me to check the ones that applied to me. I marked them off one at a time: despair, fear, hopelessness, tired . . . The doctor scanned the page after I finished. He asked me if I knew what day of the week it was. "No," I replied.

"What month is it?" he asked. How did he expect me to know these answers? I was just trying to survive from one moment to the next. I was more a zombie than a person.

Only after I signed a bunch of papers did they permit me to leave the hospital. I agreed to attend a class in the mental health wing for one hour per day, Monday through Friday. Whatever. At the time, the pronounced and painful beating in my chest interested me much more. I prayed that God would give me a heart attack and let me die. Then I wouldn't have to depend on sleep for relief.

On our return home, Judy made a few calls and located Verlan. He came to her house that night after dark, and she explained to him what the doctor said. She gave Verlan the paper that would admit me to the mental health classes at the hospital.

Without pausing to consider it, he said, "Irene will not go to any classes or see a psychiatrist." Then he turned to face me. "You're going to disrupt my whole family! In the first place, they will put you on welfare. They will make you bring your kids out into this wicked world. I may end up in prison when they discover I have all these wives. Look at you, you look terrible. Get a hold of yourself before you end up completely crazy, like my sister Lucinda!"

With that, my last hope for help vanished. Before he left, Verlan demanded I return home to Los Molinos and get back to raising the children.

I had hoped this man loved me enough to care just a little bit about my desperation. But his refusal to let me accept the help offered made me realize I had to take matters entirely into my own hands. As I mulled it all over, the idea formed in my fragmented mind to seek out my sister Becky, who now lived in Las Vegas. She and her husband were monogamous. At her first "hello," I cried out, "Becky! Help me . . . I'm losing my mind!" André, who lived near Judy, was concerned enough about my condition to pay for my bus fare to Vegas.

WHEN BECKY SAW the shape I was in, she tried to persuade me to see a doctor. I explained I couldn't seek that kind of help. I had enough burdens and guilt; I didn't want to add Verlan's being sent to jail or his family's being destroyed to the long list of things I already had to answer for. If I did, God might send me to a worse Hell than I was already experiencing. So I just stayed at Becky's house and tried to sort out my thoughts, hoping to remember why I was in this quandary in the first place.

I knew that in the late nineteenth century, Brigham Young taught the principle of blood atonement: "There are sins that men commit for which they cannot receive forgiveness [by the blood of Christ, so] they would be perfectly willing to have their blood spilt upon the ground, that the smoke thereof might ascend to Heaven as an offering for their sins; and the smoking incense would atone for their sins. . . . [These sinners] would beg of their brethren to shed their blood . . ." (Journal of Discourses, Vol. 4:51; Deseret News, 1856, p. 235). In our group, Brigham Young was always quoted as the ultimate authority. I knew I didn't deserve to continue living, but I couldn't remember which of my sins made me such a stench.

Oh, yes. I'd tied my tubes, depriving several unborn spirits of their opportunities to obtain bodies, to come to Earth and work out their salvation. And now I needed to atone for my despicable crime. A price had to be paid, and Jesus hadn't paid it—not for such a weighty sin as this. I made the decision to submit myself to the church's blood atonement ritual in order to rid myself of guilt for this sin. Verlan had just left for Nicaragua to prepare for the Church of the Firstborn's probable relocation there. I hoped to get my problem taken care of before he returned. I did not want him interfering.

A young church member allowed me to ride with him from Las Vegas to Colonia LeBaron. In the foggy prison of my mind, I grieved for myself as we traveled those fifteen sleepless hours. I would be a martyr; it was my only hope.

When we arrived at Colonia LeBaron, my young friend informed me it was Saturday night. I felt this confirmed that I was acting in accordance with God's divine plan. Most of the men were only home on weekends. The next day, they would leave the colony, and their wives, to return to their jobs in the States. If I was going to find any brethren in the colony, it would have to be tonight, late as it was.

By the urgency in my voice and appearance, I was able to persuade two brothers—Bruce and Earl—to give me an audience. I respected their positions just under Verlan in the church. I swore both men to secrecy. Then I confessed my crimes before them. Both were shocked, especially when I went on to say I knew Verlan loved me too much to see me carry out my plans. I begged them to do me the favor of slitting my throat so I might thereby redeem myself from my damnable deeds.

Seeing both my agony and my sincerity, Bruce interrupted. "Irene, blood atonement isn't being practiced by our group. We wouldn't think of doing that to you! It makes me angry that Verlan isn't here when you're suffering so much emotionally. Does he know how you feel?"

"He knows," I answered. "When I revealed to him that I wanted to commit suicide, he said he recognized the demons that possessed me. They should have fled when he laid his hands on my head and rebuked them in the name of God."

Earl realized I'd gone over the edge. He assured me he'd be responsible for me, and he promised Bruce he would stay and counsel me. I'd known Earl for twelve years. He moved to Colonia LeBaron after being convinced by Joel that the United States was about to be annihilated, that fire and brimstone would soon wipe it off the map, and that our group alone would be spared by fleeing to Mexico for safety. I thought I knew Earl well. I respected his priesthood. But the solution he offered to my problem seemed very foreign to me.

This supposed man of God confessed that he'd been trained in the latest techniques of hypnosis. I cringed. How could a man possessing such godly powers suggest I resort to using the Devil's tactics? But Earl promised me that through hypnosis, he could remove all my fears and imagined sins. Only because I had nowhere else to turn and I knew I would perish if I wasn't rescued immediately did I give in to Earl's suggestion. I confessed to Earl my fear that hypnosis was from the Devil. I asked him if he thought I'd lose my salvation if I let him do it. He said, "Trust me. I promise that you'll be okay. Now, sit in this recliner and relax. I'll count to ten, and when I get there, just quietly listen to my voice. Close your eyes."

I tried to calm my restless mind, hoping the Devil wouldn't completely overtake me. I focused on the sound of Earl's monotone voice. "One, you're getting sleepy. . . . Two, you're getting a little more drowsy. . . . Three, be calm, just relax. . . . Four, that's it, let your body relax more. . . ." By the time Earl counted to ten, I was completely under. Then he told me that tying my tubes spared my life and would help me to take better care of the thirteen children I had. He told me I would sleep like a baby that night. He assured me I was not an unredeemed sinner. "You will not grieve over your operation anymore," he said. "You are a beautiful woman. You need to listen to yourself." Then he paused. "I do not need to put you under next time. When you see me raise my index finger, you'll automatically go under." Then Earl started counting from ten back to one. "Now open your eyes," he instructed.

When I opened them, I felt as though I'd been asleep for hours. I was surprised to see my dear friend Rhonita, one of Earl's five wives, in the room. She smiled. "I hope you don't object to me having come in without your permission," she said. I had opened my mouth to answer her when Earl held up his index finger. Immediately, I flopped into that soft chair like a rag doll. I was under again. He then repeated the previous injunctions, making sure I understood I was a good person and had done nothing wrong. His voice soothed my heart. Counting from ten to one again, he gently ordered me to open my eyes.

"You should feel better now that I've taken you under twice," he said. "Come back tomorrow so we can reinforce your mind again." He smiled as I rose to my feet. "I'm available twenty-four hours a day, Irene. Come anytime you need me."

That night I passed out from sheer exhaustion and slept for thirteen hours without a hint of insomnia. In each subsequent session with Earl, my twisted mind unraveled some. My new friend helped erase many of my deepest fears. Most of all, he opened my mind to a promising new sense of myself—a self that not only wanted life and love but who wasn't evil for wanting it. I'd come to the colony seeking death, but there of all places I rediscovered the will to live. And as the rigid religious constructs in my mind began to crumble, I felt myself emerging from the darkness. Before me was something I hadn't seen in a long, long time. I saw hope.

CHAPTER THIRTY-FOUR

The day finally came when Verlan decided to move me to our place of refuge in the wilderness of Nicaragua, in Central America. We spent almost two unforgettable years there, fighting for survival against malaria, diarrhea, intestinal worms, mosquitoes, and especially loneliness.

Our journey down there, like most all of our journeys, was a waking nightmare. Verlan drove us in his pickup with the camper on the back, all thirteen of us packed in with whatever clothes, dishes, pots, pans, and other minimal necessities we could fit. From Colonia LeBaron, we went south for seven days, stopping to recuperate just long enough at night to hold out through the following fourteen-hour day. We camped on the side of the road under trees or near gas stations. One night we stayed in a cheap motel and all took baths. While we traveled, those fortunate enough to get car sick were allowed to sit in the front of the truck. The rest of us fought our claustrophobia in the broiling camper. With everyone in the truck bickering and crying over the miserable conditions, we barely noticed the beautiful scenery throughout Mexico and Central America. It was a relief to finally set foot in our newest "promised land."

Verlan purchased a small property in a jungle paradise about thirty-three miles outside the small town of Jinotega. Then, planning to build a city for God, he bought a nine-hundred-acre ranch with others in our church who were preparing to flee from Ervil's murderous rampage against our Mexico colonies. It was to be the final destination for additional saints Verlan was sure would arrive in the near future.

When I first saw the rolling hills covered with vegetation, I thought Nicaragua didn't seem too bad. We passed lush foliage, trees, and hillside plantations of coffee plants, bananas, oranges, and grapefruits. I thought our living conditions and diet might actually be better here than in places we'd lived in the past. But the small plantation onto which we moved was overgrown with weeds. The soil had never even been tilled. The boys spent hours with machetes, cutting down small trees, tall grass, and shrubs just to make room for a vegetable garden. As soon as possible, we planted an acre of cabbage, hoping it would grow into a cash crop to supply us with a few meager necessities. All the older kids worked each day pulling weeds to make sure the plants survived.

Lucy and five of her children had preceded us to the jungle. We crowded right in to her tin-roofed, dirt-floored wooden shack, which was the only structure on the plantation. This made a total of seventeen of us piled into one three-room jungle hut. Our only drinking water came from a bubbling creek running along at the bottom of the high hill on which the shack was built. The water had to be boiled before we drank it because the creek was used for bathing and washing clothes by neighbors on the plantations upstream from ours.

I almost ruined my hands trying to wash our clothes by scrubbing them on the huge rocks in the middle of the creek. But I soon learned the native way of washing in the creek—by beating the soapy clothes on the rocks. Then when they were clean and rinsed, I hung them on the bushes to dry between rainstorms. I welcomed the rains at first because the rainwater was cleaner than the water we drank from the creek. We had two fifty-gallon barrels to catch the raindrops as they showered down the tin roof. We often watched the clouds rapidly crossing close above us like floating herds of sheep.

As quickly as he could, Verlan built two more small lumber houses, one for Charlotte and one for Susan. They also moved to Central America, and we all settled in to make the best of what we had. Verlan of course was seldom there. He would often drive back to the

States or to check on our Mexican colonies and on other properties our people purchased in Nicaragua.

Our boys soon learned how to plant gardens and pick the wild fruits. Fourteen-year-old Steven bought a team of oxen. He often dragged big logs to our wooden shack to cut up for firewood. Most of the thousands of fruit and nut trees Verlan brought from the States and planted there died in the foreign climate. The ones that survived were eventually choked out by the tall weeds we couldn't pull fast enough. We had to buy most of our fruits and vegetables, especially green onions to replace the Mexican chilies that were such a staple of our diet but were unavailable there. Once a week, I would walk three miles with a couple of my children to catch a bus into Jinotega to buy supplies.

We soon discovered that the rainy season lasted for nine months of the year. The miserable dampness was an ideal breeding ground for mosquitoes, insects, snakes, and the sickness that assailed us constantly. It began with diarrhea and continued with everything else. Then the fleas in the dirt floors drove us wild, biting our arms and legs until they got swollen and the bites turned into open sores. I bought Merthiolate by the quart, doctoring everyone's sores each night at bedtime. But as fast as some dried up, new ones took their place.

Once, Kaylen cried with stomach pains all through the night. By the way he was doubled over, I thought his appendix was about to burst. While I waited for the bus to take him into Jinotega to the doctor the next day, I changed my baby Lothair's diaper. I noticed a flat, spaghettilike thing hanging out of Lothair's bottom about an inch. I gently pulled it, and to my horror, it stretched into an almost endless worm. When I examined the diaper stool by probing it with a small stick, I counted up to forty-five worms before I quit. At least Kaylen didn't have appendicitis.

I was mortified to tell the doctor what I discovered. I could hardly admit it, let alone tell him the details. But he nonchalantly stated, "Oh, that. Every Christian gets worms here." I wondered what Christianity had to do with it. I soon learned that was their way of referring to white foreigners in general.

The doctor wrote a prescription for all seventeen of us. "Take a tablespoon of Padrax once a day for three days. Then wait three days and repeat the process again."

I left the doctor's office almost blind with anger. The money we needed for food I had to use instead to buy medicine to deworm the whole family. I marched right over to the telegraph office and sent Verlan this message: "Come immediately—kids sick—marriage over!"

I simmered down some on the thirty-three-mile trip back to our plantation. But after the medical purge, I about died counting sixty-five worms measuring from one to twelve inches long in just one kid's bowel movement.

ALTHOUGH I DESPERATELY WANTED VERLAN to come and take us away from here, I also remember the good times we'd experienced in Nicaragua. Ironically, it was a kids' paradise. They got to go swimming, hiking, and exploring in the jungle for relics and pets. One little monkey they brought home soon developed a unique method of self-defense. Whenever he was threatened or he just wanted to be naughty, he would crap in his hand and then throw the stinky stuff on his victim. The kids thought it was rather funny, but when it happened to Verlan, good-bye monkey!

Our greatest satisfaction came from the friendships we formed among the native people there. In spite of our poverty, we shared what little we had with them. Verlan bought two milking cows that provided enough milk to share among the four wives and our collective school of children. We occasionally made cheese and cottage cheese, which added flavor to our meals. We used the male calves for meat. When we butchered an animal, our families would use the meat we needed, and the remainder went to our friends. Not a particle of anything was ever wasted, including hide, blood, entrails, head, and so forth. There was no electricity or refrigeration, and we didn't want our food to spoil in the heat. At these times, a festive spirit always prevailed.

After one such celebration, a neighbor from about three miles away sent word with one of her children for me to walk over for dinner. Rice was a luxury seldom enjoyed, but on this occasion, she served rice soup. While stirring the soup in my bowl, I discovered a small boiled egg in it, so I commented, "I've never seen whole eggs in soups before."

"Oh no," she said, "that's not an egg. That's the cow's eye. We serve them to our guests because the eyes are all-seeing. They give wisdom to those who eat them."

Good gracious! How was I going to get out of this one? Luckily, her hungry ten-year-old son was standing next to me, looking on. When she turned her back, I quickly spooned the boiled eye into his mouth, and he gobbled it down as I signaled for secrecy.

A SHORT TIME after receiving my telegram, Verlan returned to Nicaragua to find me fed up with his most recent utopian delusion. I didn't want to live with any more false hopes, so I informed him I was leaving him. That way, I wouldn't set myself up with any further expectations of him that he could proceed to dash.

He said I needed a trip. That was all. He promised that if I went back with him to Colonia LeBaron in Mexico, we could be together for a whole month. He spoke of the good times we'd enjoy. He could expedite church business and spend a little time with Lillie, Beverly, and Esther. "But," he said, "you'll be my priority."

So I agreed.

The seven-day trip through Central America and Mexico was long and tiring, but it was the most time I'd spent alone with Verlan in years. The back of the truck was loaded with some of the personal belongings of three of the other wives. Verlan was taking the load back to Mexico because the moisture of the Nicaraguan rains was ruining treasured photos and other valuables. The camper was so tightly packed, we couldn't sleep in it. So we stopped at night and slept on a blanket under the trees. Knowing I couldn't conceive but hoping to pacify me so I wouldn't divorce him, Verlan guiltily gave in to my seductive advances.

We were approximately a hundred miles from Colonia LeBaron when Verlan asked if he could share his thoughts with me. I got that sick sensation that often warned me of what was coming.

"I feel terrible that I've avoided Elizabeth like I have," he said. "She asked me six months ago if I'd marry her. Since then, I've just kept putting her off because I haven't had the money or the time. But you know how sad it is to be alone. Imagine her, a widow and no hope at all."

It amazed me how compassionate he could be about other women's desperation. For the past two years, I'd recovered only fragments of hope. I would relinquish Verlan once more, if necessary. But I would not trust him again.

He glanced in the mirror of the truck, and then looked at me. "Come on. She won't bother you, Irene! After all, you've been close friends for most of your life."

I silently watched the road.

"Hey," he said, slapping my knee. "If you don't want to let me do it this time, just say so. I'll tell her she'll have to wait, because you don't want her to."

I remained quiet.

"Come on," he probed. "What do you say? It's going to happen sometime, so why don't you just get it over with? Why not now?"

If I cried, he would just condemn me more. "Let's do it then!" I snapped.

"Don't be angry. She has so many talents. She can teach our children. She types. She's calm and humble. Why, honey, she'll be a big asset to our family."

I looked at him sarcastically. "Yeah, that's what worries me—where she'll sit her ass!"

We arrived in Colonia LeBaron after dark. He dropped me off at Linda's house while he went to see his future wife, Elizabeth. It was almost midnight when he returned with a smile on his face. "I've made arrangements to be married at noon tomorrow in Elizabeth's home. Just a private wedding—her four children, you, and me . . . and you're invited, too, Linda." He smiled, hugging me good-bye as he left to go sleep with Lillie.

It was February 22, 1976. Verlan sent me over early to help Elizabeth. She'd made a small cake, which I frosted. I made a pitcher of lemonade, putting it in the fridge to keep cold. I thought about how lucky they were to finally have electricity in the colony.

This was to be Elizabeth's third marriage. I couldn't believe she was so nervous as she primped her short gray hair. She removed her glasses to wipe the lenses clean. Couldn't she see what she was getting herself into? I wondered if she worried about her marriage affecting our friendship. It had endured longer than either of her previous marriages.

I watched as she slipped into a pink dress she had bought secondhand six months before. She had saved it just in case Verlan honored her request for marriage. She fastened her belt. "Do I look okay?" she asked me. I nodded with approval.

Alma arrived to perform the ceremony. He shook hands with us and said, "I'm sure proud of both of you. This is a step in the right direction."

Then Linda walked in with Verlan. He apologized for being late again. He'd taken the liberty of going to visit his two Mexican wives, who lived in the colony and hadn't seen him for over a month. Immediately, he motioned for me to follow him into a small bedroom adjacent to the kitchen. He enveloped me in his strong arms, holding me so tight, I could hardly breathe. He smooched me as I fought to keep him from forcing my gold wedding band off my hand. I tried to speak, but his kisses muffled my complaints. He got my ring off and hid it in his pocket. "I'll give it back to you later. Please don't say anything."

Quietly, Verlan opened the door, joining the few guests who awaited our presence in the living room. He said to Alma, "Let's get things started."

Again, I could feel the volcano welling up inside me. I breathed deeply, forcing the air from my lungs. *Don't cry; it's just a ring!* I told myself. But I couldn't help thinking how that was the only piece of jewelry he'd ever given me. Not only was I giving Elizabeth my husband but I had to share the sacred token of my marriage also. After many a deep breath, I finally regained my composure and entered the living room, where they were all waiting.

Alma offered a prayer thanking God for the wonderful occasion as I begged God not to let me cry. Immediately after the prayer, Verlan, Elizabeth, and I took our places, standing before the fireplace. I heard Alma clear his throat. Then, for the fourth time, I was asked the dreaded question. "Do you, Sister Irene, take Sister Elizabeth by the right hand and give her unto your husband to be his lawful and wedded wife?"

Obediently, I placed her sweaty hand in his and tuned out the rest of the ceremony. It seemed that all my trips with Verlan quickly evolved into his going on a honeymoon with one of my best friends. Now I wanted to run far away, where I could cry about it without being criticized.

"I now pronounce you man and wife," Alma said. As with Helen, we'd only have Elizabeth in our family for this life. After her death, she'd belong to her deceased husband, Earl. In light of that, I wondered what the advantage was to our taking her in.

Verlan surprised everyone except me by pulling out my ring and placing it on Elizabeth's finger. Elizabeth was elated. Verlan kissed his fifty-year-old bride as the congratulations began.

Elizabeth showed Linda and me her beautiful gold band. "Isn't it lovely? Can you believe he's so thoughtful?" Verlan stared at me, tacitly warning me not to deflate her.

Linda and I cut the cake, serving Elizabeth and her four children. Alma and Verlan talked over business while they ate.

"Are you ready to go, Elizabeth?" Verlan asked after a while.

"I will be in twenty minutes or so. I just need to find a babysitter for my kids."

"Oh, that's no problem. Irene can do it for you. We're family now. Besides, she's here on vacation, with nothing to do." He walked over and pulled me to him, giving me a hug. "There's no one quite like Irene. She enjoys serving everyone."

Elizabeth hugged me good-bye, suitcase in hand, as Verlan gave me a peck of gratitude. And the honeymoon was on.

Two days later, Elizabeth threw open her kitchen door and dropped her small suitcase, making a grand entrance. "Tah-rah! Oh, Irene, he is simply wonderful!"

My heart fell to the floor. I thought so myself in that particular respect, but I didn't need another woman to tell me about it.

I smiled and hugged her as I welcomed her home, knowing our friendship could never be the same. I hated to shatter her dreams, but since I was leaving, now would be as good a time as any. "Liz," I said, trying to sound light and breezy, "it's bad enough to have to give my husband to you, but could I have my wedding ring back?"

She was shocked. "You mean"—she looked at the indentation on my naked finger—"he actually used *your* ring?" She shook her head in disbelief. "I wonder about men sometimes," she said, and gave the ring back to me. Then she thanked me for caring for her four kids as I hugged her good-bye.

Walking down the street, I hoped to run into Verlan. He'd left in such a hurry after his wedding, I'd failed to congratulate him. Any man whose ego was big enough to try and keep nine women happy certainly deserved to be praised.

IN ADDITION TO our miserable living conditions in Nicaragua, a raging revolution broke out in many parts of the country. Verlan's four wives agreed on one thing: we all wanted out of there. Even Verlan realized it was futile to remain. He also realized he'd lose me if he didn't make other arrangements.

Because Elizabeth's wedding had occurred during what began as my trip, Verlan decided to make up for it by taking me with him to Dallas, Texas, where he planned to arrange things so some of his wives could live and work and become self-supporting. I had flown in a small plane once before, but this was my first commercial airline flight. I almost died of fright. At thirty thousand feet in the air, I felt I was halfway to Heaven and would probably get all the way there very shortly. Before we landed, I promised God I'd be good if he'd see me through this one. When we landed safely, I wondered if I could keep my part of the bargain.

Our friend Erv Lowther agreed to let three of us sell jewelry for him in Dallas, so Verlan and I returned to Nicaragua just long enough to wind up our affairs. It was a good thing we did, considering the revolution soon infiltrated that area. We left the properties and lost a few head of cattle. We left with very little to show for our efforts except the experience we'd gained. We could at least say we'd once lived in Nicaragua.

Before long, Susan, Lillie, and I ended up in Dallas, where we rented a couple of apartments that we crammed full of our children. My older boys were off working in other places, and my faithful Donna was married and living in California. She'd seen enough tears and heartache. She wanted to be as far as possible from poverty, polygamy, and her uncle Ervil, who was terrorizing the fundamentalist groups. My twelve-year-old daughter, Barbara, cared for all the kids while Susan, Lillie, and I went to work selling jewelry. It was summer vacation, so we didn't have to worry about babysitters until school started for the older kids in the fall.

Erv arranged to set up some tables of jewelry in various hotel lobbies. This was my first experience at selling, and I enjoyed it. I discovered I had a talent for sales. In order to keep this job, I had to get up early and come home late. I also had many things to do for the children as I made preparations to ease Barbara's load during the day.

Verlan, as usual, was seldom around. He had so many other responsibilities to take care of besides us. He was also constantly on the move to keep clear of Ervil's henchmen. On one of his trips, he took Susan with him for a short vacation. Before leaving, she asked me to take care of her mail. She requested I keep only her personal letters and throw away all the junk mail. She warned me several times to beware of con artists, "because," she said, "the big cities are full of crooks. They'll take advantage of you if you don't watch out."

Just after Susan left, our apartment manager asked me to evacuate the apartment for twelve hours so pest control could spray for cockroaches. I asked him to also fix the wooden doors below the kitchen sink, because the whole frame was loose. He hired a nice carpenter who did the job in just a few minutes. Shortly thereafter, a letter came addressed to Susan that I figured was junk mail, but out of curiosity I opened it. I found an astonishing bill: "Beatles—$6.95, Carpenters—$13.90, Bread—$13.90, Total—$34.75." It was accompanied by a letter: "Dear Miss Ray, Your account is long overdue. Remit the total amount immediately or we will have to turn the account over to a collection agency."

I couldn't believe it. The exterminator and the carpenter were trying to rip her off. This was urgent, and she wouldn't be back in time to handle it, so I figured I'd fix these villains myself. Pretending to be Susan, I wrote:

Dear Sirs:

I can't believe you'd try to rip me off. Last week I complied with your request to leave the apartment empty for the day while they sprayed for cockroaches. They were not beatles! You can't charge me for carpenters because there was only one, and the doors you fixed were the manager's responsibility. I could've glued and nailed those boards under the sink myself! It was supposed to be done for free. Next time you try to take advantage of me, think twice, because I think you're downright stupid! I know, because I've never bought bread through the mail before. I've made twelve loaves of homemade bread every other day for most of my life. Seeing that you're trying to swindle me, I don't ever want to hear from you again.

Signed, Susan Ray

When Susan returned, I told her she was right about the crooks. I began telling her about these guys trying to rip her off and the letter I sent them in her defense. She laughed between tears. "Irene, those were cassette tapes I ordered. Haven't you heard of the Beatles, the Carpenters, and Bread?" I hadn't. It was all news to me!

Our Dallas experience came to an abrupt end, like most everything else Verlan got us into. He suddenly came with overnight orders for us to pack what would fit into his pickup. The fact was he thought we were becoming too independent. His excuse was that he could no longer leave the three of us out in the wicked world, where sharks were lurking.

I had furnished my apartment from garage sales and now had the best beds and furniture I'd ever owned. Damn! It was so exasperating to have to leave all our worldly possessions behind for the umpteenth time. But the outcome was worth it, since I got to live in Las Vegas with my sister Becky for a while. I also took a step toward fulfilling one of my lifelong dreams. With Verlan's permission, and with Barbara and Lucy watching all but my youngest two kids, I took a six-week creative writing course at the University of Nevada at Las Vegas. Becky offered to let me take her car to and from my classes. She was shocked when I admitted I'd never had a driver's license.

"How did you drive all the kids to school in Mexico?" Becky asked.

"Oh, that was just on dirt roads, with no traffic lights or signs, just out in the middle of nowhere."

"Well, I'm going to see that you get your license immediately," she assured me. She became my driving instructor. One Monday, she informed me I would take my driving test on Friday. I did, but with much trepidation because it was the first time I had ever used my husband's last name for an official purpose. I also doubted myself, worrying I wouldn't be able to pass the driving test because I'd been sheltered so long. When André heard I'd received my driver's license at forty, he bought me a used, yellow Honeybee Datsun—the first vehicle I ever owned.

Shortly after I finished my studies, Verlan insisted I return to Colonia LeBaron, where he purchased a three-room adobe house for me and my younger kids. It had electricity, running water, and an indoor toilet. Other than the bathroom and one bedroom, however, there were no partitions in the unfinished house. Still, I was immensely thankful just to have electricity. The government had finally fulfilled its promise to extend power to the LeBaron Colony.

Meanwhile, Ervil's violent havoc within the Church of the Firstborn was escalating. His power to intimidate and control came home

to me personally in a terrible way. On May 10, 1977, I was walking down the gravel road in Colonia LeBaron, drinking a Coke and
laughing with Linda, when a pickup truck raced up beside us. Verlan's
anxious shouting surprised me. "Irene! They've killed your Uncle
Rulon in Salt Lake City! Ervil had it done; I'm sure of it."

I was stunned for a moment, and then I started weeping. My dear
uncle, who had been my one constant father figure since childhood,
was dead.

"Come, get in with me, Irene. I want to spend a few minutes with
you before I leave town," Verlan urged.

As we hurried home, he admitted to me fearfully, "I know if I'm
not careful, I might be next. Ervil's on his worst rampage. He's still
madly jealous over Joel making me the patriarch and president of the
church. I'm afraid he's out to kill us all. I'm really sorry to have to
leave town before I can stay with you, but I have to go into hiding
and somehow attend Uncle Rulon's funeral as well."

From that time on, Verlan slept with his clothes on and a pistol by
his side, ready to defend himself in an emergency. When he traveled,
he generally went with other elders in the church, and they were
careful to lay low. He felt safer being away from his wives so Ervil's
people wouldn't know his routine. When he was with us, he refused
to follow any organized rotation list. We never knew whose night
it would be, what to expect, or even when he was coming to town.
Understandably, we were always relieved to see him back after he'd
been gone.

MEANWHILE, JUST AS VERLAN FEARED, Susan's time in Dallas
convinced her she could make it on her own. A few months after
Uncle Rulon's death, she left Verlan and moved with her five children to Cedar City, Utah, to live around her brothers. Her leaving
affected Verlan as though she'd died. He neglected his other wives
while he mourned her and tried to win her back with songs and
poetry he composed himself. But nothing he said or did persuaded
her to return.

I remember accompanying Verlan on a thirteen-hour trip to San Diego after one of his long absences. The despair was written plainly on his face as he told me how lost he felt without Susan.

"Forgive me for using you as a sounding board, Irene. None of my other wives want to hear a word about her. I appreciate you listening to me, because a part of me is dying. I love her so."

I was trying to understand his pain, but I also hoped he'd try to comprehend mine. Wanting reassurance he hadn't canceled out his love for me, I said, "Verlan, I know you love all of your wives. It's evident you have tried to be fair by treating us all the same. Even though you say you do love us, I feel that Susan is the only woman you have ever really been in love with."

Wanting desperately for him to deny it, I watched the tears forming in his blue eyes. "You know what?" he said. "You're right! I hate to admit it because I don't want to hurt you, but I've never loved another woman as much as I love Susan."

CHAPTER THIRTY-FIVE

Priscilla (at whose home Verlan proposed to Helen a few years earlier) was Joel LeBaron's widow. She'd been married two other times as well, but she divorced both men. Priscilla was thin, cute, and had an air of arrogance about her.

Verlan tried in vain to persuade her to marry him when she was only sixteen. I remember my resentment when they sat in his truck most of the night in front of my bedroom window. He felt I had no right to feel bad. After all, they were both in plain sight. He admitted to me later how he stole her first kisses. Before the night was over, she promised to marry him, but two months later she secretly married a younger man, becoming his plural wife without the knowledge of his first one. That union lasted only six months.

Verlan got all excited after her failed marriage, hoping she realized what a good position he was in to exalt her. But Priscilla wanted prestige and the highest glory she could obtain in exchange for her sacrifices. She snubbed Verlan again and instead asked Joel, our self-proclaimed prophet, if she could become his seventh wife. He gladly agreed, and she gave birth to three daughters in rapid succession. Then Ervil had Joel brutally murdered.

Verlan was sick over his brother's untimely death, but he felt certain Priscilla would now consent to marry him. The Old Testament says that if a man dies, his brother should marry his widow and raise up seed unto his dead brother. Perhaps that's all Verlan was proposing.

He took every opportunity to reaffirm his love and devotion to Priscilla. Well, scripture or no scripture, this time Priscilla chose to become the second wife of a good-looking convert named Bruce. She gave him a daughter as well, but then divorced him when he wanted to move her to the States. She believed in the prophecies of her dead husband that the United States would soon be destroyed.

Verlan pled with Priscilla to become his wife before and after each of her three marriages, and it seemed to me he should've taken no for an answer already. How much more battering could his ego take from the same woman?

I'd agonized over Priscilla for years. The more Verlan desired her, the more determined I was to see he didn't get her. I tried not to be jealous, but I wanted to be the one he pursued, the one he needed and desired. Instead, I usually felt like a number, merely a tool by which he hoped to fulfill his dreams for eternity.

In late August, about a year after Susan left, my fourteen-year-old son, Kaylen, woke me up from a deep sleep. "Mom, why did Daddy go into Priscilla's bedroom, and then all the lights went off in her house?"

Although I was still exhausted from hoeing tomatoes for ten hours that day in the hot sun, I dressed in a flash and almost ran to the corner. Then I crossed the street and walked right up to the back of Priscilla's house. Every step I took was familiar. On many an evening, I'd let myself in her back door and gone down to her room, where we talked, read poetry, and shared our intimate feelings.

Just as Kaylen said, I didn't see a flicker of light on anywhere in the house. It was dark, but it wasn't silent. With my heart in my throat, I approached Priscilla's outside bedroom door. Once I calmed my breath, I could clearly hear their playful giggles on the other side. I raised my hand to knock, but their sudden laughter restrained me. Resolving to put a stop to it, I pounded violently on the door. Their laughter hung in midair. Then silence.

When I realized they didn't intend to answer, I called loudly, "Priscilla?"

"It's late," she said, "I'm in bed. Can't you come back tomorrow?"

"No," I insisted. "I need to come in now."

"What do you want?" she asked, perturbed.

"My husband!" I shouted.

Immediately the light went on. Verlan opened her bedroom door just wide enough to make his exit. He grabbed me and forced me out the wrought-iron gate as I fought to go back inside Priscilla's house and give her a piece of my mind. He overpowered me and led me down the gravel road, insisting I cut out my nonsense. "I'm ashamed of you, Irene! Why don't you mind your own business?"

"You, ashamed of me?" I cut in. "How do you justify this? Why are you sneaking behind my back? You know there's no reason for it. Why try and hide the fact that you're seeing Priscilla?"

"I didn't want to hurt you. I figured I'd mention it to you later when I knew for sure what her decision would be. But don't worry, she'll probably ignore me after your scene just now."

Making sure I got into my bed, Verlan shut my door and quietly left. It was almost midnight, and Elizabeth was supposedly waiting for him to spend the night with her. I was furious when I found out later that both Elizabeth and Lucy forfeited the first parts of their evenings with Verlan so he could court Priscilla.

Too angry to sleep, I lay awake instead and tried to make sense of Verlan's strange behavior. For the most part, I thought, I'd upheld him in living the Principle. I'd even supported him courting one or two of his wives. When I hadn't been quite so supportive, he'd charged right on anyway, telling me all the while that I ought to be happy God was continuing to shower us with such blessings. So why was he trying to hide Priscilla from me?

As I mulled it over, it came to me. All summer long, I'd been taking twelve to fifteen of Verlan's kids to the tomato fields each day to hoe weeds with me from dawn until dark. At about 9 A.M., I'd take the crew to my house for hotcakes, and then we'd return to our hoeing until about 2 P.M. By then the burning sun made it impossible to continue, but at five in the afternoon, I'd force the tired group to resume work.

I did it because I thought Verlan needed the help to feed his giant families. Happy to help ease his burdens, I'd slaved away, uncomplaining, while he was supposedly busy with other important matters. Now I saw just what those matters were.

But my nights with Verlan were too few and far between to ruin things by fighting with him. By the time it was my turn again, I'd repented of my anger and jealousy, and we made up. Hoping to snuggle up to him, I awoke earlier than usual, needing his touch. "What are your plans for today?" I asked, knowing it was my turn to enjoy it with him.

"I'm going to Casas on business," he said, then quickly added, "but you need to get all the kids and finish weeding the tomato field."

"It's my turn! I'm taking the day off so I can go with you."

"No. I really can't let you go this time. The kids won't work if you're not there."

My daughter Connie came late to the field. She stayed behind to clean the house for me. "Mama, Priscilla's girl said that Daddy is taking her mom to Casas with him. I thought it was your turn to go."

Irate, I left the kids hoeing, and I drove like mad over the bumpy road in my yellow Datsun. When I turned the corner, sure enough, there was Verlan's gray truck in front of Priscilla's house. I came to a stop five feet in front of his vehicle, facing it.

Out came Verlan with Priscilla at his side, all smiles until they glanced up and realized they'd been caught. Ignoring me, Priscilla jumped into his truck and slammed the door as if to show me who was boss. Verlan waved to me as he walked between our vehicles. With no explanation at all, he slid into the driver's seat beside Priscilla.

What I did next, I did by pure instinct. My intellectual self just looked on, amazed, as I started my little car and drove head-on into Verlan's truck. The sound of crunching metal and breaking glass was awful. I remember congratulating myself that I'd finally made an impression on them. I'd put a nice big dent in their day.

Priscilla looked daggers at me. Verlan tried backing up his truck so he could pull away. Again I stepped on the gas, lunging forward and smashing his headlights. Verlan was clearly shocked. I'd never been a violent wife. Perhaps he would think I was possessed again.

The third time Verlan tried backing up, his rear tires fell into the irrigation ditch behind his truck. I could see him getting angrier as his wheels spun in the mud. He motioned for me to leave them alone, but I didn't give a damn by then. I charged forward again, banging his truck for all it was worth.

Verlan jumped out and walked briskly over to my open window. "Are you crazy?"

"About you!" I screamed. "You take that bitch to town on my day, and you'll never see me again." I hoped Priscilla would realize how ungodly I was and refuse to become a part of our family kingdom.

Exasperated, Verlan returned to his truck, determined to leave. After several tries, he backed through the ditch, splashing water all over the dirt road as they took off. With hatred and disgust, I watched him zoom away with his new love in flagrant preference over me. I drove home so hysterical, I could hardly see the road. Dejected and furious, I decided what I had to do. A polygamous husband wasn't supposed to marry without his wives' consent, and for the first time in our marriage, I wasn't going to give mine.

When my fifteen-year-old son, Brent, saw my suffering, he got so angry, he jumped into my car, flew over the dirt roads to the paved highway, and drove at top speed until he caught up with his father. He came up beside Verlan's truck, honking for him to stop. Verlan angrily refused, so Brent pulled ahead, hollering for him to pull over.

Verlan finally did. "What do you want?" he yelled out his window at Brent.

"Please, Daddy, come here for a minute."

Verlan refused. "If you want to talk to me, be decent enough to come over here."

Trembling with anger, hardly able to speak, Brent went over to Verlan's truck and blurted out right in front of Priscilla, "If you take that woman to town, you'll never see us again!"

"Just mind your own business and go home!"

"I mean it. We'll be gone by the time you get back."

Verlan drove off, leaving Brent standing there alone on the road.

Hours later, I woke up with Verlan trying to kiss me. "Hey, Priscilla and I broke up. She decided she didn't want to be part of such a family after the way you and Brent acted. See what you've done?

"But don't feel too bad. I guess I shouldn't have been courting her without at least telling you. Looks like we'll both have to pay for our mistakes. I want you to apologize in the morning and tell her how sorry you are that you banged my truck. That was absolutely uncalled for!"

"*Who* owes *whom* an apology? I'll never apologize! I can't understand you, Verlan. It's wrong for me to bang your damn truck, but it's not wrong for you to want to bang her!?"

VERLAN PLANNED FOR ME to go pine-nut picking in the Sierra Nevada with him and his older children, as we'd done several times before. First we would set up our tent camp, where I'd do all the cooking for fifteen to thirty people. I always got up at dawn, then got busy making a fire between three big rocks on which I'd set a round barrel lid and make breakfast, usually consisting of fried potatoes, eggs, and pancakes along with oat or wheat cereal. While the group ate, I'd pack everyone's lunch.

As soon as the crowd left each day, I would do the breakfast dishes, clean camp, and wash any dirty clothes left by the crew. Then I'd start in on supper. The famished pickers usually loved the hot soups, chicken, potatoes, gravy, and vegetables I made for them. I always had a carrot salad or coleslaw and hot biscuits. This rich diet was a rare treat for us. Verlan supplied all the scrumptious food because he wanted the children to keep animated while working the long hours.

Except for the baking, I did all the cooking over the campfire. For the baking, we set up an apartment-size gas stove in an improvised kitchen Verlan made by wrapping black plastic around four upright posts, then covering the top. There I would bake twelve loaves of bread almost every day. When the family came home, starved from working hard, they'd often find I'd made twenty-five pies at a whack. I would also make applesauce and carrot and gingerbread cakes, and I'd set big pans of Jell-O in the cold creek to make fruit Jell-O for salad. We never ate better than we did on those trips.

This year, Donna paid my bus fare to Stockton, California, so I could visit with her and her husband, Marshall, for a week before the camp started. In the middle of this vacation, Verlan called and asked me to come immediately so we could be the first to pick pine nuts and therefore make more money.

I got to San Diego early in the morning and found Verlan all ready to go. He'd gotten a trailer to haul supplies and for the two of us to sleep in. It was already packed full of tents, food, and several hundred gunnysacks for the pine nuts. Also ready to go were seven of my children, plus eight of his other kids.

Shortly before we were to leave, Charlotte showed up, wanting to go with us. I asked Verlan in private if he'd forgotten his promise to me. He said, "Well, if you don't want her to go, just tell her she can't."

"You promised if I worked in the fields, hoeing tomatoes eight to ten hours a day, I could go to the pine nuts for two weeks. You promised I could be your only wife there, and we could be alone. You never keep your promises. Tell Charlotte yourself she can't go." I wasn't about to be the one to tell Charlotte.

At the appointed hour for our departure, instead of telling her not to come, Verlan merely asked her to drive my Datsun so I could spend the night driving with him. I hadn't seen him for two weeks, and she'd just had a fourteen-hour trip with him from Mexico to San Diego. When Charlotte refused, he finally put his foot down. He made her stay in San Diego for a week and come later with her son Mark. So I looked forward to spending one week alone with him.

The previous year, we stored our ladders, camp stove, and other equipment on a ranch near Ione, Nevada. Verlan was going to drive over there before dark to pick it all up. He insisted I stay at the camp to help the kids, but I refused. All the young kids were doing just fine pitching their own tents and preparing to settle in for the night. I'd come to work, but I needed to spend some time with my husband. Baffled that he didn't want me to go, I insisted he take me with him.

The truck was so weighted down with ladders, we had to drive slowly over the rough, rocky mountain roads. We had plenty of time to talk. I shouldn't have even mentioned her name, but the last time we discussed Priscilla, Verlan promised me it was all over between them. My kids had been telling me something different, so I figured this would be a good time to ask about it. "How's your little Miss Priss doin'?" I asked.

Verlan stared ahead at the road long and hard. Then he said, "You better make your mind up right now, because whether you fight me or not, I've promised I'd marry her."

"If that's the way it is, then I'm leaving you," I said. "You don't love me! If you did, you'd consider how I feel about it. Can you break my heart and still be exalted in the celestial kingdom, Verlan? For this hussy, you'd give up a good wife, like me, who has stood by you, who's given you all these other wives? Can't you see you're hurting me by marrying another man's widow when she won't be with you in eternity anyway?" I started crying.

As soon as he saw my tears, he yelled, "I'm damn sick and tired of seeing you cry! That's all you've ever done, and I'm sick and tired of it. So shape up!"

This time Verlan had lied to me outright. He'd never given Priscilla up at all. And now, the bitterness in his voice told me I didn't matter to him. A new resolve took hold of me as I vowed, "The day will come when you'll beg to see me cry. I'll never shed another tear over you again!"

"I hope you'll keep your word."

I told him I was leaving in the morning. He figured I was bluffing because I'd always broken down before. Then I asked, "Would you please give me just enough money for gas to get to Vegas?"

"No. I don't want to be held accountable before God for helping you leave."

Enraged, I didn't say another word. Glad when we finally arrived back at the camp, I went straight to Brent and Steven's tent. They hadn't gone to sleep yet but were snuggled down in their sleeping bags. I told them I was leaving their father. Between the two of them, they gave me $125 from the money they had earned as tapers working with drywall in San Diego. My boys knew for years of my heartache, but they also felt a strong loyalty to their father. I'd never carried out my threats before, and they didn't expect me to now.

Verlan pretended to be asleep when I crawled into bed next to him. Throughout the long, sleepless night, we never spoke or touched. Then, early in morning before I left his trailer, he again assailed me, forbidding me to tell my kids I was leaving him. He insisted they all belonged to him. If I left him, he was going to make me do it alone and empty-handed, just as the laws of the fundamentalist Mormon faith authorized him to do.

I retorted, "Where were you when my kids were born? Where were you when they were sick at night? They've never had a father. This is preposterous!"

"Do you think you'll take these kids from me? I want you to sign them over to me legally when we return home to Mexico," he countered.

I hissed at him. "It will be over my dead body. You'll have to kill me first!"

"Well, I'll allow you to take the younger ones for now, but only because I've given my consent until we can settle this. Don't upset them by telling them you're thinking of divorcing me."

Verlan kept Steven, Brent, Kaylen, and Barbara with him because he wouldn't be able to make much money without their help with the pine nuts. He loaded up the truck with gunnysacks and ladders and left with a dozen or more of his children to start work for the day. I left shortly after with my three youngest nut pickers.

I drove with LaSalle, Margaret, and Lothair from Ione, Nevada, toward my sister Becky's house in Las Vegas. I'd never driven by myself on the highways before. My car overheated when I was only an hour from Vegas. I pulled to the side of the road, waiting for someone to help me and concluding this was God's punishment for leaving Verlan. But the highway patrol soon came to my rescue. The cop phoned Becky, told her where I was, and said she needed to call a tow truck for me. She showed up instead with a thick tow rope and informed me we were taking the freeway. I put the three kids in her car, praying I could safely steer the Honeybee at the end of the rope.

In Vegas, Becky's husband, Garlin, let me borrow his car. He got a notarized statement allowing me to take the vehicle into Mexico. I left alone, feeling vulnerable and afraid as I drove fifteen hours back to Colonia LeBaron to pick up my other four young children. I went directly to Linda's house.

"I thought you were in the pine nuts. What're you doing back here?" she asked.

"I did it, Linda. I left him! I'm just here to get the children before any of the brethren try to stop me."

"You're serious? I figured it would eventually come to this. Boy, am I gonna miss you!"

My four children I left at home were overjoyed to see me and thrilled with the news that we were all moving to Las Vegas. As I sorted through my personal belongings, I opened a small blue suitcase filled with photographs that reminded me of the decades of poverty and suffering I was finally choosing to leave behind. I flung the suitcase, scattering the pictures in all directions. Verlan could pick up the memories when he came home. I took only one change of clothes, two of my best blankets, and the children.

CHAPTER THIRTY-SIX

I saw Priscilla walk down the aisle of the church and kneel beside my husband at the altar. Loudly, I cried out to Verlan, hoping I could stop the ceremony. But it was too late. He kissed the bride as I ran hysterically outside and fell into Linda's arms for comfort. My remorseful sobs woke me. It was only a dream, but I knew it was true.

Obsessed with this premonition, I was glad two days later, when Becky offered to take all seven of my kids to the park and let me stay home alone. Once they were gone, I turned on the radio to try and drown out my torment. Bonnie Tyler was belting out "It's a Heartache." "Love him till your arms break, then he lets you down . . ."

Didn't Verlan realize he'd let me down? He hadn't called or seen us for five months. If he didn't show up in Las Vegas soon, I'd be granted a divorce by the church. I wondered if he was just trying to punish me. How could he ignore his children for so long?

The music from the radio was loud enough that I didn't hear his footsteps. I jumped in fear as someone sprawled on top of me. In my shock, I fought off his rapid kisses. Then Verlan rolled me over, pinning me beneath his large frame.

Yes, a part of me still wanted to respond to his advances and let him kiss away my fears. But I knew where it would end, and I fixated on that.

"How's my little sweetheart doing?" he said.

I tried to push his body off mine. "Not as good as you!" I snapped. "You married Priscilla, didn't you?"

Instantly, he fell to hedging. "Where did you get that idea?"

"Friday I dreamed you married her. I've cried for two days, hoping it wasn't true, but it is . . . isn't it?"

He buried his head on my shoulder. "Please don't ask me that, Irene . . . please." He clung to me as though he wanted to shut out the world. "I married her, but I'm here with you. Doesn't that mean something?"

I went berserk. He tried holding me down, but I pulled myself from his grip. I ran out to the carport, just steps ahead of him, and jumped into the Honeybee. As I started up the motor, he forced himself into the passenger seat beside me.

"Get out! Out of my car! Out of my life!" I screamed.

He begged me to just listen to him, to try and understand why he'd done it. I didn't need to listen. This time, I knew exactly why he'd done it. Wheels spinning, I backed the car out blindly, driving so fast, I skidded around the corner. "Please calm down, Irene," Verlan whined. But I drove faster onto Marilyn Parkway. "Just stop somewhere before you kill us!" he demanded.

I came very close to giving into my rage and deadly impulses, to driving head-on into the semitruck coming toward us and thereby ending it for us both, forever. But I finally pulled into an abandoned gas station instead, too blinded by tears to drive any farther. Verlan turned off the car and tried to force me into his arms. I fought and screamed, pushing him away.

"Irene, I love you. You've got to understand. I love you!"

Hissing as I spoke, I gritted my teeth. "If this is love, for God's sake, Verlan, don't love me one minute longer!"

He let me rage at him for several minutes until I eventually wound down, exhausted. Then he told me, "I have your interest at heart, Irene. Believe me, I love you."

I felt so numb. My head was throbbing like crazy as I sat in silence, collecting my thoughts. "Verlan, I'm going to tell you one final time how I feel. Don't you say a word until I'm through. You've ruined my life. I married you, thinking you could exalt me. You promised if I obeyed you, I'd one day be a goddess. I've done everything you told me to, and look at me. I've become a devil!

"I was a beautiful green plant when you married me, but you neglected me! All I ever wanted, all I ever asked was to be watered with your love. I never asked you for money. I took whatever you gave me, but even that became less and less. The beautiful green plant wilted, withered, and finally dried up completely. Then one day, you happen to come along and see that there's nothing left of the plant except for one small sprig. So you say, 'Oh my, I've got to save it!'" My voice cracked then, but I shed no tears. I went on. "You say, 'I'll revive the plant.' So you piss on it!

"That's how it is, Verlan. It's too late. I've been threatened with Hell for so many years, I'm not afraid anymore. No one can send me to Hell, because I'm already there."

I paused, so he tried to kiss me. But I pushed him away.

"I knew things were bad, but not that bad," he said. "Irene, what you've got is a broken heart. And I can fix that if you'll give me another chance."

"No, Verlan, it's too late."

"I can mend it, glue the pieces back together again—"

"There are no pieces."

"Ah, come on! Not even little tiny ones?"

"No. Not even dust."

VERLAN WENT TO GREAT LENGTHS to try and get me back into his fold. He even tricked me into going on a trip to Europe with him and my oldest son, André. I'd always wanted to see Europe, and I had a wonderful time on the trip. While we toured those sixteen countries and met so many kind and loving people, I kept remembering how Joel taught us that God would send them all to Hell. I wondered how it was that God favored only our small group in Mexico.

Throughout the trip, Verlan and I shared no intimacy, not even holding hands (although he tried many times). I slept alone each night while André shared a bed with his father. Verlan mourned the whole time about my hard-heartedness, especially since he was spending so much money to try and soften me up. I felt sorry for him, but not sorry enough to trust him again with my heart.

When we arrived in San Diego, all twelve of our other children came to meet us, and we took our first and last family photo. It was July 3, 1978, twenty-five years to the day after Charlotte, Verlan, and I hid under some trees in Memory Grove and she placed my hand in his "for time and all eternity."

That evening, after our photo shoot, Verlan took us to a Mexican restaurant, where all fifteen of us sat at one long table. This was the only time we'd ever gone out to eat together as a complete family. It may have been the only time we all sat down to a meal together anywhere. I watched the people seated around us, smiling and staring at such a large family. I was proud, but at the same time sad. I knew what they didn't: In many ways, this was just an illusion.

I SPENT THE NEXT THREE years out in the world—away from Verlan and his other wives, away from almost all polygamist influences. Becky and her husband, Garlin, tried to help me and my kids acclimate to life outside our little fundamentalist enclave. Becky was one of my mother's children to have completely avoided polygamy. She was a free thinker who gave up on organized religion altogether, but she lived my nightmare as a child and knew from where and what I was coming. She had a great deal of compassion for me.

Since I was now free from Verlan and my children were all of school age, I suddenly had time for myself. Considering I'd only graduated ninth grade, I seldom gave my educational ambitions any serious thought. But now I felt compelled to get further schooling. I enrolled in several classes at the community college in Las Vegas. I loved the creative writing, public speaking, and self-awareness courses. As a result of these classes and the place in which I found myself in life, I began to wonder if I might have something important to say. It was the birth of a dream I would nurture for many years—to one day write and talk to people about my experiences living in plural marriage.

My hunger for knowledge led me to read avidly. I consumed four or five books a week in the areas of psychology, philosophy, biography, self-help, and world religions. And as my mind expanded, I experienced something I would never have expected: anger. As a fundamentalist Mormon woman, I'd been admonished not to "delve into the mysteries" or listen to others' counsel. We were to believe and follow the narrow edicts of our husbands, our teachers, and our leaders—period. We weren't to bother ourselves with anything else.

Heber C. Kimball, First Councilor to Brigham Young, once stated, "Learn to do as you are told, . . . if you are told by your leader to do a thing, do it. *None of your business whether it is right or wrong.*" (*Journal of Discourses,* Vol. 6) When I began to explore outside my faith, I saw why they'd gone to such lengths to keep us ignorant. There were so many other ways to think about things, some of them quite persuasive. A part of me wanted to find out about them all, as frightening as it was.

Eventually, though, the fear began to win out. Life on the outside proved to be just plain uncomfortable. I felt like a zoo animal let loose in the wild. I had no job skills, so we lived off welfare. When the children told Verlan how well we were eating and that we had food stamps and welfare, he was furious. He actually wrote a letter to the welfare department telling them he was supporting me and I had no right to be in their system. He said he had always supported me and was willing to continue if I came back to the home I'd abandoned in Mexico. I trembled when they called me in to interrogate me and read me Verlan's letter. They wanted an explanation, and I tearfully splattered polygamy all over the social worker's desk. Seeing my hopeless plight, they decided I was more than qualified for their help.

There were many other vexations as well. A couple of men I met wanted to date me, but I turned them down because I was sure they'd lose interest as soon as they found out I had so many children, seven of whom still lived at home with me. Frankly, I think I was scared of going on a date at that point. It was just too contrary to my religious training and my past way of life.

Everything was different. The variety among the people and ideas I encountered was itself a huge shift from my prior life, in which everyone thought and acted the same way, and believed almost exactly the same things. And then there was my constant doubt and guilt over the choices I made to leave Verlan and the church. Overcoming forty-plus years of indoctrination is a monumental task, no matter how much the bottom seems to have dropped out of your belief system. To fuel the guilt, I could always fall back on that handy mind-bender with which our early prophets encouraged us: plural marriage is a high calling that damns more people than it saves. That is, fallible people fail polygamy, but polygamy itself is infallible.

As hard as all this was for me, it may have been even harder for my kids. I had at least lived in the United States before, but all my kids ever knew was life within our various church colonies down in Mexico and Central America. The culture and people they encountered in Las Vegas and later in McKinleyville, California (when we followed Becky and her husband there to live in a rental house they purchased), was totally foreign to them. This was highlighted for me when I enrolled them in American public schools for the first time.

A week after Seth entered kindergarten, I received a note from a psychologist asking me to come up to the school for a conference with him. When I arrived, he was tactful but very serious. "I want to talk to you about your son Seth. I've given him several tests, and he's failed every single one. From my evaluation, he appears retarded and needs to be in a special class."

I couldn't help but laugh out loud. "Retarded! He's one of the smartest kids I have."

The look on the psychologist's face told me he thought I was the problem and that I was living in complete denial. Still smiling to myself, I asked, "May I see the tests he took? Something is certainly wrong, because I know he's a bright child."

"Excuse me," he cut in, "I'm the psychologist here. I'm sorry if you disagree with me, but he must go into special classes. Still, I'll be glad to show you the tests we gave him."

He opened a picture book. On the first page was a baseball mitt. "See," the psychologist said, trying to convince me. "He couldn't even tell what that was!"

Then he turned the page. "And look here. He couldn't identify Mickey Mouse, a fireman, a policeman, a fire hydrant—"

I put my hand over the page with the fire hydrant, stopping him before he could go any further. "Seth's never seen *any* of those things," I informed him. "He's lived in Mexico and Nicaragua all his life. Had you asked him what a burro was or a three-toed sloth, or a monkey, ox, coconut, banana, machete, or sugarcane, he could have told you." I continued, pointing to the next page. "This lightbulb, for instance. He's never seen one. We've always lived without electricity. In fact, I have to reprimand Seth most every time I hear the toilet flush. He's in there tearing squares of toilet paper from the roll, watching excitedly as the tissue disappears. It's all new to him. We've never had a flushing toilet before."

The psychologist was amazed. Together, we scanned through all three books. Not one thing pictured in them was familiar to Seth. The psychologist shook his head.

"I want you to know this is the first time I've been made aware of the unfairness of these tests. Now I can see we may have been improperly screening children from other countries, placing them in unsuitable circumstances. I'm so sorry, but I'm very thankful you've brought this to our attention, Mrs. LeBaron.

"By the way, when I was in my internship at the Utah State Mental Hospital in Provo, I met one of the nicest men I'd ever met, and his name was LeBaron also. He was a friendly, tall, blond man who had a flawless character. I was so impressed by him, I named my son after him."

"What do you call him?" I asked.

"LeBaron," he said.

"Did you know the man's first name?"

"No, I never did. But he was a great guy."

I opened my wallet, pulling out a photo of Verlan taken while he was working at the State Mental Hospital, almost thirty years before. I put it on the man's desk.

"Oh my, this is him! I can't believe it. Why, I'd recognize him anywhere." He smiled. "So, it's your husband?"

"Yes," I said. "I can't believe it either."

LIVING IN THE STATES also made it impossible for my children to see their grown brothers and sisters, half siblings, cousins, and extended family in Mexico. The three oldest—Margaret, Sandra, and Connie—begged me repeatedly to take them back there. Most of all, they wanted their father and reprimanded me constantly for taking them so far away from him. Their tears wore me down, producing a new uneasiness in me.

In his own way, Verlan was a good father, and they needed him. But I knew what it was like to submit to him, and I didn't think I could stand being one of ten wives any longer. Besides, I hoped I could ultimately give my kids more by living in the States and outside polygamy.

Then again, it was not just the kids who longed for the familiarity of Mexico. I fit in so much better there than here. If I returned, I could also stop living off welfare and just maybe assuage my guilt about abandoning God and Verlan. Perhaps I could bear it at least until all my kids were out of the house. I felt utterly conflicted.

I was weary of defending myself to my children and looking for any good excuse to go back to Mexico, but I also dreaded and felt foolish making that decision. I called Becky, hoping she could tell me what I should do. Over pie and coffee at Denny's, I expressed my concerns to her. I wanted a good future for my children. I also wanted one for myself.

Becky was heartbroken at the possibility that I might leave, but she also wanted me to do what was best for me and my kids. Not certain what that was, she recalled a friend of hers recently recommending a palm reader who was supposedly very accurate in predicting the future. Becky was rather into that sort of thing, and in this case she hoped it might help me think more positively. She felt so strongly about my going to this psychic, she said she'd accept all responsibility for taking me there. I had many misgivings about it, but I went along because I simply fell back into my old habit of listening to other people rather than trusting myself. Besides, I felt I was drowning and needed answers.

Still, I felt great apprehension as we approached the door. A thousand voices from my past screamed at me to stay away from psychics because the Bible forbids any interaction with divination or sorcery, witchcraft, consultation with the dead, and the like. As Mormon fundamentalists, we'd been taught instead to listen only to the brethren (whose intuition was supposedly far better). But Becky was unencumbered by any of those voices. She walked right up and rang the doorbell and then turned to me. "Hey, sis, maybe Lady Maria will see some good-looking man in your future who'll take you, kids and all!"

I was so racked by guilt, I could barely laugh. According to Mormon fundamentalist beliefs, I'd already sinned by leaving my husband. Even worse, I'd all but abandoned my personal commitment to the overall practice of polygamy. Now I wondered if I'd be damned for coming to see a fortune-teller as well.

A portly, dark-haired woman with colored ribbons in her thick black braids invited us in. I watched her intently as my mind spun. Was she Italian? Mexican? From the Devil?

"How much do you charge?" Becky asked her.

"Forty dollars each."

I wondered if Maria thought her big smile would make me feel better about being ripped off. "Thanks anyway," I heard myself say, "but I can't afford forty dollars right now." I silently thanked God I was getting out of this creepy situation.

But I got pulled right back in when Becky said, "You go first, sis. I'll be glad to pay for both of us." Maria motioned for me to follow her. When Becky came, too, Maria stopped and said, "I only take one person at a time. We must have complete privacy so I can concentrate."

I sat at a small table with a red linen tablecloth. Smoke from burning incense rose from the table, and the acrid smell stung my nostrils. Maria sat on a wooden chair opposite me. "Give me your right hand," she ordered, spreading my fingers wide apart as she peered at my palm. "I see you going to Mexico."

My heart fell. Why did she say that? Why not New York or Paris?

"I see you left your husband because of another woman. But don't worry. He didn't love her as he did you. You have thirteen, maybe fourteen children?" she asked quizzically. When I nodded she was right, she continued, "I know you won't like this—I can feel it—but you must return to your husband."

"Why?" I asked, wondering how she knew all these things.

"Because only you can teach him certain things."

I shook my head. "I'll never go back."

"I know how you feel," she assured me. "As I said, there are certain lessons in life that only you can teach him. I can promise you this—in one year, you'll know why you went back."

While Becky had her fortune told, I reprimanded myself for being crazy enough to have come here. I didn't believe in soothsayers. But if she was a fake, how did she know so much about me? I returned home, wishing I'd minded my own business. Now I just had one more thing to worry about.

Next Becky was given two tickets to a psychic fair at the College of the Redwoods. Her friend suggested to Becky that she take me along. I decided since I'd gotten myself in this deep already, it wouldn't hurt to have a second opinion.

Becky and I took seats on opposite sides of the conference room, hoping not to influence each other. I don't remember the speaker's name. She was a pretty blonde woman who worked in Florida as a psychic for a police department. After an hour of amazing demonstrations, she announced she'd show us how to do what she called "psychometry." Passing around an empty cigar box, she instructed us to place a ring or watch or some other small article in it if we wanted to participate.

As the box went around, I held my gold ring, which had LOVE inscribed on it. My daughter Donna had given it to me for my birthday. I knew after watching her that this woman was amazingly accurate. I put my ring in the box while praying, *God, I must know for sure what I should do about my future. Please let the psychic pick out my ring when she does the demonstration.*

Someone handed the box back to the psychic, who turned to a woman in the front row and asked her to pick out an article. She told the woman to stand up, holding the wristwatch she'd just chosen from the box. "Now, say the very first thought that comes into your mind."

"Oh, this sounds silly," the woman remarked, embarrassed to say what she'd thought.

"Go ahead, flow with it. Say it no matter how silly you think it is."

"Well, I see early European sailing ships on the ocean." She laughed, embarrassed.

"Whose watch is this?" The psychic motioned for the woman to hold it up high so it could be identified.

A tall man in his thirties came forward to retrieve his timepiece. "Wow! That's exactly right. I'm working with friends, diving in the ocean to recover treasure from a sunken fifteenth-century ship."

For the next fifteen minutes or so, we were amazed by the accuracy of the participants' "first thoughts."

"Now, I'll do the last one myself," the psychic said. She reached in and drew my ring from the box, holding it up. "I see this woman going to Mexico. She won't like it, but she must go. My, this person has suffered; she's been a pioneer. I see she has thirteen or fourteen children. Whose ring is this?"

As I came forward, she continued, "I see you left your husband or companion. You must go back to this man, even though I see you left him because of another woman. In fact, I see many women in his life. You must return, for he has some very important lessons he must learn, and only you can teach them to him." Sensing my unwillingness, she added, "Don't be downhearted. I promise, in exactly one year, you'll know why you returned. I also see happiness and success in your future."

Faced with a clear answer to the question I'd been asking, I found it nearly impossible to accept. I made myself almost sick going back and forth in my mind, weighing the horrors of both of my choices. Finally, exhausted by my own fear and ambivalence, I took a walk, seeking the answer from God. I told him I would do whatever he wanted me to, whether it meant going back to Verlan or doing everything it would take to make my life work right where I was. In that moment of surrender, I had a miraculous, spiritual experience that comforted me. It was so profound, I knew beyond a shadow of a doubt I would be able to return to Mexico for a year and trust God with the outcome.

Armed with that God-given courage, I called Verlan the next morning. He was shocked when I told him to come and get me and take me back to Mexico with him. He'd tried so often to coax me back, promising me all sorts of things if only I would return. Now he was baffled by my unexpected change of heart, but tickled that I wanted to come.

On August 16, 1980, Verlan brought his truck, pulling a U-Haul trailer behind it. We loaded up my possessions and drove to San Diego. We left there the next evening, driving across the scorching Southwest, and arrived in Colonia LeBaron on August 18.

Even today, I wonder about this event and the involvement of psychics in my experience. I've told this story as it happened, so I can't deny the facts. However, I know psychics are not godly sources of counsel. All I can now surmise is God loves me so much that, like Balaam in the Bible, he'd have a donkey talk to me if it would help me down his path.

CHAPTER THIRTY-SEVEN

B y the next summer, with my yearlong encore as a plural wife drawing to a close, nothing eventful had happened. It was early August already. Nearly the whole town of Colonia LeBaron was attending the annual rodeo, which immediately followed the second session of our church conference. Not being a member of the church anymore, I'd chosen to withdraw from all religious activities, even the rodeo.

While others attended the festivities, I spent my time preparing huge kettles of spaghetti, fresh corn on the cob, toasted green chilies, and homemade wheat bread. Word spread fast of the open invitation to come to my home for a free meal. More than sixty friends and family showed up to partake.

I wasn't on Verlan's calendar that day until suppertime, but I knew he'd join his friends anyway so we could all enjoy his presence as we ate. He had just self-published a book titled *The LeBaron Story*. It was about the LeBaron family and Joel's claims to be the true prophet. I took great exception to a remark he published in his book, asserting, "Irene's one wish was for a can of Franco-American spaghetti, while Charlotte would have been satisfied to attend just one evening of the Summer Festival at the University of Utah." It crushed me. He told the world, in essence, that I had no aspirations. At times in our poverty, yes, I'd mentioned how nice it would be to enjoy a can of spaghetti; but I cajoled Verlan far more about the finer aspects of life than about food. To prove my point, I told everyone who came in that day to read the spaghetti story on page 103. Then I served them a great meal as we all laughed about it.

Seeing I was being a good sport about his book and that I'd been a good host to his friends, Verlan whispered to me as he left, "I'll be late, about midnight, because I have a lot of business to take care of, but I'll be coming back to spend the night with you."

That was nice, especially since it wasn't my night, but it didn't make up for much. In the year I'd been back, circumstances hadn't changed at all. I just quietly accepted whatever life, and Verlan, dished out. Now I was merely marking time until I found the right moment to tell Verlan that I'd be leaving for good within the next couple of weeks.

I forced myself awake as Verlan crawled into bed beside me a few hours later. I didn't want him to zonk out in a flash as he usually did. It had been six weeks since I spent a night with him because he'd been busy traveling back and forth to Texas, publishing his book. On each trip, he took one of his wives, but my turn hadn't come up yet.

He took me in his arms and held me, but he was completely silent. Despite my own plans to leave, I felt a sudden surge of that old, familiar fear that Verlan would soon abandon me. It had always been the same story: wait and wait for weeks on end, longing for his return, then start over.

Not wanting to be pushy but starved for his love, I let my fingers roam. He grabbed my hand. "Please don't pressure me. I'm too tired to make love to you."

I'd heard the same excuse the last three times. Didn't he realize it had been four months since he'd loved me physically? He always came to me late, and always, he was exhausted. As usual, I was dying from neglect, but I was determined not to complain and cause a fight.

I held my face close to him. His familiar scent made my tears well up as I recalled that old shirt of his I'd clung to and wept over all those years ago in the mountains. I wanted to catch and hold onto a part of him, even now, but I made myself turn over so he could go to sleep. As I did, he grabbed me, holding me as he began to convulse with soul-wrenching sobs.

"What's the matter?" I asked, perplexed. "Tell me why you feel so bad."

"I had a dream," he said between sobs. "All I can tell you is, I had a dream."

His need for me canceled out my every complaint. It wasn't like Verlan to show such emotion. He always seemed strong and able to bear any trials that came his way. I knew that whatever was bothering him had to be serious. I ran my fingers through his hair, comforting him. "What did you dream?" I asked.

His voice was hoarse with emotion as he said resolutely, "In a few days, you'll know what it was."

I held him but remained silent as he sobbed. I didn't insist he relate his dream.

When he calmed down, Verlan apologized for not accompanying me earlier that day when I went to the cemetery to take a new headstone to Leah's grave. Then he wistfully added, "I hope you left the old cement marker I made on her grave. Was it still intact after so many years?"

"Yes." I reassured him. "I left it standing exactly where you placed it. We flattened the mound and then laid the new marker level on top of the grave. She would have been twenty-seven years old today."

"Unbelievable," he whispered.

After a moment's silence, he continued, "I haven't slept for five nights. I'm so tired I feel sick, but I need to talk to you. I know you've had so many doubts about my love for you. I know you feel I've always taken you for granted, but it's because of you I've been able to organize my family and accomplish my utmost dream. You've been my pillar of strength. Your heart hasn't been in it all, but you've been steadfast anyway throughout the years. I can't help but love you for doing it. God has taken that into consideration, and I know you'll gain your reward."

I decided it might be a good time to tell Verlan about what God showed me that afternoon almost a year before. "Have you ever had a revelation, or can you say you know anything beyond a shadow of a doubt?" I asked him.

"No," he admitted sadly. This surprised me some, since he'd always seemed sure of so much. But tonight he was exposing his vulnerabilities. That was why I felt I needed to tell him this.

"Well, I have. I have a sure knowledge about God."

"Let's hear it," he said, sounding truly interested.

"The night before I called you to come and get me, I had a spiritual experience that happened very suddenly. I can barely put into words what it was like. The spirit of the Lord seemed to come upon me, and instantly the scales of confusion and disbelief fell from my eyes. Everything I perceived seemed more alive, maybe even alive for the first time. There was no time or space, no beginning or end. All was an eternal now. It was as if I merged with the divine, removing all my fear, even the fear of death. In that moment, the doubt and despair that had claimed so much of my energy over the past few years was replaced with a joy and peace that surpassed all understanding.

"It was made known to me that I didn't have to try and do or be anything. I simply needed to be still. I know the experience came about because I surrendered. When I quit trying to control my life and mind, it was made known to me that God is the doer. It's our strong sense of self that brings about our delusions and pain. By surrendering, we tell God, 'Not my will, Lord, but thy will be done.' The essence revealed to me that everything was on time and okay exactly as it was."

Verlan was quiet for a long time. Then he said, "That's beautiful, Irene. I hope you're right. But if your experience is true, it may just do away with Mormonism." He sighed heavily. "You know, I never thought Joel would die. He held the highest priesthood office on Earth. He gave me the second highest. Without these two head priesthood offices, the church can't function." He paused, in deep thought. "Irene, if something should happen to me, you can know that Joel was merely a good man, and we all just barked up the wrong tree. In that case, please teach the kids simply to be honorable people and keep God's commandments."

Before I realized it, the morning light was beginning to filter in. It was 5 A.M., and sleep hadn't been a consideration for either of us as we'd reminisced and shared some of our deepest feelings. Then

Verlan said he needed to leave early to go to his office and get some writing done. His office was in Lillie's house. He read my mind.

"Irene, I'm not leaving you to go spend time with Lillie, honest. I need to try and accomplish a few things. I can't sleep, anyway. Will you forgive me if I leave so early?"

"Of course, go ahead," I said.

I spent the next day with my kids, but I was preoccupied with thoughts of Verlan. Very soon, I'd need to tell him I was separating myself completely from him and his religion. Although it would be hard to come by, I would need more than a few minutes with him in order to do it. What I had to tell him couldn't be settled quickly.

I retired early and extra tired because of the sleep I'd missed the night before, but I was awakened by a violent dream. I woke up my eighteen-year-old daughter, Barbara, who was sleeping with me. "Someone is going to die," I said. "I wonder who it could be."

I told her I'd seen a car wreck. Three people were in the crash. Two of them were covered with blankets and lying on the side of a freeway. Then a stranger appeared on the scene, yelling at me, "Someone you love has been killed." In the dream, I cried out to God, "Please give me strength to bear this." Just as I was going to lift the blanket so I could see who it was, I woke up.

Barbara reached out to comfort me. "It's only a dream, Mama, just a silly nightmare."

"No," I answered stubbornly. "I know someone is going to die. I feel it." Would it be one of my sons? I tried to force those thoughts from my mind. If I dwelt on it, I warned myself, it might come to pass.

I BARELY SAW VERLAN for the next two days. He was about to leave town again. I was filled with anxiety, worn down emotionally from the year of disappointments and loneliness, and dreading what I had to tell my husband. I found him packing his suitcase and his sleeping bag into the trunk of John Adams's Volkswagen, parked between the church and Lillie's house. I shook hands with John, a curly-haired convert I'd known for several years. He had driven from Utah to attend our annual church conference.

Verlan shook the seat of the car as he spoke to John. "Boy, this little car sure is flimsy! If we had a wreck, neither of us would survive. I hope we make it to Nicaragua and back safely," he said. They were going to check on some property Verlan maintained there in case he ever needed it for a refuge.

"Don't worry," John answered. "This little Rabbit is great on the road. We'll make it to Mexico City just fine. We'll spend two days there and then go on to Nicaragua."

Verlan excused the two of us, promising John he'd return shortly. He had some important things he had to do before they could leave. He guided me down the dirt road, hugging me. Wearily, he said, "I hate to go, I really do. I have a feeling I won't be coming back."

I stopped in my tracks. "Damn it, Verlan, then don't go!"

"No," he said, resuming our pace, "when your time's up, there's nothing you can do about it."

I didn't want to hear such nonsense. We walked down Lillie's sidewalk toward his office. I knew if I didn't say my piece now, I wouldn't get another chance until he returned. I didn't want another wife showing up to interrupt me, either. I thought about the psychics. They prophesied I'd be here a year, and then I would know the reason I had to return to Verlan. Another week, and my year would be up. Verlan planned to be gone for at least a month, so I must tell him now.

He put the key into the lock on his office door. After a couple of twists, it opened, and he led me inside. "I know you're in a hurry," I began, "but I need to take this opportunity to talk to you."

"Hurry up then. I'm rushed, and John is anxious to leave."

"Verlan, I think you're a great man and I respect you, but I'm miserable living here in this situation, and I want a divorce. I want to move to the States before school starts.

"Please," he interrupted, "we'll discuss this when I return." Then he added, "Maybe I'll solve all of your problems by not coming back at all."

"Verlan," I pleaded, "I'm living the biggest lie. I don't want this life another minute! I'm being stifled. Try to understand. It's not you. I take full responsibility for my actions. I just want out! I cannot continue to live like this anymore."

He opened his desk drawer. I knew he wasn't hearing a word I said. "Now listen carefully," he demanded as he held up a stack of papers. "This is my will. It'll be right here in this top right-hand drawer. Please see to it that there are no fights over it. I tried my best to treat you all equally."

"Please, Verlan. This is ridiculous," I cut in.

"Pay attention," he continued. "I have two insurance policies in here also. I know it won't be much, but it'll help out a little anyway."

"Verlan, please don't act like this."

He stood up and took a picture he had painted off his office wall. "This is for André. You'll notice I wrote a name on all these pictures, photos, and books. They're for whoever's name is written on them." He made me look in the desk drawer again. "All the important papers are right here, okay?"

I must have looked abashed as he took me in his arms. We silently held one another. Then his lips urgently found mine. Unable to fight back our tears, we both cried openly and brokenheartedly—me because I had to leave, him because he thought he was never coming back. Then he pulled away and took his hanky from his pocket to wipe his tears. "Just say a prayer for me," he said sadly.

I didn't turn back to look at him again for fear I would lose all self-control. I walked rapidly, yet resolutely away. I couldn't tell him the reason I had to give up loving him was simply for survival. He would never have been able to understand that it was only when I didn't care that I could bear it all. No woman would ever again receive Verlan's tender affection within my view. I'd rather have nothing at all of him than share him any longer. So I was going away again, this time for good. It left me feeling numb, yes, but at least I was free.

John kept the motor running as Verlan dashed into my house a couple of hours later on their way out of town. My daughter Margaret, who is a spitting image of me, was in the kitchen when he came in. Her father spoke out of breath, "Where's your mother?"

"She just left a few minutes ago for San Diego to be with Kaylen's wife, Jean, while she has her baby."

Verlan engulfed Margaret in his arms and wept. When he pulled away from her, he was clearly embarrassed. "I'm sorry I missed her," he said, then added gravely, "Please give her a message for me, will you? Tell her I . . . loved her. She never believed me, but I truly loved her."

The following week, Jean and I prepared for the arrival of her first child. I was anxious for her labor pains to start. Her due date was six days away, but I impatiently longed to have the ordeal over with so I could get on with my own life.

It was August 18, 1981. A mild breeze blew in through the open screen of the trailer house door. The air felt good on my face as I relaxed on the floor, enjoying the peace and quiet, trying to rest my overworked body and mind. A ringing telephone brought me out of my trance. Thinking me asleep, Kaylen snatched up the receiver and softly said, "Hello?" After a moment, he shouted into the phone, "Are you sure?"

I bolted upright, begging God, as I had in my dream, *Please, Lord, let me be able to bear whatever it is.*

Tears were forming in Kaylen's eyes. "Is John dead, too?" Then, covering the mouthpiece, he turned toward me. "It's Daddy. He and John got killed in a car wreck near Mexico City."

In shock and disbelief, I asked, "What is the date today?"

"It's the eighteenth, Mom. He died three hours ago."

It was far too surreal. My mind flashed back. Verlan saw it in a dream. Then I saw it in a dream. And even the psychics said I'd know in one year why I had to go back to Mexico. Verlan died exactly one year after the day I returned.

They also said I would teach or show Verlan something no one else could. In the years since, I've pondered what that might have been. For one thing, I let him know I hadn't given up on him even though I was walking away from all the rest. I'd also been able to share with him my certainty of God's existence, goodness, and sovereignty. Who else in his life could have shown him all that?

It's hard to recall the next few hours. Kaylen and I tried to comfort each other as we contacted all of Verlan's children and close friends by phone. I relayed the message to Charlotte's mother, Aunt Rhea, in Salt Lake City, who, in turn, called reporters. The LeBarons were well-known in Utah because of Ervil's threats and violence. So Verlan and John's deaths appeared on the ten o'clock news. Word of their deaths came through Elizabeth, Verlan's ninth wife, who received a call from the Red Cross stating that Verlan and John had been in a terrible car accident near Puebla, Mexico. John died instantly. A "flight for life" helicopter arrived and transported Verlan to a hospital in Mexico City, where he died approximately two hours later. Their friend Harvard Stubbs, who was also in the accident, was hospitalized briefly, but he recovered completely.

Three vehicles packed with wives, children, in-laws, and friends started on the fifteen-hour trip from San Diego to Colonia LeBaron. I drove all night while my children cried, tormented by the thought of losing their father. They all tried to catch what snatches of sleep they could so they'd be rested for the funeral.

Charlotte and Chad, Lucy's oldest son, flew to Mexico City and made arrangements to have Verlan's body flown to Chihuahua. Then it was to be driven to Colonia LeBaron.

A strange quiet pervaded the large crowd of mourners we found waiting on the lawn of Charlotte's ranch-style brick home. The silence was eerie. People spoke in hushed tones as they awaited the arrival of the hearse. Most of them were Verlan's own wives, children, and other relations.

Forty-two of Verlan's fifty-six children were able to attend. Priscilla and Lillie were both pregnant and in a few short months would give him a grand total of fifty-eight children. At the time of his death, Verlan had only six wives left—Charlotte, Lucy, Lillie, Elizabeth, Priscilla, and me. The other four wives—Helen, Susan, Beverly, and Esther—had withdrawn from his fold, divorcing him. Their divorces caused him to feel tremendous failure.

The six of us wives milled around quietly, hoping the hearse would arrive soon. We all wanted to spend a few private moments with the man we loved.

I walked into Charlotte's house to sit down and rest. Right then, Kaylen came to the screen door. "Mom, they're bringing Daddy now."

Ten or twelve of Verlan's sons huddled around the door of the hearse. The driver motioned for people to stand back, out of his way. Then they slid a large wooden crate out the rear door of the hearse onto the graveled road. All was silent except the screeching of nails as the boys pried them out with crowbars. They ripped the nails from the pine boards, tearing the wooden crate completely apart, revealing a masculine gray casket inside.

The crowd moved aside to make room for six of Verlan's older sons—Verlan Jr., Mark, Steven, Pierre, Kaylen, and André. They took the handles of the shiny casket, lifting it off the baseboards of the disassembled crate. Reverently, they carried their father's body into Charlotte's living room and placed his casket on a sturdy coffee table.

The moment of truth had arrived. As the lid was raised high, an explosion of sobs burst forth. Wives and children cried out in unison, the reality piercing our ears and hearts. Our husband and father had truly expired.

After an hour or so, Verlan Jr. requested that only the immediate family remain in the room, allowing each one to offer his or her final respects. Hanging onto Linda while the others left, I stood back and watched as Verlan's five other remaining wives touched him, each trying however inadequately to express her innermost final thoughts and feelings. I wanted to cry out loud, to tell Verlan how lucky he was just to be at peace! There would be no more quarreling. No more being fought over for a little of his time. No more jealous fits of anger. And no more turns.

Lillie patted Verlan's stocking-covered feet. Lucy kissed his large, cold hands. I sensed that all our hearts were bursting with the same agonizing grief. Tears of sadness mingled with anger streamed down my face. In death, just as in life, we had no damn privacy. We were always intruding on each other, always having to postpone feeling our own personal feelings.

I wanted to cry out to Verlan one last time, to reassure him of our friendship and thank him for my freedom. I needed to validate his worth as a wonderful human being, but also suggest to him we'd both been victims caught up in the tangled web of a fanatical religion. I wanted to yell and get it all out.

This dedicated man, just fifty-one years old, tried for so many years to pull me toward heaven, insisting I accompany him to a celestial glory. Silently now, I confessed to him that I didn't think I ever really wanted to be a goddess. All I truly wanted was to live a normal life, loving him and enjoying his undivided love. Most of all, I wanted to fulfill his needs and mine together as the only woman he ever desired.

I reflected on my wedding night, recalling the aspirations and dreams Verlan shared with me. It seemed like such a far-fetched illusion then—his desire for at least seven wives and fifty children. But he exceeded even his own wild expectations.

Violent tears blurred my vision. Linda slipped her arm comfortingly around my waist. "Come on, kid. Be strong. You'll be all right."

As the lid of the coffin was about to be lowered, dozens of weeping, screaming children reached in to touch their father for the last time. I watched as his wives quickly kissed his hands and his lips, trying to hold on to one more moment of him.

Linda tugged at my arm. I stood before the casket in a trance; I didn't move. But I couldn't bring myself to touch him, either. I wanted to treasure the good times, remember his kisses being warm.

The lid closed with a thud. Immediately, frantic, crying children forced it open about six inches for one final peek. His son Mark called out in agonizing despair, "D - a - d - d - y!"

My mind was exploding. I wanted to send everyone outside and raise the lid again to say all that was really in my heart. But how does a wife bare her soul with five other wives present?

I peered at his face for one short moment as the casket closed for the final time. Then, feeling Verlan's presence and knowing he'd understand, I whispered, "Good-bye, lover!"

EPILOGUE

After all my struggles to finally choose freedom, it was tragedy that actually ended my twenty-eight-year marriage to Verlan LeBaron. The timing of these two events haunts me to this day. Was it just one of life's synchronicities? Was his death preordained or merely an accident? Did I leave him, somehow knowing subconsciously we'd reached the end of our marriage anyway?

During my first twenty-one years as Verlan's polygamous wife, I became the mother of fourteen of his children. I shared my husband with nine other women and a total of fifty-eight kids. We lived in utter poverty, laboring to raise our own food, make our own clothes, and build our own houses. Most of that time, we lived without electricity or indoor plumbing.

Six of my children at some point in their lives became entangled in a polygamist lifestyle, but today, all but three of them are living in monogamy. I still keep in contact with some of Verlan's other wives. We remain friends and stay with each other during funerals and weddings. I currently have 118 grandchildren, the oldest only twenty-six. I have thirty-seven great-grandchildren, with more on the way. Yes, I do know all their names. Six of them are named Irene, after me. I guess I must have done something right, after all. When people ask me about my family tree, I tell them I have a family forest!

I'm grateful I've been able to treasure the many good memories I have of the years described in this book. It wasn't all bad, though it was all tainted by a terrible delusion. After sacrificing so much to try and attain "celestial glory," I think my greatest accomplishment is the bond of love and friendship I share with all my children and grand-children. In this way, Verlan was right—I truly am a blessed woman. Still a close family, we visit each other as often as we can.

Now, at last, I have a husband who's devoted to me alone. Hector J. Spencer married me nineteen years ago, making me his only wife. I treasure his love. It may seem simple to him, but he fulfilled my life-long dream of being the favorite.

I value the drive and honesty I found within myself as I struggled through trials and suffering in my life. I learned to trust myself, to appreciate and believe in my lifestyle and the choices I make as I live each day. Somewhere along the way, I learned to follow my own path rather than blindly obeying what others wanted or demanded of me.

Twenty years ago, I became a born-again Christian, as did many of my children. It took me very much by surprise, most especially because it cost me nothing. At my son Kaylen's insistence, I moved to Anchorage, Alaska, taking my Book of Mormon with me to show him how he'd been misled when he converted to Christianity a few years before. There was no sacrifice in being a Christian. It seemed too easy to just confess Christ as your savior and think you were saved. I knew we needed to work for our salvation. I couldn't believe Kaylen turned against Mormonism so easily. (As I've said, the roots of effective brainwashing can extend quite deep, and my deep roots had never been fully extracted, despite all my experiences.)

Once I arrived in Alaska, Kaylen invited me to Abbott Loop Christian Center. I accompanied him, mostly to check out what the devil he'd gotten himself into. As I entered the large sanctuary, taking my seat in a pew next to him and his wife, Jean, I felt guilty. After all my years of devotion to the one-and-only-restored-true-gospel-on-the-earth, what was I doing in a gentile church? But it was while I sat there in that open and free spiritual space that I experienced a mirac-ulous conversion. For how long had I thirsted after God, begged him to speak to me personally, and then done whatever others told me he wanted for and from me? Now I finally heard him speaking directly to my own heart. He called me by name. "Irene, where have you been that you have never worshipped me?" Then the Holy Spirit simply revealed to me God's unconditional, divine love, fully available right now through the sacrifice *already* paid by his son. I wept, ashamed to think of all the years I struggled to become a goddess and one day join my husband as the rulers of our own world. I was overcome by God's mercy and love that had been there all along, just waiting for me to receive them. After years of religious sacrifice and suffering, I finally understood that Christ really is sufficient.

Never again would I have to jump through strange, agonizing hoops in order to cajole God into accepting me. In fact, the god I'd been taught all my life to worship and obey didn't really exist at all. That god was not very powerful, not very good, and he required us to completely reject some of the most beautiful things the true God had for us. The deep human desire to unite exclusively with one person of the opposite sex is not evil and is not to be shunned. God set it up that way before the Fall, and he never changed it. He certainly never declared it a sin. My belief in what the Mormon fundamentalists taught about God and salvation had been so sincere, I embraced their miserable prescription for life and marriage. One can be sincere and at the same time be sincerely wrong.

Mormonism adopted polygamy from an ancient social custom from biblical times and made it into an essential principle for exaltation in heaven. Along the way, polygamy became a means of controlling believers and turning them into submissive pawns. Through it, prophets controlled believers and men controlled women, all allegedly in accordance with God's will. No one seemed to acknowledge how terrible it was for everyone to live it—women, children, and men as well. I certainly couldn't look at Verlan's life and say that his many marriages brought him more joy than hardship. The hardship itself is taken as a reason to carry on; it's held as a martyr's badge of honor. Mostly, though, it's just denied. The only reason polygamy works at all is because the people who practice it so fiercely believe they are living God's will.

I decided it was finally time for someone to tell it like it is. All the books I'd read on Mormon polygamy were vivid accounts of sacrificing women who upheld and emphatically stated they loved the Principle. I was convinced that these committed women simply did as I'd been taught to do—doggedly affirm the truth and righteousness of plural marriage and stubbornly maintain its advantages over monogamy. Forbidden to acknowledge their true feelings, they smothered their own agony and wrenching pain, just as I'd so emphatically been instructed to do.

I've personally known hundreds of plural wives. Their smiles are a façade required of them by their husbands and spiritual leaders. It's up to the women to make plural marriage appear to be the superior mode of marriage. It's demanded that the wives present themselves as united with one another, with their husbands, and with their religious communities. The success of plural marriage depends entirely on their willingness to play the sacrificial role and play it well.

At one time or another, when their tender hearts were bursting, many of these women broke the rules by revealing to me the strain and sorrow they experienced every day. I've seen polygamous wives stamp their feet in defense of their lifestyle, even while the truth is engraved on their faces. I've seen wives who have no light left in their eyes, who have relinquished all their rights and dreams. I've seen many manic-depressive wives who succumb to complete emotional/nervous breakdowns and many neglected ones who succumb to the tantalizing lure of adultery. Almost all the faithful polygamous women I've known have been resigned to lives of bare existence, their joys, hopes, and dreams forfeited until the next life.

Like them, I'd vehemently defended polygamy for decades. It was my only sense of identity. I sacrificed everything else for it, so I desperately needed it to be true. I remember parroting the inane arguments of early Mormon prophets who claimed that polygamy would do away with all of society's ills. There would be no adultery because if a woman fell in love with a married man, she could honorably have him. There would be no prostitution because if one wife didn't "understand" or welcome her husband sexually, he had several other wives there to satisfy his needs.

After all, no one woman can fully satisfy a man anyway. I'd heard it said many times that a man may love one woman sexually, another for her intelligence, and yet another for her cooking (that was me). Though every man vowed he loved his wives equally, the obvious truth was very different. Every man I knew had a legal wife, who was usually the dominant wife, and a favorite wife, whom all the others resented most. And many polygamous men, no matter how earnest they are about obeying God's laws, at some point use plural marriage to justify adultery. Perhaps they consider it their due for all the rest they go through.

A product of four generations of polygamy, I'd been trapped in that closed society, believing we were God's chosen people. I'd been taught to dread intermingling with the "wicked gentiles" outside our sect. God commanded that we become a "peculiar people," keeping ourselves separated from the vile customs of society. But my distrust diminished with each outsider I met. Their warm acceptance, which I thought I'd have to beg for, was freely given. People "outside" esteemed me as an individual, not because of my religious beliefs.

Writing my story has brought me healing. But this book doesn't tell it all. It doesn't describe the terror to which my infamous brother-in-law, Ervil LeBaron, subjected us for several years. He ordered the deaths of at least twenty-eight of our family, friends, and church members. I was one of the people on his death list, which helped inspire me to go along with many of our moves throughout Mexico and Central America. While I wrote this book, Ervil cunningly seemed to be taking it over, as he was prone to do with everything. So I ripped out page after page about him, realizing that this has to be my story—the story of my shattered dreams as a polygamist's wife and my journey into the light of God's unconditional love.

VERLAN M. LEBARON, 1930–1981
FATHER OF 29 BOYS AND 29 GIRLS

Wives	1. Charlotte†	2. Irene†	3. Lucy**	4. Beverly	5. Esther	6. Susan	7. Lillie	8. Helen (widow)	9. Elizabeth (widow)	10. Priscilla
Children	Verlan Jr.	Leah*	Chad	Marcelo*	Oscar*	Melanie	Christian			Garlan
	Rhea	Donna	Norman*	Lorraine*	Judah	James	Albert			Sydney
	Laura	André	Roland*	Julie	Edith	Jeannette	Shawn			
	Mark*	Steven	Verla	Theron	Ruben	Forrest	Francine			
	Pierre	Brent	Clara*	Olivia	Aurora	Lance	Stephanie			
	Susanna	Kaylen	Byron	Dorian	Veronica		Caroline			
	Beth	Barbara	Norine							
	Loretta	Margaret	Virginia							
	Natalie	Sandra*	Catherine							
		Connie	Walter							
		LaSalle								
		Verlana								
		Seth								
		Lothair								

*Deceased
†Charlotte and Irene are sisters (same father)
**Lucy is second cousin of Charlotte and Irene.